Marriage Discourses

Marriage Discourses

―

Historical and Literary Perspectives on
Gender Inequality and Patriarchic Exploitation

Edited by
Jowan A. Mohammed and Frank Jacob

The publication of this work in Open Access was made possible by the financial support from Nord Universitet.

ISBN 978-3-11-075133-8
e-ISBN (PDF) 978-3-11-075145-1
e-ISBN (EPUB) 978-3-11-075153-6

This work is licensed under a Creative Commons Attribution-NonCommercial-NoDerivatives 4.0 International License. For details go to http://creativecommons.org/licenses/by-nc-nd/4.0/.

Library of Congress Control Number: 2021944786

Bibliographic information published by the Deutsche Nationalbibliothek
The Deutsche Nationalbibliothek lists this publication in the Deutsche Nationalbibliografie; detailed bibliographic data are available on the Internet at http://dnb.dnb.de.

© 2021 with the authors, editing © 2021 Jowan A. Mohammed and Frank Jacob,
published by Walter de Gruyter GmbH, Berlin/Boston.
This book is published with open access at www.degruyter.com.
Cover illustration: Charlotte, NC, Rally Against Prop 8, November 15, 2006, photograph by James Willamor
Printing and binding: CPI books GmbH, Leck

www.degruyter.com

Table of Contents

Frank Jacob and Jowan A. Mohammed
1   Idealized Romantic Love, Legal Issues, and Patriarchic Exploitation: An Introduction to Historical and Literary Marriage Discourses —— 1

Section I: Marriage Discourses in Law and Politics

Sabine Müller
2   Political Marriage in Antiquity —— 25

Mariela Fargas Peñarrocha
3   Marriage Discourses in Conflict: Public and Private Order in Early Modern Spain —— 51

Marion Röwekamp
4   Challenging Patriarchy: Marriage and the Reform of Marriage Law in Imperial Germany and the Weimar Republic —— 73

Section II: Marriage Discourses and Social Criticism

Vincent Streichhahn
5   On the Discourse of the "New Sexual Morality" in the German Empire: Robert Michels' *Sexual Ethics* between Women's Movement, Social Democracy, and Sociology —— 105

Frank Jacob
6   Marriage as Exploitation: Emma Goldman and the Anarchist Concept of Female Liberation —— 133

Jowan A. Mohammed
7   To End the Yoke of Marriage: Mary Hunter Austin and the Struggle Against Patriarchal Norms —— 159

Section III: Marriage Discourses in Literature

Jamie Callison
8   Redefining Marriage in Interwar Britain: Internal Transformation and Personal Sacrifice in the Poetry of H.D. —— 187

Jessica Allen Hanssen
9   Scenes from a Marriage: *The Age of Innocence* as Discourse on the Transactional Value of Marriage —— 207

Margaret Stetz
10   "Marriages are just performances": Staging Fashion, Comedy, and Feminism in *Love, Loss and What I Wore* —— 231

Contributors —— 255

Index —— 257

Frank Jacob and Jowan A. Mohammed

1 Idealized Romantic Love, Legal Issues, and Patriarchic Exploitation: An Introduction to Historical and Literary Marriage Discourses

> The latest … dilemma I've encountered is a big one. Until I told my friends I was getting married, I didn't know marriage and feminism could be considered mutually exclusive. I mean, just because a bride's engagement ring is a symbol of ownership, and just because changing her name erases her identity as a separate individual, and just because the whole thing is ludicrously assumed to be the woman's domain…[1]

The British journalist and feminist Laura Bates here describes a marriage discourse that can be observed since and traced back to the 19th century. Marriage is often related to a romanticized image of love, due to which it is considered the final union of two lovers or the highest stage of a love relationship.[2] On the other hand, very often marriage is disadvantageous for women and represents a form of patriarchic exploitation. Another question Bates asks in her reflection consequently points to one basic dilemma: "Can a woman who's fought for equality and respect, against sexism and misogyny, become a bride?"[3] Of course, "[i]t's not easy to go about your daily feminist business without encountering multiple dilemmas,"[4] but when it comes to love, expressed by a legal union, i.e. marriage, that has been used by men to suppress women for centuries, the dilemma turns into a crux. What has been the backbone of the private form of living, i.e. the family, and the traditional criteria for living together as a couple and/or family

---

[1] Laura Bates, "How to Have a Feminist Wedding," *The Guardian*, June 28, 2014, https://www.theguardian.com/lifeandstyle/2014/jun/28/can-a-feminist-be-a-bride-laura-bates.
[2] The present anthology does predominantly apply a concept of marriage and family that is Western per se, and and also functioned as an instrument of colonial domination, especially in regions where such concepts did not exist before the cultural penetration by expanding European powers. For a discussion of marriage as a political element in a colonial context see, among others, Margot Lovett, "On Power and Powerlessness: Marriage and Political Metaphor in Colonial Western Tanzania," *The International Journal of African Historical Studies* 27, no. 2 (1994): 273–301; Tim Fulford, "Poetic Flowers/Indians Bowers," in *Romantic Representations of British India*, ed. Michael Franklin (New York: Routledge, 2006), 113–130, especially 61–63.
[3] Bates, "How to Have a Feminist Wedding."
[4] Ibid.

OpenAccess. © 2021 Frank Jacob and Jowan A. Mohammed, published by De Gruyter. This work is licensed under the Creative Commons Attribution-NonCommercial-NoDerivatives 4.0 International License. https://doi.org/10.1515/9783110751451-001

have changed over the last decades in particular.[5] The Slovenian philosopher Slavoj Žižek also pointed to some problems related to marriage and argued that "beneath the surface of the standard bourgeois notion of marriage lurk many unsettling implications," especially since "we humans no longer just make love for procreation, we get involved in a complex process of seduction and marriage by means of which sexuality becomes an expression of the spiritual bond between a man and a woman, and so forth."[6]

Along with the changes to what we have considered marriage to be since the early 19th century, a feminist debate about it developed and, as American philosopher Debra B. Bergoffen outlined, "[t]o date most feminist discussions of marriage have been either critical or reactive. Having declared that it is immoral to treat married women as property and unjust to position the wife as subject to the husband, feminists have either rejected the institution of marriage as exploitive or argued that they as individuals have found ways to make marriage work."[7] She consequently argues that "[i]t is not enough for feminists who value marriage to declare that marriage can escape its patriarchal trappings. To reclaim marriage for feminists we need to do more. We need to make the case that patriarchal marriage is a perversion of the meaning of marriage and that this perversion is of concern to feminists."[8] As marriage nowadays determines multiple levels of a relationship between people, i.e. "the erotic, the ethical, and the political,"[9] the discourse about marriage needs to take different aspects of it into account when defining the necessities for change with regard to the character and structure of the marital union of the future. Since marriages are legally and socially "seen as a prerequisite to the provision of certain rights and material benefits"[10] that are determined by societies in their specific chronological contexts, they are also considered "a public institution that creates a right to private sexual relations, and yet is defined by public policy."[11] The famous US law professor William Eskridge, Jr. highlighted correctly in this regard that "marriage

---

[5] Anja Steinbach, "Mutter, Vater, Kind: Was heißt Familie heute?" *Aus Politik und Zeitgeschichte* 67, no. 30–31 (2017): 5. Also see Pamela J. Smock, "The Wax and Wane of Marriage: Prospects for Marriage in the 21st Century," *Journal of Marriage and Family* 66, no. 4 (2004): 966–973.
[6] Slavoj Žižek, "Hegel on Marriage," *E-Flux Journal* 34 (2012): 1, accessed March 4, 2021, http://worker01.e-flux.com/pdf/article_8951758.pdf.
[7] Debra B. Bergoffen, "Marriage, Autonomy, and the Feminine Protest," *Hypatia* 14, no. 4: *The Philosophy of Simone de Beauvoir* (1999): 18.
[8] Ibid.
[9] Ibid., 19.
[10] Jyl Josephson, "Citizenship, Same-Sex Marriage, and Feminist Critiques of Marriage," *Perspectives on Politics* 3, no. 2 (2005): 270.
[11] Ibid.

is an institution that is constructed, not discovered by societies."[12] This means that the role marriages are supposed to play for individuals and societies as a whole need to be continuously debated, and marriage-related discourses represent a source to better understand the history of a given society in a specific time frame and can be used to analyze formerly existent norms and values related to this form of human relationship. These changes of marriage in regard to norms and social practices have also been stressed by legal scholar Renata Grossi, who argues that "[m]arriage has meant different things at different times. It has transmogrified from being a religious sacred institution to a contractual legal one, from a patriarchal institution to a more equal partnership based on freedom and equality."[13]

Very often, the patriarchal social structure is identified as one of the core issues for marriage discourses[14] as it has caused many problems for women all around the globe. A long history of forced marriages,[15] the economic exploitation of women who are married, as criticized and legally challenged by feminists since the 19th century,[16] and the issue of abuse within marriage are major concerns about the concept as such. Women, whether feminist or anti-feminist, and men, often representing the patriarchic system that was reluctant to accept change, struggled about what marriage meant as well as if and how it could be ended, especially by wives who were demanding to get divorced.[17] However, not only is the marriage discourse complicated by the issue's public and private implications but also "questions raised by same-sex marriage ... [indicate] a need to rethink many aspects of the legal regulation of families as they affect democratic citizenship."[18] It is therefore not surprising, as political scientist Jyl Joseph-

---

12 William N. Eskridge, Jr., "A History of Same-Sex Marriage," *Virginia Law Review* 79, no. 9 (1993): 1485, cited in Renata Grossi, *Looking for Love in the Legal Discourse of Marriage* (Canberra: Australian National University Press, 2014), 17.
13 Grossi, *Looking for Love*, 17.
14 Mary Becker, "Patriarchy and Inequality: Towards a Substantive Feminism," *University of Chicago Legal Forum* 1 (1999): 23.
15 E. g. in the UK. See Sundari Anitha and Aisha Gill, "Coercion, Consent and the Forced Marriage Debate in the UK," *Feminist Legal Studies* 17 (2009): 165–184. For a more global perspective of the issue, see in particular Kaye Quek, *Marriage Trafficking: Women in Forced Wedlock* (London: Routledge, 2018).
16 Mary Ziegler, "An Incomplete Revolution: Feminists and the Legacy of Marital-Property Reform," *Michigan Journal of Gender & Law* 19, no. 2 (2013): 261.
17 For a detailed discussion of this "silent revolution" in the United States, see Herbert Jacob, *Silent Revolution: The Transformation of Divorce Law in the United States* (Chicago: University of Chicago Press, 1988).
18 Josephson, "Citizenship," 269.

son further remarks, that "[a]dvocates of same-sex marriage compare their quest to those of other social movements, particularly the civil rights movement, that sought equal status as citizens before the legal institutions of the state."[19] A continuation of the patriarchic instrumentalization of marriage norms would therefore not only prevent women from acting as equal citizens with the same political and social rights as men but also representatives of the LGBTQ+ community, whose ostracization from equal marriage rights would represent a limitation of their rights as individuals as well. In this regard, one can only agree with the evaluation of marriage of Josephson, who argues that it "has a significant place in our understanding of responsible citizenship in a democratic polity"[20] and that "[m]arriage has become a centerpiece for both opponents and proponents of greater rights for the members of the gay, lesbian, bisexual and transgender community."[21] It took, however, a long time for such aspects to become part of the marriage discourse, which itself was not very prominent or taking place in the form of a truly public debate before the 19th century.

Early Debates about Marriage

Before the Enlightenment stimulated debates about existent social norms like marriage,[22] the demands for and the social role of the latter, which also means the position of women as part of such relations or unions, were solely determined by men, who used marriages in many ways as a repressive measure to keep women in their unequal social and political position. While marriages were considered an important element of diplomacy as well lineage protection and legitimization in antiquity,[23] in the Middle Ages, "the Roman Church count-

---

19 Ibid., 270.
20 Ibid., 269–270.
21 Ibid., 269.
22 For some recent works about debates about marriage related to the Enlightenment see, among others, E. Claire Cage, *Unnatural Frenchmen: The Politics of Priestly Celibacy and Marriage, 1720–1815* (Charlottesville, VA: University of Virginia Press, 2015); Edward T. Potter, *Marriage, Gender, and Desire in Early Enlightenment German Comedy* (Cambridge: Cambridge University Press, 2013); Sian Reynolds, *Marriage and Revolution: Monsieur and Madame Roland* (New York/Oxford: Oxford University Press, 2012).
23 For a detailed survey of marriage policies in antiquity, see Sabine Müller's chapter in the present volume. Marriage remained an important diplomatic element until modern times and secured ties between European rulers. The Habsburg Empire's diplomacy in particular used marriage as an important cornerstone of its political relations in Europe. See Paula Sutter Fichtner,

ed the marital union of man and woman among the seven sacraments, had placed it under its special protection, thoroughly regulated betrothal and divorce with canon law, and laid down norms for sexual behavior in and outside of marriage."[24] In later centuries, the Church continued to control the perception of and rules for marriage when "papal and episcopal courts ... exercised an enormous influence on the marital behavior of men and women, enforced legally defined impediments to marriage, and drew couples wanting to marry as well as already married couples before ecclesiastical tribunals."[25] Throughout medieval times, marriage as such was considered a public issue and legal institution rather than something related to romantic feelings. Although, as Italian historian Silvana Seidel Menchi affirms, "[t]here is no consensus as to exactly what a marriage was in early modern society," it was nevertheless more a legal than a romantic institution because "eroticism and passion are aspects that [were] alien to the traditional marriage"[26] in early modern times. A dichotomy between differing views on marriage, however, existed in the centuries leading from the medieval to the modern period, before the dispute eventually gained importance and became more central in the 19th century. These centuries, to quote Seidel Menchi once more, were—more or less—characterized by two main perspectives on marriage:

> The tension between the model of the disciplined marriage and the particularity of individual choices was a constant of European social history from the waning of the Middle Ages until the early nineteenth century. The tendentiously uniform model recommended by the ecclesiastical and secular authorities is counterpoised by a plurality of individual conjugal initiatives. A lively nuptial experimentation paralleled and challenged the norm. The model of a disciplined, regulated, socially conforming marriage, as formulated by jurists and theologians, found itself in competition with a variegated and undisciplined category of marriage, obeying individual impulses and emotions.[27]

From the 18th century, "debates about 'policing the family,' with marriage as its linchpin, through the state"[28] began to intensify. From "a global perspective on

---

"Dynastic Marriage in Sixteenth-Century Habsburg Diplomacy and Statecraft: An Interdisciplinary Approach," *The American Historical Review* 81, no. 2 (1976): 243–265.
24 Ludwig Schmugge, *Marriage on Trial: Late Medieval German Couples at the Papal Court* (Washington, DC: Catholic University of America Press, 2012), 1–2.
25 Ibid., 2.
26 Silvana Seidel Menchi, "Introduction," in *Marriage in Europe, 1400–1800*, ed. Silvana Seidel Menchi (Toronto: University of Toronto Press, 2016), 3.
27 Ibid., 7.
28 Julia Moses, "Introduction: Making Marriage 'Modern'," in *Marriage, Law and Modernity: Global Histories*, ed. Julia Moses (London: Bloomsbury, 2017), 1.

the modern history of marriage," which is represented in Julia Moses' recently published anthology *Marriage, Law and Modernity* (2017), this century "witnessed the creation of global marital norms that, to a certain extent, became enshrined in international law."[29] The debates related to the establishment of the new norms "had contradictory effects, enabling love to thrive in various forms, yet discouraging or outright banning certain types of relationships" as, for some of those, defining the new set of norms related to marital relationships was an expression of "modernity."[30]

Hence it was not only legal debates that characterized the discourse about marriage, as in the 18th and 19th centuries, philosophers also participated in the discourse about the role of the martial relationship between women and men for the family and society.[31] For the German philosopher Georg Wilhelm Friedrich Hegel (1770–1831), to quote Žižek's evaluation here,

> marriage is "a contract to transcend the standpoint of contract": contract is a deal between two or more autonomous individuals, each of whom retains their abstract freedom (as is the case in exchange of commodities), while marriage is a weird contract by means of which the two concerned parties oblige themselves precisely to abandon/surrender their abstract freedom and autonomy and to subordinate it to a higher organic ethical unity.[32]

Hegel therefore endorsed the "'sacrifice of personality' as the only suitable basis for marriage,"[33] especially since his idea of the family is not based on equality between men and women. The family Hegel has in mind, according to US women's studies scholar and historian Joan B. Landes, "is not a simple model for politics. He therefore rejects the idea that authority relationships throughout society are homogeneous, a view which underlies the patriarchalist argument that the father's relationship to his wife and children is analogous to the king's relationship to his subjects."[34]

For Hegel, the family can also not be separated from the society it exists in, which is why he "rejects the proposition that the family constitutes a wholly independent sphere of social existence, a refuge from an unpleasant social

---

29 Ibid.
30 Ibid.
31 For the 18th century, see Marlene LeGates, "The Cult of Womanhood in Eighteenth-Century Thought," *Eighteenth-Century Studies* 10, no. 1 (1976): 21–39.
32 Žižek, "Hegel on Marriage," 2. The direct Hegel quotes refer to *Philosophy of Right* (1820), accessed March 4, 2021, http://www.marxists.org/reference/archive/hegel/works/pr/prfamily.htm.
33 Kathryn Wilkinson, "Hegel, The Sacrifice of Personality and Marriage" (PhD diss., University of Sheffield, 2006). For a more detailed discussion of this sacrifice, see ibid., 111–162.
34 Joan B. Landes, "Hegel's Conception of the Family," *Polity* 14, no. 1 (1981): 5.

world."³⁵ In his work *Philosophy of Right* (1820), he nevertheless points to problems of legal contracts in their relation to marriage: "[T]hough marriage begins in contract, it is precisely a contract to transcend the standpoint of contract, the standpoint from which persons are regarded in their individuality as self-subsistent units."³⁶ Hegel therefore shows some ambivalence in his elaborations about marriage, as this relationship tends to "transcends the standpoint from which man and wife are deemed to have property in each other, especially in one another's sexual faculties."³⁷ The described ambivalence expressed about the nature of marriage in Hegel's writings consequently points to the discourses of his time and provided what German-American scholar Rudolf J. Siebert called "[t]he Origin of Subjective Freedom."³⁸ Regardless of this origin, Hegel continued to consider women and men to be different with regard to their nature. In his *Philosophy of Right*, Hegel argued the following:

> Women are capable of education, but they are not made for activities which demand a universal faculty such as the more advanced sciences, philosophy, and certain forms of artistic production. Women may have happy ideas, taste, and elegance, but they cannot attain to the ideal. The difference between men and women is like that between animals and plants. Men correspond to animals while women correspond to plants because their development is more placid and the principle that underlies it is the rather vague unity of feeling. When women hold the helm of government, the state is at once in jeopardy, because women regulate their actions not by the demands of universality but by arbitrary inclinations and opinions. Women are educated – who knows how? – as it were by breathing in ideas, by living rather than by acquiring knowledge. The status of manhood, on the other hand, is attained only by the stress of thought and much technical exertion.³⁹

Although Hegel's works and thoughts are still important today and kept their actuality in many regards,⁴⁰ these views are nevertheless now outdated. However, they show how marriage and the role of the two sexes within it were perceived in the first third of the 19th century.

Beyond the philosophical level of marriage discourses, the relationships themselves and the motives to engage in them were and still are very often relat-

---

35 Ibid., 6.
36 Cited in ibid., 8.
37 Ibid., 10.
38 Rudolf J. Siebert, *Hegel's Concept of Marriage and Family: The Origin of Subjective Freedom* (Washington, DC: University Press of America, 1979).
39 Cited in Landes, "Hegel's Conception of the Family," 22.
40 As exemplars, see, among others, Marina F. Bykova and Kenneth R. Westphal, eds. *The Palgrave Hegel Handbook* (Cham: Palgrave, 2020); Slavoj Žižek, *Hegel im verdrahteten Gehirn*, trans. Frank Born (Frankfurt am Main: Fischer, 2020).

ed to the "main economic behaviors of workers and consumers."[41] American economist Shoshana Grossbard therefore correctly emphasizes that multiple questions and the way marriage might relate to them or provide specific answers determines the human decision to legally bond with another: "How much people work, how much they earn, what kind of work they engage in is partially motivated by their marriage goals and commitments."[42] That especially working-class women were driven into marriage by their exploitative working conditions, just to be exploited as mothers and workers once fulfilling their role as wives, was criticized early on by leading figures of the socialist and workers' movements.

Marriage Roles and Social Questions

The German Social Democrat August Bebel (1840–1913) emphasized the capitalist nature of marriage in his work *Woman and Socialism* (1879).[43] He argues that "[m]onogamic marriage as has been sufficiently shown, is the outcome of the system of gain and property that has been established by bourgeois society, and therefore undoubtedly forms one of its basic principles."[44] In this important work, Bebel outlined that "marriage, which depends upon the bourgeois system of property, is a more or less forced relation, having many disadvantages, and frequently fulfilling its purpose only insufficiently or not at all."[45] These considerations were essential for the re-evaluation of marriage in the late 19th century, and many feminists who also shared a political identity of the left would emphasize this issue as part of the larger "woman question" that they increasingly connected with a female view on the ongoing class struggle.[46] Another important representative of the political left who similarly emphasized the problems related to marriage as a form of exploitation was Friedrich Engels (1820–1895).[47] In his

---

[41] Shoshana Grossbard, *The Marriage Motive: A Price Theory of Marriage* (New York: Springer, 2015), 5.
[42] Ibid.
[43] August Bebel, *Woman and Socialism* (New York: Socialist Literature Co., 1910 [1879]), accessed March 4, 2021, https://www.marxists.org/archive/bebel/1879/woman-socialism/index.htm.
[44] Ibid., chap. VIII.
[45] Ibid.
[46] For a more detailed discussion of this connection, see Vincent Streichhahn and Frank Jacob, eds., *Geschlecht und Klassenkampf: Die "Frauenfrage" aus deutscher und internationaler Perspektive im 19. und 20. Jahrhundert* (Berlin: Metropol, 2020).
[47] On Engels's position toward and his role in the debate of the "woman question" during the 19th century, see Vincent Streichhahn, "Friedrich Engels: From the 'Woman Question' to Social

work *The Origin of the Family, Private Property and the State* (1884), Engels characterized marital relationships as follows:

> Monogamous marriage was a great historical step forward; nevertheless, together with slavery and private wealth, it opens the period that has lasted until today in which every step forward is also relatively a step backward, in which prosperity and development for some is won through the misery and frustration of others. It is the cellular form of civilized society, in which the nature of the oppositions and contradictions fully active in that society can be already studied. ... But a second contradiction thus develops within monogamous marriage itself. At the side of the husband who embellishes his existence with hetaerism stands the neglected wife. And one cannot have one side of this contradiction without the other, any more than a man has a whole apple in his hand after eating half. But that seems to have been the husbands' notion, until their wives taught them better. With monogamous marriage, two constant social types, unknown hitherto, make their appearance on the scene – the wife's attendant lover and the cuckold husband. The husbands had won the victory over the wives, but the vanquished magnanimously provided the crown. Together with monogamous marriage and hetaerism, adultery became an unavoidable social institution – denounced, severely penalized, but impossible to suppress.[48]

Many women and men would eventually share such views and criticize marriage as a form of patriarchic exploitation and suppression. Although they had been contested by men as well, both of these elements were particularly harsh for the women who got married, or as British historian Philippa Levine expressed it:

> Marriage, for the nineteenth-century woman, was perhaps the single most profound and far-reaching institution that would affect the course of her life. For the woman who did not marry, whether by choice or by chance, spinsterhood marked her as one of society's unfortunates, cast aside from the common lot of the sex. For the woman who did enter wedlock, marriage spelled, simultaneously, a loss of freedom in both political and financial matters, perhaps domestic drudgery and frequent pregnancy, but undoubtedly a clear elevation in social status.[49]

Marriage expressed power over many women's lives, as, to quote Levine once more, "[i]t was undoubtedly one of the major agencies of socialization to

---

Reproduction Theory," in *Engels @ 200: Reading Friedrich Engels in the 21st Century*, ed. Frank Jacob (Marburg: Büchner, 2020), 235–270.

48 Friedrich Engels, *Der Ursprung der Familie, des Privateigenthums und des Staats* (Hottingen-Zurich: Verlag der Schweizerischen Volksbuchhandlung, 1884). English text taken from https://www.marxists.org/archive/marx/works/1884/origin-family/ch02d.htm, accessed March 4, 2021.

49 Philippa Levine, "'So Few Prizes and So Many Blanks': Marriage and Feminism in Later Nineteenth Century England," *Journal of British Studies* 28, no. 2 (1989): 150. Although Levine focused her evaluation on Victorian England, it can be applied for women in other national contexts of the 19th century as well.

which women were exposed; the pressures it imposed were enormously persuasive and difficult to resist."[50] The contestation of marriage by women during the 19th century was nevertheless taking place and consequently one of the elements that would stimulate the genesis of the "First Wave" feminists in many national contexts.[51]

During the 19th century, the discourses about marriage intensified, especially since they "were really about who should be included as full citizens in the polity"[52] and represented a stronger demand by women to be treated equally. This also involved the debate about the legal right to divorce. In the 18th century, in his posthumously published work *The History of the Pleas of the Crown* (1736), the influential English barrister and judge Sir Matthew Hale (1609–1676) emphasized the right of men in marital relations by arguing that husbands cannot be considered guilty for "a rape committed by himself upon his lawful wife, for by their mutual matrimonial consent and contract the wife hath given herself in this kind unto her husband which she cannot retract."[53] Divorce, which had long not been an option for women at all[54] and controlled exclusively by the Church, was secularized during the 19th century, although "[t]he grounds upon which divorce could be granted were different for men and women (the infamous divorce double standard)."[55] Step by step, and in accordance with other rights women began to demand,[56] "married women had won a number of important rights in relation to the ownership of property and the right to leave a marriage."[57]

---

[50] Ibid.
[51] Olive Banks, *Becoming a Feminist: The Social Origins of "First Wave" Feminism* (Brighton: Wheatsheaf Books, 1986); Valerie Sanders, "First Wave Feminism," in *The Routledge Companion to Feminism and Postfeminism*, 2nd ed., ed. Sarah Gamble (London: Routledge, 2001), 15–24.
[52] Josephson, "Citizenship," 270.
[53] Matthew Hale, *History of the Pleas of the Crown 1736*, vol. 1, ed. Peter R. Glazebrook (London: Professional Books, 1971), 629, cited in Grossi, *Looking for Love*, 20. In Germany, to name just one example here, rape in a marriage could not be legally charged until 1992. For a broader contextualization, see Melanie Randall, Jennifer Koshan and Patricia Nyaundi, eds., *The Right to Say No: Marital Rape and Law Reform in Canada, Ghana, Kenya and Malawi* (Oxford: Hart, 2017).
[54] In Britain, between 1670 and 1857, only four of the 325 people who successfully obtained a divorce were women. Grossi, *Looking for Love*, 22.
[55] Ibid.
[56] For a survey of women's struggles to gain political rights, first and foremost the right to vote, see, among others, Hedwig Richter and Kerstin Wolff, eds., *Frauenwahlrecht: Demokratisierung der Demokratie in Deutschland und Europa* (Hamburg: Hamburger Edition, 2018).
[57] Grossi, *Looking for Love*, 23.

The 20th Century and the Struggle for Equality

Once the "First Wavers" had begun their quest for more political and social equality, it was the 20th century that witnessed substantial changes. Marriage and its image as such seemed to have reached a crisis around 1900[58] and, as Austrian historian Christa Putz emphasized, "[i]t could not be overlooked that the zeal of sex researchers was also driven by a larger social problem. Around 1900 it is a question of 'saving' marriage or at least making its crises manageable."[59] The traditional relationship between man and woman was supposed to face a general crisis, as represented by "[t]he legal disadvantage of women in marriage, the increase in the divorce rate, the decline in marital births and the failure of romantic ideals in practice."[60] This was also related to the change of the considerations about marriage, love, and sex.[61] Especially sexual passion as part of a marital relationship was debated as well, and in the early 1900s, guide books, reflecting feminist demands, "no longer teach spouses how to curb their lust and, if possible, subordinate it to conception, but how it could succeed in igniting passion and maintaining it permanently. It is downright prescribed for the couple to realize themselves sexually in marriage."[62]

Marital relations and how they could be emotionally, socially, and politically reframed were also a subject in literary works that began to focus on such relationships.[63] "New Woman fiction" challenged traditional images of women in literature, and the new female heroines that were presented also struggled with ex-

---

[58] Christa Putz, *Verordnete Lust: Sexualmedizin, Psychoanalyse und die "Krise der Ehe," 1870–1930* (Bielefeld: Transcript, 2011), 123–154.
[59] Ibid., 16.
[60] Ibid.
[61] Christina Simmons, *Making Marriage Modern: Women's Sexuality from the Progressive Era to World War II* (New York: Oxford University Press, 2009), 58–104.
[62] Putz, *Verordnete Lust*, 16. Also see Lesley Hall, "'Good Sex': The New Rhetoric of Conjugal Relations," in *The Facts of Life: The Creation of Sexual Knowledge in Britain 1650–1950*, eds. Roy Porter and Lesley Hall (New Haven, CT: Yale University Press, 1995), 202–223.
[63] One example would be H. G. Wells, *Marriage* (Auckland, NZ: The Floating Press, 2011 [1912]). Wells in a way describes Marjorie, the female protagonist of his novel, as resembling the fact that women were demanding more than society was actually offering them: "That was the visible Marjorie. Somewhere out of time and space was an invisible Marjorie who looked out on the world with those steady eyes, and smiled or drooped with the soft red lips, and dreamt, and wondered, and desired." Ibid., 8.

istent marital norms.[64] Literature studies scholar Sevinç Elaman identified a "juxtaposition of a multiplicity of conflicting voices on the New Woman question" in the early 20th century, "particularly as these are expressed in the heroines' inner dilemmas and conflicts and around the issues of marriage, divorce and sexuality."[65] Elaman further emphasized that "[t]he New Woman was one of the most dramatic symbols of the crisis of gender relations that occurred during the fin-de-siècle period in a number of societies. Her image was first brought to public attention worldwide in the 1890s as she became a subject of discussion and controversy in magazines, periodicals and newspapers."[66] Dichotomic gender norms, including the ones related to emotions[67] or the female capacity with regard to work, were more and more contested, especially by transnational events like the First World War that challenged not only political systems and social orders[68] but also the existent gender roles,[69] including traditional considerations about marriage.[70]

The First World War nevertheless also laid the ground for a hyper-masculinity[71] that would determine a reversed course against the emancipatory efforts that had been achieved so far.[72] The interwar period as well as the Second

---

[64] Sevinç Elaman, "A Feminist Dialogic Reading of the New Woman: Marriage, Female Desire and Divorce in the Works of Edith Wharton and Halide Edib Adıvar" (PhD diss., University of Manchester, 2012), 4.
[65] Ibid.
[66] Ibid., 9. On the "New Woman" narrative and some of its main represenatatives, see Ann Heilmann, *New Woman Strategies: Sarah Grand, Olive Schreiner, Mona Caird* (Manchester: Manchester University Press, 2004).
[67] Manuel Borutta and Nina Verheyen, "Vulkanier und Choleriker? Männlichkeit und Emotion in der deutschen Geschichte 1800–2000," in *Die Präsenz der Gefühle: Männlichkeit und Emotion in der Moderne*, eds. Manuel Borutta and Nina Verheyen (Bielefeld: Transcript, 2010), 12.
[68] For a global perspective on these protests, see Marcel Bois and Frank Jacob, eds. *Zeiten des Aufruhrs (1916–1921): Globale Proteste, Streiks und Revolutionen gegen den Ersten Weltkrieg und seine Auswirkungen* (Berlin: Metropol, 2020).
[69] See, among others, Susan A. Grayzel, *Women's Identities at War: Gender, Motherhood, and Politics in Britain and France During the First World War* (Chapel Hill, NC: University of North Carolina Press, 1999).
[70] Sandra Brée and Saskia Hin, eds., *The Impact of World War I on Marriages, Divorces, and Gender Relations in Europe* (London: Routledge, 2020).
[71] George L. Mosse, *The Image of Man: The Creation of Modern Masculinity* (New York: Oxford University Press, 1996).
[72] On marriage norms during the Second World War, see Ulrike Jureit, "Zwischen Ehe und Männerbund: Emotionale und sexuelle Beziehungsmuster im Zweiten Weltkrieg," *WerkstattGeschichte* 22 (1999): 61–73.

World War proved to be disastrous for the emancipatory course of the feminist movements around the globe, and as legal scholar Mary Becker emphasizes,

> Human beings, whether men, women, or children, do not flourish when hyper-masculinity is glorified and traditionally feminine qualities (such as care, caretaking, and valuing relationships) are denigrated. Nor do human beings flourish when all males are pressured to adopt hypermasculine attributes and repress feminine ones, and all females are pressured to adopt traditionally feminine attributes and repress masculine ones.[73]

Regardless of such setbacks, feminists, like the sociologist Jessie Bernard (1903–1996) in her work *The Future of Marriage* (1972),[74] argued that the future of marital relationships would rely upon its re-definition to match female demands for a more equal and emancipated form of marriage. Bernard highlighted the continuation of two different forms or norms of marriage: a female one and a male one.[75] This double standard could cause trouble for the patriarchy, especially "when women in traditional marriages assume a feminist identity, they and their relational expectations change a great deal but their husbands have little interest in changing their beliefs and behaviors,"[76] expressing their unease with an emancipated form of relationship that would challenge their ruling position. Feminists have consequently pointed to the exploitative and repressive aspects of marriage, which functioned rather as a means of patriarchic suppression than the fulfillment of romantic ideals.

In addition, the pressure of marital relations on wives is manifold: "Women are the marital partners responsible for a family's emotional intimacy, for adapting their sexual desires to their husbands', for monitoring the relationship and resolving conflict from a subordinate position, and for being as independent as possible without threatening their husbands' status."[77] While women began to struggle for a better form of marriage, conservative forces, especially male elites, were not willing to change the existent patriarchic norms.[78] Since the 1990s and early 2000s, the LGBTQ+ community has also demanded changes with regard to the traditional concepts of marriage.[79] Next to the public debate

---

[73] Becker, "Patriarchy and Inequality," chap. 22.
[74] Jessie Bernard, *The Future of Marriage* (New York: Bantam Books, 1972).
[75] Karen R. Blaisure and Katherine R. Allen, "Feminists and the Ideology and Practice of Marital Equality," *Journal of Marriage and Family* 57, no. 1 (1995): 5.
[76] Ibid.
[77] Ibid., 6.
[78] William N. Eskridge and Christopher R. Riano, *Marriage Equality: From Outlaws to In-Laws* (New Haven, CT: Yale University Press, 2020), 113.
[79] John Mazurek, *The Road to Marriage Equality* (New York: Rosen Publishing, 2018), 47–58.

about same-sex marriage, there were legal implications that were hotly debated, especially in the United States:

> Marriage is an institution that many people view as the ultimate commitment between two partners, but it is also a legal institution that confers rights and protections. That is why for most of American history, same-sex partners had been denied something far greater than a piece of paper when they were turned away from their attempts to receive a marriage license. To be denied marriage also meant to be denied protections that included the right to exist as a family unit, the right to make legal decisions as a parent or spouse, and the right to self-govern one's family in a way that is agreeable to the law.[80]

Naturally, and not only in the United States, the debates about marriage and the changes achieved,[81] in relation to its nature and form as well as its meanings and implications, were continued in the late 20th and early 21st centuries and present an ongoing process that is unlikely to stop soon,[82] as societies are leading fierce debates about gender norms at the moment, especially with regard to the use of an appropriate gendered language.[83]

Marriage in the 21st Century

A new approach toward marriage is already being expressed by a new generation, i.e. the millennials. According to American scholar Brian J. Willoughby,

> millennials are approaching marriage with more hesitation and caution than ever before, even if it appears to bring happiness and fulfillment. Marriage, once the clear front-runner when it came to romantic unions, has now come under fire. There are numerous potential hypotheses as to why marriage may have lost its beneficial luster in the last few decades. For our purposes, however, we will focus on perhaps the most lingering yet important potential cause of this shift: that millennials have changed what marriage means and how it works.[84]

---

80 Ibid., 8.
81 Rebecca Probert, Joanna Miles and Perveez Mody, "Introduction," in *Marriage Rites and Rights*, eds. Joanna Miles, Perveez Mody and Rebecca Probert (Oxford: Hart Publishing, 2015), 3.
82 Laura L. Paterson and Georgina Turner, "Approaches to Discourses of Marriage," *Critical Discourse Studies* 17, no. 2 (2020): 136.
83 Felix Bohr et al., "Ist das * jetzt Deutsch?" *Der Spiegel*, March 5, 2021, https://www.spiegel.de/panorama/gesellschaft/gendergerechte-sprache-der-kulturkampf-um-die-deutsche-sprache-a-ad32de9a-0002-0001-0000-000176138596.
84 Brian J. Willoughby, *The Millennial Marriage* (London/New York: Routledge, 2020), 10.

Considering the historical discourses about marriage, this means that there is another and currently evolving "growing tension between the ideal of marriage held in the past and the new approach to marriage."[85] This tension is created "between one's personal ambitions and goals and the marital relationship's needs and goals"[86] and in a way repeats earlier negotiations between those parties who engage in martial relations to secure the best possible but first and foremost equal outcome of such an engagement. What if an essential precondition for such an achievement is the end of toxic patriarchy with regard to marriage?

The question of the ideal marriage is interesting not just for the intellectuals who reflect on it, nor for the state as the organizing institution for marriages, but for all human beings who are interested in a better, i.e. more equal, society.[87] This also opens the question of whether marriages are needed at all for a future society, although marriage is not at its end yet because it is still a strong aspect of our value system, maybe because human beings still want to rely upon romantic images that are often too far away from the repressive and exploitative realities of marriage. Some works on marriage also point out the "beneficial effects of marriage" that can exist: "Married people are generally healthier; they live longer, earn more, have better mental health and better sex lives, and are happier than their unmarried counterparts. Further, married individuals have lower rates of suicide, fatal accidents, acute and chronic illnesses, alcoholism, and depression than other people."[88] However, it must be emphasized that it is the quality and equality of the marital relationship that guarantees these advantages, not marriage per se. At the same time, as American sociologist Steven L. Nock pointed out, the advantages as such were quite unequal for women and men: "Even though marriage contributes to the well-being of both men and women, husbands are the greater beneficiaries. Men reap greater gains than women for virtually every outcome affected by marriage. When women benefit from marriage, it is because they are in a satisfying relationship; but men appear much less sensitive to the quality of their marriages and gain by simply *being married.*"[89] Nock therefore clearly pointed to the gender gap within marital relations: "Marriage itself improves men's lives; the quality of the marriage affects women's lives."[90] This also leads to different gender experiences in relation to marriage,

---

85 Ibid., 32.
86 Ibid.
87 Elizabeth Brake, *Minimizing Marriage: Marriage, Morality, and the Law* (Oxford: Oxford University Press, 2012), 1.
88 Steven L. Nock, *Marriage in Men's Lives* (Oxford: Oxford University Press, 1998), 3.
89 Ibid. Emphasis in the original.
90 Ibid.

which, of course, must also be considered when taking a look at historical marriage discourses. Women have a reason to challenge the marriage norms of their times, as they were rarely considered equal partners within such relationships. They were systematically put at a disadvantage, one that was legally sanctioned to allow husbands to rule, exploit, and abuse their wives. Without any doubt, as Renata Grossi correctly outlined, "the most decisive of the institution's meanings comes from the fact that it entrenched the dominance of the male/husband, and the complete subordination of the female/wife."[91] Historically, marriage meant "in fact a 'civil death' for women, who were treated like children, idiots, criminals and even slaves."[92] One can consequently only agree with Lawrence Stone's dictum that it was, next to economic necessities, only the "skillful resistance of many wives and the compassion and goodwill of many husbands"[93] that kept marriage, especially as a romantic ideal, alive over time.

Whatever the future of marriage and the discourses about it will be, it is essential to abolish its patriarchic nature. For far too long, marriage has continued to reproduce patriarchic norms,[94] and the generations of the 21st century will have to end this inequality. As "[m]ost men are aware of women's second shift and its unfairness, but are uninterested in change,"[95] it is important that the necessity for change is acknowledged and accepted by a majority of men as well to support, and not in a patronizing way, the establishment of further gender equality, especially with regard to marriage. This also means that feminists need to be fully supported by other political movements, especially from the left, which had failed to do so in the past, particularly since "there is ample evidence of the persistence of sexual violence, gendered discrimination and hostility to feminism across sites of left politics, old and new."[96] The image of modern marriage is at the same time too closely related to stereotypes that have remained uncontested for too long and abused by patriarchic elites around the globe. Becker, in this regard, makes it clear that it is important to contest such images and believes that

---

91 Grossi, *Looking for Love*, 19.
92 Ibid.
93 Lawrence Stone, *Broken Lives: Separation and Divorce in England, 1660–1857* (Oxford: Oxford University Press, 1993), 26, cited in ibid., 19–20.
94 Carol Smart, *The Ties that Bind: Law, Marriage and the Reproduction of Patriarchal Relations* (London: Routledge, 1984).
95 Becker, "Patriarchy and Inequality," 21–22.
96 Kirsty Alexander, Catherine Eschle, Jenny Morrison and Mairi Tulbure, "Feminism and Solidarity on the Left: Rethinking the Unhappy Marriage Metaphor," *Political Studies* 67, no. 4 (2019): 973.

[b]ecause patriarchy rests on the belief that women and men are essentially different, patriarchy values and rewards women and men for conforming to gender stereotypes. For example, in custody disputes, many courts consider economic stability as a reason for awarding custody to the father, who has been the primary breadwinner throughout the marriage. In contrast, mothers who have worked for wages throughout the marriage, most of whom have also been primary caretakers of the children, often lose custody because they work outside the home. It is important to break the link between sex and valuation.[97]

As mentioned before, it is therefore important to discuss what marriage actually is, and if it continues in the future, what it should look like and what it should stand for. The present anthology in this regard provides some examples from history and literature to show the manifold forms of marriage discourses that have been witnessed in the past.

The Contributions

The editors hope that the contributions will stimulate further and necessary debates about marriage, no matter if they are related to its institutional and legal aspects or to romantic aspects of an equal union between lovers, regardless of their self-declared and self-expressed gender norms.

The first section of this volume begins with some reflections about marriage discourses with regard to law and politics. Depending on its historical and geographical context, the understanding of marriage could be quite different from our modern day considerations. The contributions in the initial part of the volume will therefore show, that marriage was for centuries a political or legal aspect of human life, but nothing related to romance of human emotions at all. Sabine Müller provides a detailed survey and analysis of the roles of marriage in ancient societies, namely the Persian, Greek, and Roman ones. She shows that marriage has rather been considered a political institution and that it was an expression of alliances, lineage, and legitimization and not related to any romantic images that would later become attached to it by socially constructed narratives. That marriage was rather related to the public order and the display of gender roles followed ideas of order and rule is then discussed by Mariela Fargas Peñarrocha in her chapter on marriage discourses in early modern Spain. As in antiquity, the determination of what marriage was supposed to mean for the public and private order continued to be stipulated by men, securing the rule of the patriarchy. How First Wave feminists would later challenge these traditional struc-

---

97 Becker, "Patriarchy and Inequality," 51.

tures is discussed by Marion Röwekamp, who shows how women contested existent legal norms in relation to marriage in Imperial Germany and the Weimar Republic. The section as a whole therefore gives a first impression of how legal aspects of marriage were established, which purposes they served, and what efforts it took to change them.

The second section takes a closer look at some critics of social norms in relation to marriage during the latter part of the "long" 19th century.[98] Scientists and political activists alike questioned the existent gender relations in the late 1800s and began to actively demand a change, based on their theoretical considerations as well as practical experiences. Vincent Streichhahn opens the section and takes a closer look at the German sociologist Robert Michels (1876–1936) and his *Sexual Ethics*. Streichhahn locates the latter between the women's movement during the German imperial period and social democracy, showing that marriage discourses politically overlapped and found supporters or stimulated debates in different spheres in the early 1900s. Frank Jacob's analysis of Emma Goldman's (1869–1940) anarcha-feminist views on marriage and sexual liberation further highlights the amalgamation of early or proto-feminist positions with the political ideas of class struggle during the late 19th and early 20th centuries, in which women who represented the broad spectrum of the political left also acted as agents for gender equality, especially with regard to the further advancement of marriage as a truly equal form of relationship. Jowan A. Mohammed's chapter on Mary Hunter Austin (1868–1934) and her struggle against patriarchic norms, especially with regard to the marital relations of women in her times, shows that while this struggle was a political one, it was also expressed in literary works. Like Goldman, Austin reflected on marriage according to her personal experiences, but at the same time in their literary or political writings made clear statements for more gender equality. Mohammed with her analysis thereby bridges the second and the last sections of the present volume.

In the final part, Jamie Christopher Callison, Jessica Allen Hanssen, and Margaret Stetz provide chapters on literary discourses about marriage that show how authors dealt with marriage from the late 19th to the early 21st century and in which ways they used their texts as a way to stimulate and sometimes provoke their readers' thoughts about marriage and what it stood for. The single cobtributions consequently show in what way the literary texts in specific time periods can be read and positioned with regard to their respective take on marriage as

---

[98] Franz J. Bauer, *Das "lange" 19. Jahrhundert (1789–1917): Profil einer Epoche*, 4th rev. ed. (Stuttgart: Reclam, 2017).

an important social issue. After a discussion of marriage discourses in interwar Britain based on the poetry of the American writer H.D., i.e. Hilda Doolittle (1886–1961), in which Callison provides a close reading of the motifs of internal transformation and personal sacrifice, Allen Hanssen analyzes *The Age of Innocence*, the 1920 novel by Edith Wharton (1862–1937). Last but not least, Stetz shows how marriage-related images were combined with feminism and fashion in Ilene Beckerman's novel *Love, Loss and What I Wore* (1995) and the play of the same name written by Nora and Delia Ephron (2008).

What all the chapters provide is a glimpse into the long history of marriage discourses which, in their totality, paved the way to the 21st-century concept of marital relationships. This concept will be sure to stimulate further discourses and debates, especially since each generation has to redefine the existent social norms to adequately adjust them to its own necessities and demands. The editors hope that these discourses will contribute to a future form of marriage that is truly equal and might thereby also gain more accuracy in regards to the romantic images related to it.

Works Cited

Alexander, Kirsty, Catherine Eschle, Jenny Morrison and Mairi Tulbure. "Feminism and Solidarity on the Left: Rethinking the Unhappy Marriage Metaphor." *Political Studies* 67, no. 4 (2019): 972–991.

Anitha, Sundari and Aisha Gill. "Coercion, Consent and the Forced Marriage Debate in the UK." *Feminist Legal Studies* 17 (2009): 165–184.

Banks, Olive. *Becoming a Feminist: The Social Origins of "First Wave" Feminism*. Brighton: Wheatsheaf Books, 1986.

Bates, Laura. "How to Have a Feminist Wedding." *The Guardian*, June 28, 2014. https://www.theguardian.com/lifeandstyle/2014/jun/28/can-a-feminist-be-a-bride-laura-bates.

Bebel, August. *Woman and Socialism*. New York: Socialist Literature Co., 1910 [1879]. Accessed March 4, 2021. https://www.marxists.org/archive/bebel/1879/woman-socialism/index.htm.

Becker, Mary. "Patriarchy and Inequality: Towards a Substantive Feminism." *University of Chicago Legal Forum* 1 (1999): 21–88.

Bergoffen, Debra B. "Marriage, Autonomy, and the Feminine Protest." *Hypatia* 14, no. 4: *The Philosophy of Simone de Beauvoir* (1999): 18–35.

Bernard, Jessie. *The Future of Marriage*. New York: Bantam Books, 1972.

Blaisure, Karen R. and Katherine R. Allen. "Feminists and the Ideology and Practice of Marital Equality." *Journal of Marriage and Family* 57, no. 1 (1995): 5–19.

Bohr, Felix et al. "Ist das * jetzt Deutsch?" *Der Spiegel*, March 5, 2021. https://www.spiegel.de/panorama/gesellschaft/gendergerechte-sprache-der-kulturkampf-um-die-deutsche-sprache-a-ad32de9a-0002-0001-0000-000176138596.

Brée, Sandra and Saskia Hin, eds. *The Impact of World War I on Marriages, Divorces, and Gender Relations in Europe*. London: Routledge, 2020.

Bois, Marcel and Frank Jacob, eds. *Zeiten des Aufruhrs (1916–1921): Globale Proteste, Streiks und Revolutionen gegen den Ersten Weltkrieg und seine Auswirkungen*. Berlin: Metropol, 2020.

Borutta, Manuel and Nina Verheyen. "Vulkanier und Choleriker? Männlichkeit und Emotion in der deutschen Geschichte 1800–2000." In *Die Präsenz der Gefühle: Männlichkeit und Emotion in der Moderne*, edited by Manuel Borutta and Nina Verheyen, 11–39. Bielefeld: Transcript, 2010.

Brake, Elizabeth. *Minimizing Marriage: Marriage, Morality, and the Law*. Oxford: Oxford University Press, 2012.

Bykova, Marina F. and Kenneth R. Westphal, eds. *The Palgrave Hegel Handbook*. Cham: Palgrave, 2020.

Cage, E. Claire. *Unnatural Frenchmen: The Politics of Priestly Celibacy and Marriage, 1720–1815*. Charlottesville, VA: University of Virginia Press, 2015.

Elaman, Sevinç. "A Feminist Dialogic Reading of the New Woman: Marriage, Female Desire and Divorce in the Works of Edith Wharton and Halide Edib Adıvar." PhD diss., University of Manchester, 2012.

Engels, Friedrich. *Der Ursprung der Familie, des Privateigenthums und des Staats*. Hottingen-Zurich: Verlag der Schweizerischen Volksbuchhandlung, 1884. Accessed March 4, 2021. https://www.marxists.org/archive/marx/works/1884/origin-family/ch02d.htm.

Eskridge, William N., Jr. "A History of Same-Sex Marriage." *Virginia Law Review* 79, no. 9 (1993): 1419–1513.

Eskridge, William N. and Christopher R. Riano. *Marriage Equality: From Outlaws to In-Laws*. New Haven, CT: Yale University Press, 2020.

Fulford, Tim. "Poetic Flowers/Indians Bowers." In *Romantic Representations of British India*, ed. Michael Franklin, 113–130. New York: Routledge, 2006.

Grayzel, Susan A. *Women's Identities at War: Gender, Motherhood, and Politics in Britain and France During the First World War*. Chapel Hill, NC: The University of North Carolina Press, 1999.

Grossbard, Shoshana. *The Marriage Motive: A Price Theory of Marriage*. New York: Springer, 2015.

Grossi, Renata. *Looking for Love in the Legal Discourse of Marriage*. Canberra: Australian National University Press, 2014.

Hale, Matthew. *History of the Pleas of the Crown 1736*, vol. 1, edited by Peter R. Glazebrook. London: Professional Books, 1971.

Hall, Lesley. "'Good Sex': The New Rhetoric of Conjugal Relations." In *The Facts of Life: The Creation of Sexual Knowledge in Britain 1650–1950*, edited by Roy Porter and Lesley Hall, 202–223. New Haven, CT: Yale University Press, 1995.

Heilmann, Ann. *New Woman Strategies: Sarah Grand, Olive Schreiner, Mona Caird*. Manchester: Manchester University Press, 2004.

Jacob, Herbert. *Silent Revolution: The Transformation of Divorce Law in the United States*. Chicago: University of Chicago Press, 1988.

Josephson, Jyl. "Citizenship, Same-Sex Marriage, and Feminist Critiques of Marriage." *Perspectives on Politics* 3, no. 2 (2005): 269–284.

Jureit, Ulrike. "Zwischen Ehe und Männerbund: Emotionale und sexuelle Beziehungsmuster im Zweiten Weltkrieg." *WerkstattGeschichte* 22 (1999): 61–73.
Landes, Joan B. "Hegel's Conception of the Family." *Polity* 14, no. 1 (1981): 5–28.
LeGates, Marlene. "The Cult of Womanhood in Eighteenth-Century Thought." *Eighteenth-Century Studies* 10, no. 1 (1976): 21–39.
Levine, Philippa. "'So Few Prizes and So Many Blanks': Marriage and Feminism in Later Nineteenth Century England." *Journal of British Studies* 28, no. 2 (1989): 150–174.
Lovett, Margot. "On Power and Powerlessness: Marriage and Political Metaphor in Colonial Western Tanzania." *The International Journal of African Historical Studies* 27, no.2 (1994): 273–301.
Mazurek, John. *The Road to Marriage Equality*. New York: Rosen Publishing, 2018.
Moses, Julia. "Introduction: Making Marriage 'Modern'." In *Marriage, Law and Modernity: Global Histories*, edited by Julia Moses, 1–23. London: Bloomsbury, 2017.
Mosse, George L. *The Image of Man: The Creation of Modern Masculinity*. New York: Oxford University Press, 1996.
Nock, Steven L. *Marriage in Men's Lives*. Oxford: Oxford University Press, 1998.
Paterson, Laura L. and Georgina Turner. "Approaches to Discourses of Marriage." *Critical Discourse Studies* 17, no. 2 (2020): 133–137.
Potter, Edward T. *Marriage, Gender, and Desire in Early Enlightenment German Comedy*. Cambridge: Cambridge University Press, 2013.
Probert, Rebecca, Joanna Miles and Perveez Mody. "Introduction." In *Marriage Rites and Rights*, edited by Joanna Miles, Perveez Mody and Rebecca Probert, 1–16. Oxford: Hart Publishing, 2015.
Putz, Christa. *Verordnete Lust: Sexualmedizin, Psychoanalyse und die "Krise der Ehe", 1870–1930*. Bielefeld: Transcript, 2011.
Quek, Kaye. *Marriage Trafficking: Women in Forced Wedlock*. London: Routledge, 2018.
Randall, Melanie, Jennifer Koshan and Patricia Nyaundi, eds. *The Right to Say No: Marital Rape and Law Reform in Canada, Ghana, Kenya and Malawi*. Oxford: Hart, 2017.
Reynolds, Sian. *Marriage and Revolution: Monsieur and Madame Roland*. New York/Oxford: Oxford University Press, 2012.
Richter, Hedwig and Kerstin Wolff, eds. *Frauenwahlrecht: Demokratisierung der Demokratie in Deutschland und Europa*. Hamburg: Hamburger Edition, 2018.
Schmugge, Ludwig. *Marriage on Trial: Late Medieval German Couples at the Papal Court*. Washington, DC: Catholic University of America Press, 2012.
Seidel Menchi, Silvana. "Introduction." In *Marriage in Europe, 1400–1800*, edited by Silvana Seidel Menchi, 3–30. Toronto: University of Toronto Press, 2016.
Simmons, Christina. *Making Marriage Modern: Women's Sexuality from the Progressive Era to World War II*. New York: Oxford University Press, 2009.
Smart, Carol. *The Ties that Bind: Law, Marriage and the Reproduction of Patriarchal Relations*. Routledge: London, 1984.
Smock, Pamela J. "The Wax and Wane of Marriage: Prospects for Marriage in the 21st Century." *Journal of Marriage and Family* 66, no. 4 (2004): 966–973.
Steinbach, Anja. "Mutter, Vater, Kind: Was heißt Familie heute?" *Aus Politik und Zeitgeschichte* 67, no. 30–31 (2017): 4–8.
Stone, Lawrence. *Broken Lives: Separation and Divorce in England, 1660–1857*. Oxford University Press, Oxford, 1993.

Streichhahn, Vincent and Frank Jacob, eds. *Geschlecht und Klassenkampf: Die "Frauenfrage" aus deutscher und internationaler Perspektive im 19. und 20. Jahrhundert*. Berlin: Metropol, 2020.

Sutter Fichtner, Paula. "Dynastic Marriage in Sixteenth-Century Habsburg Diplomacy and Statecraft: An Interdisciplinary Approach." *The American Historical Review* 81, no. 2 (1976): 243–265.

Wells, H. G. *Marriage*. Auckland, NZ: The Floating Press, 2011 [1912].

Wilkinson, Kathryn. "Hegel, The Sacrifice of Personality and Marriage." PhD diss., University of Sheffield, 2006.

Willoughby, Brian J. *The Millennial Marriage*. London/New York: Routledge, 2020.

Ziegler, Mary. "An Incomplete Revolution: Feminists and the Legacy of Marital-Property Reform." *Michigan Journal of Gender & Law* 19, no. 2 (2013): 259–292.

Žižek, Slavoj. *Hegel im verdrahteten Gehirn*. Translated by Frank Born. Frankfurt am Main: Fischer, 2020.

Žižek, Slavoj. "Hegel on Marriage." *E-Flux Journal* 34 (2012). Accessed March 4, 2021. http://worker01.e-flux.com/pdf/article_8951758.pdf.

Section I: Marriage Discourses in Law and Politics

Sabine Müller
2 Political Marriage in Antiquity

Introduction

According to an ancient description of a kind of utopian society, located in the realm of the Indian ruler Sopeithes (4th century BC) west of the Hydaspes (Jhelum), physical qualities counted the most: "So they plan their marriages without regard to dower or any other consideration, but consider only beauty and physical excellence."[1] This image of an "ideal" society is thought to originate from a Greek writer of the 4th century BC: Onesikritos (ca. early 4th century BC – ca. late 4th century/early 3rd century BC), an admiral of Alexander III of Macedonia (356– 323 BC).[2] Onesikritos and his co-members of the Greek and Macedonian elites will have perceived the local marriage patterns in Sopeithes' realm as very remote from their own practices, even as an inversion. In their view, it was another element of the literary tales about India as an *alter orbis* at the edge of the world imagined as a land of marvels, strange peoples, and peculiar customs such as this marriage practice.

Throughout antiquity, marriage in leading circles was a matter of politics and social and/or economic status, not of beauty of body or soul or of love and affection.[3] Marriage was crucial to the establishment, consolidation, and ex-

---

1 Diod. 17.91.6–7. Trans. C. Bradford Welles. Also see Curt. 9.1.26–27; Strab. 15.1.30.
2 Onesikritos, *BNJ* 134 F 21.
3 On ancient marriage policy (a) of early Greek tyrants: Loretana De Libero, *Die archaische Tyrannis* (Stuttgart: Steiner, 1996), 393, 405–406; (b) in the Persian royal house: Maria Brosius, *Women in Ancient Persia (559–331 B.C.)* (Oxford: Oxford University Press, 1996), 35–82, 189– 190; (c) in Classical Athens: Cheryl A. Cox, *Household Interests: Property, Marriage Strategies, and Family Dynamics in Ancient Athens* (Princeton: Princeton University Press, 1998); Elke Hartmann, "Heirat und Bürgerstatus in Athen," in *Frauenwelten in der Antike: Geschlechterordnung und weibliche Lebenspraxis*, eds. Thomas Späth and Beate Wagner-Hasel (Stuttgart/Weimar: Metzler, 2000), 16–31; (d) in Argead Macedonia: Elizabeth D. Carney, "Marriage Policy," in *Lexicon of Argead Makedonia*, eds. Waldemar Heckel, Johannes Heinrichs, Sabine Müller and Frances Pownall (Berlin: Frank & Timme, 2020), 331–335; (e) in Hellenistic times: Jakob Seibert, *Historische Beiträge zu den dynastischen Verbindungen in hellenistischer Zeit* (Wiesbaden: Steiner, 1967); Daniel Ogden, *Polygamy, Prostitutes and Death: The Hellenistic Dynasties* (London: Duckworth, 1999); Sheila Ager, "Symbol and Ceremony: Royal Weddings in the Hellenistic Age," in *The Hellenistic Court*, eds. Andrew Erskine, Lloyd Llewellyn-Jones, and Shane Wallace (Swansea: The Classical Press of Wales, 2017), 165–188; (f) in Rome: Christiane Kunst, "Eheallianzen und Ehealltag in Rom," in *Frauenwelten in der Antike: Geschlechterordnung und weibliche Leben-*

OpenAccess. © 2021 Sabine Müller, published by De Gruyter. This work is licensed under the Creative Commons Attribution-NonCommercial-NoDerivatives 4.0 International License.
https://doi.org/10.1515/9783110751451-002

pansion of socio-political networks. Hence, potential spouses were chosen in accordance with politically useful factors: their families' political standing and influence, wealth and possessions, and symbolic capital such as reputation, wealth, interpersonal connections, and genealogical prestige. Marriages were either matters of alliances or means of access to and control of wealth, privileges, political influence, heritage, or sources of legitimacy.

The parties involved may or may not have had long-term goals in mind. However, a marital bond was essentially a matter of political usefulness at the moment of the marriage. Its value depended on situational, changeable power constellations and could fade away when the tides of politics turned. Thus, some political marriages could remain important and endure till death, whereas others were ephemeral and substituted by new, more profitable marriages. In general, both parties involved in a political marriage expected to profit the most from it in the situation when it was planned.

This paper analyzes different examples of political marriage in antiquity and discusses their aims and motivations. After some general remarks about the various reasons for political marriages that can be found in the extant evidence, selected examples from ancient Persia, Greece, Macedonia, and Rome will be discussed. These cases illustrate the most frequent motivations and circumstances of political marriages in antiquity: seizure of power, war, conquest, pacification, legitimization, and consolidation. Thereby, the categories can overlap. Due to the limited nature of our extant evidence, the focus of the paper is necessarily on ancient leading circles, especially ruling houses; our sources, in particular the literary ones, tend to focus on male members of the elites and to mention their wives (and the reason for the marriages) only *en passant*.

Some General Remarks on Marriage Patterns, Aims, and Motivations

Political marriages in ancient leading circles served various ends that can be categorized according to matters of alliance, control, legitimization, heritage,

---

spraxis, eds. Thomas Späth and Beate Wagner-Hasel (Stuttgart/Weimar: Metzler, 2000), 32–52; Francesca Cenerini, *Dive e donne. Mogli, madri, figlie e sorelle degli imperatori romani da Augustus a Commodo* (Imola: Angeli Editore, 2009); Francesca Cenerini, "Il matrimonio con un'*Augusta*: forma di legittimazione?" in *Femmes influentes dans le monde hellénistique et à Rome, IIIe siècle avant J.-C. – Ier siècle après J.-C.*, eds. Anne Bielman Sánchez, Isabelle Cogitore and Anne Kolb (Grenoble: UGA Éditions, 2016), 119–142.

and finances. Often, these categories do not exclude each other but overlap. On the basis of the extant evidence, one can make some generalizations about ancient political marriages and discern the following reasons divided into the categories of diplomacy, social advancement, financial advancement, legitimization, and familial politics.

a) Diplomacy:
   - to prepare a new alliance,
   - to revive, intensify, or cement existing alliances,
   - to solve a conflict or end a war/initiate peace,
   - to win allies against a common enemy,
   - to counter a military threat,
   - to pacify a conquered region/defeated family or ethnic group,
   - to integrate oneself into a family/elite/ethnic group,

b) Social advancement:
   - to expand one's political influence and/or social prestige,
   - to inscribe oneself in the spouse's genealogy,
   - to increase the number of one's followers,
   - to take control over a family, its possessions, privileges, followers, and claims,
   - to ensure the loyalty and gratefulness of the members of the spouse's family,
   - to prevent rivals from marrying into a specific family and lay claims to their possessions, privileges, followers, and claims and thus surpass them,

c) Financial advancement:
   - to inherit wealth and solve one's financial problems and control sources of wealth,
   - to keep property within a certain circle and prevent heritage from being split,

d) Legitimization:
   - to justify one's political, social, and/or economic position,
   - to reproduce legitimate heirs and provide them with a promising future,

e) Familial politics:
   - to tie a specific member of the spouse's family closer to oneself,
   - to take care of an otherwise unprotected female member of a family who lacks male relatives.

Most of the marriages about which we have information in our ancient literary sources seemed to function as marriage alliances. They were understood to establish or confirm *philia* relationships that were regarded as reciprocal. In consequence, in ancient leading circles, it was not love and marriage but alliance and marriage that went together like a horse and carriage.

Polygamy, practiced as a royal privilege in some ancient dynasties (i.e., Egypt, Persia, Parthia, Argead Macedonia), was a strategy to increase the number of marriage alliances (as well as to secure a sufficient number of candidates for the succession and distinguish the polygamous rulers from their leading circles).[4] However, in the eyes of monogamous Greek and Roman writers who tended to misunderstand the motivation of polygamous marriage policy, polygamy was perceived as an indicator of cultural difference.[5] While not universally seen as a symptom of decadence, it could occasionally be misjudged as a symptom of the rulers' lack of moderation and loss of morals.[6] In fact, royal polygamy was often a sign of the respective ruler's territorial expansion, wide-spanning networks, and diplomatic efforts. Of course, polygamy was not always but at least occasionally proof of a capable and well-connected politician.

Another marriage strategy often practiced as a royal prerogative in ancient dynasties (Egypt, Persia, Ptolemies, Seleucids, Hellenistic Pontos) was endogamy, next-of-kin marriage in its different forms.[7] Endogamy served to the end of the restriction of political influence, privilege, and property within a specific circle, status group, or family.[8] Practiced in royal houses, it could contribute to dy-

---

[4] Brosius, *Women*, 35; Sabine Müller, *Das hellenistische Königspaar in der medialen Repräsentation: Ptolemaios II. und Arsinoë II.* (Berlin/New York: De Gruyter, 2009), 21.

[5] Dominique Lenfant, "Polygamy in Greek Views of the Persians," *Greek, Roman, and Byzantine Studies* 59 (2019): 15–37.

[6] For instance, Plut. *Demetr.* 14.2–3; Ath. 13.557d; Plut. *Artax.* 23. Also see Brosius, *Women*, 35; Irene Madreiter, *Stereotypisierung – Idealisierung – Indifferenz: Formen der Auseinandersetzung mit dem Achaimeniden-Reich in der griechischen Persika-Literatur* (Wiesbaden: Harrassowitz, 2012), 92–93, 144–145, 161.

[7] Paul John Frandsen, *Incestuous and Close-Kin Marriage in Ancient Egypt and Persia: An Examination of the Evidence* (Copenhagen: Museum Tusculanum Press, 2009); Sabine Müller, "Endogamy," in *The Encyclopedia of Ancient History*, eds. Roger S. Bagnall, Kai Brodersen, Craige B. Champion, Andrew Erskine and Sabine R. Hübner (Oxford: Blackwell, 2013), accessed January 11, 2020, https://onlinelibrary.wiley.com/doi/10.1002/9781444338386.wbeah22094; Sheila Ager, "Royal Brother-Sister Marriage, Ptolemaic and Otherwise," in *The Routledge Companion to Women and Monarchy in the Ancient Mediterranean World*, eds. Elizabeth D. Carney and Sabine Müller (London/New York: Routledge, 2020), 346–358. As for Argead Macedonia, it has been suggested that some Argead rulers married their predecessors' widows, often their own step-mothers, as tokens of legitimacy (Ogden, *Polygamy*, xix–xxi, 8–9). However, such a pattern of "step-mother marriages" is based on scholarly reconstruction of gaps of knowledge. In fact, there is no reliable proof that such a marriage pattern existed in the Argead house.

[8] In Classical Athens, endogamy was part of heirship strategies to prevent the fragmentation of a family estate and the flow of political power out of an *oikos*: Cherly A. Cox, *Household Inter-*

nastic loyalty and avoid the risk of political entanglement produced by exogamy: any foreign political actor was denied the chance to lay claim to the throne through exogamous marriage.

As for the role of the bride, in the Persian, Graeco-Macedonian, and Roman worlds, it was the head of the respective house, thus usually her father (and in case of his death, her brother), who arranged the marriage.[9] In scholarly works, not at least due to the scarcity of ancient evidence, there is a focus on women from royal houses in marriage alliances. Recent studies of royal women have shown that contrary to the traditional assumption, they were not always or necessarily passive pawns or merely tokens in an alliance. Some of them could act as agents of their dynasty and/or natal house, which they continued to represent, and play a role in diplomacy, representation, patronage, legitimization, succession policy, religious cult, or euergetism.[10]

Marriage and Political Rise

Archaic Athens is the setting of a prime early example of a marriage alliance for the sake of political control. The source is one of the most important ancient historiographers, Herodotos, the "father of history" (ca. 490/80 – 420s BC).[11] In the mid-6th century BC, an age in Greek history when tyranny as a constitution was in bloom, Athens was also governed by a tyrant, Peisistratos (ca. early 6th century – ca. 520s BC).[12] However, his opponents Lykourgos and Megakles,

---

ests: *Property, Marriage Strategies, and Family Dynamics in Ancient Athens* (Princeton: Princeton University Press, 1998), 132–136.
9 Brosius, *Women*, 35–82; Hartmann, "Heirat," 17; Helen King, "Bound to Bleed. Artemis and Greek Women," in *Sexuality and Gender in the Classical World. Readings and Sources*, ed. Laura McClure (Oxford: Blackwell, 2002), 79; Carney, "Marriage Policy," 334.
10 Elizabeth D. Carney and Sabine Müller, "Introduction to Thinking about Women and Monarchy in the Ancient World," in *The Routledge Companion to Women and Monarchy in the Ancient Mediterranean World*, eds. Elizabeth D. Carney and Sabine Müller (London, New York: Routledge, 2020), 3–7. Carney, "Marriage Policy," 334. On the traditional view, see Ogden, *Polygamy*, 155.
11 Cic. *leg.* 1.5.
12 On Peisistratos, see Helmut Berve, *Die Tyrannis bei den Griechen* (München: Beck, 1967), I, 47–63; II, 543–55; Brian M. Lavelle, "The Compleat Angler: Observations on the Rise of Peisistratos in Herodotos (1.59–64)," *Classical Quarterly* 41, no. 2 (1991): 317–324; De Libero, *Tyrannis*, 41–134; Heleen Sancisi-Weerdenburg, "The Tyranny of Peisistratos," in *Peisistratos and the Tyranny: A Reappraisal of the Evidence*, ed. Heleen Sancisi-Weerdenburg (Leiden/Boston: Brill, 2000), 1–15; Brian M. Lavelle, *Fame, Money, and Power: The Rise of Peisistratos and 'Democratic' Tyranny at Athens* (Ann Arbor: University of Michigan Press, 2005), 66–115.

a member of the noble Alkmeonidai (from which the famous politician Perikles (ca. 490s–429 BC) would descend), allied against him and expelled him from the city in ca. 561/60 or 560/59 BC.[13] Shortly after, Megakles fell out with Lykourgos and reconciled with Peisistratos: "Megakles made proposals to Peisistratos asking if he were willing to marry his daughter and regain the tyranny on that condition."[14] Peisistratos agreed, established his second tyranny in Athens with Megakles' help (in ca. 557/56 or 556/55 BC), and married the latter's daughter. It was his third marriage. Herodotos terms their arrangement *homologie* (ὁμολογίη),[15] the Ionian form of *homologia* (ὁμολογία), "agreement." It is clear that Peisistratos' profit was his re-establishment in power. However, the politician Megakles was not content with being only Peisistratos' steppingstone. Apparently, he expected Peisistratos to grant the Alkmeonidai a future share in power: he wanted his male grandchildren, the future offspring of his daughter and Peisistratos, to succeed the latter as tyrants.[16] Such a prospect would also have increased Megakles' own standing in Athens. If this was part of the ὁμολογία, it would have meant a complete change of Peisistratos' own ideas about succession policy, as Herodotos makes clear: "But since he had sons who were already young men and the Alkmeonidai were said to be accursed, he did not want to have children by his new bride and therefore had intercourse with her *ou kata nomon* (οὐ κατὰ νόμον [not in accordance with the rule/custom])."[17]

The phrase οὐ κατὰ νόμον in the sense of avoiding the bride getting pregnant reflects that, according to the Greek view, procreation was of course a major aim of marriage to the end of ensuring the continuation of the house and thus was the "customary way" of being together with one's wife.[18] When he discovered that he had been tricked by Peisistratos, an insulted Megakles al-

---

[13] Hdt. 1.60.1. Also see Berve, *Tyrannis*, I, 48. On the (uncertain) chronology see Peter J. Rhodes, "Pisistratid Chronology Again," *Phoenix* 30 (1976): 219–233; Peter J. Rhodes, *A Commentary on the Aristotelian Athenaion Politeia* (Oxford: Oxford University Press, 1981), 198.
[14] Hdt. 1.60.2.
[15] Hdt. 1.61.1.
[16] Herodotos fails to mention the name of Megakles' daughter. Apparently, it was Koisyra (Schol. Aristoph. *Nub.* 48): Berve, *Tyrannis*, II, 545.
[17] Hdt. 1.61.2.
[18] See Hartmann, "Heirat," 22; King, "Bound to Bleed," 80. Writing in the 2nd-century AD Roman Empire, the Greek moral philosopher Plutarch advises men who want to become fathers of notable offspring to abstain from random cohabitation with courtesans and concubines: only children of a well-born, honorable father *and* mother (which implies a marriage) have the chance to become distinguished persons (*Mor.* 1a-b).

lied himself with Peisistratos' enemies and drove him into his second exile in ca. 556/55 BC.[19]

The scabrous part about Peisistratos' sexual trickery looks suspiciously like an exaggeration that contributes to the portrayal of the tyrant as a cunning trickster.[20] It is better not to be taken literally. While Herodotos' audience may have enjoyed the punchline that birth control ruined the Peisistratid-Alkmeonid cooperation, there is no need for any "unusual" sexual practices to explain why Megakles was disappointed by the outcome of the alliance. The marriage produced no future grandchildren for him and Peisistratos carried on supporting his three sons from his first marriage with an Athenian wife, among them Hippias and Hipparchos.[21] He did not want to endanger their future succession by siring a half-Alkmeonid son.

The marital bond had served Peisistratos well in order to seize power in Athens again, but it lost its political value and even turned into an obstacle as soon as his new father-in-law's ideas about succession policy collided with his own plans. Peisistratos was not willing to sacrifice his sons' future for the sake of the alliance that soon dissolved. As a result, he had to flee with his sons but came back in ca. 546/45 BC to establish his third tyranny by military force. After his death in ca. 528/27 BC, Hippias and Hipparchos succeeded him.[22]

Peisistratos' marriage alliance with the Alkmeonidai illustrates that, although one party had long-term goals in mind, the political constellations and calculations of the moment took priority. The value of the marriage was a matter of the politics of the day and faded when the interests of the parties involved collided. The example also shows that while the reproduction of legitimate heirs was a highly important factor of political marriages, not every ancient political marriage was intended to produce children.

Another example of marriage connected with the seizure of power is provided by the marriage policy of the Persian king Dareios I, founder of the Achaimenid dynasty (reg. 522/21–486 BC). Due to his need to legitimize and consolidate his rule, he concluded marriage alliances on a particularly wide scale that was

---

19 Hdt. 1.61.1–2; *Ath. Pol.* 15.1.
20 Berve, *Tyrannis*, I, 48–50; Lavelle, "Compleat Angler," 318; Carolyn Dewald, "Humour and Danger in Herodotus," in *The Cambridge Companion to Herodotus*, eds. Carolyn Dewald and John Marincola (Cambridge: Cambridge University Press, 2006), 151: an Athenian story of political humor. Peisistratos seems to have used the curse as a pretext.
21 *Ath. Pol.* 17.3.
22 *Ath. Pol.* 18.1; Thuc. 1.20.2; 6.55.1–3. Also see Berve, *Tyrannis*, I, 63–77; II, 554–60.

not repeated by his successors.²³ The political circumstances of his accession after the end of the Teispid dynasty of the Persian Empire's founder Kyros II (reg. ca. 559–530 BC) shed light on the background of Dareios' marriage policy.

Dareios paved his way to the throne by overthrowing the reigning king in a palace coup. The prime source for the events, the Behistun inscription, was commissioned by Dareios himself and reflected his propaganda. According to his version, he overthrew an evil usurper named Gaumata, who had pretended to be Kyros II's (already dead) son Bardiya.²⁴ This Bardiya would have been next in line to the throne after his childless brother Kambyses II (reg. 530–522 BC) had died in 522 BC. According to Dareios, he killed a "false" Bardiya and restored the kingship to his family, claiming that he belonged to the house of Kyros II.²⁵ However, it is controversial if his version can be trusted.²⁶ The circumstance that in 522/21 BC, various parts of the empire including the central regions of Persis, Media, and Babylonia revolted against Dareios' accession, seems to indicate that he had some problems with his legitimacy. His marriage policy may also hint at this. After Dareios had put down the revolts, he married *all* the remaining Teispid royal women: Kyros II's daughters Atossa and Artystone, Bardiya's daughter Parmys, and the Persian noble Otanes' daughter Phaidymie, the widow of the two previous kings.²⁷ To quote Sancisi-Weerdenburg: "It looks as if he wanted to leave no loose ends."²⁸

---

23 On Dareios I, see Josef Wiesehöfer, *Das antike Persien von 550 v. Chr. bis 650 n. Chr.* (Düsseldorf/Zurich: Artemis & Winkler, 1993), 33–43; Brosius, *Women*, 47–64, 194; Pierre Briant, *Histoire de l'empire perse de Cyrus à Alexandre* (Paris: Fayard, 1996), 119–173; Maria Brosius, *The Persians: An Introduction* (London/New York: Routledge, 2006), 15–25.
24 *DB* §§ 11–13.
25 *DB* §§ 3–4.
26 Wiesehöfer, *Das antike Persien*, 33–43; Briant, *L'empire Perse*, 113–127; Robert Rollinger, "Ein besonderes historisches Problem: Die Thronbesteigung des Dareios und die Frage seiner Legitimität," in *Pracht und Prunk der Großkönige*, ed. Historisches Museum der Pfalz Speyer (Darmstadt: WBG, 2006), 43; Brosius, *Persians*, 15–18; Amélie Kuhrt, *The Persian Empire: A Corpus of Sources from the Achaemenid Period* (London/New York: Routledge, 2007), 135–140; Bruno Jacobs,"'Kyros der große König, der Achämenide': Zum verwandtschaftlichen Verhältnis und zur politischen und kulturellen Kontinuität zwischen Kyros dem Großen und Dareios I.," in *Herodotus and the Persian Empire*, eds. Robert Rollinger, Brigitte Truschnegg and Reinhold Bichler (Wiesbaden: Harrassowitz, 2011), 635–663. Dareios may have been a remote relative of Kyros.
27 Hdt. 3.88.2–3. Also see Kuhrt, *Persian Empire*, 138.
28 Heleen Sancisi-Weerdenburg, "Exit Atossa: Images of Women in Greek Historiography on Persia," in *Images of Women in Antiquity*, eds. Averil Cameron and Amélie Kuhrt (Detroit: Croom Helm, 1983), 24.

Dareios' polygamous marriages served various political ends. The marital bond with the female descendants of the founder-figure Kyros II and the widows of Kambyses II and Bardiya increased Dareios' royal prestige and helped him to create an illusion of political continuity and to cover up the impression that he himself may have been a usurper. In addition, by tying all the Teispid women to himself, Dareios prevented rivals from marrying them, claiming the throne, or producing sons descending from Kyros' line who could raise claims.

Brosius characterizes Dareios' marriages as a complex arrangement designed to eliminate the danger of rivals to the throne and secure the loyalty of the most important Persian nobles.[29] As for the latter aspect, the families of his supporters Otanes and Gobryas were tied to Dareios by double marriage alliances: Otanes and Gobryas were simultaneously Dareios' fathers-in-law and brothers-in-law.[30] The endogamy went on: Gobryas' son Mardonios, Dareios' nephew, was married to a daughter of Dareios. The case of Mardonios, who became his and Xerxes' foremost general, shows that such interfamilial marriages served to create reliable, loyal next-of-kin candidates for the highest military and political offices.[31]

Dareios' marriage to his niece Phratagoune is interpreted by Herodotos, according to his Greek view, as a measure to concentrate family wealth since she was his brother's only child.[32] It may also have served to strengthen and unite the family core. In sum, due to the problems associated with his accession, Dareios' marriage policy illustrated a major effort to use marital bonds to the end of securing his position, legitimating his seizure of power, establishing links to the Teispid past, uniting his family, and excluding rivals from the outside. Perhaps it was a lesson he had learned by considering how he himself had ascended the throne.

The next example illustrates the connections between marital bonds, *clientelae*, and political career in the late Roman Republic. It is about a prestigious and profitable marriage alliance of the Roman politician and general L. Corne-

---

29 Brosius, *Women*, 61–62. The authenticity of Herodotos' account (3.84.2) that Dareios and his six Persian noble accomplices agreed before their palace coup that the future king would marry into one of their families is debated. See Wiesehöfer, *Das antike Persien*, 64; Brosius, *Women*, 51; Kuhrt, *Persian Empire*, 173, n. 3.
30 Gobryas had already been Dareios' father-in-law before his accession (Hdt. 7.2.2).
31 Hdt. 7.5.1. Also see Brosius, *Women*, 61; Briant, *L'empire Perse*, 168–169, 267–268, 541–558.
32 Hdt. 7.224.2. This means that property was inherited through the male line, and in order to safeguard his brother's property, Dareios married her. Kuhrt, *Persian Empire*, 626, n. 5. However, Brosius points out that due to our lack of knowledge about Persian inheritance customs, we cannot be sure if this is true or an *interpretatio Graeca*. Brosius, *Women*, 61. See, however, Briant, *L'empire Perse*, 972.

lius Sulla (ca. 138–78 BC).³³ Sulla came from an old patrician family that, however, had not produced a consul for generations. Also, his father had known how to marry in a profitable way. He had solved his financial problems by his second marriage to a wealthy heiress, Sulla's stepmother, who left her fortune to her stepson so that he became moderately well off.³⁴

Of Sulla's five marriages, we know most about the third, which was of major political significance: in 88 BC, Sulla divorced his second wife Cloelia and married Caecilia Metella.³⁵ This was a respectable tie to the Metelli, one of the most influential houses in Roman politics in his time. Plutarch calls it a *gamos endoxotatos* (γάμος ἐνδοξότατος), a most illustrious marriage, and adds that many members of the Roman elite were indignant at it because they thought he was unworthy of the woman.³⁶ Since in the competitive atmosphere of the late Roman Republican leading circles, the familial background of a wife and her prestige were important parts of the symbolic capital of a politician, it is understandable that some nobles were envious of Sulla's marriage coup. The marital bond increased Sulla's prestige and followers. Furthermore, it testified to his own political rise. To quote Badian: "This was official recognition."³⁷ The marriage also emphasized Sulla's political stand: Caecilia Metella, the widow of the eminent politician M. Aemilius Scaurus, was the niece of Q. Caecilius Metellus Numidicus, the arch-enemy of Sulla's major opponent (and former patron) C. Marius.³⁸ Sulla probably owed his consulship in the same year to this alliance.³⁹ His colleague in consulship in 88 BC, Q. Pompeius Rufus, also formed part of the network—the circle of the Metelli and M. Aemilius Scaurus—in which Sulla had now been integrated through his marriage.⁴⁰

In 83 BC, Sulla used his stepdaughter Aemilia, Caecilia Metella's child from her previous marriage, in order to establish an alliance. Plutarch reports: "In the case of Pompeius Magnus, at least, wishing to establish relationship with him, he ordered him to divorce the wife he had, and then gave him in marriage Aemi-

---

33 On Sulla, see Ernst Badian, *Lucius Sulla: The Deadly Reformer* (Sydney: Sydney University Press, 1970); Karl Christ, *Sulla: Eine römische Karriere* (München: Beck, 2002); Arthur Keaveney, *Sulla, the Last Republican* (London/New York: Routledge, 1982); Federico Santangelo, *Sulla, the Elites, and the Empire: A Study of Roman Politics in Italy and the Greek East* (Leiden/Boston: Brill, 2007).
34 Plut. *Sull.* 2.4.
35 Plut. *Sull.* 6.10–12, 33.3, 34.3, 37.2.
36 Plut. *Sull.* 6.10.
37 Badian, *Sulla*, 13.
38 Christ, *Sulla*, 199.
39 Plut. *Sull.* 6.5–6.
40 Badian, *Sulla*, 13, 20.

lia, daughter of Scaurus and his own wife Metella, whom he tore away from Manius Glabrio when she was with child by him."[41] This example illustrates the pragmatic and calculating attitude toward matrimony employed by the Roman leading circles; if a marriage lost its political value or if there was the option of another, more prestigious and profitable (in terms of either alliance, finances, or reproduction) marriage, divorce was the solution and pregnancy was no reason for not doing it.[42] Thus, the fate of Aemilia was not unusual.

Marriage in Connection with War and Pacification

The following section is concerned with one dynasty, the Macedonian Argeads. Before its consolidation and rise under the reign of Philip II (reg. 360/59 – 336 BC), Argead Macedonia was constantly threatened and pressed hard by ambitious neighbors such as the Illyrians and Thracians and also by Athens, due to her aspirations regarding Northern Greece. Consequently, an Argead ruler had to prove himself a good warrior and know how to use marriage policy as another diplomatic strategy in order to protect his position and realm.

An early example dates to 429 BC when, with the spiritual support of the Athenians, the Thracian ruler Sitalkes (reg. ca. 430s – 424 BC) invaded Argead Macedonia with a huge army, ravaged the country, and tried to overthrow the ruler Perdikkas II (reg. ca. 450 – 414/3 BC) and install the latter's nephew Amyntas on the throne.[43] However, Sitalkes' efforts were in vain: the Macedonians kept off in fortified places, while Perdikkas played cool and entered into negotiations with Sitalkes' nephew Seuthes who acted as his uncle's representative while the latter was on campaign. Perdikkas promised to give Seuthes his sister Stratonike in marriage and a large dowry. Seuthes accepted the offer; as a consequence, Sitalkes retreated from Macedonia.[44] The marital bond between the Argead and Odrysian houses signaled a return to friendly relations. Furthermore, Sitalkes also let down the Athenians, at that time Perdikkas' enemies. Thus, the marriage of Stratonike was a strategy in an emergency situation to reconcile with the invader and make him shift alliances.

---

41 Plut. *Sull.* 33.3; Plut. *Pomp.* 9.2 – 3. Trans. Bernadotte Perrin. Also see Kunst, "Eheallianzen," 33 – 34. However, Aemilia had a tragic end since she died in childbirth at Pompeius' house.
42 Kunst, "Eheallianzen," 40.
43 Thuc. 2.95.1 – 2, 100.3; Diod. 12.50.4 – 6.
44 Thuc. 2.101.5 – 6. Also see Sabine Müller, *Perdikkas II., Retter Makedoniens* (Berlin: Frank & Timme, 2017), 155 – 164.

The next example from Argead Macedonia illustrates how marriage could serve after a defeat to the end of taking precautions against another attack. In 393/92 BC, at the beginning of his reign, Amyntas III (reg. 394/3–370/69 BC) was expelled from his realm by the invading Illyrians, a traditional threat to Argead Macedonia.[45] Since the autonomous Upper Macedonian region of Lynkestis that controlled a route into Central Macedonia was the corridor of the Illyrians and the local Lynkestian dynasts were frequently hostile to the Argeads, Lynkestian involvement in the Illyrian invasion is possible. In ca. 390 BC, after his return, Amyntas married Eurydike, who was likely of Illyrian *and* Lynkestian descent.[46] Hence, Amyntas may have killed two birds with one stone by establishing ties to the Illyrian and Lynkestian elites in order to seal the peace and integrate himself into the ruling circles of his former opponents. In Eurydike's case, the political value of the marriage remained important since the Illyrians and Lynkestians did not cease to be sources of danger.[47] In addition, Amyntas' marriage to Eurydike produced three sons who succeeded him one after the other. The most important of them was Philip II, the Macedonian master of political marriage.

Polygamous marital bonds on an unprecedentedly wide scale were one of Philip's characteristic strategies to consolidate his conquests, appease defeated elites, and seal a peace or truce.[48] He married seven wives. Citing Satyros' *Life of Philip*, the 2nd-century AD writer Athenaios describes the way Philip concluded marriage alliances associated with his military campaigns and political ambitions:

> But Philip always married in connection to a war (*kata polemon egame*, κατὰ πόλεμον ἐγάμε) ... Wishing to govern the Thessalians as well, he begat children by two Thessalian women ... And, in addition, he also gained the kingdom of the Molossians, having married Olympias, by whom had Alexander and Kleopatra. And when he conquered Thrace, Kothe-

---

45 Diod. 14.92.3.
46 Plut. *Mor.* 14b; Suda *s.v.* Karanos κ 356 Adler; Strab. 7.7.8; Just. 7.4.4–5. Also see Elizabeth D. Carney, *Eurydice and the Birth of Macedonian Power* (Oxford: Oxford University Press, 2019), 23–31.
47 A female Argead's (flexible) symbolic capital consisted of the political and ancestral prestige of her natal family, the influence of her faction at court, her ability to give birth to a potential successor, and her personal ability to create useful personal connections.
48 Elizabeth D. Carney, *Olympias, Mother of Alexander the Great* (London/New York: Routledge, 2006), 21; Müller, *Königspaar*, 18–21; Sabine Müller, "Philip II," in *Blackwell Companion to Ancient Macedonia*, eds. Joseph Roisman and Ian Worthington (Oxford/Malden: Wiley-Blackwell, 2010), 169; Carney, "Marriage Policy," 332; Gerhard Wirth, "Philip II," in *Lexicon of Argead Makedonia*, eds. Waldemar Heckel, Johannes Heinrichs, Sabine Müller and Frances Pownall (Berlin: Frank & Timme, 2020), 416.

las the king of the Thracians came over to him, bringing his daughter Meda and many gifts.⁴⁹

While this passage tends to simplify more complex matters, it confirms the ancient understanding of Philip's marriage as a political alliance and a tactical marriage. At the beginning of his reign, in the context of expelling the Illyrians from Upper Macedonia, Philip married Audata, a female member of the Illyrian ruling house.⁵⁰ The establishment of his control over the formerly autonomous Upper Macedonian regions was likely prompted by his marriage to an Upper Macedonian noble, Phila from Elimeia.⁵¹ In ca. 357 BC, Philip sealed an alliance with Epeiros' ruler Arrhybas by marrying the latter's niece Olympias.⁵² Philip's interventions in strategically important Thessaly that finally led to the establishment of Argead control over the region were sealed by two political marriages when Philip integrated himself into the leading houses of the two major Thessalian cities, Larisa and Pherai.⁵³ All of these marriages formed part of his efforts to secure the borders of his realm. The marital bond to Meda, the daughter of the Thracian local dynast, in the late 340s BC mirrors the expansionist success of Philip and the rapidly extending frontiers of his realm.⁵⁴ Philip's last marriage in 337 BC was to Kleopatra, a member of the most influential Macedonian clan at his court. Ancient claims that it was love are misleading and serve to illustrate Philip's (alleged) moral flaws.⁵⁵ In fact, it was another political marriage to the end of ensuring the loyalty of Kleopatra's clan to Philip's war against Persia. Significantly, Kleopatra's guardian Attalos and his father-in-law Parmenion commanded Philip's advance force sent out in 336 BC to secure Asia Minor's coast.⁵⁶ Thus, by conferring the honor on them to marry into their clan, Philip wanted to tighten the links to his two influential generals.

---

49 Ath. 13.557b-e. Trans. Elizabeth D. Carney.
50 Ath. 13.557c; Just. 9.8.1; Paus. 8.7.6; Elizabeth D. Carney, *Women and Monarchy in Macedonia* (Norman: Gerald Peters Gallery, 2000), 57–58; Waldemar Heckel, *Who's Who in the Age of Alexander the Great* (Oxford: Wiley, 2006), 14.
51 Ath. 13.557c; Heckel, *Who's Who*, 129, 210.
52 Ath. 13.557c–d; Plut. *Alex.* 2.1; Carney, *Olympias*, 19–24; Heckel, *Who's Who*, 181; Elizabeth D. Carney, "An Exceptional Argead Couple: Philip II and Olympias," in *Power Couples in Antiquity: Transversal Perspectives*, ed. Anne Bielman Sánchez (London/New York: Routledge, 2019), 16–31.
53 Ath. 13.557c.
54 Ath. 13.557d; Carney, *Women*, 68; Heckel, *Who's Who*, 158.
55 Ath. 13.557d; Plut. *Alex.* 9.4.
56 Diod. 16.91.2, 93.9; 17.2.4; Just. 9.5.9; Sabine Müller, *Alexander der Große: Eroberung—Politik—Rezeption* (Stuttgart: Kohlhammer, 2019), 62–63; Wirth, "Philip II," 420.

Comparable to Herodotos' account on Peisistratos that may have served the Alexander historiographers as a blueprint, Attalos is said to have had high hopes for his ward's future sons and insulted Philip's son Alexander, raised as the heir apparent.[57] However, Philip carried on supporting the future succession of Alexander. One strategy to strengthen his son's courtly faction was provided by marriage policy. Philip emphasized the importance of Alexander's maternal descent from the Epeirote house of Olympias by giving Alexander's full sister Kleopatra in marriage to Olympias' brother Alexander I of Epeiros (reg. 343/42–331 BC) and staged it as a huge and splendid festival intended to impress the spectators.[58]

Comparably modestly, Alexander III "only" took three wives, each time in association with his campaigns and conquests in Asia. In 328/27 BC, his first marriage alliance was concluded in the context of his efforts to put down the fierce Baktrian-Sogdian resistance against the Macedonian rule. Alexander tried to weaken the circle of the leaders of the resistance by marrying Rhoxane, the daughter of one of them, the Baktrian noble Oxyartes. The strategy was successful: Oxyartes surrendered, and the marriage alliance helped to pave the way to the establishment of Macedonian control in the area (although it remained troubled).[59]

In 324 BC in Susa, Alexander took two Achaimenid brides, the daughters of the Persian kings Artaxerxes III (reg. 359–338 BC) and Dareios III (reg. 338–330 BC). He also gave his most influential generals (such as Ptolemy) Persian wives and registered the liaisons of his soldiers with Asian women.[60] These so-called mass marriages, organized in accordance with the Persian ritual, served to integrate the Macedonians into the Persian power structures and family networks, thus neutralizing the threats of Persian interfamily connections throughout the empire. Since Alexander could not marry into *all* of the numerous, widespread influential Persian families, this Herculean task was divided among his officials. Alexander's own marriages at Susa were limited to the illus-

---

[57] Plut. *Alex.* 9.4–5; Ath. 13.557d-e; Just. 9.7.3–5.
[58] Just. 7.6.3–4; Diod. 16.2.5–3.1; Müller, *Alexander*, 63–64; Carney, "Marriage Policy," 335.
[59] Arr. *An.* 4.19.4–5; Plut. *Alex.* 47.4; Plut. *Mor.* 332c, 338d; Curt. 8.4.24–26. Though the ancient sources claim that Alexander married Rhoxane for love, ending the rebellion was his motivation. Also see Carney, *Women*, 105–107; Heckel, *Who's Who*, 241–242; Marek Jan Olbrycht, "Macedonia and Persia," in *A Companion to Ancient Macedonia*, eds. Joseph Roisman and Ian Worthington (Oxford: Wiley-Blackwell, 2010), 360; Müller, *Alexander*, 174–177.
[60] Arr. *An.* 7.4.4–8; Diod. 17.107.6; Brosius, *Women*, 77–78; Carney, *Women*, 108–113; Waldemar Heckel, *The Conquests of Alexander the Great* (Cambridge: Cambridge University Press), 137–141; Olbrycht, "Macedonia," 360; Müller, *Alexander*, 198–201.

trious royal Achaimenid house. By marrying two of the remaining marriageable Achaimenid women himself and giving the third (another daughter of Dareios III) to his deserving general Hephaistion as a reward,[61] Alexander left no loose ends for any potential pretender with high hopes of marrying into the Achaimenid house. Thus, marriage policy was central to his plans concerning the consolidation of his conquests. However, his early death in 323 BC and the subsequent wars of his generals interfered. Not much is heard of the Persian-Macedonian marital bonds afterward, partly due to the lack of interest of our Greek and Roman writers in the fate of the Persian women and maybe also partly due to some Macedonian bridegrooms' lack of interest in keeping their Persian wives.[62]

Marriage and Legitimization

Kassandros (ca. 354–297 BC) was one of the Macedonian protagonists involved in the wars over Alexander's legacy. He fought for control over Macedonia and Greece. His marriage policy illustrates his urgent need to legitimize himself as a Macedonian ruler by profiting from his spouse's personal prestige. Compared to his rivals, Kassandros had to overcome a major disadvantage: unlike Polyperchon (ca. 390s/80s–after 301 BC) and Antigonos (ca. 382–301 BC), he had not participated in any of the battles of Alexander's Asian campaigns. He had stayed at home and failed in distinguishing himself in military matters. Hence, he could neither measure up to his opponents' military glory nor base his claims to rule parts of Alexander's empire on any achievement under Alexander's military command. Kassandros had to find another way to distinguish himself and justify his pose as the legitimate successor of the Argeads. His solution was marriage policy.

In 316 BC, he captured his opponent Olympias and her entourage at Pydna, among them Thessalonike, the daughter of Philip II and his Thessalian wife Nikesipolis. Since Thessalonike was still of marriageable age, Kassandros hurried to establish this prestigious link to the traditional Macedonian ruling house. He married Thessalonike immediately after the capture of Pydna.[63] The marriage

---

61 Arr. *An.* 7.4.5.
62 According to the traditional view, most of the bridegrooms hurried to get rid of their Persian wives after Alexander's death; Seleukos, who kept Apame, was an exception. Seibert, *Historische Beiträge*, 72. In the current debate, this is seen as an exaggeration based on meager evidence. Müller, *Alexander*, 201.
63 Diod. 19.52.1–2; *Heidel. Epit.*, FGrH 155 F 2.4; Franca Landucci Gattinoni, *L'arte del potere: Vita e opera di Cassandro di Macedonia* (Stuttgart: Steiner, 2003), 79–82; Franca Landucci Gat-

served as one of his strategies to style himself as Philip II's spiritual and "true" heir and create the illusion of political continuity (by abandoning Alexander, whom he was said to have disliked).[64] Kassandros might have hoped to become particularly popular with the Macedonians by triggering feelings of nostalgia and memories of Macedonia's rise to supremacy under Philip II.[65] The first-century BC historiographer Diodoros comments: "he began to embrace in his hopes the Macedonian *basileia*. For this reason he married Thessalonike, who was Philip's daughter and Alexander's half-sister, since he desired to establish a connection (*syngeneia*) with the royal house."[66] Diodoros also mentions that Kassandros' opponent Antigonos accused him of having forced this marriage upon the bride.[67] The authenticity of Antigonos' claim is a matter of scholarly dispute.[68] In any case, as a captive in the hands of the victor, Thessalonike had no chance to resist.[69] However, the marital bond endured. Thessalonike bore three sons to Kassandros and remained significant at his court—and his only wife; he chose not to practice polygamy. Apparently, her Argead prestige did not cease to be of legitimizing and ideological value. Her name was inscribed into the landscape for

---

tinoni, "Cassander's Wife and Heirs," in *Alexander and His Successors: Essays from the Antipodes*, eds. Pat Wheatley and Robert Hannah (Claremont: Regina Books, 2009), 260; Franca Landucci Gattinoni, "Cassander and the Legacy of Philip II and Alexander III in Diodorus," in *Philip II and Alexander the Great, Father and Son, Lives and Afterlives*, eds. Elizabeth D. Carney and Daniel Ogden (Oxford: Oxford University Press, 2010), 113–114. On Thessalonike see further Elizabeth D. Carney, *Women and Monarchy in Macedonia* (Norman: Gerald Peters Gallery, 2000), 155–159; Elizabeth D. Carney, "The Sisters of Alexander the Great: Royal Relics," *Historia* 37 (1998): 385–392.
64 Plut. *Alex.* 74.2–4; Landucci Gattinoni, *L'arte del potere*, 80–82; Carney, *Olympias*, 108; Landucci Gattinoni, "Cassander's Wife," 261–263; Landucci Gattinoni, "Cassander and the Legacy," 114, 116, 121. On Kassandros' propaganda see also Gerhard Wirth, "Alexander, Kassander und andere Zeitgenossen: Erwägungen zum Problem ihrer Selbstdarstellung," *Tyche* 4 (1989): 204–208. To the same end, Kassandros re-issued Philip's coins.
65 Landucci Gattinoni, "Cassander and the Legacy," 114.
66 Diod. 19.52.1–2. Trans. Russell M. Geer.
67 Diod. 19.61.2.
68 Carney, "Sisters," 388; Carney, *Women*, 156–157; Carney, *Olympias*, 70–87. She argues that it is plausible since Kassandros had Olympias killed, probably Thessalonike's foster-mother who had brought her up after Thessalonike's mother had died soon after her birth. This is accepted by Heckel, *Who's Who*, 265. However, Landucci Gattinoni argues that Thessalonike was also interested in marrying Kassandros since he guaranteed her a leading role for the first time. Landucci Gattinoni, "Cassander's Wife," 261–262.
69 On the fate of female captives in ancient warfare, see Kathy L. Gaca, "Girls, Women, and the Significance of Sexual Violence in Ancient Warfare," in *Sexual Violence in Conflict Zones*, ed. Elizabeth Heineman (Philadelphia/Oxford: University of Pennsylvania Press, 2011), 73–88.

eternity when he founded the city of Thessalonike in her honor, presumably soon after the marriage.⁷⁰

The following example from Severan Rome is a case of a failure of marriage policy: the arrangements did not have the desired effects regarding the impression made on the Roman recipients and the public image of the bridegroom. In 218 AD, the 14-year-old Varius Avitus Bassianus (204–222 AD), soon known as Elagabalus, was acclaimed emperor under the name Marcus Aurelius Antoninus Augustus.⁷¹ His accession was engineered by his grandmother Julia Maesa and her supporters such as the soldier P. Valerius Comazon.

Antoninus descended from an influential Syrian family from Emesa whose members had traditionally been priests of the main local deity Elagabalus.⁷² Also, the teenager had been groomed to be Elagabalus' high priest. His short reign was an unhappy experiment in emperorship; Antoninus was a manipulated youth, misguided and misused by his family as a political instrument. The idea of his clan to stress his priesthood of the god Elagabalus as the key factor of his legitimacy as Roman emperor (due to the youth's lack of any political or military deeds) proved to be unfortunate. The conservative Roman leading circles disliked an emperor who was first of all a high priest of a foreign deity. In addition, they disapproved of the god Elagabalus' translocation to Rome via his cult statue, integration in the Roman *pantheon*, and treatment as equal to Jupiter.⁷³

The marriage policy of Antoninus designed by the managing forces behind him mirrors the fruitless efforts to legitimize his position. Bertolazzi characterizes the marriages as a reflection of the differing views of Julia Maesa and Antoninus' mother Julia Soaemias: they "pushed him to alternately pursuing traditional and theocratic styles of rule."⁷⁴ In consequence, the marriage policy seems inconsistent.

---

70 Diod. 19.52.1; Elizabeth D. Carney, "Eponymous Women: Royal Women and City Names," *The Ancient History Bulletin* 2 (1988): 136–137; Carney, *Women*, 207; Heckel, *Who's Who*, 265.
71 Dio 80.4.1–2, 80.21.2; Hdn. 5.5.1. On Antoninus' reign, see Leonardo De Arrizabalaga y Prado, *The Emperor Elagabalus: Fact or Fiction?* (Cambridge: Cambridge University Press, 2010); Martijn Icks, *The Crimes of Elagabalus: The Life and Legacy of Rome's Decadent Boy Emperor* (London: L.B. Tauris, 2011); Riccardo Bertolazzi, "Women in the Severan Dynasty," in *The Routledge Companion to Women and Monarchy in the Ancient Mediterranean World*, eds. Elizabeth D. Carney and Sabine Müller (London/New York: Routledge, 2020), 455–457.
72 Dio 79.30.2; HA *Heliog.* 1.5; De Arrizabalaga y Prado, *Emperor*, 6; Edward Lipinski, "Elaha Gabal d'Émèse dans son context historique," *Latomus* 70 (2011): 1081–11.
73 Hdn. 5.3.5, 5.5.8, 5.6.6–9; Dio 80.11.1; HA *Heliog.* 1.6, 3.4. The decision to force the nobility to participate in the Emesan cultic services (Dio 80.11.1, Hdn. 5.5.7) by no means improved the situation.
74 Bertolazzi, "Women," 456–57.

In 219 AD, Antoninus arrived in Rome and was married to Julia Cornelia Paula from an old distinguished Roman family: an attempt to make the Syrian priest-emperor compatible with Roman society.[75] However, in ca. 220 AD, he had to divorce her to marry Aquilia Severa, a Vestal Virgin (who actually had to live a chaste life).[76] Apparently, the marriage was intended to link the traditional Roman religious cults, represented by a priestess of Vesta, with the newly imported Syrian cult of Elagabalus, represented by Antoninus as Elagabalus' high priest.[77] Significantly, the sacral union seems to be connected to another *hieros gamos:* symbolically, the sun god Elagabalus was married to the Carthaginian moon goddess Urania, both represented by their cult statues.[78] The staging of this sacral bond is suggested to have symbolized cosmic harmony.[79] However, since Antoninus' marriage to the Vestal Virgin was an outright violation of Roman religious tradition, it did not produce any harmony but caused a scandal and increased his unpopularity.

His clan tried to revise its policy: Antoninus had to divorce Aquilia Severa and marry Annia Faustina, a descendant of the emperor Marcus Aurelius, whose memory was held in great esteem in Rome.[80] However, the attempt to tie the youth to a prestigious Roman ancestry could not turn the tide. The marriage policy took another chaotic turn when he divorced Annia Faustina and returned to the priestess of Vesta, abandoning ancestral legitimization in favor of sacral legitimization. It was a lost cause. Maesa and her faction dropped Antoninus; in order to keep control over the throne, they had already groomed his younger cousin for the royal role, the future Severus Alexander (208–235 AD).[81] In 222 AD, 18-year-old Antoninus was murdered, his body was mutilated, and he fell victim to *damnatio memoriae*.[82] The failure of the marriage policy designed for him was one of the multiple unfortunate political decisions his clan took for him and can be regarded as symptomatic.

---

[75] Icks, *Elagabalus*, 18.
[76] Dio 80.9.3.
[77] Icks, *Elagabalus*, 32.
[78] Dio 80.12.1–2; Hdn. 5.6.3–5.
[79] Martin Frey, *Untersuchungen zur Religion und zur Religionspolitik des Kaisers Elagabal* (Stuttgart: Steiner, 1989), 91–93; Icks, *Elagabalus*, 34.
[80] Icks, *Elagabalus*, 38; Bertolazzi, "Women," 457.
[81] Dio 80.17.2–3 (Xiph.), 80.19.4 (Xiph.); Hdn. 5.7.1–5; HA *Heliog.* 10.1.
[82] Dio 80.20.2 (Xiph.); HA *Heliog.* 16.5–17.4, 18.1, 33.7; Hdn. 5.8.8–9.

Marriage and Dynastic Unity

This last section is concerned with dynastic unity associated with next-of-kin marriage. An interesting example of a family sticking together through thick and thin is provided by the influential Persian house of Artabazos (satr. reg. 363/2–ca. 353/52 BC) from 4th-century BC Asia Minor. Artabazos was a member of a satrapal dynasty residing in Daskyleion. His parents were Pharnabazos (satr. reg. ca. 413–374/73/70 BC), the famous satrap of Hellespontine Phrygia, and Apame, the daughter of King Artaxerxes II (reg. 404–359/58 BC).[83] As a deserving official, Pharnabazos had been honored by this marriage: it was a royal reward in order to ensure his continued loyalty to the Great King.[84]

Artabazos married an (anonymous) woman from Rhodes. Reportedly, the marriage produced eleven sons and ten daughters, but it is considered that the Rhodian wife was the stepmother of some of them.[85] Besides the relevance of procreation and the importance of geo-strategical links to Rhodes, the major advantage of the marriage was the integration of the wife's two brothers into Artabazos' house: the mercenary generals Mentor and Memnon of Rhodes. They became most influential political figures in the Aegean and were focal persons of political networks linking Greek politicians and mercenary generals with the Persian court.[86] Artabazos could rely on them, even in times of trouble that were frequent in his life. Apparently a strongly united house, Mentor and Memnon tried to free their brother-in-law when the neighboring satrap of Lydia captured him at the end of the 360s BC.[87] In about 356/55 BC, Artabazos fell from grace with Artaxerxes III and went into revolt.[88] When he lost the struggle and had to flee in ca. 353/52 BC, Memnon, his sister, and the children shared his

---

[83] Michael Weiskopf, *The So-Called "Great Satraps' Revolt"* (Stuttgart: Steiner, 1989), 54–55 with reference to Xen. *Hell.* 5.1.28 and *IG* II² 356. See Briant, *L'empire Perse*, 800–802, 805, 808, 810–812; Heckel, *Who's Who*, 55.
[84] Xen. *Hell.* 5.1.28; Plut. *Artax.* 27.7; Nep. 9.2.1; Briant, *L'empire Perse*, 720; Brosius, *Women*, 78.
[85] Diod. 16.52.3–4; Heckel, *Who's Who*, 55.
[86] See Briant, *L'empire Perse*, 810–812, 841–842; Maxim Kholod, "Achaemenid Grants of Cities and Lands to Greeks: The Case of Mentor and Memnon of Rhodes," *Greek, Roman, and Byzantine Studies* 58 (2018): 177–197; Sabine Müller, "Argead Macedonia and the Aegean Sea," *Ricerche Ellenistiche* 1 (2019): 10–11, 15–17; Sabine Müller, "Memnon of Rhodos," in *Lexicon of Argead Makedonia*, eds. Waldemar Heckel, Johannes Heinrichs, Sabine Müller and Frances Pownall (Berlin: Frank & Timme, 2020), 337–339.
[87] Dem. 23.154–155; Julia Heskel, *The North Aegean Wars, 371–360 B.C.* (Stuttgart: Steiner, 1997), 119–121.
[88] Diod. 16.22.1, 34.1; Polyain. 7.33.2. The background of the rebellion is unclear. See Kuhrt, *Persian Empire*, 662, n. 5.

exile in Macedonia.[89] Through the influence of Mentor, who helped to secure Artaxerxes III's conquest of Egypt, Artabazos was pardoned and allowed to return to Persia with his family in the late 340s BC.[90]

His house was additionally unified by endogamy: first Mentor and then, after his death, his brother Memnon married Artabazos and their sister's daughter Barsine, thus their niece, and produced children with her.[91] Under Dareios III, Artabazos and his male relatives enjoyed a high position.[92] When the Macedonian invasion of Persia began and Dareios III organized the resistance, Artabazos, his eleven sons, his brothers-in-law, and his grandchild Thymondas played a central role. A firmly united house, the male members of the core family shared the same political stand and supported Dareios until his end became inevitable.[93] Their role in Persian politics was literally a family matter.

The last example also involves at least the image of a harmonious couple, of unity, peace, and mutual love in the family. In ca. 278 BC, Ptolemy II (reg. 283/82–246 BC) married his older full sister Arsinoë II. It was the first sibling marriage in the Ptolemaic house.[94] To understand Ptolemy II's decision, it is important to look at the problems he had had with his accession. His father, Ptolemy I, the founder of the Ptolemaic Empire, had taken efforts to secure Ptolemy II's succession and made it clear that he was his desired heir by making him his co-regent in 285 BC. However, when Ptolemy I died in 282/1 BC, Ptolemy II's succession as sole ruler was contested by his half-brothers.[95] While he overcame the intradynastic rivalry, he needed to legitimize his contested position. To this end, he stressed the ruling qualities of his specific family branch as a token of his legitimacy. This theme formed part of the carefully arranged public image of the inseparable loving royal couple, Ptolemy II and Arsinoë II.

Being a master of the theme of dynastic love, Ptolemy II styled her as the Brother-Loving Goddess (Arsinoë *Philadelphos*) and a part of the Sibling Gods (*Theoi Philadephoi*).[96] Thus, their family branch was glorified and the message circulated that the royal couple was able to convey double benefits. The siblings

---

89 Diod. 16.52.3–4.
90 Diod. 16.52.1–3; Briant, *L'empire Perse*, 706–707, 802.
91 Curt. 3.13.14; Carney, *Women*, 101.
92 Arr. *An.* 3.27.7; Briant, *L'empire Perse*, 718.
93 Curt. 5.12.7–8; Stephen Ruzicka, "War in the Aegean, 333–331 B.C.: A Reconsideration," *Phoenix* 42 (1988): 131–151; Müller, "Aegean Sea," 15–18; Müller, *Alexander*, 107, 109, 111, 142.
94 Ager, "Brother-Sister Marriage," 346; Elizabeth D. Carney, *Arsinoë of Egypt and Macedon. A Royal Life* (Oxford: Oxford University Press, 2013), 82–85. On the uncertain date of the marriage, see Müller, *Königspaar*, 90.
95 Paus. 1.6.6, 1.7.1; Müller, *Königspaar*, 105–111, 385.
96 Müller, *Königspaar*, 139–382, 385–386; Carney, *Arsinoë*, 83–128.

represented a legitimate, safe, and just rule, promising their empire's inhabitants a good, wealthy life. This ideology was visualized by Arsinoë's unique attribute, a double cornucopia wrapped in the royal diadem. Related to abundance, thus echoing expectations concerning royal wealth and generosity, the *dikeras* contained cake and fruits. Ptolemy II is said to have been responsible for its creation as an iconographic code of the images of his sister-wife.[97] After her death in ca. 270 BC, he never married again (and died in 246 BC). The dead Arsinoë continued to play the role of his *basilissa* in his representation. According to this ideology, caring for the empire worked even better as, freed from her earthly being, she was now omnipresent.

However, dynastic representation was not the only reason why Ptolemy II chose to marry his full sister. The claims of his half-brothers to his throne had taught him the dangers of the polygamy that his father had practiced. Ptolemy II had learned his lesson well and tried to reverse the disadvantages polygamy had produced by restricting power within the immediate family through endogamy. Thus, he shut the gates and denied any outsider claims to the Ptolemaic throne. Furthermore, the marriage to his full sister served to have a trustworthy person at his side to assist him in securing the succession of one of his sons from his first (exogamous) marriage. Arsinoë II adopted her nephews and seems to have been a loyal confidante in whose support for the sake of his sons Ptolemy II could trust.[98]

Conclusion

Among ancient elites, marriage policy formed part of the art of diplomacy. Marriages were a matter of alliances and networking, of financial profit, or of prestige and status. Love and affection were not among the reasons. Marital bonds were central to the strategies of influential ancient houses in order to establish, refresh, or intensify alliances, to gain, preserve, or limit influence, privileges, or wealth, to secure the family's continuation, or to legitimize a social position or political actions. Often, marriages occur in the context of a war, conquest, or another situation of political change. While one party involved or both may have had long-term goals in mind, political marriages, dependent on the unpredictable and changeable power constellations, were first of all made for the moment. Their value depended on political developments. Therefore, some mar-

---

97 Ath. 11.497b-c; Müller, *Königspaar*, 373–380; Carney, *Arsinoë*, 114–115.
98 Schol. *Theokr.* 17.128; Müller, *Königspaar*, 100–103.

riages were ephemeral while others endured. However, comparable to non-political marriages, at the moment of the wedding, nobody could tell if this bond would last.

Works Cited

Ager, Sheila. "Royal Brother-Sister Marriage, Ptolemaic and Otherwise." In *The Routledge Companion to Women and Monarchy in the Ancient Mediterranean World*, edited by Elizabeth D. Carney and Sabine Müller, 346–358. London/New York: Routledge, 2020.

Ager, Sheila. "Symbol and Ceremony: Royal Weddings in the Hellenistic Age." In *The Hellenistic Court,* edited by Andrew Erskine, Lloyd Llewellyn-Jones, and Shane Wallace, 165–188. Swansea: The Classical Press of Wales, 2017.

Badian, Ernst. *Lucius Sulla. The Deadly Reformer*. Sydney: Sydney University Press, 1970.

Bertolazzi, Riccardo. "Women in the Severan Dynasty." In *The Routledge Companion to Women and Monarchy in the Ancient Mediterranean World*, edited by Elizabeth D. Carney and Sabine Müller, 452–462. London/New York: Routledge, 2020.

Berve, Helmut. *Die Tyrannis bei den Griechen*. 2 vols. München: Beck, 1967.

Briant, Pierre. *Histoire de l'empire perse de Cyrus à Alexandre*. Paris: Fayard, 1996.

Brosius, Maria. *The Persians. An Introduction*. London/New York: Routledge, 2006.

Brosius, Maria. *Women in Ancient Persia (559–331 B.C.)*. Oxford: Oxford University Press, 1996.

Carney, Elizabeth D. "An Exceptional Argead Couple: Philip II and Olympias." In *Power Couples in Antiquity: Transversal Perspectives*, edited by Anne Bielman Sánchez, 16–31. London/New York: Routledge, 2019.

Carney, Elizabeth D. *Arsinoë of Egypt and Macedon. A Royal Life*. Oxford: Oxford University Press, 2013.

Carney, Elizabeth D. "Eponymous Women: Royal Women and City Names." *The Ancient History Bulletin* 2 (1988): 134–142.

Carney, Elizabeth D. *Eurydice and the Birth of Macedonian Power*. Oxford: Oxford University Press, 2019.

Carney, Elizabeth D. "Marriage Policy." In *Lexicon of Argead Makedonia*, edited by Waldemar Heckel, Johannes Heinrichs, Sabine Müller and Frances Pownall, 331–335. Berlin: Frank & Timme, 2020.

Carney, Elizabeth D. *Olympias, Mother of Alexander the Great*. London/New York: Routledge, 2006.

Carney, Elizabeth D. "The Sisters of Alexander the Great: Royal Relicts." *Historia* 37 (1998): 385–404.

Carney, Elizabeth D. *Women and Monarchy in Macedonia*. Norman: Gerald Peters Gallery, 2000.

Carney, Elizabeth D., and Sabine Müller. "Introduction to thinking about Women and Monarchy in the Ancient World." In *The Routledge Companion to Women and Monarchy in the Ancient Mediterranean World*, edited by Elizabeth D. Carney and Sabine Müller, 3–7. London/New York: Routledge, 2020.

Cenerini, Francesca. "Il matrimonio con un'*Augusta:* forma di legittimazione?" In *Femmes influentes dans le monde hellénistique et à Rome, IIIe siècle avant J.-C. – Ier siècle après J.-C.*, edited by Anne Bielman Sánchez, Isabelle Cogitore and Anne Kolb, 119–142. Grenoble: UGA Éditions, 2016.

Cenerini, Francesca. *Dive e donne. Mogli, madri, figlie e sorelle degli imperatori romani da Augustus a Commodo.* Imola: Angeli Editore 2009.

Christ, Karl. *Sulla. Eine römische Karriere.* München: Beck, 2002.

Cox, Cheryl A. *Household Interests: Property, Marriage Strategies, and Family Dynamics in Ancient Athens.* Princeton: Princeton University Press, 1998.

De Arrizabalaga y Prado, Leonardo. *The Emperor Elagabalus. Fact or Fiction?* Cambridge: Cambridge University Press, 2010.

De Libero, Loretana. *Die archaische Tyrannis.* Stuttgart: Steiner, 1996.

Dewald, Carolyn. "Humour and Danger in Herodotus." In *The Cambridge Companion to Herodotus*, edited by Carolyn Dewald and John Marincola, 145–164. Cambridge: Cambridge University Press, 2006.

Frandsen, Paul John. *Incestuous and Close-Kin Marriage in Ancient Egypt and Persia. An Examination of the Evidence.* Copenhagen: Museum Tusculanum Press, 2009.

Frey, Martin. *Untersuchungen zur Religion und zur Religionspolitik des Kaisers Elagabal.* Stuttgart: Steiner, 1989.

Gaca, Kathy L. "Girls, Women, and the Significance of Sexual Violence in Ancient Warfare." In *Sexual Violence in Conflict Zones*, edited by Elizabeth Heineman, 73–88. Philadelphia/Oxford: University of Pennsylvania Press, 2011.

Hartmann, Elke. "Heirat und Bürgerstatus in Athen." In *Frauenwelten in der Antike. Geschlechterordnung und weibliche Lebenspraxis*, edited by Thomas Späth and Beate Wagner-Hasel, 16–31. Stuttgart/Weimar: Metzler, 2000.

Heckel, Waldemar. "Artabazos in the Lands beyond the Caspian." *Anabasis* 9 (2019): 93–109.

Heckel, Waldemar. *The Conquests of Alexander the Great.* Cambridge: Cambridge University Press, 2008.

Heckel, Waldemar. *Who's Who in the Age of Alexander the Great.* Oxford: Wiley, 2006.

Heskel, Julia. *The North Aegean Wars, 371–360 B.C.* Stuttgart: Steiner, 1997.

Icks, Martijn. *The Crimes of Elagabalus. The Life and Legacy of Rome's Decadent Boy Emperor.* London: L.B. Tauris, 2011.

Jacobs, Bruno. "'Kyros der große König, der Achämenide.' Zum verwandtschaftlichen Verhältnis und zur politischen und kulturellen Kontinuität zwischen Kyros dem Großen und Dareios I." In *Herodotus and the Persian Empire*, edited by Robert Rollinger, Brigitte Truschnegg and Reinhold Bichler, 635–663. Wiesbaden: Harrassowitz, 2011.

Keaveney, Arthur. *Sulla, the Last Republican.* London/New York: Routledge, 1982.

Kholod, Maxim. "Achaemenid Grants of Cities and Lands to Greeks: The Case of Mentor and Memnon of Rhodes." *Greek, Roman, and Byzantine Studies* 58 (2018): 177–197.

King, Helen. "Bound to Bleed. Artemis and Greek Women." In *Sexuality and Gender in the Classical World. Readings and Sources*, edited by Laura McClure, 77–97. Oxford: Blackwell, 2002.

Kuhrt, Amélie. *The Persian Empire. A Corpus of Sources from the Achaemenid Period.* London/New York: Routledge, 2007.

Kunst, Christiane. "Eheallianzen und Ehealltag in Rom." In *Frauenwelten in der Antike. Geschlechterordnung und weibliche Lebenspraxis*, edited by Thomas Späth and Beate Wagner-Hasel, 32–52. Stuttgart/Weimar: Metzler, 2000.

Landucci Gattinoni, Franca. "Cassander and the Legacy of Philip II and Alexander III in Diodorus." In *Philip II and Alexander the Great, Father and Son, Lives and Afterlives*, edited by Elizabeth D. Carney and Daniel Ogden, 113–122. Oxford: Oxford University Press, 2010.

Landucci Gattinoni, Franca. "Cassander's Wife and Heirs." In *Alexander & his Successors. Essays from the Antipodes*, edited by Pat Wheatley and Robert Hannah, 261–275. Claremont: Regina Books, 2009.

Landucci Gattinoni, Franca. *L'arte del potere. Vita e opera di Cassandro di Macedonia*. Stuttgart: Steiner, 2003.

Lavelle, Brian M. "The Compleat Angler: Observations on the Rise of Peisistratos in Herodotos (1.59–64)." *Classical Quarterly* 41, no. 2 (1991): 317–324.

Lavelle, Brian M. *Fame, Money, and Power. The Rise of Peisistratos and 'Democratic' Tyranny at Athens*. Ann Arbor: University of Michigan Press, 2005.

Lenfant, Dominique. "Polygamy in Greek Views of the Persians." *Greek, Roman, and Byzantine Studies* 59 (2019): 15–37.

Lipinski, Edward. "Elaha Gabal d'Émèse dans son context historique." *Latomus* 70 (2011): 1081–1011.

Madreiter, Irene. *Stereotypisierung – Idealisierung – Indifferenz, Formen der Auseinandersetzung mit dem Achaimeniden-Reich in der griechischen Persika-Literatur*. Wiesbaden: Harrassowitz, 2012.

Müller, Sabine. *Alexander der Große. Eroberung—Politik—Rezeption*. Stuttgart: Kohlhammer, 2019.

Müller, Sabine. "Argead Macedonia and the Aegean Sea." *Ricerche Ellenistiche* 1 (2019): 9–20.

Müller, Sabine. *Das hellenistische Königspaar in der medialen Repräsentation. Ptolemaios II. und Arsinoë II*. Berlin/New York: de Gruyter, 2009.

Müller, Sabine. "Endogamy." In *The Encyclopedia of Ancient History*, edited by Roger S. Bagnall, Kai Brodersen, Craige B. Champion, Andrew Erskine and Sabine R. Hübner. Oxford: Blackwell, 2013. https://onlinelibrary.wiley.com/doi/10.1002/9781444338386.wbeah22094.

Müller, Sabine. "Memnon of Rhodos." In *Lexicon of Argead Makedonia*, edited by Waldemar Heckel, Johannes Heinrichs, Sabine Müller and Frances Pownall, 337–339. Berlin: Frank & Timme, 2020.

Müller, Sabine. *Perdikkas II., Retter Makedoniens*. Berlin: Frank & Timme, 2017.

Müller, Sabine. "Philip II." In *Blackwell Companion to Ancient Macedonia*, edited by Joseph Roisman and Ian Worthington, 166–185. Oxford/Malden: Wiley-Blackwell, 2010.

Ogden, Daniel. *Polygamy, Prostitutes and Death. The Hellenistic Dynasties*. London: Duckworth, 1999.

Olbrycht, Marek Jan. "Macedonia and Persia," in *A Companion to Ancient Macedonia*, edited by Joseph Roisman and Ian Worthington. 342–369. Oxford: Wiley-Blackwell, 2010.

Rhodes, Peter J. *A Commentary on the Aristotelian Athenaion Politeia*. Oxford: Oxford University Press, 1981.

Rhodes, Peter J. "Pisistratid Chronology again." *Phoenix* 30 (1976): 219–233.

Rollinger, Robert. "Ein besonderes historisches Problem. Die Thronbesteigung des Dareios und die Frage seiner Legitimität." In *Pracht und Prunk der Großkönige*, edited by Historisches Museum der Pfalz Speyer, 41–53. Darmstadt: WBG, 2006.
Ruzicka, Stephen. "War in the Aegean, 333–331 B.C.: A Reconsideration." *Phoenix* 42 (1988): 131–151.
Sancisi-Weerdenburg, Heleen. "Exit Atossa: Images of Women in Greek Historiography on Persia." In *Images of Women in Antiquity*, edited by Averil Cameron and Amélie Kuhrt, 20–33. Detroit: Croom Helm, 1983.
Sancisi-Weerdenburg, Heleen. "The Tyranny of Peisistratos." In *Peisistratos and the Tyranny: A Reappraisal of the Evidence*, edited by Heleen Sancisi-Weerdenburg, 1–15. Leiden/Boston: Brill, 2000.
Santangelo, Federico. *Sulla, the Elites, and the Empire. A Study of Roman Politics in Italy and the Greek East.* Leiden/Boston: Brill, 2007.
Seibert, Jakob. *Historische Beiträge zu den dynastischen Verbindungen in hellenistischer Zeit.* Wiesbaden: Steiner, 1967.
Weiskopf, Michael N. *The So-Called "Great Satraps' Revolt".* Stuttgart: Steiner, 1989.
Wiesehöfer, Josef. *Das antike Persien von 550 v. Chr. bis 650 n. Chr.* Düsseldorf/Zürich: Artemis & Winkler, 1993.
Wirth, Gerhard. "Alexander, Kassander und andere Zeitgenossen. Erwägungen zum Problem ihrer Selbstdarstellung." *Tyche* 4 (1989): 193–220.
Wirth, Gerhard. "Philip II." In *Lexicon of Argead Makedonia*, edited by Waldemar Heckel, Johannes Heinrichs, Sabine Müller and Frances Pownall, 415–420. Berlin: Frank & Timme, 2020.

Mariela Fargas Peñarrocha
3 Marriage Discourses in Conflict: Public and Private Order in Early Modern Spain

There was a time when discourses on marriage flourished, as never before, in the form of political, moral, and legal books, as well as fictional literature. That time was the early modern age.[1] There are several reasons and historical causes that explain why there was so much interest in writing and publishing books on marriage.

First, a political element, the consolidation of authoritarian monarchies. The new European states since the Renaissance needed to show a new legitimacy, and this was found in the political metaphor that realized the king as a good father and the anonymous father as the king of the small space of his family. Political power and domestic power lived in authentic harmony. This was the wish. For that reason, the family was thought and built, or rebuilt, and this family policy produced a very important line of thought with discourses that spoke of the father's relationship with his family, with his wife, so they spoke about marriage. The gradual development of the new states, in turn, required an unprecedented legal development. In this field, there was legislation and doctrine on the family that accepted their hierarchy, the conservation of their heritage, in which males were given preference, the secondary role being given to women. These were important issues, overall, for the maintenance of the order and peace of the old feudal families because their stability automatically affected the monarchy.

Second, a social element—the new space of power, the court, needed to educate the courtiers. Most of the political literature had one objective, among others, and this was to design a behavioral model for use in both public and private, i.e. in the family, that addressed problems like parental relationships with their sons and, of course, the marriage. At that time, public and private were undifferentiated spaces, its borders were almost imperceptible. All these books started from the classic premise that the good ruler knew how to successfully rule his

---

Note: Research project financed by AEI / 10.13039/501100011033, PID2019–103970GB-I00.

1 Carlos Lechner, "La influencia de la familia, el Estado y la Iglesia en la construcción del matrimonio en los manuales matrimoniales españoles de la época moderna," in *Actas Congreso de la Asociación Internacional del Siglo de Oro* (Madrid: Vervuert, 1999), 782–792; M. Luisa Correia Fernandes, *Espelhos, cartas e guias: Casamento e espiritualidade na península ibérica 1450–1700* (Porto: Instituto de cultura portuguesa-Universidade do Porto, 1995).

∂ OpenAccess. © 2021 Mariela Fargas Peñarrocha, published by De Gruyter. [CC BY-NC-ND] This work is licensed under the Creative Commons Attribution-NonCommercial-NoDerivatives 4.0 International License.
https://doi.org/10.1515/9783110751451-003

house. Consequently, the rules of marriage spoke of good coexistence, harmony. If the rules affected the life of a courtier, a prince, or a good family and were not followed, they became problems that interested politics as a form of public behavior. Keep in mind that this interest was not new. It had its roots in ancient times. Xenophon (c. 430–354 BC), the author of *Oykonomikos*, compared the good citizen and the good manager of his own *oykos*. And Aristotle, in his *Politics*, regards the family as the origin of the *polis* and domestic life as a political space subjected to power relations.[2] During the Renaissance, these works would greatly inspire the arguments of the new writers. At this point, the rise of the bourgeoisie, a social and political phenomenon throughout early modern Europe, should also be considered. Since the late Middle Ages, a new social group was developing, especially in the cities, that had a high interest and a genuine passion in accessing these new courtly environments and establishing relationships with the traditional nobility. The upward process was unstoppable in the early modern ages. This new social group was the bourgeoisie. Books about the new civility were necessary to this new group. They became great consumers of books of all kinds, especially on moral and family education. The new and rising bourgeoisie needed to know how to govern their marriage. Enjoying a perfect marriage was an endorsement to rise in the social hierarchy and in the court. Lastly, the collapse of the Christian world and its cohesion, with the breakdown of Protestantism in the 16th century and the consequent desacralization of marriage, caused a rise in canonical-moral and sacred literature throughout the territories of Catholicism. A lot of books destined to defend the marriage sacrament, especially after the Council of Trent, became an important part of the confessor's recommendations principally addressed to women. But the rise of religious discourses was also due to the evolution of the canonical discipline of marriage. During the Middle Ages, there were great discussions about the definition of legitimate marriage. The persistence of different theories, of different rituals, made clandestine marriage possible. The secret troubled the honor of families and made control of their women difficult. When the Council of Trent began, this problem was widespread. The council fathers condemned clandestine marriage. And so, the form, in addition to the essence, was the subject of many writings. From this moment, there was only one model of legitimate marriage, celebrated with a specific and public liturgy. Informal unions that did not respect this liturgy were condemned and persecuted. It was necessary to teach families

---

[2] M. Dolores Mirón Pérez, "El gobierno de la casa en Atenas clásica: género y poder en el Oikos," *Studia Histórica: Historia antigua* 18 (2000): 103–117.

how to prepare for the marriage of their sons and, in particular, to teach young women what the true legitimate union was.

In summary, the power of monarchies, the social, cultural, and political convergence of the nobility with the new bourgeoisie, and the Catholic indoctrination of society are contextual elements that together explain the rise of marriage and family literature from the beginning of the early modern age.[3] My approach in this text defends that all literature, regardless of the different topics, e. g. politics, moral theology, law, talks about marriage and about family in general, meaning that it is not possible to understand our object of study from limited or monodisciplinary readings. All this literature shares an objective, the preservation and consolidation of the social and political order under the moral rules of Catholicism, which transcended from the public to the private and from the private to the public. But I also think it is necessary to underline the contradictions of the family and marriage rules that the writers and moralists were developing in those books. This is my hypothesis. On the one hand, they wanted to promote harmony; on the other, if these rules based on a concept of hierarchical society and gender inequality were applied in everyday life, they really could produce conflict. Certainly, though, these discourses cannot be taken out of their context; at that time, no one believed that order was possible from a perfect consensus, but rather from obedience or repression.

Throughout the texts, there are many opinions and reflections about order-conflict tensions. Early modern literature is a very interesting observatory of this tension. I think the discourses show conflicts and, at the same time, their authors wanted to eliminate them. Apparently, this is a contradiction. But they needed to do it to show the error against the rule, to show the disorder against the order. This makes theological sense, which was very logical at the time. And, above all, it offers a wealth of nuances about married life. For this reason, it is also useful to look at fictional literature on marriage. Its discourses were freer, sometimes escaping censorship with subterfuges of style, and its reading opens the door to get to know dilemmas and ways of directly negotiating order and resolving conflicts by both men and women, and not *only* according to the rules. Finally, I want to remind the reader that this text is focused on the early modern age, from the 16th century to the beginning of the 17th century. This is the time that saw the development of a wide and interdisciplinary range of marriage and family literature. The following sections constitute the main top-

---

3 Ofelia Rey, "Literatura y tratadistas de la familia en la Europa de la edad moderna," in *Familia y organización social en Europa y América: siglos XV–XX*, eds. Francisco Chacón et al. (Murcia: Universidad de Murcia, 2007), 211–232.

ics of this discourse: a portrait of married life, gender roles, and the difficulty of applying power and moral rules in a pre-modern society.[4]

Honor in Marriage and the Education of Women.

Honor was a very significant social and cultural code from classical Mediterranean societies. The Hispanic societies of early modern times were also honor societies. Honor was at the top of social representation in the oldest lineages, and descending down the social pyramid to the poorer classes, it disappears. However, if there was no antiquity of lineage, there could be antiquity in faith. Thus, along with honor, the idea of old Christian blood (*limpieza de sangre*) was expanded to designate people and families who could show that they had been Christian for many generations.[5] Honor and faith gave great meaning to social relations.

Within the family, honor also meant the desired order, as everyone knew what the position, and therefore the honor, of each individual in the hierarchy of the domestic government was, as moral conscience and reputation had different nuances.[6] For that reason, classical anthropology contrasted male honor, as a matter of precedence linked to the social space, with the honor of women, which was rather a question of virtue and sexual purity typical of a private space:[7] "the woman founds her honor only on her virtue," wrote Gaspar Lucas Hidalgo in 1605.[8] Female honor implied being a virgin (*doncella*) before marriage and then keeping her fidelity.[9] For M. Luisa Candau, on this scale of honor, women were undervalued, which is just what medieval scholasticism defended.[10] Women were the true guardians, in the family, of men's social honor, and female honor derived from that of the men: the father or the husband. It was an element that sustained the patriarchal culture and family power. The dis-

---

4 Tom Brandenberger, *Literatura de matrimonio (Península Ibérica, S. XIV–XVI)* (Lausanne: Sociedad Suiza de Estudios Hispánicos, 1996).
5 Margarita Torremocha, ed., *Mujeres, sociedad y conflicto* (Valladolid: Castilla ediciones, 2019).
6 Carmel Cassar, *Honor y vergüenza en el Mediterráneo* (Barcelona: Icaria, 2004).
7 Francisco Galvache Valero, *La educación familiar en los humanistas españoles* (Pamplona: Eunsa, 2001), 140.
8 J. Alonso Asenjo et al., eds., *G.L. Hidalgo. Diálogos de apacible entretenimiento* (Valencia: Publicacions de la Universitat de València, 2010), 172.
9 Carlos Maza Ozcoidi, "La definición del concepto del honor. Su entidad como objeto de investigación histórica," *Espacio. Tiempo y Forma. Historia Moderna* 8 (1995): 191–209.
10 M. Luisa Candau Chacón, ed. *Las mujeres y el honor en la Europa moderna* (Huelva: Universidad de Huelva, 2014), 11–25.

courses describe the attributes of women's honor (*honra*): silence, modesty, posture.[11] It was therefore essential to educate women, to preserve the honor of their family, of the husband. And so many moral books and treatises were written for the education of married women.

The education of wives covered more issues. Marriage was a trade that came with its own duties.[12] Man and woman, each had their own different duties. And in the hands of the woman, there was a very special one: leading the marriage to a life of concord and peace. With that objective in mind, Juan Luis Vives wrote *De institutione feminae christianae* (*The Education of a Christian Woman*, 1523) and *De officio mariti* (*The Husband's Trade*, 1538). In his *De institutione*, we can observe these words:

> Among the virtues of a wife, it is convenient to have two that are very important ... If she has these two virtues, marriages will be stable, long-lasting, easy, bearable, sweet, and pleasant ... These virtues are chastity and a great love for her husband ... If you add knowing how to govern the house, marriages will be more pleasant and happy; without this third virtue, there will be no family patrimony, without chastity and love there is no marriage, but a terrible and perpetual cross.[13]

The success of the marriage was entrusted to the wife. These moralists did not forget the difficulties that this represented. Another emblematic work on women's education was *La perfecta casada* (*The Perfect Wife*, 1583) by Fray Luis de León. Like the previous author, Fray Luis warned about the harshness of the marriage occupation: "Many women deceive themselves because they think that getting married is just leaving the father's house, moving to the husband's house, and getting out of servitude and coming to freedom." He continued: "When the wife does her job, the husband loves her, the family agrees, the children learn virtues and peace reigns ... on the contrary, if the wife does not like the house, there everything is bitterness." [14]

Some time after, Fray Antonio Arbiol, the author of a frequently republished work entitled *La familia regulada según doctrina de la sagrada escritura* (*The*

---

[11] Aurelio Martín Casares, "Las mujeres y la "paz en la casa" en el discurso renacentista," *Chronica Nova* 29 (2002): 217–244.
[12] E. Teresa Howe, *Education and Women in the Early Modern Hispanic World* (London/New York: Routledge, 2016).
[13] Juan Luis Vives, *Instrucción de la mujer cristiana*, accessed September 1, 2020, https://www.bivaldi.gva.es/es/corpus/unidad.do?posicion=1&idCorpus=1&idUnidad=10066libro; Isabel Morant, *Discursos de la vida buena: Matrimonio, mujer y sexualidad en la literatura humanista* (Madrid: Cátedra, 2002). Unless otherwise indicated, all translations into English are by the author.
[14] Luis de León, *La perfecta casada* (Zaragoza, 1584), 2, 12.

Family's Rules According to the Sacred Scripture Doctrine, 1715), dedicated a whole chapter to "The importance of peace in marriage," and wrote:

> Peace and harmony between husband and wife is not only wanted by God, it is also good for the construction of the world (...). Peace and harmony in holy matrimony is the main thing to live happily in marriage (...). An unhappy house where there is no union or peace but a continual war, troubles, disputes, regrets, and discords does not seem like a house of Christians.[15]

The moralists considered that the obligations of the wife were natural, but curiously they also saw that it was necessary to indoctrinate them. Of course, every natural thing unites people to God, so it is essential to guide them well. According to Fray Luis de León, marriage meant work and fidelity for the woman, an opportunity to obtain sanctifying grace. The grace that the Sacrament gave helped her to live in harmony. Humanistic thought had already insisted on this. Let us take a look at another reference, *Encomium matrimonii* (1518) by Erasmus. In 1597, when Fray Gaspar de Astete titled a chapter of his *Tratado sobre el gobierno de la familia* (*Treatise on the Government of the Family*) as "What is perfection in marriage," he considered it a generally consensual matter. Gaspar de Astete pointed out that perfection was linked to the many obligations of marriage. For that reason, marriage was as worthy of salvation as ecclesiastical celibacy. From this perspective, the long centuries of the medieval period were now overcome. This effort to dignify marriage was equal to the commitment to direct the woman's life. Both clergy and the new authoritarian monarchies were very interested in it. This was logical for the Catholic clergy because it had to underline the sacramentality of marriage that the Protestants denied. On the other hand, the new monarchies needed the collaboration of strong and supportive families, built on stable marriages, in their courts. A huge body of texts would do this work throughout the early modern age.

In addition, married life was a working space for a woman. Her work and dedication here were an example of harmony, welfare, and good coexistence for the community in general. Incidentally, customs indicated that this coexistence should be between socially equal people. The letters written by Fray Antonio de Guevara (from 1541) are very clear on this point: "husband and wife must be equal in blood and status."[16] His words tell us about the arranged marriage, which was decided by the families. For the moralists, social differences in mar-

---

15 Antonio Arbiol, *La familia regulada con doctrina de la Sagrada escritura y santos padres de la Iglesia católica* (Madrid, 1778), 85.
16 Antonio de Guevara, *Epístolas familiares* (Madrid: 1673), 275.

riage are the result of the disobedience of young people when faced with the advice of their parents. This led to misery. And in *Microcosmia y gobierno universal del hombre cristiano* (*Microcosm and Universal Government of Christian Man*, 1592), a work destined for the education of princes and rulers, Marco Antonio de Camós insists on this: "If a virtuous man marries a woman of bad habits, a nobleman with a commoner ... if he has some characteristics and she the opposite ones, how do you want love to exist between them and for them to keep peace and conformity, what is the main thing in this sacrament?"[17] With these words, Camós addresses the husband: if his wife is of the same social condition, he can exercise his power over her without limits, even using humiliation. Was gender violence allowed? Yes, but within the limits of Christian charity and when it was necessary to control a rebellious wife. Fortunately, a wife could complain in court if her husband mistreated her. And although she could not divorce, the judge could dictate a separation of bodies. Fray Juan de la Cerda, in his *Vida política de todos los estados de mujeres* (*Political Life of All Women's Status*, 1599), spoke about this violence: "When this similarity and equality does not exist in marriage, there are scorn and offenses, because one calls the other one infamous ... and quarrels, hatreds, and resentments increase."[18] However, the social factor did not completely guarantee the obedience of women. Moral rules clashed with the heterogeneity of everyday life. Consequently, Catholic authors did not forget another element, affection, a concept that is different in all cultures at all times.[19] According to these writers, affection was important for married peace. The *Coloquios matrimoniales* (*Marriage Dialogues*, 1550) by Pedro de Luján talk about love: "hatred separates the badly married very quickly and love preserves the marriage to death ... we have the obligation to love our husbands ... believe me, if love does not exist in marriage, no good will come of it," Dorotea, the protagonist, tells us.[20] The problem of the marriage union appears again, but now affection is the key to achieving that union. Now, the compliant silence of the wives is not so important. Arbiol himself, whose work also touches on sentimental education, would write that "love makes work soft and sweet ... if love does

---

[17] Marco Antonio de Camós, *Microcosmia y gobierno universal del hombre cristiano* (Barcelona, 1592), 73.
[18] Juan de la Cerda, "Vida política de todos los estados de mujeres," *Lemir* 14 (2010): 290.
[19] M. Luisa Candau, "Entre lo permitido y lo ilícito: la vida afectiva en los tiempos modernos," *Tiempos Modernos* 18 (2009–1), accessed July 1, 2020, http://rabida.uhu.es/dspace/handle/10272/11165.
[20] Pedro de Luján, *Coloquios matrimoniales*, ed. A. Rallo (Sevilla: Junta de Andalucía-Consejería de cultura, 2010), 57, 104, accessed July 1, 2020, http://www.bibliotecavirtualdeandalucia.es/catalogo/es/catalogo_imagenes/grupo.cmd?path=1014397.

not exist between married people, it becomes unbearable." [21] Marriage was a school of affection, of love. This affection was built in everyday life. And it was good for the republics. Camós wrote: "The first light of natural and supernatural love (through the Sacrament, God gives his grace) that exists in the marriage union, later increases between parents and children, between brothers and relatives."[22]

Another virtue attributed to wives, essential for marital peace and community peace, was silence. Women had the obligation to be the guardians of the marriage secrets. Nothing could be known outside the home. It was important to control what the servants knew or did not know. Marriage was a space of intimacy. The early modern era conquered the notion of domestic intimacy, unknown in the Middle Ages when life was ruled by lineages and open kinship structures. Women, wives, were now in charge of its surveillance. Although knowing secrets, keeping them, or correcting them gave authority to the wife, the truth is that this obligation, or diligence, could be a problem for the wives who silenced the violence of their husband. This was good for patriarchal culture and less so for the woman. Vives, in *De institutione*, suggested, "nothing said or done with your husband in your bedroom, do not discover it, do not tell anyone, the main thing is that it is secret and unknown."[23] Fray Antonio de Guevara did not forget this problem either:

> The bad life of women with their husbands does not derive from day-to-day life, it derives from the things they talk about outside the home. If the wife is silent when the husband reprimands her ... but this is not the case when the husband begins to protest, she begins to scream even more, in the end they fight loudly and the neighbors hear everything.[24]

Female education was essential to the formation of marriage and as a regulator of peace. The representation of the social order depended on learning. A social order that took the honor of marriage as one of its main elements and this feminine honor, so prudent and silent, reproduced the patriarchal culture. But was it possible to bring this ideal behavior into reality? It must have been difficult in a world of strong relationships between relatives and neighbors. The authors of these books knew it, and consequently they wrote about (patriarchal) rules

---

21 *La familia regulada*, 60.
22 *Microcosmia*, 36.
23 Juan Luis Vives, *Instrucción de la mujer cristiana, que tradujo a la lengua castellana Juan Justiniano* (Madrid, 1793), 144, 297, 301.
24 Antonio de Guevara, *Libro primero de las epístolas familiares* (Valladolid, 1542), 309.

but also about emotions, perhaps looking for a possible balance inside the conflict.

Marriage and Politics: Jobs and Government in the House

The foundation of the family and marriage as a social hierarchy was theorized in ancient times by Aristotle. For him, the family was a space governed by the father, who was obeyed by the mother, as well as by the sons and servants. The father had a natural power. This power consisted of deciding on the house, its members, and managing the patrimony, the inheritances. Political and civic literature from the Renaissance, which would follow classical ideas so passionately, was concerned with offering advice to fathers and husbands.[25] Thus, Fray Antonio de Guevara wrote a detailed comparison of the tasks at home:

> The husband's job is to earn wealth and the wife's one is to keep it. The husband's job is to go out and look for resources and the wife's one is to stay in the house. The husband's job is to look for money and the wife's one is not to waste money. The husband's job is to make relationships with everyone and the wife's one is to talk to very few people … The husband's job is to know and the wife's one is to keep quiet … The husband's job is to be the owner of everything and the wife's one is to be responsible for everything.[26]

Hard words, certainly, which produce a hierarchy and gender differences. But the same author changes his tone radically in another famous text, *Reloj de príncipes* (*The Dial of Princes*, 1529): "married women and men have more authority than single men and between well-married husband and wife there is true love, and they can be perfect and perpetual friends. Other friends and relatives, if they love us today, it may be that tomorrow they will hate us." Guevara recommends marriage highly because "the benefit that follows from marriage is the peace and reconciliation made with enemies through marriages." This was very important to the republic. In the Middle Ages, feudal families fought wars for dominance over territory. At the beginning of the early modern age, these wars persisted and joined other more subtle conflicts to control positions in courts and defeat the new competitors, the bourgeoisie. In this context, kings or princes were interested in keeping their servants in peace. Marriage was in all these cases a

---

25 James Casey, *España en la edad moderna. Una historia social* (Valencia: Publicaciones de la Universitat de Valencia, 2001), 298.
26 De Guevara, *Libro primero*, 90.

business for peace. However, Fray Antonio de Guevara was not unaware that within marriages there were also wars, for which he blamed especially women: "the sane man must be careful to choose whom he marries, but after marrying he must be like the one who enters the war ... the life that the badly married have in their home is a war." [27]

It was necessary to find a solution to this problem. For that reason, he wrote a lot of instructions addressed to the head of the house, who had the ultimate responsibility for order and peace. I have chosen a small selection: "the husband must suffer and be patient when the wife is angry ... he must ensure that his wife interacts with good people ... he must sometimes be happy with his wife and other times sad ... he must try to make his wife not confront neighbors ... he should not lay his hands on his wife to punish her ... if he wants to have peace with his wife, he should praise her a lot in front of the neighbors."[28]

This male role of undisputed authority, as a king or a prince in his kingdom, was justified by Gaspar de Astete: "just as the King gives various offices and offices to his vassals ... so that the kingdom is well-governed and all live in peace and obey the laws ... the father of the family in your house must order his children and servants a trade and occupation ... so that their home is well arranged and everyone enjoys peace and is obeyed."[29] The link between diligent work at home and marital peace should be noted again. If the children are well educated, they will help their parents in the future and, consequently, will also help to maintain the happiness and harmony of the whole family. Fray Miquel Agustí wrote about this in *Llibre dels secrets de agricultura, casa rústica y pastoril* (*Book of the Secrets of Agriculture, Rural House and Herding House*, 1615). His sentence "peace made, house made" is very significant.[30] It is important to note that, despite gender differences, if the common good was peace in marriage, everyone, both men and women, had the obligation to collaborate in it. Just as education was a joint affair of father and mother, so both had their importance in the little republic of the family. On this point, Marco Antonio de Camós, in his *Microcosmia*, explains that marriage, of husband and wife, is an important part of the body of the republic. All the elements of that body are bound to peace and harmony. Husband and wife have the same degree of responsibility.

---

27 Ibid.
28 Antonio de Guevara, *Relox de Príncipes*, Proyecto filosofía en español, accessed July 3, 2020, http://www.filosofia.org/cla/gue/gue00.htm.
29 Gaspar de Astete, *Del gobierno de la familia y estado del matrimonio: donde se trata, de como se han de auer los casados con sus mugeres, y los parientes con sus hijos, y los señores con sus criados* (Valladolid, 1597), I.
30 Miquel Agustí, *Libro de los secretos de agricultura* (Barcelona, 1626), 412.

Camós insists that "married people have to get along so as not to live discontent all their lives." Among the advice that the author indicated is, above all, "mutual aid ... because the perfection of marriage does not consist in the *copula carnalis* but in faith in the sacrament and in union and love." The first goal of marriage, says Camós, is "union, loyalty, and charity." Then this author introduces the rules to achieve this union: "if one gets angry the other must suffer ... This must be done mainly by the woman to respect her husband." The man's wife is silenced, she must be subordinate to her husband: "you honor, respect, serve and entertain your husband, recognize in him a superiority, do not fear being his subject." To achieve peace in marriage, following his work, some could command or rule, others should obey: "the woman who commands then becomes the enemy of her husband ... the husband must not be very good and allow her to command, he must be the one who dictates the last rule or a decision with his own *libero arbitrio*." However, the sense of the Christian government of the home urged man to exercise his power with charity, with subtlety: "man will do it according to his customs. He can re-educate his wife like him."[31] The need to approach this relationship between husband and wife from the Christian virtues led Fray Luis de Granada to exhort couples to an examination of conscience: "The husband must be attentive to his attitude and not treat his wife badly in words, in facts, or not give her the necessary things. The same thing happens if the woman treats her husband badly by insulting him."[32]

Going back to Camós, if "charity, love, and patience to raise children are greater in women, in men wisdom is greater, and thus they can teach them." On the one hand, moralists believe in balance in marriage, but he admits "the woman has something unknown in her nature that makes her indomitable," and that produced discord in the marriage: "very few women do not seek entanglements, domestic litigation, and anger." Fortunately, God endows man and woman with "reason to consult, judge and resolve private and home matters ... grace and spirit on their thoughts to better agree and confirm them." After all these statements, it is obvious that there is a game of balances that puts forward contradictions and conflicts inside and outside the discourses. Camós insists that the wife is the ultimate guardian of the peace: "it was a custom in some places for women to fix problems between friends, and even today they are the ones who make peace."[33] The sacramental grace of marriage would definitely help to redirect the weaknesses and mistakes of the spouses. For centuries, the Catholic

---

31 De Camós, *Microcosmia*, 65, 69, 80, 86.
32 Luis de Granada, *Obras, Biblioteca de Autores Españoles*, II (Madrid, 1860), 231–232.
33 De Camós, *Microcosmia*, 58.

faith had contributed to sustaining the patriarchal order, of course, but from the Renaissance and due to the influence of humanism, new nuances are observed in discourses to rebalance relationships in marriage. It is essential to think in terms of politics. The marriage or family is a metaphor for the kingdom; marriage relationships are a metaphor for the relationships between rulers and the common people. The common good requires limits to be observed by everybody.

Sacrament, Legitimacy, and Peace in Marriage

The marriage was a sacred institution: it "gives a special grace to married people to live patiently," wrote Gaspar de Astete.[34] But the canonical rules like the civil ones that do not ignore reality offer an image of risk. A risk that needs the assistance of the sacraments, a life of piety and devotions, and a fear of God: "loving and fearing God and obeying the Divine Law makes homes and families prosper," as the heading that Antonio Arbiol uses to talk about marital happiness goes.[35] All Catholic catechisms insisted that this sacrament meant union: "The sacrament is the bond of marriage that can never be broken ... it means the union of Christ with the Church ... the husband should never separate from his wife."[36]

Important in making visible this vulnerability were the rules on the formation of marriage and the criminalization of clandestine marriage. This modality symbolizes the stress between order and conflict and had an important public perspective. Since the late Middle Ages, both the Catholic canons and civil and criminal law insisted on punishing clandestine marriage. In the early modern age, people of all social classes considered that problem an epidemic that harmed families. But contradictorily, families practiced marriage rituals similar to clandestine marriage, such as the kidnapping of rebellious daughters or daughters who had more than one suitor when this marriage was a very interesting prospect with an important dowry. But there was also kidnapping as a way of escape from family pressure for young people. In any case, many women were kidnapped, raped, seduced, deceived, or hidden and officially controlled by their parents. The doctrine of the Council of Trent, finally, as stipulated by the Tametsi decree in 1563, regulated the formation of marriage and guaranteed the order desired by authoritarian monarchies. This rule also tried to restore the lost peace in

---

[34] De Astete, *Tratado del gobierno*, 63.
[35] Arbiol, *La familia regulada*, 135.
[36] *Catecismo del Santo concilio de Trento para los párrocos ordenado por disposición de San Pío V* (Roma, 1761), 204.

the families and to protect the status of women who were convinced to marry in secret and later abandoned, probably victims of a promise with seduction. Trent made celebration in secret a canonical interdict for a marriage's validity. There were many theologians, moralists, and canonists who spoke about it, but without a doubt the most influential was Tomas Sánchez, who wrote *Disputationes de sancto matrimonii sacramento* (*Disputes over the Holy Sacrament of Marriage*, 1601–1605).[37] Pedro de Ledesma also left us an extensive work titled *Summa de sacramentis*, in which he said the following about this problem:

> Those married clandestinely are obliged to marry later under the ritual performed by a priest and several witnesses, and not to consolidate the contract, but to repair the damage done. For example, if a man and a woman were married in secret, that verbal contract allowed the man to have *copula carnalis* with his woman, so he has an obligation to marry her because of the damage he did to her.[38]

The Church had forbidden secrecy. It was not lawful to run away from home and marry without a priest. The families saw their suffering averted. But the Tametsi decree highlighted an element that would cause concern again: marriage had to be a free and voluntary decision of those who were going to marry. No one, not even parents, could meddle in it or force it. Therefore, the families lost control. Tension was guaranteed. Fortunately, the commandment of God's law required honoring one's parents. To achieve this balance, the clergy indoctrinated obedience to sons from the pulpit, in the confessional, and in the catechisms: "everyone in the family should highly value obedience to the one who governs it because he represents God," writes Fray Antonio Arbiol. The author continues: "marriage is a very important matter for parents and they receive God's help … disobedient sons who want to marry against the will of their parents will not prosper."[39] Thus, the celebration of marriage continued for a long time to be the result of the social and power relationships of families and communities who found in that transaction or deal, and according to their social status, a way of survival, preservation, or social mobility.

---

37 Celestino Carrodeguas, *La sacramentalidad del matrimonio. Doctrina de Tomás Sánchez, s.j.* (Madrid: Universidad Pontificia de Comillas de Madrid, 2013).
38 Pedro de Ledesma, *Summa* (Zaragoza, 1611), 37.
39 Arbiol, *La familia regulada*, 535.

The Marriage, Mirror of Justice: Conflict Resolution and Defiance in the Family

At a time when some echoes of the old system of lineage self-protection still survived, a form of private justice very present at the beginning of the 16th century,[40] in a family, headed by the husband and father, there was a certain power to do a small domestic justice with a marriage. This meant that the father had the right to correct his own. The right of correction, *ius correctionis*, came from the parental authority—*patria potestas*—that was converted into the father's *officium*.[41] Juan Luis Vives wrote a chapter in *De officii mariti* (1538) about rebuke and correction. These are some of his considerations:

> [T]he husband's correction should be brief ...; because censorship and constant reproach ... destroy conjugal love, provoke lasting hatreds and transform the sweetness of coexistence and mutual treatment into disputes ... The husband can reprimand his wife in a way that she understands that this reprimand is love, because he wants the best for her.[42]

Of course, it was critical that someone within the family ruled on and determined the punishment for disobedience. If it was not soon corrected, the disorder or vices born inside the home could become known and be a cause of scandal among the neighbors. This frequent possibility caused fear. Disorder easily contaminated everything and attacked the honor and shame of the family. The task of the husband and father to be vigilant was important. The moral treatises refer to this role of the husband as a domestic judge. Once again, Arbiol perfectly described that task: "The father of the family knows that his house is the House of God ... so that the judgment of God begins there, he must examine the behavior of everyone in his house to see if someone lives badly and is in God's misfortune."

It was basically a judgment of good manners. It is convenient to consider the description of Arbiol in *The Family's Rules*, where he offers us the best account of what would be called domestic judgment. It is a mixture of reminiscences of the old private justice—now generally eliminated—and the conversion of the family into an ideal space for Catholic moralization: "Another rule for the father of the

---

40 James Casey, *Historia de la familia* (Madrid: Espasa Calpe, 1990), 186.
41 M. Eva Fernández Baquero, "El paterfamilias y el *consilium domesticum*," *Revista de la Facultad de Derecho de la Universidad de Granada* 8 (1985): 163.
42 Juan Luis Vives, *Los deberes del marido*, accessed Juny 15, 2020, https://bivaldi.gva.es/va/corpus/unidad.do?idUnidad=10109&idCorpus=1.

family is that no one repress or punish without first hearing the declaration of his guilt and that the accused confess it ... No one can punish without hearing his discharge ... then he must be harsh in the correction and in the punishment until throwing him out of the house if the matter is very serious."[43]

It is important to note that family or marriage literature tells us how to pacify the family because it was not so easy: married relationships were difficult due to male domination, and relationships with sons were also complicated by parental interference, without forgetting the tense relations between siblings due to the implementation of the privileges of hereditary exclusion and the monopoly of the oldest son. The books could not hide the diversity of situations: separations, transgressions of written norms, men who forgot their responsibilities, husbands who cheated on their wives, women who resisted, adulteries, etc. The submission of wives, for example, clashed with the theory when they had a greater dowry or wealth than their husbands. This could happen even in indivisible inheritance systems, where some women collected significant real estate due to the high mortality of their brothers. When death devastated a family, the survival of at least one woman was essential. In such cases, a daughter inherited a great heritage from the male line. This was the generalized situation in the territories of the *ius commune*. In the areas of Germanic tradition and egalitarian heritage, it was not very different either. So those daughters were married to poorer males, although of the same social status, to preserve the surname. These husbands were in an inferior social position and without a doubt depended on the economic power of the wife, who ruled her great house. On the other hand, it was not easy for all widows to accept control of their brothers or brothers-in-law. They, in our legal framework, had the right to use and enjoy the property of deceased husbands until their dowries were recovered. But the husband's family preferred to retain that dowry. Nor should we forget the lives of the married couple who had not chosen to be married. Literature has imagined those lives and their adversities. Even an *auto sacramental* (sacramental play) like Calderón de la Barca's *El pleito matrimonial del alma y el cuerpo (The Marriage Dispute Between the Soul and Body,* 1634) offers a reading of real marital problems against the background of man's pain in the face of death. Body and soul, in this work, are the allegory of a marriage with a lot of disagreements:

> Body: You are my wife, and you must obey me.
> Soul: Yes, but only in what is fair.
> Life: How sad the life of married people without peace is!
> Body: All that I wish is fair.

---

43 Arbiol, *La familia regulada*, 63, 321, 367, 368, 406, 410, 482, 558–559.

Soul: No, that's why I'll go away.
Body: You will have to file a marriage lawsuit.
Soul: Yes, I will.
Music: Only one son of both has forced them peacefully.[44]

Comedies about honor were the most prolific literature on the marriage subject. Among the issues included in them are social and domestic hierarchies, honor, obedience, and shame, which appear as values that characterize marriage and its gender roles. Almost all comedies evoke the debate between the marriage of convenience with the intervention of the family and, on the other hand, sentimental love. For example, *La Celestina* (originally titled *The Tragicomedy of Calisto and Melibea*, 1499) by Fernando de Rojas represented young people who wanted to move far away from the advice of their families. The unfortunate Melibea expressed her annoyance in this way: "I ask my parents to let me enjoy him [Calisto] if they want to enjoy me; I ask them not to think about vanities or arranged marriages, because it is better to be a good friend than a badly married one."[45]

It is logical that the moralists advised against reading this kind of work, especially by women. It was dangerous to let the female imagination fly, allowing the idea that a woman could decide who to marry or not to marry. Humanists such as Vives or Fray Luis de León advised only religious literature for the female sex. Nor was it advisable to go to the performance of plays that placed secret marriages at the center of their plots because these stories revealed personal choices contrary to the family. Parental authority was defied by the daring of disobedient sons who loved someone against the will of the parents.[46] It is interesting in this sense to read *El casamiento fingido* (*The Feigned Marriage*, 1700) by Cristóbal de Monroy y Silva. The plot of this comedy shows different secret marriages at the same time, and it allows us to understand different situations that led to the same problem: the young Doña Aña feels secretly married to Don Carlos. But her father does not know. He wants to marry her to a richer and more powerful man, Don Diego de Cabrera. She dares not disappoint him. She admits to the courtship of the official suitor but continues to love Don Carlos. When her father arranges the wedding date, the lovers decide to run away. Unfortunately, they are discovered. She takes refuge with her father-in-law, and Don Carlos, who

---

[44] Pedro Calderón de la Barca, *El pleito matrimonial*, ed. M. Roig (Pamplona-Kassel: Universidad de Navarra-Reichenberger, 2011).
[45] Fernando de Rojas, *La Celestina: o tragicomedia de Calisto y Melibea* (Madrid, 1822), 326–327.
[46] Gabriela Carrión, *Staging Marriage in Early Modern Spain. Conjugal Doctrine in Lope, Cervantes and Calderón* (Lanham, MD: Bucknell University Press, 2011), 150.

confronts Don Diego and believes he has killed him, disappears and travels to Aveiro, Portugal. A long time passes, and one day Doña Aña and her father-in-law discover the place where Don Carlos is. They decide to go looking for him. But Don Carlos seems to be married to a lady. In fact, this lady is the mistress of the nobleman whom Don Carlos serves, who cannot marry her due to the difference in status. The ending represents a hymn to freedom and love, and the main couple get their reward. This comedy demonstrates the existence of unions that are illicit because they do not conform to social rules or because they do not conform to parental dictates. Unlike what the moral discourses seemed to hide, the family strategy, a sign of order and the result of parental authority, was not always peaceful. In the following text, we see Don Carlos describing that he is already the husband of Doña Aña, but that he has married her in secret:

> [D]on Diego de Cabrera lives in this city ... he is very powerful and rich, and he aims (this is my misfortune!) to marry her ... as his nobility and wealth is so great, Doña Aña's parents have offered him their daughter to marry ... and since they are already suspicious of my courtship, they have almost violently decided to force the wedding and do it very soon ... with good words I have said that she has already chosen a husband, that it is me, that she has already who enjoys her as owner, and has someone to serve her.[47]

In addition to the difficulties of choosing and celebrating a marriage, Miguel de Cervantes, in *El juez de divorcios* (*The Judge of the Divorce Court*, 1615), presents a diversity of marriages with disagreements, where men and women confront each other, tired of living together. In this *entremés* (interlude), there are four troubled couples who ask the judge for a divorce. The typology of these couples collects stereotypes of failure, such as the marriage between an old man and a young woman or between a lady and a poor, lazy man.[48] One of the divorce applicants expresses her grief in this way: "In well-ordered kingdoms and republics, the duration of marriages should be limited, and every three years they could be broken or reconfirmed, like a lease."[49]

In the *Novelas ejemplares* (*Exemplary Novels*, 1613), Cervantes treats marriage very extensively. The work consists of thirteen novels. Of these, nine are dedicated to the marital issue. Lucía López Rubio has studied the conflicts caused between freely desired marriage and arranged marriage, such as in *La fuerza de*

---

47 Cristóbal de Monroy y Silva, *El casamiento fingido* (Madrid, 1700).
48 Enrique Vivó de Undabarrena, "El teatro de Cervantes y su casuística matrimonial," *Boletín de la Facultad de Derecho* 12 (1997): 228–243.
49 Miguel de Cervantes Saavedra, *Entremés del juez de los divorcios*, accessed July 15, 2020, http://www.cervantesvirtual.com/nd/ark:/59851/bmcsf2s7.

la sangre (*The Power of Blood*, 1613).[50] Here Leocadia is raped by Rodolfo, and they have a son. When his parents meet this child, they arrange a marriage and force Rodolfo to return from Italy. On returning to his parents' house, his mother shows him a false portrait of his future wife who does not like anything and reacts with these words: "it is good that sons obey their parents (...) but it is also convenient, and better, that parents give their sons the state they please (...) in the sacrament of marriage there must be the delight that married couples enjoy, and if this does not exist the marriage will fail."[51]

His statement contains messages about marriage: about the freedom to contract it, about the importance of personal choice, about the virtues that parents want compared to the wishes of young people, and also about the fear of not being happy during married life. Like the previous texts, it speaks of the intervention of the parents, which was not consistent with the law of Trent, which preached the free will of the spouses in their choice. But we already know that everyday experiences were far from the rule. Freedom was a recurring discourse in baroque comedies, proof of the ineffectiveness of that rule. In *El laberinto de Amor* (*The Labyrinth of Love*, 1615) by Cervantes, we also read a determined woman defend freedom of choice: "Can't it happen, unsurprisingly, that a woman looks for a man, just as a man looks for a woman?"[52]

In the same way, Pedro Calderón de la Barca tells us about the conflicts of married life derived from a strict code of conjugal honor. In *A secreto agravio, secreta venganza* (*Secret Vengeance for Secret Insult*, 1637), the innocent wife, Doña Leonor, is sacrificed by her husband, Don Lope, just for having secretly loved a gentleman. Jealousy, social appearance, possession, and gender violence are signs of lives that offer a perverse face of marriage. And to get rid of that nightmare, some authors present empowered women, agents of their own lives. So, in *Las bizarrías de Belisa* (*The Gallantries of Belisa*, 1634), Félix Lope de Vega draws a female personality opposite to the usual gender role: daring, defiant, and independent. The protagonist enjoys intervening in love and marriage matters, disobeying the wishes of the families and building her own wishes. She seduces and conquers men. She decides if she wants to marry or not to

---

50 Lucía López, *El matrimonio en las Novelas ejemplares y El Quijote: la influencia del modelo histórico, social y legal de los siglos XVI y XVII* (Madrid: Universidad Complutense de Madrid, 2016).
51 Miguel de Cervantes Saavedra, *La fuerza de la sangre* (Madrid, 1842), 25.
52 Miguel de Cervantes Saavedra, *Comedia famosa el laberinto de amor*, Jornada II, accessed September 30, 2020, http://www.cervantesvirtual.com/obra-visor/el-laberinto-de-amor-1/html/ff31fba4-82b1-11df-acc7-002185ce6064_10.html#I_0_.

marry; in fact, it is a message on the notion of marriage as an option and not as an obligation:

> I was born leaning/
> to all love so contrary/
> that I did not think that in my life/
> to want to hold her.[53]

In real life, some cultured women, those belonging to privileged classes, were aware that one of the great evils of marriage was the absence of freedom to decide for themselves. Some of them wrote short discourses denouncing this situation. In *El verdugo de su esposa (The Executioner of His Wife)*, included in the collection of novels titled *Desengaños amorosos (Love Disappointments*, 1647), María de Zayas decides that the protagonist rejects the marriage with her suitor and enters a convent: "the beautiful Lysis is closed due to the fear that some deception will disappoint her … It is not a tragic end, but the happiest there was, because, coveted and desired by many men, she did not submit to any of them."[54] Note the few alternatives to marriage, with the exception of the religious path or dependence on siblings and other relatives; however, the satisfaction shown by these women for choosing non-submission is very inspiring.

Conclusion

An innocent reading of the texts from the early modern age that spoke about marriage lets us deduce that all conceived it as an idealized space in imitation of the republics. A small, intimate space where men and women learned to put into practice the principles of social and political order that governed them: obedience, social rules, and the masculine hierarchy. For them, the small family was the small republic, or more precisely the mirror of the real republic, and everyone must be governed according to these principles. But this is the theoretical discourse. The writers—both clergy and laity—whose works pleased the rulers, because otherwise they would be censored, knew the real ex-

---

[53] Félix Lope de Vega, *Las bizarrías de Belisa*, acto III, accessed September 30, 2020, http://www.cervantesvirtual.com/obra-visor/las-bizarrias-de-belisa-0/html/feea9ad4-82b1-11df-acc7002185ce6064_4.html#I_7_.

[54] María de Zayas y Sotomayor, "Desengaños amorosos," *Lemir* 18 (2014); Carmen Solana Segura, "Las heroínas de las Novelas amorosas y ejemplares de María de Zayas frente al modelo femenino humanista," *Lemir* 14 (2010): 27–33.

periences did not accord with the ideal. Accordingly, marriage appears in all these discourses as a laboratory, a testing space for political and social rules. Marriage life was a balance between order and conflict. The books on family and marriage looked for moral and theological solutions to guarantee peace and concord, the union of spouses; they were discourses of order and, at the same time, a denunciation of disorder. When the proposed solutions meant strengthening the power of the man in the house, then the conflict increased. That is why they began to talk about feelings and affection between the spouses, although families still wanted to marry their sons according to their economic or power interests. The contradictions and balances are numerous. But the obsession with public order and the final need to guarantee it from the private order was producing a slow change in marriage toward a more intimate, less rigid model, though it took a long time to implement. The most widespread and well-known discourses on marriage in the early modern age presented it as the perfect place to observe and solve political, social, and moral problems: the functioning of social relations, small-scale conflict and peace management, and a moral and theological culture based on antagonistic notions; just as men and women were conceived as antagonistic, so their lives were built between evil and good, vice and virtue, abuse and forgiveness. This microcosm built the concept of marriage for centuries.

Works Cited

Agustí, Miquel. *Libro de los secretos de agricultura*. Barcelona, 1626.

Arbiol, Antonio. *La familia regulada con doctrina de la Sagrada escritura y santos padres de la Iglesia católica*. Madrid, 1778.

Asenjo, J. Alonso and Abraham Madroñal, eds. *G.L. Hidalgo. Diálogos de apacible entretenimiento*. Valencia: Publicacions de la Universitat de València, 2010.

Astete, Gaspar de. *Del gobierno de la familia y estado del matrimonio: donde se trata, de como se han de auer los casados con sus mugeres, y los parientes con sus hijos, y los señores con sus criados*. Valladolid, 1597.

Brandenberger, Tomás. *Literatura de matrimonio (Península Ibérica, S. XIV–XVI)*. Lausanne: Sociedad Suiza de Estudios Hispánicos, 1996.

Camós, Marco Antonio de. *Microcosmia y gobierno universal del hombre cristiano*. Barcelona: 1592.

Candau Chacón, M. Luisa, ed. *Las mujeres y el honor en la Europa moderna*. Huelva: Universidad de Huelva, 2014.

Candau Chacón, M. Luisa, "Entre lo permitido y lo ilícito: la vida afectiva en los tiempos modernos." *Tiempos Modernos*, no. 18 (2009). Accessed July 1, 2020. http://rabida.uhu.es/dspace/handle/10272/11165.

Carrión, Gabriela. *Staging Marriage in Early Modern Spain. Conjugal Doctrine in Lope, Cervantes and Calderón*. Lanham, MD: Bucknell University Press, 2011.
Carrodeguas, Celestino. *La sacramentalidad del matrimonio. Doctrina de Tomás Sánchez, s.j.* Madrid: Universidad Pontificia de Comillas de Madrid, 2013.
Casey, James. *Historia de la familia*. Madrid: Espasa Calpe, 1990.
Casey, James. *España en la edad moderna. Una historia social*. Valencia: Publicacions de la Universitat de Valencia, 2001.
Cassar, Carmel. *Honor y vergüenza en el Mediterráneo*. Barcelona: Icaria, 2004.
Cerda, Juan de la. "Vida política de todos los estados de mujeres." *Lemir* 14 (2010): 1–628.
Cervantes Saavedra, Miguel de. *Comedia famosa el laberinto de amor*. Accessed September 30, 2020. http://www.cervantesvirtual.com/obra-visor/el-laberinto-de-amor-1/html/ff31fba4-82b1-11df-acc7-002185ce6064_10.html#I_0_.
Cervantes Saavedra, Miguel de. *Entremés del juez de los divorcios*. Accessed July 15, 2020. http://www.cervantesvirtual.com/nd/ark:/59851/bmcsf2s7.
Cervantes Saavedra, Miguel de. *La fuerza de la sangre*. Madrid, 1842.
Correia Fernandes, M. Luisa. *Espelhos, cartas e guias. Casamento e espiritualidade na peninsula ibérica 1450–1700*. Porto: Instituto de cultura portuguesa, Universidade do Porto, 1995.
Fernández Baquero, M. Eva. "El paterfamilias y el *consilium domesticum*." *Revista de la Facultad de Derecho de la Universidad de Granada* 8 (1985): 163–177.
Galvache Valero, Francisco. *La educación familiar en los humanistas españoles*. Pamplona: Eunsa, 2001.
Granada, Luis de. *Obras, Biblioteca de Autores Españoles*, II. Madrid: 1860.
Guevara, Antonio de. *Relox de Príncipes*. Proyecto filosofía en español. Accessed July 3, 2020. http://www.filosofia.org/cla/gue/gue00.htm.
Guevara, Antonio de. *Libro primero de las epístolas familiares*. Valladolid, 1542.
Howe, E. Teresa. *Education and Women in the Early Modern Hispanic World*. London/New York: Routledge, 2016.
Lechner, Carlos. "La influencia de la familia, el Estado y la Iglesia en la construcción del matrimonio en los manuales matrimoniales españoles de la época moderna." In *Actas Congreso de la Asociación Internacional del Siglo de Oro*, 782–792. Frankfurt am Main/Madrid: Vervuert/Iberoamericana, 1999.
Ledesma, Pedro de. *Summa*. Zaragoza, 1611.
Ledesma, Pedro de. *Tractatus de magno matrimonii sacramento*. Venecia, 1592.
León, Luis de. *La perfecta casada*. Zaragoza, 1584.
Lope de Vega, Félix. *Las bizarrías de Belisa*. Accessed September 30, 2020. http://www.cervantesvirtual.com/obra-visor/las-bizarrias-de-belisa-0/html/feea9ad4-82b1-11df-acc7002185ce6064_4.html#I_7.
López, Lucía. *El matrimonio en las Novelas ejemplares y El Quijote: la influencia del modelo histórico, social y legal de los siglos XVI y XVII*. Madrid: Universidad Complutense de Madrid, 2016.
Luján, Pedro de. *Coloquios matrimoniales*. Edited by Antonio Rallo. Sevilla: Junta de Andalucía-Consejería de cultura, 2010. Accessed July 1, 2020. http://www.bibliotecavirtualdeandalucia.es/catalogo/es/catalogo_imagenes/grupo.cmd?path=1014397.
Martín Casares, Aurelio. "Las mujeres y la "paz en la casa" en el discurso renacentista." *Chronica Nova* 29 (2002): 217–244.

Maza Ozcoidi, Carlos. "La definición del concepto del honor. Su entidad como objeto de investigación histórica." *Espacio. Tiempo y Forma. Historia Moderna* 8 (1995): 191–209.

Mirón Pérez, M. Dolores. "El gobierno de la casa en Atenas clásica: género y poder en el Oikos." *Studia Histórica. Historia antigua* 18 (2000): 103–117.

Monroy y Silva, Cristóbal. *El casamiento fingido*. Madrid, 1700.

Morant, Isabel. *Discursos de la vida buena: matrimonio, mujer y sexualidad en la literatura humanista*. Madrid: Cátedra, 2002.

Rey, Ofelia. "Literatura y tratadistas de la familia en la Europa de la edad moderna." In *Familia y organización social en Europa y América: siglos XV–XX*, edited by Francisco Chacón, Juan Hernández y Francisco García, 211–232. Murcia: Universidad de Murcia, 2007.

Rojas, Fernando de. *La Celestina: o tragicomedia de Calisto y Melibea*. Madrid, 1822.

Solana Segura, Carmen. "Las heroínas de las Novelas amorosas y ejemplares de María de Zayas frente al modelo femenino humanista." *Lemir* 14 (2010): 27–33.

Torremocha, Margarita, ed. *Mujeres, sociedad y conflicto*. Valladolid: Castilla ediciones, 2019.

Vives, Juan Luis. *Instrucción de la mujer cristiana, que tradujo a la lengua castellana Juan Justiniano*. Madrid, 1793.

Vives, Juan Luis. *Los deberes del marido*. Accessed June 15, 2020. https://bivaldi.gva.es/va/corpus/unidad.do?idUnidad=10109&idCorpus=1.

Vivó de Undabarrena, Enrique. "El teatro de Cervantes y su casuística matrimonial." *Boletín de la Facultad de Derecho* 12 (1997): 228–243.

Zayas y Sotomayor, María. "Desengaños amorosos." *Lemir* 18 (2014).

Marion Röwekamp

4 Challenging Patriarchy: Marriage and the Reform of Marriage Law in Imperial Germany and the Weimar Republic

"If it were not for husband and wife," the German social historian and writer Wilhelm Heinrich Riehl (1823–1897) wrote in 1855, "one could think people on earth [are] destined for freedom and equality. However, because God created women and men, he made inequality and dependence basic elements of all human development."[1] Gender according to Riehl not only constituted ideas of inequality and domination but contributed significantly to the construction of humanity, to the construction of the modern state. Gender was, he argues, not only one of the most powerful producers of inequality, but *the most* powerful. This meant that the existence of the traditional family was defended just as much as the traditional position of women, indeed that the subordination of women in marriage was regarded as a paradigm of human inequality and subordination par excellence. As a consequence, the exclusion of married women from the state necessarily resulted from their subordination in the family. The patriarchally organized family thus was not only a mirror image but also a basic element of the state.

No wonder that women within the context of the Enlightenment started to question why all humans, including women, were not equal and why not in the family. "Wife, marriage and love exhibit the brand of slavery," expressed the feminist and philosopher Louise Dittmar (1807–1884) in 1849. "The man is master over his wife, the absolute monarch with unlimited power to give orders in his realm, and not even lip-service is paid to constitutional guarantees that may be applied to wives,"[2] argued Hedwig Dohm (1831–1919) almost forty

---

[1] Wilhelm Heinrich Riehl, *Die Naturgeschichte des Volkes als Grundlage einer deutschen Social-Politik: Die Familie*, vol. 3 (Stuttgart/Augsburg: Cotta, 1855), 3.
[2] Louise Dittmar, "Das Wesen der Ehe," in *Das Wesen der Ehe nebst einigen Aufsätzen über die soziale Reform der Frauen*, ed. Louise Dittmar (Leipzig: Verlag von Otto Wiegand, 1849), 51; Louise Dittmar, "Die männliche Bevormundung," in *Das Wesen der Ehe nebst einigen Aufsätzen über die soziale Reform der Frauen*, ed. Louise Dittmar (Leipzig: Verlag von Otto Wiegand, 1849), 15; Renate Möhrmann, *Die andere Frau: Emanzipationsansätze deutscher Schriftstellerinnen im Vorfeld der Achtundvierziger-Revolution* (Stuttgart: Metzler, 1977); Renate Möhrmann, ed., *Frauenemanzipation im deutschen Vormärz: Texte und Dokumente* (Stuttgart: Reclam, 1980); Gilla Dölle, ed., *Eine "ächt weibliche Emancipation": Die Diskussion der Geschlechterbeziehungen um 1848* (Kassel: Archiv der deutschen Frauenbewegung, 1998); Marion Freund, *"Mag der Thron in Flammen glühn!" Schriftstellerinnen und die Revolution 1848/49* (Königstein/Taunus: Helmer,

years later for the necessity of suffrage for women as a tool to end the subordinate position of women in law in general, but especially within marriage.³ Women's first experiences with the law were often encounters of injustice such as the one Dittmar and Dohm formulated in the revolution of 1848 and in the restoration years, which saw the emergence of a tender and loosely organized women's movement in Germany. "It is not inappropriate and unfeminine to have knowledge of the sad and unworthy situation of one's own sex and to rebel against it, but it is *inhuman* and a disgrace to close your eyes and ears in cowardly egoism and keep these worst things quiet," argued Marie Stritt (1855–1928) around the turn of the century. "The women ... demand *more*, they finally demand the recognition of their human rights and their human dignity—*they demand justice!*"⁴ The idea of equal rights for all humans, as expressed here by Marie Stritt and previously especially by Hedwig Dohm, embraced for the first time also humans of the female sex who, by law, had not been treated as subjects or citizens in their own right (but very much so in terms of obligations).

Not accidentally, parallel to raising their voices, women were immediately silenced after 1848. Women were not allowed to organize themselves in political organizations or edit newspapers and journals. The claim for female suffrage within the politically suffocating atmosphere of Imperial Germany was unthinkable, thus the women's movements focused first on the mothers, these demands seemed at first sight to be relatively harmless.⁵ Similarly, as it had been proven that educated mothers could better perform educational tasks, it could be shown that it was now only natural, as feminist Louise Otto-Peters (1819–1895) put it, "to inquire about the laws that affect these living conditions, to inquire what duties women, who marry, take on, what rights or protection the laws grant, recognize or deny them."⁶ Women claimed they were just trying to improve their legal

---

2004); Birgit Mikus, *The Political Woman in Print: German Woman's Writing 1845–1919* (Oxford et al: Peter Lang, 2014).
3 Hedwig Dohm, *Der Frauen Natur und Recht* (Berlin: Wedekind & Schwieger, 1876), 141–142.
4 Marie Stritt, *Frauen-Landsturm: Flugblatt zum Familienrecht im bürgerlichen Gesetzbuch* (Berlin: n.p., 1896), reprinted in *Die Rechtsstellung der Frau im 1900: Eine kommentierte Quellensammlung*, eds. Stephan Meder, Arne Duncker and Andrea Czelk (Cologne: Böhlau, 2010), 809, emphasis in the original.
5 Dittmar, "Das Wesen der Ehe," 47–75; Helene Lange, "Über das Frauenwahlrecht," *Neue Bahnen* 33, no. 7 (1898): 68–69.
6 Louise Otto-Peters, Einige deutsche Gesetzes-Paragraphen über die Stellung der Frau, ed. Archiv der deutschen Frauenbewegung (ADF), NL-K-08 Deutscher Staatsbürgerinnenverband, Nachlass Louise Otto-Peters, 3; Marion Röwekamp, "Olympe de Gouges, Louise Otto-Peters und der Kampf um das Familienrecht in Frankreich und Deutschland," in *Die Rechte der Frauen 1791–1866–2016*, eds. Sandra Berndt and Gerlinde Kämmerer (Markkleeberg: Sax-Verlag Beu-

position within the realm they worked in according to their "natural" roles in the interest of the family and the state.[7] The idea of equal rights in a more extended way they stressed less in order not to raise hackles. But, almost unnoticed, these demands meant much more; they were the demand for the granting of full legal capacity to married women and thus the basis for full legal capacity for all women. The fight for equal rights in family law thus meant, on the one hand, the demand for equality under private law as a first step on the road to political equality and to break one of the locks that held them down legally, but also, at the same time, the more or less hidden fight for the right to vote for women, years before the women's movement was "open" about it. Indeed, until the 20th century, suffrage law and family law were closely linked because the exclusion of women from both rights was the starting point for their discrimination throughout the law. They conditioned each other in a form of deadlock or double bind, as historian Gisela Bock has called it.[8] It was hard to escape discrimination within the family without gaining suffrage, and it was logically impossible to gain suffrage without gaining full legal capacity in private law (even though it later happened exactly like that).

While initially not successful, the idea of equal rights for women was in the world. It was not only in Germany that women claimed equal rights in the family. In fact, it was one of the major topics for international feminism during the last decades of the 19th and the first decades of the 20th century.[9] All Western legal

---

cha, 2017), 21–43; Susanne Schötz, "'Einige Deutsche Gesetzes-Paragraphen' – Louise Otto-Peters und das Engagement des Allgemeinen Deutschen Frauenvereins für Frauenrechte," in *Menschenrechte sind auch Frauenrechte*, eds. Ilse Nagelschmidt et al. (Leipzig: Leipziger Universitätsverlag, 2002), 53–78.

[7] Marie Stritt, "Die Ehefrau und das bürgerliche Gesetzbuch," in *Die Rechtsstellung der Frau im 1900: Eine kommentierte Quellensammlung*, eds. Stephan Meder, Arne Duncker and Andrea Czelk (Cologne: Böhlau, 2010), 812.

[8] Gisela Bock, "Frauenwahlrecht. Deutschland um 1900 in vergleichender Perspektive," in *Geschichte und Emanzipation: Festschrift für Reinhard Rürup*, eds. Michael Grüttner et al. (Frankfurt am Main/New York: Campus, 1999), 119; Marion Röwekamp, "The Double Bind: Von den Interdependenzen des Frauenwahlrechts und des Familienrechts vor und nach 1918," in *100 Jahre Frauenwahlrecht: Kampf, Kontext, Wirkung*, eds. Hedwig Richter and Kerstin Wolff (Hamburg: Verlag des Hamburger Instituts für Sozialforschung, 2018), 99–121.

[9] Karen Offen, "National or International? How and Why the Napoleonic Code Drove Married Women's Legal Rights onto the Agenda of the International Council of Women and the League of Nations: An Overview," in *Family Law in Early Women's Rights Debates*, eds. Stephan Meder and Christoph-Eric Mecke (Cologne: Böhlau, 2013), 42–59; Sara Kimble and Marion Röwekamp, "Legal Cultures and Communities of Female Protest in Modern European History, 1860–1960s," in *New Perspectives on European Women's Legal History*, eds. Sara Kimble and Marion Röwekamp (New York: Routledge, 2017), 1–24; Marion Röwekamp, "Reform Claims in Family Law

cultures permeated a patriarchal foundation of civil law and legalized the subordination of married women. Though the legal cultures and means were different in each country, women found themselves in a common struggle.[10] At first the fight did not lead to results. This changed not only in Germany in the aftermath of World War I, emerged and prevailing ideas about democracy as well as with the ideas of the League of Nations to facilitate not only global peace but also the protection of the human rights of minorities, among them increasingly also women. Progressive forces in German society had by now adopted the idea that women deserved something called "equality." In fact, women's equality was an intrinsic part of the idea of democracy. Accordingly, suffrage rights were granted almost immediately by the new Social Democrat government in 1918. "Germany has the honor to be the first republic founded on true principles of democracy, universal and equal suffrage for all citizens and all men and women," marveled Marie Stritt happily.[11]

There was a wide variety of ideas about what equality might mean in practice beyond enfranchisement. The period of the Weimar Republic in Germany was, as in most other European countries, a time of negotiation about the extent of women's citizenship rights. There was mostly an agreement that women should have suffrage rights, but further rights than suffrage needed to be bargained within the context of their specifically gendered place in society. Society felt that the extent of their citizenship rights should be defined by women's supposed nature and be based on their distinct roles as mothers and wives. These ideas were generally shared by women and men alike, even by large parts of the women's movements; they just argued that women's nature was different but equally important for society and that it would "heal" the existing problems of the state that were caused by women not participating. But many women also believed that equality should, in principle, not be determined by gender and thus that women and men should be treated equally in terms of the law. This, however, was also claimed by women who thought women were different by na-

---

and Legal Struggles within the International Council of Women, 1888–1914," in *Forging Bonds Across Borders: Transatlantic Collaborations for Women's Rights and Social Justice in the Long Nineteenth Century*, eds. Anja Schüler and Britta Waldschmidt-Nelson (Washington, DC: Bulletin of the German Historical Institute, Supplement 13, 2017), 75–93.
10 Meder and Mecke, *Family Law*; Stephan Meder and Christoph-Eric Mecke, eds., *Reformforderungen zum Familienrecht International*, vol. 1: *Westeuropa und die USA (1830–1914)* (Cologne: Böhlau 2015); Kimble and Röwekamp, "Legal Cultures," 1–43.
11 Marie Stritt, "Germany: Victory for Woman Suffrage," *International Women's News* 13, no. 4 (1919): 44–48.

ture. The difference should not emphasize their exclusion from enjoying equal rights with men but justify it.

These demands were raised in many different legal areas of the interwar years: in criminal law, in the access to all professions plus civil service, but especially in family law. But as women were felt to have their natural vocation and space within the family, the claim for equality within the family was the punchline for equality claims. It was one thing for some women to be parliamentarians or to work in small numbers in male-dominated professions, but women being equal within the family was a totally different matter. Here, the entire setup of society and thus a nerve of society was touched. This claim was the most threatening one women raised within the years of the Weimar Republic, and the strongest fight for or against reform emerged as a consequence. Here, the limits of the negotiation over how much equality Germany's first democracy was to bring to women ended clearly for the majority of society.

The timeframe of this chapter will cover the beginning of the debates about marriage across two attempts by the women's movement to change family law. The process of becoming aware of injustice led gradually, helped by the organization also on an international level, to an understanding that women should be treated equally by the law, especially in the family, and should be citizens with equal citizenship laws to men. I will analyze this discourse within the time of Imperial Germany and the Weimar Republic, showing how the process of negotiating an equal position for women in German society and in the family unfolded over time. While women started to claim this from early on, within the stifling context of the monarchy, men tended to ignore their plights completely. This changed in Germany's first democracy. The chapter shows how the limits of equality and of the rights guaranteed in the constitution were reached as far as changes as rights in the family were concerned. And, thus, how democracy failed in one of the areas usually not assumed to be connected to be a pillar of democracy: full equal rights for all female citizens.

Re-Enforcing Patriarchy: Marriage and the Family in Imperial Germany

The far-reaching changes in the social and economic foundations of society, which began at the end of the 18th century, especially with the increasing industrialization of the second half of the 19th century, did not remain without effects on the family constitution and form the background of the intellectual-historical development to be described in the following. Of central importance in the present context is the separation of domestic and professional spheres, which characterized the new family forms and enforced the separation of different roles for men and women. The felt dissolution of life and state as well of the family into single units supported by the growing ideas of emancipation of women were interpreted as threatening the entire life of the state and had to be counteracted. German political and legal doctrine thus set out in search of a new basis that could secure supra-individual validity and duration for the family. They invented the "traditional family" by trying to adjust to the reality of the modern state on the one hand but, on the other, by incorporating ideas of the natural subordination of women.[12] "The home is still the articulation of the existing union, the organizational foundation of the social body, the strong pillar of the moral and economic order," wrote the lawyer Otto von Gierke (1841–1921), reflecting ideas of not only the legal profession but broad parts of society that were reflected within the new German civil law.[13]

The German Civil Code (*Bürgerliches Gesetzbuch*, BGB), which came into effect in 1900, was one of the last civil laws codified within Europe following the founding of Germany as a nation in 1871.[14] Its idea was to bring an equal law to all citizens of formerly 39 different territories. Partly it was also a reaction to the imposition of French law on German land, as parts of the empire were still ruled by the French Civil Code. It was also a vital part of the political ideas and project of German liberals to dismantle the old feudal society (*Ständegesellschaft*), to secure the separation of church and state, and, besides all that, to achieve national unity and contribute to the strength of the nation-state. As such, the BGB was, besides a legal project, also a social, highly political, and cultural project. This is especially obvious also in the family law which embodied the interests and values that were able to prevail in the German Empire at the end of the 19th century. It reflected the changes to which the position of the family was subject over the course of the century. Here, it did not reflect the real position of women, as was often criticized, but was intended to protect a model of the family

---

12 Ursula Vogel, "Is Citizenship Gender-Specific?" in *The Frontiers of Citizenship*, eds. Ursula Vogel and Michael Moran (New York: St. Martin's Press, 1991), 66–67.
13 Otto von Gierke, *Der Entwurf eines bourgeoisen Gesetzbuchs und das deutsche Recht* (Leipzig: Dunker & Humblot, 1899), 34.
14 For the situation of women in law before 1900, see Barbara Dölemeyer, "Frau und Familie im Privatrecht des 19. Jahrhunderts," in *Frauen in der Geschichte des Rechts: Von der frühen Neuzeit bis zur Gegenwart*, ed. Ute Gerhard (Munich: C.H. Beck, 1997), 633–658; Ute Gerhard, *Gleichheit ohne Angleichung: Frauen im Recht* (Munich: C.H. Beck, 1990); Ute Gerhard, "Legal Particularism and the Complexity of Women's Rights in Nineteenth Century Germany," in *Private Law and Social Inequality in the Industrial Age: Comparing Legal Cultures in Britain, France, Germany, and the United States*, ed. Willibald Steinmetz (Oxford: Oxford University Press, 2000), 137–154.

that had never existed in this form; the "traditional nuclear family" was re-invented on the basis of old ideas of women's subordination in the family to preserve the patriarchy within the family. Designed to support and reinforce the power of men, marriage and the family acquired a more and more public character.[15]

Beyond its modern outlook in terms of legal formality and methodology as well as of granting women some rights such as legal capacity and parental power, in its content, the BGB tightened the legal situation of women and notably gave men the power over all her property besides making them the sole decision-making authority in the house. It was set up so that the head of the conjugal community continued to be the husband, he was entitled to decide on all matters concerning the conjugal life, and he determined in particular the place of residence and domicile and had the last word in the marriage. The husband was obliged to support his wife, and she was obliged to manage the household and to cooperate. The reason given for this order in marriage was that it was the "natural order of the relationship."[16]

In terms of property law, it disenfranchised women fully. By stating that they wanted to clean up the complicated property regimes, of which there were more than 100 the German states, the BGB rationalized the pre-existing ideas and reinforced male patriarchy. In the final version, the man was granted his own right of administration and would appear in his own name "as head of the family." In addition, women could seldom file a case without the consent of the husband. So even if the husband mismanaged the property of the wife, she had no legal means to protect it.

The BGB formally introduced parental power over children, but then legislated that the "father has, by virtue of his parental power, the right and duty to take care of his child's person and property" (§ 1627 BGB). And, also with regard to the kids, the father had the last word in terms of decisions. Only in the event of the father's death did parental authority transfer to the mother. In the end, mothers were as lawless as before; they had obligations toward their children but no new rights besides formally receiving parental guardianship. Furthermore, the proposed law removed the rights of illegitimate children to make material or familial claims to their fathers.

---

15 Margaret Barber Crosby, "The Civil Code and the Transformation of German Society: The Politics of Gender Inequality, 1814–1919" (PhD diss., Brown University, 2001), 226–251.
16 Benno Mugdan, *Die gesammten Materialien zum Bürgerlichen Gesetzbuch für das Deutsche Reich*, vol. 4 (Berlin: G. Schenck, 1899), 59.

Finally, the BGB tightened the divorce law as compared to the ARL.[17] Divorce was only possible in cases of adultery and other exceptions and rested on the guilt principle. In divorce cases, if the woman was declared the guilty party, she would take her maiden name in order for status to be taken from her, and she would not receive alimony. Declarations of guilt affected custody, too.

In reality, all claimed legal progress was solely paper rights to women. It was a cross-influence of all norms that only made clear how much women were disenfranchised. Besides formal differences, the laws concerning marriage and family mirrored those of other earlier European civil codes such as the Napoleonic Code, the Austrian Civil Code of 1811, and the Prussian Civil Code of 1794. As a result, the maintenance of the existing order of marriage was placed above the individual interests of the wife—the content of the traditional family law was preserved in new legal forms. As far as the effect of the BGB is concerned, it seems to be true that it hardly differed from the marriage law of the "*Sachsenspiegel*"; marriage law has remained almost static over a period of at least one thousand years. The BGB again designated women as second-class citizens in private law.[18]

Culture of Protest: Women's Reaction against the BGB

Thus, the women's movement had, almost right from the moment of its institutional founding, begun to challenge a wife's legal subordination to her husband. In fact, it was the process of the codification of the BGB which led in the German women's movement to an early awareness of the role of law for the discrimination of women in general and in the family in particular.[19] Realizing that women

---

17 Hannelore Schröder, *Die Rechtlosigkeit der Frau im Rechtsstaat: Dargestellt am Allgemeinen Preußischen Landrecht, am Bürgerlichen Gesetzbuch und an J.G. Fichtes Grundlage des Naturrechts* (Frankfurt am Main/New York: Campus, 1979); Marianne Weber, *Ehefrau und Mutter in der Rechtsentwicklung: Eine Einführung* (Tübingen: J. C .B. Mohr, 1907), 331–341; Susanne Weber-Will, *Die rechtliche Stellung der Frau im Privatrecht des Preußischen Allgemeinen Landrechts von 1794* (Frankfurt am Main/New York: Peter Lang, 1983), 281–286.
18 Ute Rosenbusch, *Der Weg zum Frauenwahlrecht in Deutschland* (Baden-Baden: Nomos, 1998), 275.
19 Christiane Berneike, *Die Frauenfrage ist Rechtsfrage: Die Juristinnen der deutschen Frauenbewegung und das Bürgerliche Gesetzbuch* (Baden-Baden: Nomos, 1995); Orla-Maria Fels, "Die Deutsche Bürgerliche Frauenbewegung als juristisches Phänomen" (PhD diss., Freiburg University, 1959); Sabine Klemm, *Frauenbewegung und Familienrecht 1848 bis 1933: Eine Betrachtung*

were mostly lawless within the area that was supposedly the center of their life, the family, the newly founded General German Women's Club (*Allgemeiner Deutscher Frauenverein*, ADF) focused more and more on the law of the family from 1869. The situation was dire as women rightly feared that within the context of the codification process of the German Civil Code, the new law would repeat or even tighten the subordination of women in the family. Louise Otto-Peters collected the complaints and the demands of women as far as their situation in the family was concerned. Based on this material, she published a memorandum in 1876 on the legal situation of women in the family and warned women about the legal consequences a marriage had for them.[20] One year later, a commission of the ADF worked out the first legal demands of women, which turned out to be one of the first petitions of women to the Reichstag, signed by around 10,000–12,000 women.[21] This was the genesis of the first mass-organized movements of German women and the beginning of debates over marriage law, debates which would keep going well into the 21st century.

In the petition, they requested the removal of provisions that deemed women "incapable," modifications to divorce law, and changes to custody rights for both parents. In addition, they asked that women be allowed control over their own property and inheritance. They requested the removal of patriarchal authority and custody over children in the event of divorce and the elimination of "general stylistic elements in the law" that reduced women to the same status as minorities and invalids.

When the publication of the first draft of the BGB was published in 1888, this brought heavy disappointment as none of their claims had been considered. But when the second committee came together in 1890 and the women could observe the way the public debate was turning against their claims, a new wave of more

---

anhand von Quellen (Tübingen: Campus, 1999); Stephan Meder, Arne Duncker, and Andrea Czelk, eds., *Die Rechtsstellung der Frau um 1900: Eine kommentierte Quellensammlung* (Cologne: Böhlau, 2010); Stephan Meder, Arne Duncker, and Andrea Czelk, eds., *Frauenrecht und Rechtsgeschichte: Die Rechtskämpfe der deutschen Frauenbewegung* (Cologne: Böhlau, 2006); Tanja-Carina Riedel, *Gleiches Recht für Mann und Frau: Die bürgerliche Frauenbewegung und die Entstehung des BGB* (Cologne: Böhlau, 2008); Schröder, *Die Rechtlosigkeit*; Weber, *Ehefrau und Mutter*, 407–505.

20 AddF, NL Louise Otto-Peters aus Bestand NL-K-08, 6–7/2. Louise Otto-Peters, *Einige deutsche Gesetzes-Paragraphen über die Stellung der Frau*, ed. ADF, aus: Schötz, "Einige Deutsche Gesetzes-Paragraphen," 53–78; Röwekamp, "Olympe de Gouges," 21–43.

21 "Petition of the Allgemeinen Deutschen Frauenverein to the Reichstag," *Neue Bahnen* 12, no. 8 (1877): 57–59, printed in Meder et al., *Rechtsstellung der Frau*, 36–41.

serious protests emerged.²² This time it was helped by the founding of the German branch of the International Council of Women, the *Bund Deutscher Frauenvereine* (BDF), in 1894. The BDF and ADF together pooled all their efforts into fighting the BGB. In fact, for the first time, women formulated that the legal question was at the center of the so-called woman's question. The Swiss-educated Anita Augspurg (1857–1943), one of the first German female lawyers, phrased that the women's question was to a considerable degree a question of economics, but first and foremost a legal question.²³ The BDF formed a legal committee and published several pamphlets, while a number of petitions were written and launched at different sessions of parliament and the drafting committee of the BGB.²⁴ In the same year, the first organized strike of female workers occurred as a protest against the Civil Code and was joined by 500 middle-class women.²⁵

But women's protests were to no avail. Other protests against the BGB came from the Socialist Party as well as the Center Party and Catholics. The latter in general opposed the new law because, in their view, the state interfered too much within the sphere of the church; marriage was understood as a holy sacrament and not as a matter of the worldly state. Since the mandatory introduction of civil marriages in 1875, the matter of marriage law and the focus on the family became the focus and defining issue the Catholics turned around. For them, every change meant an attack on their identity. This trauma was still alive in the interwar years, though Catholics in general started to feel more "German"

---

22 Riedel, *Gleiches Recht für Frau und Mann*; Meder et al., *Frauenrecht und Rechtsgeschichte*; Berneike, *Die Frauenfrage ist Rechtsfrage*.
23 Anita Augspurg, "Gebt acht, solange noch Zeit ist!" *Die Frauenbewegung* 1, no. 1 (1895): 4–5, printed in Meder et al., *Rechtsstellung der Frau*, 41–42.
24 For example: Auguste Schmidt and Henriette Goldschmidt, *Petition und Begleitschrift betreffend das "Familienrecht" in dem Entwurf des neuen bürgerlichen Gesetzbuches für das Deutsche Reich* (Leipzig: Schäfer, 1896); Olga von Beschwitz, *Begleitschrift zu der Petition des Bundes Deutscher Frauenvereine an den Reichstag betr. das Familienrecht des neuen BGB für das Deutsche Reich* (Frankenberg: L. Reisel, 1899); Cäcilie Dose and Alma Kriesche, *Die Stellung der Frau und Mutter im Familienrecht der ausserdeutschen Staaten und nach den Bestimmungen des neuen bürgerlichen Gesetzbuches für das Deutsche Reich* (Frankenberg: L. Reisel, 1900).
25 On socialist women, see Beatrix Geisel, *Klasse, Geschlecht und Recht: Vergleichende sozialhistorische. Untersuchung der Rechtsberatungspraxis von Frauen- und Arbeiterbewegung (1894– 1933)* (Baden-Baden: Nomos, 1997), 102–105; Joseph Joos, *Die sozialdemokratische Frauenbewegung in Deutschland* (Mönchen-Gladbach: Volksvereins Verlag, 1912); Heinz Niggemann, *Emanzipation zwischen Sozialismus und Feminismus: Die sozialdemokratische Frauenbewegung im Kaiserreich* (Wuppertal: Hammer, 1981); Hanna Szymanski, *Theorie und Lebenswirklichkeit: Ehe und Eherechte im Spiegel sozialdemokratischer Forderungen im deutschen Kaiserreich* (Köln: Böhlau, 2013).

than only Catholic.²⁶ For the socialists, it was the other way around. They claimed the same as the women's movement.²⁷ Without considering the broad protests of different groups of society, the law was approved in August 1896 and came into effect on 1 January 1900.

With the introduction of the BGB, gender relations were reinforced and redefined in such a way that it reflected its entrance into daily life as positive law. But it also symbolized a growing civil society that was unequal from the core; the reform of the law was not only demanded by the women's movement but by broader parts of society such as socialists and others who saw changes as basic democratic rights. As Anita Augspurg argued, the BGB had imposed new political duties on women but denied them every political right.²⁸ The civil code made it obvious to women that they were not considered citizens.

Negotiating Equality: The Constitution and Women's Equality in the Family in the Weimar Republic

However, when Germany was defeated in World War I and in the wake of the November Revolution in 1918, women could at last see a potential for equal rights within a democratic republic. Women's suffrage became an almost overnight reality to the great surprise of the BDF, socialist women, and other women's organizations who had fought for this right for decades and who celebrated it as a major victory. That women's equality involved political rights was soon generally agreed on, even by those who had been opposed to women voting and participating in politics such as the conservative parties, who rapidly began to rely heavily on their women's voters. But despite this acceptance of women's voting rights, there still remained the question of whether and how far their equality should extend outside of the arena of voting rights. The official narrative of granting women equality runs counter to the reality of the complex struggle of

---

26 Ellen Lovell Evans, *The German Center Party, 1870–1933: A Study in Political Catholicism* (Carbondale: Southern Illinois University Press, 1981); Michael B. Gross, *The War Against Catholicism: Liberalism and the Anti-Catholic Imagination* (Ann Arbor: University of Michigan, 2004).
27 Wolfgang Plat, "Die Stellung der deutschen Sozialdemokratie zum Grundsatz der Gleichberechtigung der Frau auf dem Gebiet des Familienrechts bei der Schaffung des Bürgerlichen Gesetzbuches des Deutschen Reiches" (PhD diss., Humboldt University Berlin, 1966); Szymanski, *Theorie und Lebenswirklichkeit*, 100–134.
28 Augsburg, "Gebt acht," 4–5.

women, who soon came to realize that the aftermath of suffrage meant a reinforced struggle for all the other equal rights that by no means came as a logical consequence of women's suffrage. Suffrage was the tool and leverage they needed to go on with the new struggles. The reform of family law was one of the evergrowing varieties of this struggle, probably at the center of it, as here women had to free themselves from the second "lock" that kept them in a state of legal discrimination in order to become citizens with full rights.[29]

In consequence of World War I, the number of women in comparison to men doubled. Many women who had been responsible heads for the household in war time were relieved to go back to their homes and duties as only wives and mothers, willing to embrace the idea of a domestic sphere for women and a public one for men as often represented in women's magazines and the popular press.[30] But many women had also experienced the war time with the greater necessity for women to work a new independence and self-determination. Managing the families by themselves as heads of the household, besides often working to support them, had made them escape the domestic sphere in big numbers. For many women, even those who were not active in the women's movement, the opportunities created by the war shaped a will to keep on working and participating in the public sphere. Especially the younger ones without families were keen on keeping their independence from the war times. This independence at times went hand in hand with a loosening of sexual and moral codes. The embodiment of male fears was the so-called "new woman," single and childless, sexually emancipated with a "*Bubikopf*" (bob haircut), and into fashion, who symbolized the liberating changes in gender roles and raising the fears of the German nation that was about to falter with this egoism of women. Throughout the 1920s, many women, especially young women, rejected the exclusively domestic role in favor of gainful employment outside the home, economic independence, and the postponement of marriage because it suggested the end of freedom with its still patriarchal structure and traditional gender roles. Mass en-

---

29 Röwekamp, "The Double Bind," 99–121; Marion Röwekamp, "'Männer und Frauen haben grundsätzlich die gleichen staatsbürgerlichen Rechte': Weimar – Meilenstein auf dem Weg zur Gleichberechtigung der Geschlechter?" in *Die Weimarer Verfassung, Wert und Wirkung für die Demokratie*, ed. Friedrich-Ebert-Stiftung (Erfurt: Friedrich-Ebert-Stiftung, 2009), 235–264; Dieter Schwab, "Gleichberechtigung und Familienrecht im 20. Jahrhundert," in *Frauen in der Geschichte des Rechts: Von der Frühen Neuzeit bis zur Gegenwart*, ed. Ute Gerhard (Munich: C.H. Beck, 1997), 790–827; Inge Schwanecke, "Die Gleichberechtigung der Frau unter der Weimarer Reichsverfassung" (PhD diss., University of Heidelberg, 1977).
30 Birthe Kundrus, *Familienpolitik und Geschlechterverhältnisse im Ersten und Zweiten Weltkrieg* (Hamburg: Christians, 1995), 124–141.

tertainment, fashion, and leisure time reshaped unmarried women's lives. At the same time, Germany experienced a flood of marriages (*Heiratsflut*) but reduced the number of children in the family to a maximum of two. Marriage counseling, sexuality, birth control, abortion, eugenics, and racial hygiene characterized the public debate and reality of women. The family was seen as the key to society's health; it was just that the left and right drew different conclusions about how to improve the family. Society and women especially were torn between the idea of a new future with more freedom and the traditional family. In this way, they were, as historian Atina Grossman has phrased it, at once "modernity's agents, victims, and mediators."[31]

Returning soldiers found their wives changed, and they in turn did not find the same men who had left; their situation had changed. Divorce rates as well as birth rates of illegitimate children were rising while marriage rates were sinking.[32] But the possibility of granting divorce based on the BGB was still difficult; the most potent discontent that emerged with the family law and especially the divorce rules came from veterans and their wives. This all made the so-called "crisis of the family" obvious, yet calls for new socio-political measures were heard not only from the women's movement.

Mostly, it was demands for the better protection of mothers and children within the family that were made. This change of perspective was not due to the ideas of rights of equality in the sense of securing the rights of individuals notwithstanding their gender. Instead, the emphasis was on the preservation of family and state. Thus, in 1919, the family was for the first time placed under constitutional protection in the Weimar constitution. Welfare programs

---

[31] Atina Grossman, *Reforming Sex: The German Movement for Birth Control and Abortion Reform 1920–1950* (New York: Oxford University Press, 1995), 5. See also Julia Sneeringer, *Winning Women's Votes: Propaganda and Politics in Weimar Germany* (Chapel Hill: University of North Carolina Press, 2002), 12; Helen Boak, *Women in the Weimar Republic* (Manchester: Manchester University Press, 2015), 200–205; Cornelie Usborne, *The Politics of the Body in Weimar Germany: Women's Reproductive Rights and Duties* (Ann Arbor: University of Michigan Press, 1992), 84–85; Katharina von Ankum, ed., *Women in the Metropolis: Gender and Modernity in Weimar Culture* (Berkeley: University of California Press, 1997); Hanna Vollmer-Heitmann, *Wir sind von Kopf bis Fuß auf Liebe eingestellt: Die zwanziger Jahre* (Hamburg: Kabel, 1993); Michelle Mouton, *From Nurturing the Nation to Purifying the Volk: Weimar and Nazi Family Policy, 1918–1945* (Cambridge/New York: Cambridge University Press, 2007).

[32] Ida Rost, *Die Ehescheidungen der Jahre 1920–1924 von in Sachsen geschlossenen Ehen, unter besonderer Berücksichtigung der Dauer der Ehen und des Heiratsalters der geschiedenen Ehegatten* (Leipzig: Vieweg & Teubner, 1927); Dirk Blasius, *Ehescheidung in Deutschland (1794–1945)* (Göttingen: Vandenhoeck & Ruprecht 1987), 155–187; Karen Hagemann, *Frauenalltag und Männerpolitik: Alltagsleben und gesellschaftliches Handeln von Arbeiterfrauen in der Weimarer Republik* (Bonn: Dietz, 1990), 179–185.

for mothers, children, babies, and youth were the beginning not only of the welfare state but also of state-regulated family policy.[33]

This understanding of the family clashed with the claims for equal rights of women, which were also reinforced after the war and placed under constitutional protection. The Constitution itself was not clear in its priority in terms of how it suggested the protection of family and women's equality at the same time. Art. 119 protected the idea of the "traditional" family which needed to keep women within the home and subordinate to the husband, while at the same time it stated that men and women were equal in marriage.[34] Art. 109 specified that "all Germans are equal before the law. Men and women have in principle the same civic rights and duties." This was the first time that the principles of gender equality were embodied in the constitution.

The problems the new constitution posed for women had already become apparent during the negotiations over its content in the Constitutional Assembly. Female parliamentarians such as the socialists Marie Juchacz (1879–1956), Luise Zietz (1865–1922), and Marie Baum (1874–1964) of the German Democratic Party (DDP) had quickly identified the problems in the draft of Hugo Preuss (1860–1925) and asked for changes. They wanted different wording for Art. 109 and suggested a broader equality clause, because "we want this constitution to state that this reform of civil law must be started immediately and that the provisions that disadvantage the legal position of women in this area must be removed."[35] They wanted to make sure that a reform of the family law was enforced and claimed that the law as it was did not grant equal rights to all citizens and thus needed to be changed. Only by considering the rights of women fully, beyond only in prin-

---

[33] Karin Hausen, "Arbeiterinnenschutz, Mutterschutz und gesetzliche Krankenversicherung im Deutschen Kaiserreich und in der Weimarer Republik: Zur Funktion von Arbeits- und Sozialrecht für die Normierung und Stabilisierung der Geschlechterverhältnisse," in *Frauen in der Geschichte des Rechts*, 759–771; Young-Sun Hong, *Welfare, Modernity, and the Weimar State* (Princeton, NY: Princeton University Press, 1998).

[34] Heinrich Aldag, *Die Gleichheit vor dem Gesetz in der Reichsverfassung: Eine öffentlichrechtliche Abhandlung auf rechtsvergleichender Grundlage* (Berlin: Heymann, 1925); Alfred Wieruszowski, "Artikel 119: Ehe, Familie, Mutterschaft," in *Die Grundrechte und Grundpflichten der Reichsverfassung*, vol. 2: *Artikel 118–142*, ed. Hans Carl Nipperdey (Berlin: Hobbing, 1930), 72–94; Rebecca Heinemann, *Familie zwischen Tradition und Emanzipation: Katholische und sozialdemokratische Familienkonzeptionen in der Weimarer Republik* (Munich: Oldenbourg 2004), 67–108.

[35] *Verhandlungen der verfassunggebenden Deutschen Nationalversammlung* 328 (1919/20), 57. session July 15, 1919 (Berlin: Norddeutsche Buchdruckerei, 1920), MP Juchacz: 1560, MP Zietz: 1563–64, MP Quarck: 1565–66; see Heinemann, *Familie zwischen Tradition und Emanzipation*, 151–212; Heide-Marie Lauterer, *Parlamentarierinnen in Deutschland 1918/19–1949* (Königstein, Taunus: Ulrike Helmer, 2002), 139–147.

ciple, would the state be truly democratic.[36] But their opponents notably rejected this idea; they wanted to keep the man as head of the household model and felt that a reform would threaten the concept of the family and, by extension, the state itself. Lawyer and DDP member of parliament Hermann Luppe (1874–1945) pointed out that the constitution never intended to grant women equal rights within the family.[37]

This group interpreted the principle of equality in a way that did not threaten the established order of gender relations, especially in the family, and did not want to challenge it. According to this interpretation, women should have equality but only within the context of their specifically historically gendered place in society, meaning, if at all, outside of the family. The reason for their extended citizenship would be not equality with men as such but be based on their distinct roles as wives and mothers and thereby limited. Consequently, their opponents could make sure that their new roles would not conflict with their place in the family and that they would remain subordinate to men. Accordingly, women were not seen as individual citizens but as members of a unit, which kept on mirroring the natural differences between men and women.

Independently from the two opinions about the direct extent of the constitutional law on the family law, factually both articles contained a limitation to this citizenship for women: Art. 109 only granted equality "in principle" and Art. 119 protected the family at the same time and thus immediately compromised the promised equality for women. In effect, the protection of the family meant that the law had the duty to treat its citizens as gendered beings and bestow rights upon them based on the roles they fulfilled as women and as men. Men would still be seen as the head of the household, and women still as being at home as mothers and wives. This implied a conflict with the formulation that granted women equal rights with men. It claimed equality while at the same time saying that the law should keep discriminating between them as far as the relationship within the family was concerned. So, the reality of gender difference was implanted within the constitution and gave way to further arguments against the abolishment of the privileges of sex that men had enjoyed for centuries and kept on enjoying. The writers of the constitution did not resolve this contradiction; the clashing formulation of the equality of men and women in the constitution in Arts. 109 and 119 was the compromise that could be achieved and, in consequence, the reason for a number of new struggles about the extent

---

36 *Verhandlungen Nationalversammlung*, 1565.
37 MP Luppe, ibid., 1561, 1567–1568; MP Teusch, ibid., 1560–1561; MP Heinze, ibid., 1564; MP Quidde, ibid., 1566.

of the concrete meaning of women's equality. It created a tension over how women should be seen in the state and the extent to which they were treated as active citizens or still as legal subjects to their husbands. Central among them was the question of the reform of family law.

Attempts to Reform Family Law

With women's suffrage, the conditions for political work for women changed dramatically. Prior to 1918, women's organizations had had to rely on addressing petitions to the German Reichstag and had no means of legal redress. Now, with the BDF being so much stronger, including in numbers—it now consisted of around half a million members and around 2,200 member organizations[38]—, women were able to use parliamentary tools such as committees in order to bring petitions, file their demands via a political party, or become parliamentarians themselves. Thus, they could participate directly in the political process and use the arguments of the new constitution to claim new rights. The two parties which favored their claims were the DDP and the Social Democratic Party (SPD), which often brought in the suggestions of the BDF as their own legal claims. The women's movement gained influence not only via the female parliamentarians who often were also members of the women's movement but also via male supporters whom they asked to work as go-betweens for them. But in many instances, all female parliamentarians came together, regardless of the pressure of their parties, to push through their claims such as in the areas of peace, social welfare, and in the admission of female lawyers to the profession.[39] The family law reform was not one of these areas; here, the female parliamentarians were far too divided by their different ideologies. Even among feminists, the different ideas about the family were so strong that neither the female parliamentarians nor the women in the BDF and other women's organizations could find common ground.

---

38 Klaus Hönig, *Der Bund Deutscher Frauenvereine in der Weimarer Republik 1919–1933* (Frankfurt am Main: Hänsel-Höhenhausen, 1995), 14.
39 See, for example, Max Hachenburg, "Interfraktioneller Antrag der weiblichen Reichstagsabgeordneten auf Zulassung von Frauen zu den juristischen Prüfungen," *Deutsche Juristen Zeitung* 26 (1921): 174; Marie-Elisabeth Lüders, "Interfraktionelle Frauenarbeit," *Die Frau* 27, no. 5 (1920): 154–156.

This became especially obvious in the debate on divorce, which was at the center of the reform proposals.[40] The BDF, led by the reform proposals of its female lawyers such as Margarete Berent (1887–1965) and Marie Munk (1885–1978), called for divorce on the grounds of irretrievable breakdown,[41] without allocation of guilt, on the grounds of mutual consent and of dislike for each other.[42] DDP member of parliament Marie-Elisabeth Lüders (1878–1966) led the fight for divorce reform together with the socialist women in the Reichstag, first raising the issue in January 1921, when she called for divorce to be made easier. She, her party, and the socialist women under the leadership of Antonie Pfülf (1877–1933) submitted petitions and drafts introducing their ideas of divorce reform.[43] In 1928, Pfülf gave a major speech in the Reichstag in which she pointed

---

40 Hilde Lion, *Zur Soziologie der Frauenbewegung: Die sozialistische und die katholische Frauenbewegung* (Berlin: Herbig, 1926); Heinemann, *Familie zwischen Tradition und Emanzipation*, 151–211; Marion Röwekamp, "Der Kampf um die Ehe: Der Katholischer Frauenbund und das Zentrum im Richtungsstreit um eine Reform des Ehescheidungsrechts," in *Die Frauen und der politische Katholizismus*, eds. Markus Raasch and Andreas Linsenmann (Mainz: Schöningh, 2018), 210–237; Blasius, *Ehescheidung*, 187–197; Michael Humphrey, *Die Weimarer Reformdiskussion über das Ehescheidungsrecht und das Zerrüttungsprinzip: Eine Untersuchung über die Entwicklung des Ehescheidungsrechts in Deutschland von der Reformation bis zur Gegenwart unter Berücksichtigung rechtsvergleichender Aspekte* (Göttingen: Cuvellier, 2006), 15–242; Marion Röwekamp, "Gedachte Grenzen. Ehescheidungsrechtsforderungen als Grenze innerhalb der Bürgerlichen Frauenbewegung, 1918–1933," *Ariadne* 57 (2010): 14–21; Werner Schubert, *Die Projekte der Weimarer Republik zur Reform des Nichtehelichen-, des Adoptions- und des Ehescheidungsrecht* (Munich/Vienna/Zurich: Ferdinand Schöningh, 1986), 82–92.
41 Marion Röwekamp, *Marie Munk: Rechtsanwältin – Richterin – Rechtsreformerin* (Berlin: Hentrich & Hentrich, 2014, Marion Röwekamp, "Margarete Berent und Marie Munk: Pionierinnen im Kampf um gleiche Rechte für Frauen," in *Streitbare JuristInnen: Eine andere Tradition*, vol. 2, eds. Tanja Hitzel-Cassagnes and Joachim Perels (Baden-Baden: Nomos, 2015), 73–108.
42 Margarete Berent and Marie Munk, *Vorschläge zur Abänderung des Familienrechts und verwandter Gebiete*, LAB Rep, 235–01 BDF, MF-Nr. 2765; Ella Bormann, "Die Gleichstellung der Geschlechter im deutschen Eherecht," *Sozialistische Monatshefte* 27, no. 19 (1921): 1036–1045; Marie-Elisabeth Lüders, "Vorschläge zum Ehescheidungsrecht," *Die Frau* 35 (1928): 325–331; Marie Munk, *Vorschläge zur Umgestaltung des Rechts auf Ehescheidung und der elterlichen Gewalt nebst Gesetzesentwurf* (Berlin: Herbig, 1923); Antonie Pfülf, "Die Reform des Ehescheidungsrechts," *Arbeiterwohlfahrt* 3 (1928): 3–9; Antonie Pfülf, "Die Auflösung der alten Familie," in *Jugendnot*, eds. Gerhard Danziger et al. (Leipzig: Oldenburg, 1922), 26–30; Emmy Rebstein-Metzger, "Scheidung schuldlos zerrütteter Ehen," *Deutsche Juristen Zeitung* 32, no. 10 (1927): 715–719; Elisabeth Röhl, "Ehereform," *Die Gleichheit* 29, no. 14 (1919): 109–111; Sophie Schöfer, "Notwendige Änderungen der ehelichen Rechtsgrundlagen," *Die Neue Zeit* 40, no. 1/10 (1921): 230–234.
43 Marion Röwekamp, "Von der Klassenkämpferin zur Republikanerin. Sozialdemokratinnen in der Weimarer Republik," in *Geschlecht und Klassenkampf: Die "Frauenfrage" aus deutscher und*

out the discrepancy between the constitution and civil law and masterfully traced the misogynistic figures of the BGB as well as touched on the strong consequences of the economic dependence of women on men.[44]

Even supporters of reform found themselves with the contradiction that they generally agreed with the model of the traditional family and the common belief that it was the moral foundation on which the family, the state, and even humanity rested. For family reform supporters, the fact that the family was a social institution justified the state's regulation of it. Especially because reform meant a separation of the Church's strong hold over the family, because it separated religious practice from legal practice, it was meant to be more reasonable, more equal, more modern, and more democratic. The reform of divorces in particular allowed, in their opinion, justice to be brought to broken marital relationships without punishing one party as being guilty for the breakup of the marriage and freeing both parties for a new life and, more importantly, securing newly functional families for the state. According to these ideas, only happy families were allowed to raise children to be stable and good citizens, and sometimes divorce was the means to free children from dysfunctional families. Both sides agreed strongly on the family as the social foundation of the new German democratic state and society and saw the need for families to rear children for the future of the nation. It was considered to be the source of morality, stability, well-being, and culture and the central base of the nation.

In the early years of the Weimar Republic, these claims found a majority within the Reichstag and the BDF (among others), but already in the second half of the 1920s, supporters of divorce reform could not reiterate their claims as conservative women's organizations became too powerful within the BDF. In addition, many women did not understand the full reform proposal and that all parts of the family law reform claims were interrelated with each other in order to protect women after divorce. As the basic agreement on divorce reform was waning, the BDF board replaced it strategically to stress and discuss the need for the reform of married women's property rights. The reorganization of matrimonial property law appealed to all women because the community of gains, as suggested by the female lawyers, had both conservative and progressive elements. Conservative women saw that the model of the family as an institution was strengthened and that gender separations work were preserved. However, it was radical at the same time because it was not only the work of the man

---

internationaler Perspektive im 19. und 20. Jahrhundert, eds. Vincent Streichhahn and Frank Jacob (Berlin: Metropol, 2020), 154–181.
44 *Verhandlungen des Reichstags, session November 20, 1928,* vol. 423 (Berlin: Druck und Verlag der Reichsdruckerei, 1929), 564–569.

within the family that had an economic impact but also that of the woman. So, this proposal found encouragement, both within the politically diverse women's movement as well as in parliament, from more groups than for the ideas for reforming divorce and the consequences of divorce. In fact, the Center Party agreed with former statements about a new order of the marital property law in order to prevent the divorce reform.[45]

The reform opponents, the Center Party and its political allies, the German National People's Party (Deutschnationale Volkspartei, DNVP) and the German People's Party (Deutsche Volkspartei, DVP), strongly objected to the proposed reforms and vigorously defended their proposed hold over marriage. According to them, the reforms, especially those relating to divorce, would taint the sacred bond of marriage and would lead to men freeing themselves from their older wives and marrying younger brides. Thus, emancipation and equality in family law would bring only suffering to married women instead of the claimed freedom. For them, the reform would lead to a weakening of the family as a social institution and thus to a weakening of the state, causing great harm to the fragile post-war German nation. They were also afraid that the possible breakup of families would lead to a further reduction of children born to a country that had lost millions in the war.[46]

In addition, these parties invoked the dangers of Bolshevism as a reason to stall reform. In Russia, the no-fault divorce was introduced besides broader family law reforms, and the supposed breakdown of the Russian state was used as a warning to all the reform claimants in the Reichstag, especially the Social Democrats and the Communists. While the Communists openly supported implementing the Russian ideas in Germany, the SPD often did not push its ideas strongly enough in order to keep the peace with its coalition partners, which

---

45 BDF Ausschuss für Ehegüterrecht, Landesarchiv Berlin (henceforth LAB B), Rep. 235–01 BDF, MF-Nr. 2126; Bormann, "Gleichstellung," 1036–1046; Emmy Rebstein-Metzger, "Gütertrennung oder Gütergemeinschaft?" *Die Frau* 34, no. 10 (1927): 522–527; Marie Munk, "Inwiefern bedürfen die familienrechtlichen Vorschriften des BGB mit Rücksicht auf den die Gleichberechtigung aussprechenden Art. 119 Abs. 1 Satz 2 RV einer Änderung?" *Deutsche Richterzeitung* 23, no. 8/9 (1931): 300–303; Camilla Jellinek, "Vom Jammer des ehelichen Güterrechts," *Die Frau* 34, no. 7 (1927): 409–417; Marion Röwekamp, "Misjudged and Underestimated: The Family Law Claims of the *Bund Deutscher Frauenvereine* on Matrimonial Property Law, 1918–1933," in *Gender Difference in European Legal Cultures: Historical Perspectives. Dedicated to Heide Wunder on the Occasion of her 70th Birthday*, ed. Karin Gottschalk (Stuttgart: Franz Steiner Verlag, 2013), 221–234.
46 See, for example, Schubert, *Projekte*, 542–544, Deutsche Volkspartei, ed., *Stichworte für den Wahlkampf 1930* (Berlin: Staatspolitischer Verlag, 1930), 621–628.

cost them lots of votes, especially from women, who turned away from the party.⁴⁷

Despite all these disagreements, by 1928, most parties understood that some kind of reform to the family law was unavoidable and were tired of the debates; even the DVP supported reform movements, such as divorce after five years of separation on the grounds of irretrievable breakdown and the end of the principle of guilt. The DNVP and the Protestant women's movement, while thinking that some reform was needed, stressed the principle of guilt and that divorce, especially based on the claim of one party, would create a problem for elderly wives. The Catholic Church, the Center Party, as well as the Catholic women's movement stood strong in their understanding of marriage as a sacrament that could not be dissolved. They went so far as to leave a debate in the Reichstag in 1929 because the Chancellor refused to postpone the debates once again based on the Center Party's protest. As Dirk Blasius has pointed out, they were willing to put the government at risk in order to hold their ground on the question of divorce law.⁴⁸

The other areas of family law, such as the reform proposals for personal marriage law, married women's property law, custody law, and the law regarding illegitimate children, suffered the same fate, even though, in the latter case, all parties agreed that the fate of these children had to be approved. The parties of the left and the women's movement asked for a reform of the civil law and claimed, based on Art. 121 of the constitution, that illegitimate children should receive the same legal position as legitimate children in terms of inheritance, alimony, and education.⁴⁹ The death rate of illegitimate children in the first years of

---

47 "Ehebolschewismus," *Schlesische Tagespost*, March 7, 1928; DNVP MP Freytagh-Loringhoven on "Ehebolschewismus," in Schubert, *Projekte*, 566–567; Deutsche Volkspartei, *Stichworte*, 64. For a positive view about the SU family law: MP Arendsee, 22. session, November 30, 1928, 578; however parts of the SPD were critical: Hedwig Schwarz, "Beruf und Mutterschaft," *Die Genossin* 5 (1928): 440. See also Heinemann, *Zwischen Familie und Emanzipation*, 99 and 145–149; Atina Grossmann, "German Communism and New Women: Dilemmas and Contradictions," in *Women and Socialism: Socialism and Women*, eds. Helmut Gruber and Pamela Graves (New York/Oxford: Berghahn, 1998), 135–168; Björn Laser, *Kulturbolschewismus! Zur Diskursemantik der "totalen Krise" 1929–1933* (Frankfurt/Main: Peter Lang, 2010).
48 Blasius, *Ehescheidung in Deutschland*, 182–187.
49 Marie Munk, *Das Recht der Unehelichen*, LAB B Rep. 235–01 BDF MF-Nr. 2765; Marie Munk, "Die künftige Regelung der Rechte des unehelichen Kindes," *Die Frau* 33, no. 3 (1925): 150–156; Marie Munk, "Der Gesetzesentwurf ueber die unehlichen Kinder und die Annahme an Kindes Statt," *Deutsche Juristen Zeitung* 31, no. 15 (1926): 1069–1074; Gertrud Bäumer, "Der Unehelichenschutz und die legitime Familie," *Die Frau* 36, no. 6 (1929): 336–341; Elsbeth Georgi, "Zur Reform des Unehelichenrechts," *Die Frau* 36, no. 10 (1929): 621–625; Hilde Eiserhardt, "Das Unehelichenrecht im Reichstag," *Soziale Praxis und Archiv für Volkswohlfahrt* 38, no. 9

their life was in fact double that of legitimate ones in 1919. But the conservative parties thought the civil law was not the right tool to improve their fate but would only endanger and destroy the traditional family and further weaken the morals of women. They suggested solving the problem through social law, and in fact the Reich Youth Welfare Law of July 1922 did give some relief to the situation of illegitimate children. The newly introduced juvenile offices and their guardians oversaw the wellbeing of the kids and that the fathers would pay child support.[50] In civil law, the draft for the equal treatment of illegitimate and legitimate children published by the government in 1925 found more common ground than the one on divorce law. People could get involved in it since the previous gender division of labor in the family and the marriage as a fundamental principle of life were not questioned here. But the Center Party again did not like the idea that it would morally encourage the wrong form of families. So the draft law again did not become law.

Conclusion

The debates over family law reform and especially over divorce reform illustrate the conflict that surrounded marriage and family as a social institution. In between all these ideologies around the marriage and family on the one hand as well as around socialism and Catholicism on the other, the reform of divorce law while keeping the family model intact was an impossible task. This became obvious in the debates in the Reichstag, in the legal science, and in the media, but also in the women's movement itself. No wonder that every suggested change to family law touched the nerves of the entire society. The family law claims of the reform proponents such as the Social Democrats communists, and the women's movement, for example, were bedded into a more complex picture than a simple law reform. The question was central to the task to redefine the new state and to modify the "traditional" family to maintain their function in society on the one hand but also to fit into the new democracy on the other. The equality of women in the family constantly clashed with the role of

---

(1929): 219–222, 288–291; Hans Maier, "Die Sozialdemokratie und das Gesetz über die unehelichen Kinder," *Die Genossin* 6 (1929): 11–16; Hanna Scherpner-Drexel, *Rechte unehelicher Kinder aus den Sozialgesetzen (Stand vom 1. Januar 1926)* (Langensalza: H. Beyer, 1926). See also: Schubert, *Projekte*, 29–81; Sybille Buske, *Fräulein Mutter und ihr Bastard: Eine Geschichte der Unehelichkeit in Deutschland 1900–1970* (Göttingen: Wallstein, 2004), 82–85; Heinemann, *Familie zwischen Tradition und Emanzipation*, 181–205.
50 Buske, *Fräulein Mutter*, 109–114.

the family in the functioning of the state. Even supporters of family law reform often did not believe in the right of women to full equality; they also believed in the fact that men and women held different roles and duties in the family (and the state) to which they were suited by nature. To fully quit the male breadwinner model was not within the mental range even of the major part of the women's movement, even less the rest of the society.

Women's main demand for political equality was fulfilled with the right to vote, and their right to vote became to some extent a symbol of the new, democratic Germany. The granting of women's suffrage was, however, only a first step toward the attainment of full citizenship rights for women, and the declaration of equality in the constitution was just that: a declaration, not a realization. The Weimar Constitution had introduced democracy just as little as equal rights for women; it was a steady process of negotiation toward realizing these goals. Analyzing this process shows us the understanding of all involved parties and what democracy meant to them, which principles of the constitution were important to them and which were not. Women's equality was introduced in the constitution, it offered a blueprint for beginning a democratization process, but the constitution was not the end product the women had hoped for to guarantee equal rights just by formulating them. The weak draft of the constitution already provided for the fact that women had to keep on fighting for every further step toward equal rights beyond the right to vote, namely civil, social and economic equality. All concrete efforts by women and the parties of the left to achieve equality in family law were a process of negotiation to determine to what extent the young democracy was now willing to implement the constitutionally guaranteed rights for women. As we have seen, these claims reached the limit of negotiability sooner than the women had hoped according to the limits the constitution provided for. The demands to bring democracy into marriage and the family reached a clear and inflexible negotiating limit.

However, the debates on equal rights for women show that there was at least room for these debates, although they rarely ended in favor of women. Above all, they had the right and repeatedly demanded the place for the debates. These debates were characterized by a generally very slow change to understanding women's role in society. Women were somehow considered to be equal but at the same time different, the difference being caused by the different "nature" of the sexes. This understanding and the fear of social disintegration, especially of the family and, in the second step, of the nation, shaped the debates on women's citizenship rights in society and within all parties. For it was precisely the rights demanded for women and the expression that the changed roles of women in the form of the "new women" found so obvious were interpreted as symbolizing that the nation was in moral disintegration. Besides, the number of women calling for change was a small group of elite women. For most of the other women, the choices the new family law might provide seemed risky as they primarily wanted to be homemakers. To be a full-time housewife was generally the ideal that not only all middle-class women but even socialist women dreamed of. The latter, being burdened by economic hardships or the double burden of paid work and the family's needs at home (and without the domestic help of the middle-class professional and stay-at-home women), understandably found the idea very attractive. And women who were full-time housewives did not want to lose the security the law provided for them as they understood it. For them, the divorce claims in particular seemed to threaten the basis of their existence. They rather saw themselves as protected by a law that disempowered them while at the same time not understanding the full mechanism of protection the reform claims provided. They wanted reforms that would strengthen their rights within an existing family, to force husbands to be responsible for the family and themselves. They wanted domestic work to be recognized as essential and important as paid work. They wanted women's power within the family, not outside the family, to be increased. And if the belief in God and the holy union came into the picture, the different roles within the family, even in the minds of reformists, and society were not only provided by nature but also by God. But of course, in the minds of reformists, divorce was a devastating concept for women as, in their view, marriage was the ideal way for women to live. So, women themselves were too ambivalent about the idea of equality in the family and in the state to push together with one idea for women's full citizenship rights. Women in general wanted more social justice and security within the new state rather than individual freedoms or full equality, and most men could live with this concept. Claims beyond these needs that maybe coincidentally also served the needs of the German nation were more difficult to negotiate.

When men were recognized as citizens by the state, they automatically filled in their new rights because they already had power within the family and because their general ability to fill the concept of them as individuals with full legal capacity was never really questioned. When women gained citizenship (in principle) in 1918, they still faced the fact that they were not full legal persons in the family and were, in general, limited to the domestic sphere. To overcome these barriers was not only a question of the law but also of overcoming mental structures and finding a new, growing consensus of women and men about women's new role in family, society, and the state. We can see how difficult this proved to be as we are still in the middle of this process.

Works Cited

Archival Material

Archiv der deutschen Frauenbewegung (ADF)

NL-K-08 Deutscher Staatsbürgerinnenverband, Nachlass Louise Otto-Peters, 3;

Landesarchiv Berlin

LAB B Rep. 235–01 BDF, MF-Nr. 2126.
LAP B Rep. 235–01 BDF, MF-Nr. 2765.

Published Sources and Secondary Works

Aldag, Heinrich. *Die Gleichheit vor dem Gesetz in der Reichsverfassung: Eine öffentlichrechtliche Abhandlung auf rechtsvergleichender Grundlage*. Berlin: Heymann, 1925.
Ankum, Katharina von, ed. *Women in the Metropolis: Gender and Modernity in Weimar Culture*. Berkeley: University of California Press, 1997.
Augspurg, Anita. "Gebt acht, solange noch Zeit ist!" *Die Frauenbewegung* 1, no. 1 (1895): 4–5.
Barber Crosby, Margaret. "The Civil Code and The Transformation of German Society: The Politics of Gender Inequality, 1814–1919." PhD diss., Brown University, 2001.
Bäumer, Gertrud. "Der Unehelichenschutz und die legitime Familie." *Die Frau* 36, no. 6 (1929): 336–341.
Berneike, Christiane. *Die Frauenfrage ist Rechtsfrage: Die Juristinnen der deutschen Frauenbewegung und das Bürgerliche Gesetzbuch*. Baden-Baden: Nomos, 1995.
Beschwitz, Olga von. *Begleitschrift zu der Petition des Bundes Deutscher Frauenvereine an den Reichstag betr. das Familienrecht des neuen BGB für das Deutsche Reich*. Frankenberg: L. Reisel, 1899.
Blasius, Dirk. *Ehescheidung in Deutschland (1794–1945)*. Göttingen: Vandenhoeck & Ruprecht 1987.
Boak, Helen. *Women in the Weimar Republic*. Manchester: Manchester University Press, 2015.
Bock, Gisela. "Frauenwahlrecht. Deutschland um 1900 in vergleichender Perspektive." In *Geschichte und Emanzipation: Festschrift für Reinhard Rürup*, edited by Michael Grüttner, Rüdiger Hachtmann and Heinz-Gerhard Haupt, 95–136. Frankfurt am Main/New York: Campus: 1999.
Bormann, Ella. "Die Gleichstellung der Geschlechter im deutschen Eherecht." *Sozialistische Monatshefte* 27, no. 19 (1921): 1036–1045.
Buske, Sybille. *Fräulein Mutter und ihr Bastard: Eine Geschichte der Unehelichkeit in Deutschland 1900–1970*. Göttingen: Wallstein, 2004.

Deutsche Volkspartei, ed. *Stichworte für den Wahlkampf 1930*. Berlin: Staatspolitischer Verlag, 1930.

Dittmar, Louise. "Das Wesen der Ehe." In *Das Wesen der Ehe nebst einigen Aufsätzen über die soziale Reform der Frauen*, edited by Louise Dittmar, 47–62. Leipzig: Verlag von Otto Wiegand, 1849.

Dittmar, Louise. "Die männliche Bevormundung." In *Das Wesen der Ehe nebst einigen Aufsätzen über die soziale Reform der Frauen*, edited by Louise Dittmar, 62–64. Leipzig: Verlag von Otto Wiegand, 1849.

Dohm, Hedwig. *Der Frauen Natur und Recht*. Berlin: Wedekind & Schwieger, 1876.

Dölemeyer, Barbara. "Frau und Familie im Privatrecht des 19. Jahrhunderts." In *Frauen in der Geschichte des Rechts: Von der frühen Neuzeit bis zur Gegenwart*, edited by Ute Gerhard, 633–658. Munich: C.H. Beck, 1997.

Dölle, Gilla, ed. *Eine "ächt weibliche Emancipation": Die Diskussion der Geschlechterbeziehungen um 1848*. Kassel: Archiv der deutschen Frauenbewegung, 1998.

Dose, Cäcilie and Alma Kriesche. *Die Stellung der Frau und Mutter im Familienrecht der ausserdeutschen Staaten und nach den Bestimmungen des neuen bürgerlichen Gesetzbuches für das Deutsche Reich*. Frankenberg: L. Reisel, 1900.

"Ehebolschewismus." *Schlesische Tagespost*, March 7, 1928.

Eiserhardt, Hilde. "Das Unehelichenrecht im Reichstag." *Soziale Praxis und Archiv für Volkswohlfahrt* 38, no. 9 (1929): 219–222, 288–291.

Evans, Ellen Lovell. *The German Center Party, 1870–1933: A Study in Political Catholicism*. Carbondale: Southern Illinois University Press, 1981.

Fels, Orla-Maria. "Die Deutsche Bürgerliche Frauenbewegung als juristisches Phänomen." PhD diss., Freiburg University, 1959.

Freund, Marion. *"Mag der Thron in Flammen glühn!" Schriftstellerinnen und die Revolution 1848/49*. Königstein/Taunus: Helmer, 2004.

Geisel, Beatrix. *Klasse, Geschlecht und Recht: Vergleichende sozialhistorische Untersuchung der Rechtsberatungspraxis von Frauen- und Arbeiterbewegung (1894–1933)*. Baden-Baden: Nomos, 1997.

Georgi, Elsbeth. "Zur Reform des Unehelichenrechts." *Die Frau* 36, no. 10 (1929): 621–625.

Gerhard, Ute. "Legal Particularism and the Complexity of Women's Rights in Nineteenth Century Germany." In *Private Law and Social Inequality in the Industrial Age: Comparing Legal Cultures in Britain, France, Germany, and the United States*, edited by Willibald Steinmetz, 137–154. Oxford: Oxford University Press, 2000.

Gerhard, Ute. *Gleichheit ohne Angleichung: Frauen im Recht*. Munich: C.H. Beck, 1990.

Gierke, Otto von. *Der Entwurf eines bourgeoisen Gesetzbuchs und das deutsche Recht*. Leipzig: Dunker & Humblot, 1899.

Gross, Michael B. *The War Against Catholicism: Liberalism and the Anti-Catholic Imagination*. Ann Arbor: University of Michigan, 2004.

Grossman, Atina. *Reforming Sex: The German Movement for Birth Control and Abortion Reform 1920–1950*. New York: Oxford University Press, 1995.

Grossmann, Atina. "German Communism and New Women: Dilemmas and Contradictions." In *Women and Socialism: Socialism and Women*, edited by Helmut Gruber and Pamela Graves, 135–168. New York/Oxford: Berghahn, 1998.

Hachenburg, Max. "Interfraktioneller Antrag der weiblichen Reichstagsabgeordneten auf Zulassung von Frauen zu den juristischen Prüfungen." *Deutsche Juristen Zeitung* 26 (1921): 174.

Hagemann, Karen. *Frauenalltag und Männerpolitik: Alltagsleben und gesellschaftliches Handeln von Arbeiterfrauen in der Weimarer Republik*. Bonn: Dietz, 1990.

Hausen, Karin. "Arbeiterinnenschutz, Mutterschutz und gesetzliche Krankenversicherung im Deutschen Kaiserreich und in der Weimarer Republik: Zur Funktion von Arbeits- und Sozialrecht für die Normierung und Stabilisierung der Geschlechterverhältnisse." In *Frauen in der Geschichte des Rechts: Von der frühen Neuzeit bis zur Gegenwart*, edited by Ute Gerhard, 759–771. Munich: C.H. Beck, 1997.

Heinemann, Rebecca. *Familie zwischen Tradition und Emanzipation: Katholische und sozialdemokratische Familienkonzeptionen in der Weimarer Republik*. Munich: Oldenbourg 2004),

Hong, Young-Sun. *Welfare, Modernity, and the Weimar State*. Princeton, NY: Princeton University Press, 1998.

Hönig, Klaus. *Der Bund Deutscher Frauenvereine in der Weimarer Republik 1919–1933*. Frankfurt am Main: Hänsel-Höhenhausen, 1995.

Humphrey, Michael. *Die Weimarer Reformdiskussion über das Ehescheidungsrecht und das Zerrüttungsprinzip: Eine Untersuchung über die Entwicklung des Ehescheidungsrechts in Deutschland von der Reformation bis zur Gegenwart unter Berücksichtigung rechtsvergleichender Aspekte*. Göttingen: Cuvellier, 2006.

Jellinek, Camilla. "Vom Jammer des ehelichen Güterrechts." *Die Frau* 34, no. 7 (1927): 409–417.

Joos, Joseph. *Die sozialdemokratische Frauenbewegung in Deutschland*. Mönchen-Gladbach: Volksvereins-Verlag 1912.

Kimble, Sara and Marion Röwekamp. "Legal Cultures and Communities of Female Protest in Modern European History, 1860–1960s." In *New Perspectives on European Women's Legal History*, edited by Sara Kimble and Marion Röwekamp, 1–24. New York: Routledge, 2017.

Klemm, Sabine. *Frauenbewegung und Familienrecht 1848 bis 1933: Eine Betrachtung anhand von Quellen*. Tübingen: Campus, 1999.

Kundrus, Birthe. *Familienpolitik und Geschlechterverhältnisse im Ersten und Zweiten Weltkrieg*. Hamburg: Christians, 1995.

Lange, Helene. "Über das Frauenwahlrecht." *Neue Bahnen* 33, no. 7 (1898): 68–69.

Laser, Björn. *Kulturbolschewismus! Zur Diskurssemantik der "totalen Krise" 1929–1933*. Frankfurt/Main: Peter Lang, 2010.

Lauterer, Heide-Marie. *Parlamentarierinnen in Deutschland 1918/19–1949*. Königstein, Taunus: Ulrike Helmer, 2002.

Lion, Hilde. *Zur Soziologie der Frauenbewegung: Die sozialistische und die katholische Frauenbewegung*. Berlin: Herbig, 1926.

Lüders, Marie-Elisabeth. "Interfraktionelle Frauenarbeit." *Die Frau* 27, no. 5 (1920): 154–156.

Lüders, Marie-Elisabeth. "Vorschläge zum Ehescheidungsrecht." *Die Frau* 35 (1928): 325–331.

Maier, Hans. "Die Sozialdemokratie und das Gesetz über die unehelichen Kinder." *Die Genossin* 6 (1929): 11–16.

Meder, Stephan and Christoph-Eric Mecke, eds. *Reformforderungen zum Familienrecht International*, vol. 1: *Westeuropa und die USA (1830–1914)*. Cologne: Böhlau 2015.

Meder, Stephan, Arne Duncker, and Andrea Czelk, eds. *Frauenrecht und Rechtsgeschichte: Die Rechtskämpfe der deutschen Frauenbewegung*. Cologne: Böhlau, 2006.

Meder, Stephan, Arne Duncker, and Andrea Czelk, eds. *Die Rechtsstellung der Frau um 1900: Eine kommentierte Quellensammlung*. Cologne: Böhlau, 2010.

Mikus, Birgit. *The Political Woman in Print: German Women's Writing 1845–1919*. Oxford et al: Peter Lang, 2014.

Möhrmann, Renate. *Die andere Frau: Emanzipationsansätze deutscher Schriftstellerinnen im Vorfeld der Achtundvierziger-Revolution*. Stuttgart: Metzler, 1977.

Möhrmann, Renate, ed. *Frauenemanzipation im deutschen Vormärz: Texte und Dokumente*. Stuttgart: Reclam, 1980.

Mouton, Michelle. *From Nurturing the Nation to Purifying the Volk: Weimar and Nazi Family Policy, 1918–1945*. Cambridge/New York: Cambridge University Press, 2007.

Mugdan, Benno. *Die gesammten Materialien zum Bürgerlichen Gesetzbuch für das Deutsche Reich*, vol. 4. Berlin: G. Schenck, 1899.

Munk, Marie. "Der Gesetzesentwurf ueber die unehlichen Kinder und die Annahme an Kindes Statt." *Deutsche Juristen Zeitung* 31, no. 15 (1926): 1069–1074.

Munk, Marie. "Die künftige Regelung der Rechte des unehelichen Kindes." *Die Frau* 33, no. 3 (1925): 150–156.

Munk, Marie. "Inwiefern bedürfen die familienrechtlichen Vorschriften des BGB mit Rücksicht auf den die Gleichberechtigung aussprechenden Art. 119 Abs. 1 Satz 2 RV einer Änderung?" *Deutsche Richterzeitung* 23, no. 8/9 (1931): 300–303.

Munk, Marie. *Vorschläge zur Umgestaltung des Rechts auf Ehescheidung und der elterlichen Gewalt nebst Gesetzesentwurf*. Berlin: Herbig, 1923.

Niggemann, Heinz. *Emanzipation zwischen Sozialismus und Feminismus: Die sozialdemokratische Frauenbewegung im Kaiserreich*. Wuppertal: Hammer, 1981.

Offen, Karen. "National or International? How and Why the Napoleonic Code Drove Married Women's Legal Rights onto the Agenda of the International Council of Women and the League of Nations: An Overview." In *Family Law in Early Women's Rights Debates*, edited by Stephan Meder and Christoph-Eric Mecke, 42–59. Cologne: Böhlau, 2013.

"Petition of the Allgemeinen Deutschen Frauenverein to the Reichstag." *Neue Bahnen* 12, no. 8 (1877): 57–59.

Pfülf, Antonie. "Die Auflösung der alten Familie." In *Jugendnot*, edited by Gerhard Danziger et al., 26–30. Leipzig: Oldenburg, 1922.

Pfülf, Antonie. "Die Reform des Ehescheidungsrechts." *Arbeiterwohlfahrt* 3 (1928): 3–9.

Plat, Wolfgang. "Die Stellung der deutschen Sozialdemokratie zum Grundsatz der Gleichberechtigung der Frau auf dem Gebiet des Familienrechts bei der Schaffung des Bürgerlichen Gesetzbuches des Deutschen Reiches." PhD diss., Humboldt University Berlin, 1966.

Rebstein-Metzger, Emmy. "Gütertrennung oder Gütergemeinschaft?" *Die Frau* 34, no. 10 (1927): 522–527.

Rebstein-Metzger, Emmy. "Scheidung schuldlos zerrütteter Ehen." *Deutsche Juristen Zeitung* 32, no. 10 (1927): 715–719.

Riedel, Tanja-Carina. *Gleiches Recht für Mann und Frau: Die bürgerliche Frauenbewegung und die Entstehung des BGB*. Cologne: Böhlau, 2008.

Riehl, Wilhelm Heinrich. *Die Naturgeschichte des Volkes als Grundlage einer deutschen Social-Politik: Die Familie*, vol. 3. Stuttgart/Augsburg: Cotta, 1855.

Röhl, Elisabeth. "Ehereform." *Die Gleichheit* 29, no. 14 (1919): 109–111.
Rosenbusch, Ute. *Der Weg zum Frauenwahlrecht in Deutschland*. Baden-Baden: Nomos, 1998.
Rost, Ida. *Die Ehescheidungen der Jahre 1920–1924 von in Sachsen geschlossenen Ehen, unter besonderer Berücksichtigung der Dauer der Ehen und des Heiratsalters der geschiedenen Ehegatten*. Leipzig: Vieweg & Teubner Verlag, 1927.
Röwekamp, Marion. "'Männer und Frauen haben grundsätzlich die gleichen staatsbürgerlichen Rechte': Weimar – Meilenstein auf dem Weg zur Gleichberechtigung der Geschlechter?" In *Die Weimarer Verfassung, Wert und Wirkung für die Demokratie*, edited by Friedrich-Ebert-Stiftung, 235–164. Erfurt: Friedrich-Ebert-Stiftung, 2009.
Röwekamp, Marion. "Der Kampf um die Ehe: Der Katholischer Frauenbund und das Zentrum im Richtungsstreit um eine Reform des Ehescheidungsrechts." In *Die Frauen und der politische Katholizismus*, edited by Markus Raasch and Andreas Linsenmann, 210–237. Mainz: Schöningh, 2018.
Röwekamp, Marion. "Gedachte Grenzen. Ehescheidungsrechtsforderungen als Grenze innerhalb der Bürgerlichen Frauenbewegung, 1918–1933." *Ariadne* 57 (2010): 14–21.
Röwekamp, Marion. "Margarete Berent und Marie Munk: Pionierinnen im Kampf um gleiche Rechte für Frauen." In *Streitbare JuristInnen: Eine andere Tradition*, vol. 2, edited by Tanja Hitzel-Cassangnes and Joachim Perels, 73–108. Baden-Baden: Nomos, 2015.
Röwekamp, Marion. *Marie Munk: Rechtsanwältin – Richterin – Rechtsreformerin*. Berlin: Hentrich & Hentrich, 2014.
Röwekamp, Marion. "Misjudged and Underestimated: The Family Law Claims of the *Bund Deutscher Frauenvereine* on Matrimonial Property Law, 1918–1933." In *Gender Difference in European Legal Cultures: Historical Perspectives. Dedicated to Heide Wunder on the Occasion of her 70th Birthday*, edited by Karin Gottschalk, 221–234. Stuttgart: Franz Steiner Verlag, 2013.
Röwekamp, Marion. "Olympe de Gouges, Louise Otto-Peters und der Kampf um das Familienrecht in Frankreich und Deutschland." In *Die Rechte der Frauen 1791–1866–2016*, edited by Sandra Berndt and Gerlinde Kämmerer, 21–43. Markkleeberg: Sax-Verlag Beucha, 2017.
Röwekamp, Marion. "Reform Claims in Family Law and Legal Struggles within the International Council of Women, 1888–191." In *Forging Bonds Across Borders: Transatlantic Collaborations for Women's Rights and Social Justice in the Long Nineteenth Century*, edited by Anja Schüler and Britta Waldschmidt-Nelson, 75–93. Washington, DC: Bulletin of the German Historical Institute, Supplement 13, 2017.
Röwekamp, Marion. "The double bind. Von den Interdependenzen des Frauenwahlrechts und des Familienrechts vor und nach 1918." In *100 Jahre Frauenwahlrecht: Kampf, Kontext, Wirkung*, edited by Hedwig Richter and Kerstin Wolff, 99–121. Hamburg: Verlag des Hamburger Instituts für Sozialforschung, 2018.
Röwekamp, Marion. "Von der Klassenkämpferin zur Republikanerin. Sozialdemokratinnen in der Weimarer Republik." In *Geschlecht und Klassenkampf: Die "Frauenfrage" aus deutscher und internationaler Perspektive im 19. und 20. Jahrhundert*, edited by Vincent Streichhahn and Frank Jacob, 154–181. Berlin: Metropol, 2020.
Scherpner-Drexel, Hanna. *Rechte unehelicher Kinder aus den Sozialgesetzen (Stand vom 1. Januar 1926)*. Langensalza: H. Beyer, 1926.

Schmidt, Auguste and Goldschmidt, Henriette. *Petition und Begleitschrift betreffend das "Familienrecht" in dem Entwurf des neuen bürgerlichen Gesetzbuches für das Deutsche Reich.* Leipzig: Schäfer, 1896.

Schöfer, Sophie. "Notwendige Aenderungen der ehelichen Rechtsgrundlagen." *Die Neue Zeit* 40, no. 1/10 (1921): 230–234.

Schötz, Susanne. "'Einige Deutsche Gesetzes-Paragraphen' – Louise Otto-Peters und das Engagement des Allgemeinen Deutschen Frauenvereins für Frauenrechte." In *Menschenrechte sind auch Frauenrechte*, edited by Ilse Nagelschmidt, Susanne Schötz, Nicole Kühnert and Melani Schröter, 53–78. Leipzig: Leipziger Universitätsverlag, 2002.

Schröder, Hannelore. *Die Rechtlosigkeit der Frau im Rechtsstaat: Dargestellt am Allgemeinen Preußischen Landrecht, am Bürgerlichen Gesetzbuch und an J.G. Fichtes Grundlage des Naturrechts.* Frankfurt am Main/New York: Campus, 1979.

Schubert, Werner. *Die Projekte der Weimarer Republik zur Reform des Nichtehelichen-, des Adoptions- und des Ehescheidungsrecht.* Munich/Vienna/Zurich: Ferdinand Schöningh, 1986.

Schwab, Dieter. "Gleichberechtigung und Familienrecht im 20. Jahrhundert." In *Frauen in der Geschichte des Rechts: Von der Frühen Neuzeit bis zur Gegenwart*, edited by Ute Gerhard, 790–827. Munich: C.H. Beck, 1997.

Schwanecke, Inge. *Die Gleichberechtigung der Frau unter der Weimarer Reichsverfassung.* PhD diss., University of Heidelberg, 1977.

Sneeringer, Julia. *Winning Women's Votes: Propaganda and Politics in Weimar Germany.* Chapel Hill: University of North Carolina Press, 2002.

Stritt, Marie. "Die Ehefrau und das bürgerliche Gesetzbuch." In *Die Rechtsstellung der Frau im 1900: Eine kommentierte Quellensammlung*, edited by Stephan Meder, Arne Duncker and Andrea Czelk, 811–820. Cologne: Böhlau, 2010.

Stritt, Marie. "Germany. Victory for Woman Suffrage." *International Women's News* 13, no. 4 (1919): 44–48.

Stritt, Marie. *Frauen-Landsturm: Flugblatt zum Familienrecht im bürgerlichen Gesetzbuch.* Berlin: n.p., 1896. Reprinted in *Die Rechtsstellung der Frau im 1900: Eine kommentierte Quellensammlung*, edited by Stephan Meder, Arne Duncker and Andrea Czelk, 805–811. Cologne: Böhlau, 2010.

Szymanski, Hanna. *Theorie und Lebenswirklichkeit: Ehe und Eherechte im Spiegel sozialdemokratischer Forderungen im deutschen Kaiserreich.* Cologne: Böhlau, 2013.

Usborne, Cornelie. *The Politics of the Body in Weimar Germany: Women's Reproductive Rights and Duties.* Ann Arbor: University of Michigan Press, 1992.

Verhandlungen der verfassunggebenden Deutschen Nationalversammlung, vol. 328. Stenographische Berichte. Von der 53. Sitzung am 10. Juli 1919 bis zur 70. Sitzung am 30. Juli 1919. Berlin: Norddeutsche Buchdruckerei, 1920.

Verhandlungen des Reichstags. IV. Wahlperiode 1928, vol. 423. Von der 1. Sitzung am 13. Juni 1928 bis zur 40. Sitzung am 4. Februar 1929. Berlin: Druck und Verlag der Reichsdruckerei, 1929.

Vogel, Ursula. "Is Citizenship Gender-Specific?" In *The Frontiers of Citizenship*, edited by Ursula Vogel and Michael Moran, 58–85. New York: St. Martin's Press, 1991.

Vollmer-Heitmann, Hanna. *Wir sind von Kopf bis Fuß auf Liebe eingestellt: Die zwanziger Jahre.* Hamburg: Kabel, 1993.

Weber, Marianne. *Ehefrau und Mutter in der Rechtsentwicklung: Eine Einführung.* Tübingen: J. C. B. Mohr, 1907.

Weber-Will, Susanne. *Die rechtliche Stellung der Frau im Privatrecht des Preußischen Allgemeinen Landrechts von 1794.* Frankfurt am Main/New York: Lang, 1983.

Wieruszowski, Alfred. "Artikel 119: Ehe, Familie, Mutterschaft." In *Die Grundrechte und Grundpflichten der Reichsverfassung,* vol. 2: *Artikel 118–142*, edited by Hans Carl Nipperdey, 72–94. Berlin: Hobbing, 1930.

Section II: Marriage Discourses and Social Criticism

Vincent Streichhahn
5 On the Discourse of the "New Sexual Morality" in the German Empire: Robert Michels' *Sexual Ethics* between Women's Movement, Social Democracy, and Sociology

Research on Robert Michels (1876–1936) tends to think of the sociologist from the end. In the reception of the public, Michels appears predominantly as an elite theorist, whose classic *Political Parties: A Sociological Study of the Oligarchical Tendencies of Modern Democracy*[1] of 1911 reflects his disappointment with representative democracy on the one hand, and in which, on the other hand, the "nucleus of an authoritarian understanding of politics" is laid out, which predestined him as Benito Mussolini's (1883–1945) later Fascism apologete. This study, read as a disappointment in Michels' former democratic hopes, would have led him ultimately from social democracy via syndicalism to Italian Fascism.[2] Other works and thus different strands of interpretation are largely unknown compared to *Political Parties*.

In the same year as Michels' classic, however, another work was published, which is the focus of this article and has the potential to shake up the previous reception, namely *Sexual Ethics: A Study of Borderland Questions*.[3] This "sexual-

---

[1] Robert Michels, *Zur Soziologie des Parteiwesens in der modernen Demokratie* (Leipzig: Klinkhardt, 1911).
[2] Terry R. Kandal, "Profile: Rober Michels' Sexual Ethics," *Sociology* 38 (2001): 62; Arthur Mitzman, *Sociology and Estrangement: Three Sociologists of Imperial Germany* (New York: Knopf, 1973), 315.
[3] In this article I quote from the German edition. The quotations have therefore been translated by me, as have the quotations from the other German books and articles listed here. Interestingly, the Italian (1912), English, and French (both 1914) editions are larger in scope than the German and were revised by Michels. It would be an exciting task to investigate the hitherto neglected revision and editing process. Robert Michels, *Die Grenzen der Geschlechtsmoral: Prolegomena – Gedanken und Untersuchungen* (Leipzig: Frauen-Verlag, 1911); Idem, *Sexual Ethics: A Study of Borderland Questions* (New York: Walter Scott, 1914); Idem, *Amour et Chasteté. Essais Sociologique* (Paris: Siard & Brière, 1914); Idem, *I Limiti della Morale Sessuale: Prolegomena: Indagini e Pensieri* (Torino: Bocca, 1914).

ô OpenAccess. © 2021 Vincent Streichhahn, published by De Gruyter. This work is licensed under the Creative Commons Attribution-NonCommercial-NoDerivatives 4.0 International License.
https://doi.org/10.1515/9783110751451-005

reform educational pamphlet"[4] goes beyond the previous limits of Michels' interpretation. While the *Political Parties*, as Timm Genett emphasizes in opposition to well-trodden paths of reception, presented itself as an effort to reform democracy by critically describing how it functions,[5] the reformist will to shape and progress optimism in *Sexual Ethics* is obvious.

The latter writing has received little attention so far. The US sociologist Terry R. Kandal is a notable exception and has been studying Michels' thinking on the "woman question"[6] in the context of classical sociological theory since the end of the 1980s.[7] At the same time, probably only the Italian Pino Ferraris was dealing with Michels' work in the area of gender relations, but it was not widely received due to language barriers.[8] Two years after the turn of the millennium, Michels' writing was re-edited in English with an introduction by Kandal.[9]

Particularly in Germany, where Michels was refused a professorship despite the protection of Max Weber (1864–1920) because of his commitment to social democracy,[10] research punished his work for a long time with the extremely one-sided perception of an elite theorist with a musty political connotation. We owe the most fundamental attempt at an overall interpretation of Michels' work and development to the German political scientist Genett, who presents the Italian-by-choice as a "pioneer of social movement research" and thus breaks

---

4 Timm Genett, *Der Fremde im Kriege: Zur politischen Theorie und Biographie von Robert Michels 1876–1936* (Berlin: Akademie Verlag, 2008), 43.
5 Ibid., 21–22.
6 The "women's question" appeared in public discourse in the mid-19th century and was initially understood by contemporaries primarily as a component of the social question. Under the term, a bundle of issues was negotiated that affected gender relations. Among them were the situation of single and married women, women's work, sexuality, and political rights for the female sex. Lucy Delap, "The 'Woman Question' and the Origins of Feminism," in *The Cambridge History of Nineteenth-Century Political Thought* (Cambridge: Cambridge University Press, 2011), 319–348.
7 Terry R. Kandal, *The Woman Question in Classical Sociology Theory* (Miami: Florida International University Press, 1988), 201–211.
8 Pino Ferraris, "Questione femminile e morale sessuale nell'evoluzione politica di Roberto Michels," in Roberto Michels, *Economia – Sociologia – Politica*, ed. Riccardo Faucci (Torino: Giappichelli 1989), 97–122.
9 Terry R. Kandal, "From Egalitarian Sexual Ethics to Gender Politics: An Evaluation of Michels' Contribution," in Robert Michels, *Sexual Ethics: A Study of Borderline Questions*, with a new introduction by Terry R. Kandal (New York/London: Routledge, 2002), XI-LXV.
10 Thomas Nipperdey, *Deutsche Gesellschaftsgeschichte, 1866–1918*, vol. 1: *Arbeitswelt und Bürgergeist* (Munich: Beck, 1991), 575.

with the hitherto established lines of interpretation.[11] In Michels' early work, the women's movement would stand on an equal footing with the labor and national autonomy movement.[12]

In this narrative, *Sexual Ethics* occupies a central place. As a result of the early creative phase, according to Genett, these serve as a "key to understanding Michels' main sociological work."[13] Kandal's thesis, according to which Michels' writings on gender relations in the period from 1903 to 1913 ran roughly parallel to the development of his sociological views, already had a similar thrust.[14] In Germany, in addition to Genett's research, political scientists Harald Bluhm and Skadi S. Krause have referred, at least in passing, to *Sexual Ethics*.[15] The Swiss historian Caroline Arni went into this in more detail in her account of the modern discourse on love.[16] More recently, Hans Geske placed the question of gender relations in Michels' work at the center of his Master's thesis, thus presenting the most detailed discussion of *Sexual Ethics* in the German-speaking world, alongside that of Genett.[17]

The present chapter does not attempt an overall interpretation of Michels' work. Instead, it focuses on the contribution and location of *Sexual Ethics* in the discourse on "new sexual morality" in the German Empire. A more detailed, contextualizing examination of Michels' critique of bourgeois marriage and sexual morality, as well as his journalistic commitment to the German women's movements, would be able to better classify and understand the ideas set out in *Sexual Ethics*. My argument is that Michels' concept of a "new sexual morality" can be interpreted as an egalitarian-feminist reaction to the transformation of the gender order in modernity. His ideas for the reorganization of gender rela-

---

11 Timm Genett, "Robert Michels. Pionier der sozialen Bewegungsforschung," in *Soziale Bewegungen zwischen Dynamik und Erstarrung*, ed. Timm Genett (Berlin: Akademie Verlag, 2008), 11–69; Timm Genett, *Der Fremde im Kriege*, 43–80.
12 Genett, "Robert Michels," 36.
13 Genett, *Der Fremde im Kriege*, 44.
14 Kandal, "Profile," 65.
15 Harald Bluhm and Skadi S. Krause, "Einleitung: Robert Michels' Soziologie des Parteiwesens: Oligarchien und Eliten – Die Kehrseiten moderner Demokratie," in *Robert Michels' Soziologie des Parteiwesens*, eds. Harald Bluhm and Skadi S. Krause (Wiesbaden: Springer, 2012), 11.
16 Caroline Arni, "Seelengesetze mit Gesellschaftswert: Weibliche Subjektwerdung und die Utopie menschlicher Perfektion in der feministisch-sexualreformerischen Liebesethik um 1900," *Feministische Studien* 27, no. 2 (2009): 196–209; Caroline Arni, "L'Amour en Europe: Ein Versuch über Robert Michels' vergleichende Liebeswissenschaft und den Liebesdiskurs in der Moderne," in *Der Eigensinn des Materials: Erkundungen sozialer Wirklichkeit: Festschrift für Claudia Honegger zum 60. Geburtstag*, ed. Caroline Arni (Frankfurt am Main: Stroemfeld, 2007), 71–89.
17 For a condensed version, see Hans Geske, "Oligarchie, Faschismus … Feminismus? Ein neuer Blick auf Robert Michels," *Berliner Debatte Initial* 31, no. 3 (2020): 99–109.

tions distinguish Michels as a border crosser between the radical factions of the reform movement of the German Empire.[18]

A Preliminary Classification Attempt

Sexual Ethics can be read as a flaming plea for a "new sexual morality ... whose sun is already seen above the horizon, but whose rays are still pale and weak, and lack sufficient force to arouse a new moral life."[19] According to Caroline Arni, the concept presented by Michels is both utopia and program at the same time, which characterizes utopian thinking in modernity. After 1800, utopia had become a program waiting to be realized "and in this way inscribed in the present as an orientation for action."[20] The basic features of Michels' vision are exemplary for "a conception of the heterosexual couple that was developed around 1900 in the context of sexual-reformist feminist thinking." At its center is the love relationship based on autonomy (voluntary love) and equality (comradeship), which "realizes the ethical potential of humanity."[21]

In the context of "sexual-reformist feminist thinking" at the turn of the century, Michels' basic concept was therefore not an isolated phenomenon. In general, according to Thomas Nipperdey (1927–1992), the turn of the century could be described as the beginning of the "sexual revolution of the 20th century."[22] Nevertheless, only a tiny minority at that time advocated a reform of sexual morality, which was rejected by large parts of the bourgeois women's movement, as it would endanger the bourgeois family and thus the foundations of bourgeois so-

---

[18] It is no coincidence that Michels first joined the Italian Socialist Party at the beginning of the 20th century and then the German Social Democratic Party (SPD). For the latter he had even been elected delegate for the party congresses by the Magdeburg SPD from 1903 to 1905. In this context, he also took part in the Social Democratic Women's Conference in Bremen in 1904. *Protokoll über die Verhandlungen des Parteitages der Sozialdemokratischen Partei Deutschlands. Abgehalten zu Bremen vom 18. bis 24. September 1904* (Berlin: Vorwärts, 1904), 342–344. Social Democracy was the natural choice for Michels, as it had taken over the historical task of reactionary German liberalism. Genett, *Der Fremde im Kriege*, 32. This view was generally shared by the SPD. Richard Evans, *Sozialdemokratie und Frauenbewegung im deutschen Kaiserreich* (Bonn: Dietz, 1979), 98.
[19] Michels, *Sexual Ethics*, 55.
[20] Arni, "Liebesethik," 196.
[21] Ibid., 196–197.
[22] Nipperdey, *Deutsche Gesellschaftsgeschichte*, 104.

ciety.²³ The importance that Michels and his feminist comrades-in-arms assigned to sexual morality, which also explains the almost hostile attitude of the majority society of the German Empire, is rooted in the transformation processes of modernity, often perceived as a danger and crisis. In this modern reorganization of social conditions, gender relations took a central position, the patriarchal character of which was defended to the hilt by some, reformed tentatively by others, and fundamentally challenged by a few.

This sexual reform discourse can be classified as part of the "woman question," which, driven by the political and economic developments of the modern age and the commitment of the women's movement at the turn of the century, had advanced far into the German public sphere. "The woman's question, when we consider its historical foundation, the diversity of its social, intellectual, and economic aspects," says Michels, "must be recognised as being no fairy tale to occupy the energies of a few unbalanced women, but a most serious problem, whose solution demands the coordinated efforts of the best."²⁴ One dimension of the "woman question," in which gender relations were generally contended with, is the aspect of sexuality, which in contemporary times could not be discussed without talking about marriage.

Sexual Ethics was published in 1911 by Frauen-Verlag²⁵ and appeared in the same year in the second and, to date, last German edition.²⁶ In the foreword, Mi-

---

23 Most representatives of the bourgeois women's movement limited themselves in the marriage discussion to the demand for reforms in divorce and property law.
24 Michels, *Sexual Ethics*, 133.
25 The same publishing house also published the monthly journal *Frauen-Zukunft*, edited by Gabriele von Lieber (life data unknown), Meta Hammerschlag (1864–1954), and Hanns Dorn (1878–1934), which appeared from 1910 to 1912 and in which Michels published a lengthy article on Neo-Malthusianism one year before *Sexual Ethics*. Robert Michels, "Neomalthusianismus," *Frauenzukunft* 1, no. 1 (1910): 42–55.
26 Until now, knowledge about the history of the edition was limited to the year of publication and the publisher. By analyzing parts of Michels' correspondence, which is kept in the Robert Michels Archive of the Luigi Einaudi Foundation in Turin, it is possible to reconstruct a piece of the buried history of the edition. Michels pursued the idea for the work from the spring of 1909 at the latest, as is clear from a letter from Helene Stöcker to Michels dated June 22 of the same year. On February 3, 1910, he received a reply from the publisher Gabriela von Lieber, to whom Michels must have submitted an offer of publication, including a project outline, in the meantime. Lieber agreed to publish the book in Frauen-Verlag. The following year, *Sexual Ethics* was published in an edition of 1,000 copies. In the same year, another edition of 1,000 copies followed, which had almost sold out by the beginning of 1915, as Lieber informs Michels in a letter dated February 22, 1915. "If the war had not intervened now, I would have tackled the 3rd thousand without further ado," Lieber writes. However, she had to refrain from an "undertaking that was not immediately profitable" due to the current circumstances. Lieber did encour-

chels openly admits that the book is the "result of many years of observation by a man who has given much and serious thought to the sexual problems of his youngest youth." In Italy, France, and Germany, he encountered everywhere "the same unsolvable problem ... of reconciling young love with old customs." Michels' descriptions "are not strictly scientific" but, he hopes, "not devoid of scientific importance." It was not written for those who have already solved the "problems of sexual morality" on the basis of some "preconceived dogma," but instead the premise of the book is based on the recognition of its unsolved nature. At the same time, Michels explicitly distinguishes himself from other works in this field, since he has drawn the conclusion from his work with "borderland problems" that "more questions should be asked than answered, more problems should be posed than solved."[27]

The term "borderland problems" plays a central role in the work. In the field of sexuality, according to Michels, it is, "to say the least, nonsense ... to speak of 'abysses,' where there are only gentle transitions and fine nuances."[28] He accordingly refuses to accept sexual morals that operate with a black and white contrast.[29] The criticism of bourgeois double morals, which would regard women as whores at night and saints during the day,[30] forms a main strand of *Sexual Ethics*. However, Michels addresses a wide range of issues in addition to sexual morals in general: prostitution, pornography, sexual education, contraception, bridal morality (*Brautstandsmoral*), and the fundamental relationship between the sexes inside and outside of marriage. On the other hand, Michels omits the issue of women's suffrage in his book, which was decidedly political and virulent at the time.[31]

Michels leaves no doubt about his fundamental perspective: on the one hand, he rejects the form of the monogamous, inseparable family as a "state institution of coercion," but on the other hand, he recognizes in it a "moral goal"

---

age Michels to tackle a new edition himself as a "popular edition" [*Volksausgabe*] at a favorable retail price, but, as is known, a third German edition did not come about. Helene Stöcker to Robert Michels, June 22, 1909; Gabriele von Lieber to Robert Michels, February 3, 1910; Gabriele von Lieber to Robert Michels, February 22, 1915. All letters from the Robert Michels Archive of the Luigi Einaudi Foundation, Turin.

27 All quotes in the paragraph from Michels, *Sexual Ethics*, VII, VIII and X.
28 Ibid., 63–64.
29 Robert Michels, "Die Zwischenstufen der Ehrbarkeit," *Die neue Generation* 2, no. 9 (1909): 351–359.
30 Michels, *Sexual Ethics*, 146.
31 In his journalism at the beginning of the 20th century, Michels publicly advocated for women's suffrage with determination. Robert Michels, "Frauenstimmrecht – schon heute eine Notwendigkeit," *Die Frauenbewegung* 8, no. 23 (1902): 177–178.

that "will certainly never be achieved, but whose pursuit is at the same time in the individual and collective interest of humanity."³² The very structure of the work is divided into four parts: 1) general borderland problems of erotic life, 2) borderland problems of the extra-conjugal erotic life, 3) pre-conjugal borderland problems, and finally 4) borderland problems of the conjugal sexual life. Genett is correct in highlighting that this structure signals "the goal of Michels' sex education: to give marriage a new legitimacy as a monogamous alliance for life."³³ Marriage, according to Michels, is "reformable but not abolishable."³⁴ Nevertheless, he recognizes the "polygamous dispositions" of human beings as an anthropological premise and compares the sex drive with a physical need, the "feeling of hunger."³⁵ Michels thus finds (not only) himself in a "good" social democratic tradition, since August Bebel (1840–1913) had already used the metaphor of food to refer to the naturalness of sexual needs in his classic *Woman and Socialism* published in 1879.³⁶

Michels had been working on the "woman question" since the beginning of the 20th century. The first essays on this subject date back to 1901, and a large number of articles were published in various periodicals of the women's movement in the years before *Sexual Ethics*. Some of them were included to a greater extent in Michels' monograph, which he describes in varying degrees of detail. In his journalistic offensive, the sociologist, who received his doctorate in 1900 in Halle, felt no shyness whatsoever toward any of the various wings of the German women's movement—excluding the patriotic women's associations. He published in *Die Frau* [*The Woman*],³⁷ edited by Helene Lange (1848–1930), as a representative of the "moderate" bourgeois women's movement, as well as in the papers of the "radical" bourgeois wing of the movement, including *Die Frauenbewegung* [*The Women's Movement*],³⁸ edited by Lily Braun (1865–1916) and Minna Cauer (1841–1922), and the journal *Mutterschutz: Zeitschrift zur Re-*

---

32 Michels, *Sexual Ethics*, VIII.
33 Genett, *Der Fremde im Kriege*, 65.
34 Michels, *Sexual Ethics*, 128.
35 Ibid., 11.
36 Bebel's book was of course known to Michels, who both mentioned it in the footnotes of his *Sexual Ethics* and had already reviewed it positively in 1904 for *Die Gleichheit*. Robert Michels, "Der vierunddreißigste Bebel," *Die Gleichheit* 14, no. 15 (1904): 113–115; August Bebel, "Die Frau und der Sozialismus," in *Ausgewählte Reden und Schriften*, vol. 10, ed. Internationales Institut für Sozialgeschichte Amsterdam (Munich: K. G. Sauer, 1996 [1879]).
37 Among others, see Robert Michels, "Die Arbeiterinnenbewegung in Italien," *Die Frau* 10, no. 6 (1902): 328–336.
38 Among others, see Robert Michels, "Entstehung der Frauenfrage als soziale Frage," *Die Frauenbewegung* 9, no. 3 (1903): 17–18.

form der Sexuellen Ethik [*Maternity Protection: Journal for the Reform of Sexual Ethics*],[39] renamed *Die neue Generation* [*The New Generation*][40] in 1908 under the editorship of Helene Stöcker (1869–1943). In quantitative terms, however, Michels wrote the most in the proletarian women's magazine *Die Gleichheit* [*The Equality*], run by Clara Zetkin (1857–1933), which was characteristically and almost exclusively about the Italian women's movement and not about questions of sexual morality.[41] Moreover, Michels was very familiar with the literature of the women's movement of his time, as is impressively demonstrated by some of his reviews and references.[42]

Michels also corresponded with activists from all factions of the German women's movement.[43] However, his longest and most intensive contact was with sex reformer Helene Stöcker, as can be seen from the correspondence with her, some of which has survived. While many other contacts broke off around 1910, the two continued to be in contact. Michels had asked Stöcker as late as 1923 if she would speak at one of his seminars.[44] This makes clear that the field of sexual morality gained in importance for Michels over the years in comparison to the other aspects of the women's question. That development can also be explained by Michels' sociological interest in these issues, which is why he published all other editions in sociological series except for the German edition of *Sexual Ethics*.[45]

Michels' preoccupation with gender relations flattened noticeably after the publication of *Sexual Ethics*. The separate foreword to the 1914 English edition, which Michels also enriched with a separate chapter on sex education for children, probably formed a provisional conclusion to his work, underlining his sex-

---

[39] Robert Michels, "Erotische Streifzüge: Deutsche und italienische Liebesformen. Aus dem Pariser Liebesleben," *Mutterschutz* 2, no. 9 (1906): 362–374.

[40] Among others, see Robert Michels, "Ein sexueller Kongreß in Italien," *Die neue Generation* 4, no. 2 (1911): 63–70.

[41] Among others, see Robert Michels, "Rückblick auf die Geschichte der proletarischen Frauenbewegung in Italien," *Die Gleichheit* 13, no. 1: 2–3; no. 2: 11–13; no. 5: 36–38; no. 8: 58–60; no. 11: 83–85; no. 17: 131–134 (all 1903).

[42] Robert Michels, "Die deutsche Frau im Beruf," *Die Gleichheit* 14, no. 11 (1904): 82–84; Robert Michels, "Das Weib und der Intellektualismus," *Dokumente der Frauen* 4, no. 4 (1902): 106–114.

[43] The inventory list of Michels' correspondence from the already mentioned archive of the Luigi Einaudi Foundation in Turin is like a who's who of the German women's and workers' movements.

[44] Helene Stöcker to Robert Michels, May 7, 1923, Robert Michels Archive of the Luigi Einaudi Foundation, Turin.

[45] While the German edition was published by a women's movement publishing house, all other editions were published in sociological series: Piccola biblioteca di scienze moderne, Bibliothèque Sociologique Internationale, and The Contemporary Science Series.

ual education claim.⁴⁶ At the end of the 1920s, however, he once again took up the "study of borderland problems," as he himself noticed.⁴⁷ At the center of Michels' later work is the topic of moral statistics as a problematic basis for statements on sexual morality, which was also a component of his early work. In a footnote, Genett makes the succinct remark that the "normative impulse of sexual reform" is completely lost in the later writings. This is true, but if one takes a closer look at the monograph *Sittlichkeit in Ziffern?* [*Morality in Figures?*], it could just as well be classified as a fulsome sociology of sexual morality or sociological sexology, the analysis of which must remain the subject of future work.⁴⁸

Michels was in demand as a discussion partner in the field of sexuality, and he had discussions on this subject with Werner Sombart (1863–1941) and Max Weber and his children, among others.⁴⁹ The nascent sociology or some of its early representatives recognized the significance of changing gender relations in modernity and became partly involved in the reform movement of the empire. Max Weber's wife, Marianne Weber (1870–1954), was herself active in the bourgeois women's movement, and both of them, like other respected intellectuals, initially supported Helene Stöcker's *Bund für Mutterschutz* [*Association for Maternity Protection*] in its efforts to strengthen the rights of illegitimate children and unmarried mothers. However, none of the classics of early sociology dealt with the relationship between the sexes as intensively as Robert Michels, whose sociological view characterizes his descriptions.⁵⁰ His studies are thus not only to be understood as "criticism in the melee" (*Kritik im Handgemenge*) but also follow a scientific interest.

These first contextualizing highlights were intended to illustrate that Michels' *Sexual Ethics* oscillate in their determination of origin between the women's movement, social democracy, and sociology—between political influence and scientific knowledge gain. In the following, I will limit myself to two aspects of Michels' remarks: 1) the criticism of bridal morality and 2) the criticism of bourgeois marriage, which are finally more precisely located in the social democratic and feminist discourse of the German Empire.

---

46 Geske, "Ein neuer Blick," 107.
47 Robert Michels, *Sittlichkeit in Ziffern? Kritik der Moralstatistik* (Berlin: Duncker & Humblot, 1928), V.
48 Robert Michels, "Altes und Neues zum Problem der Moralstatistik (Kritik der Geschlechtsmoralstatistik)," *Archiv für Sozialwissenschaft und Sozialpolitik* 57, no. 2 (1927): 417–469 and 701–745.
49 Andrew Bonnell, "Robert Michels, Max Weber, and the Sexual Question," *The European Legacy* 3, no. 6 (1998): 97–105.
50 Kandal, *The Woman Question*, 201–211.

Bridal Morality: Critique of a Primitive Rite

In a brochure dating from 1904, Michels wrote that "among all the different components of our current concept of morality ... bridal morality is the most fragile, rotten and abnormal."[51] Bridal morality refers to the social conventions that are imposed on two fiancées until marriage. The basic principle here is chastity. Although the example of bridal morals is somewhat extravagant, bourgeois double standards have been at the center of the moral movement (*Sittlichkeitsbewegung*) since the 1890s, subjecting prostitution to a fundamental critique.[52] The fundamental critique of bourgeois sexual morals, which Michels carries out with great perspicacity, could, as Genett points out, have had a biographical background. Michels' first daughter, Italia, was born in August 1900 in a small town in northern Italy, but she died just four months later. The date of birth is only three months after marriage, which is a scandal in bourgeois circles because it breaks the pre-conjugal rule of sexual abstinence.[53]

Michels' criticism of bridal morals is quite impressive in terms of the methodological approach that runs through his work in the field of gender relations. The analysis is characterized by a mixture of class analysis and cultural variation, as Kandal generally notes for Michels' work in this field.[54] In the case of bridal morality, Michels judges that the customs are strictest in those countries that have remained closest to the "medieval customs." Among these, he counts

---

[51] Robert Michels, *Brautstandsmoral: Eine kritische Betrachtung* (Leipzig: Magazin Verlag, 1904), 3. The dating of the booklet is not very easy, as both Robert Michels himself and Timm Genett date it to the year 1906. A version that has been digitized in the meantime, on the other hand, dates from 1904 and is already in its 5th edition. In a letter from Helene Stöcker, however, we learn that the text was originally intended for the Frauen-Rundschau but was rejected by Stöcker because it was too sharp in form and expression for the "women's audience." As a result, Michels came up with the idea of publishing the text as a booklet in May 1903. It is possible that it was published later that year, or in 1904 at the latest. However, at the beginning of 1904, the authorities confiscated the booklet on the grounds that it violated morality. The public prosecutor wanted to put Michels on trial. Unfortunately, it has not yet been possible to determine whether a trial actually took place and what the outcome of this incident was. Obviously, the booklet was not taken out of circulation in the long run. Helene Stöcker to Robert Michels, 13.5.1903, 12.6.1903, 17.2.1904, 19.5.1904, Robert Michels Archive of the Luigi Einaudi Foundation, Turin.
[52] Briatte Anne-Laure, *Bevormundete Staatsbürgerinnen: Die 'radikale' Frauenbewegung im Deutschen Kaiserreich* (Frankfurt am Main: Campus, 2020), 103–115; Anette Dietrich, *Weiße Weiblichkeiten: Konstruktionen von "Rasse" und Geschlecht im deutschen Kolonialismus* (Bielefeld: Transcript, 2007), 313–319.
[53] Genett, *Der Fremde im Kriege*, 165.
[54] Kandal, *The Sexual Question*, 208.

Germany, Italy, France, and the countries of the Austrian monarchy. In Holland, England, and North America, the "conditions are not quite so sad." Beyond this cultural component, Michels points to the "two moral worlds," whose border is class difference. The "dominion" of bridal morality, he says, extends only to the aristocratic, bourgeois, and petty-bourgeois bourgeoisie. The proletariat remains largely unaffected by the "regulations of sexuality."[55]

In Michels' work, the criticism of bridal morality presents itself as an implicit critique of a primitive rite, which is a modern anachronism. The three-phase model of the religious rite developed by the anthropologist Arnold van Gennep (1873–1957) in 1909, which is still used in anthropological research today, can serve as an analytical framework for the analysis of Michels' descriptions.[56] Gennep starts his analysis from the assumption that transitions are of great importance in all human societies. In this case, bridal morality would be a form of social transition to a different social status, that of wife and husband. The social boundaries broken down during the transition are a potential danger to society and are therefore accompanied by rituals "whose function is to restore the temporarily broken down boundaries and to confirm the traditional structure."[57] Gennep says that there is a regular sequence of three phases in transition rituals, which will be traced below in the light of Michels' comments on bridal morality.

The first phase is that of separation from the old status, which is carried out for the future bride and groom through the "act of so-called engagement."[58] At this stage, both become "sexless beings" who must henceforth adhere to a new morality, the bridal morality and the basic principle of sexual abstinence associated with it. This is followed by the threshold and transformation phase, the second phase of the rite of passage. In this phase of interregnum, the bride and groom belong to neither the old nor the new status. Here the couple is exposed to a kind of "spy system"[59] in which parents, relatives, friends, and sometimes even servants ensure that the couple do not get too close and are never alone together. In the following period of preparation for the wedding, the couple must carry out or endure a series of practices until the night of the wedding. Central to this is the "furnishing of the young woman," who is dressed in white linen, fine lace, and bright colors. When the groom visits the bride, he is con-

---

55 Michels, *Brautstandsmoral*, 7–8.
56 Arnold van Gennep, *Les rites de passage* (Paris: Deschamps, 1909). See also Roland Mischung, "Religionsethnologie," in *Ethnologie: Einführung und Überblick*, eds. Bettina Beer and Hans Fischer (Berlin: Reimer, 2012), 230–234.
57 Mischung, "Religionsethnologie," 231.
58 Michels, *Brautstandsmoral*, 5.
59 Michels, *Sexual Ethics*, 118.

fronted with the whole "mysterious apparatus" which serves to "hide human nudity and which, precisely for this reason, arouses so much desire and promises feelings of lust."[60]

On the wedding day, the "execution of the bridal morality" comes to an end after a long procedure in which the bride and groom first have to perform the ceremony at the registry office, then that in the church, and finally that of the banquet. "At the end of the long series of humiliations, they are thrown into each other's arms quite beastly."[61] The third and final phase is the integration phase, in which the rights and duties of the new social position are accepted and which in this case is completed by the wedding night. At the end of this phase there is a socially "made" couple, who from then on have to comply with their rights and duties as defined by the hegemonic bourgeois sexual morality.

Michels openly admits that he feels a "disgust" for this kind of morality. A "'morality' whose immorality we unfortunately no longer notice because of the tiresome habit of seeing it before us every day." The criticism focuses on bourgeois double morality, which, although it puts the "chastity of the bride" above all else, does not prevent the mother of the bride from "inquiring very brutally about the day when she will be able to lose her," before setting the date of the wedding. According to Michels, who sees the height of immorality in the fact that the bride is "not only allowed to connect sexually, but even has to connect sexually on the night of the wedding,"[62] the "transition in the pleasure of love" from prohibition to compulsion is a traumatizing event for a majority of young brides, which for some women "almost feels like rape."[63] The interrelation between rape and power, which establishes a hierarchy and dominance beyond sexualized violence, remains under-theorized by Michels.

The class character of bridal morality is obvious. Only a few working women had no sexual experience before marriage, because "the maintenance of virginity is a result of constant surveillance and satisfactory housing conditions. The female worker possesses neither one nor the other."[64] However, proletarian sexual morals do not presuppose the virginity of the bride either. It would not be considered immoral in the proletarian milieu for the fiancées to already live to-

---

60 Michels, *Brautstandsmoral*, 11–12.
61 Ibid., 13.
62 All four quotations ibid., 10–11 and 13–14..
63 Michels, *Sexual Ethics*, 122–123.
64 Ibid., 65.

gether. In most cases, premarital children are also considered acceptable.[65] In an early article published by Michels in 1903 in *Die Neue Zeit*, the theory journal of the Social Democratic Party, he even went so far as to claim that "morality in the lower classes is far more natural and for this reason alone is truly moral."[66] In the following years, Michels somewhat reduced this normative-idealizing impetus of a proletarian counter-model of sexual morality in favor of more sober descriptions, although his sympathy remained obvious. Thus, he counters the trauma of the wedding night with the idea of a "gradual evolution" of sexual life.[67] Although this is only intended for those couples who actually intend to marry, Michels nevertheless detaches sexuality from an exclusive tie to conjugal status. The process of getting to know each other can also include the result, which in Michels' case sounds rather implicit, of denying a couple the ability to marry each other on the basis of the experiences made and of separating again.

Genett's assessment is that, in Michels' early works, the scientific interest in questioning customs and morals for their implicit meaning seems only to be limited in relation to bridal morality.[68] The implicit meaning of bridal morality remains largely hidden in Michels' phenomenological description. He explicitly excludes the causes of its emergence, which he locates both ethically and economically.[69] Instead, Michels uses the presentation and criticism of bridal morality as an opportunity to demonstrate the "primitive state" of bourgeois sexual morality and to call for a fundamental revision of it.[70]

---

[65] Robert Michels, "Beitrag zum Problem der Moral," *Die neue Zeit: Wochenschrift der deutschen Sozialdemokratie* 1, no. 15 (1903): 471–472.
[66] Ibid., 472.
[67] Michels, *Sexual Ethics*, 124.
[68] Genett, *Der Fremde im Kriege*, 57.
[69] In his book *The Origin of the Family*, Friedrich Engels does not criticize bourgeois bridal morals, but his comments offer an economic explanation for this rite. While the groom is by no means subject to strict monogamy before the engagement, as Michels himself notes, for women of the bourgeoisie abstinence applies both before and during the engagement. Sexuality is granted to her after marriage only with her husband. For the woman, abstinence transfers itself into strict monogamy. With Engels it could be argued that this strict sexual discipline of the wife is intended to ensure that the husband can be sure of his possible paternity so that the inheritance is only passed on to legitimate descendants. Friedrich Engels, "Der Ursprung der Familie, des Privateigentums und des Staats," in *Marx-Engels-Werke* (henceforth *MEW*), vol. 21 (Berlin: Dietz, 1962 [1884]), 25–173.
[70] Michels, *Brautstandsmoral*, 20.

Individual and Collective Scope for Action in Marriage

"The old marriage bleeds from a thousand wounds," says Michels, "which a criticism as astute as it is unrelenting has beaten into it."[71] Michels presses hard into this open wound. In the first article after his dissertation, he also deals with patriarchal marriage law, which was manifested in the German Empire by the Civil Code that came into force in 1900 and was the subject of criticism from the women's movements and social democracy.[72] However, Michels did not express his criticism in a German journal but in the Italian *Riforma Sociale*.[73] In it, Michels complained, among other things, of the disregard for women as "independent personalities in state and society" codified in marriage law.[74] In *Sexual Ethics*, he also judged that marriage was basically an "officially licensed breeding ground" (*offiziell konzessionierte Notzuchtanstalt*), since it was based on the conjugal duty of sexual coercion. The husband can correct the grievance of this "legal situation" through his individual conduct.[75]

In Michels' reform discourse on marriage, there are at least three dimensions. The first two are the legal and material dimensions. The gender inequality manifested in the legal situation must be reduced, but the legal debate is not a focal point in Michels' work. He also only marginally discusses economic issues, though this does not mean that he does not attach importance to them. Instead, Michels focuses on the individual dimension, which includes aspects of sexuality, bringing up children, the general relationship between the married couple, and the domestic division of labor. This emphasis points to the enlightening character of the book, which points individuals to their own scope and possibilities for action within the existing order, the exhaustion of which can contribute to a happier marriage.

Before Michels' proposals in the following part are located in the discourse of the social democracy and women's movement of the German Empire, a few aspects of internal marriage should be particularly emphasized, which Michels

---

71 Michels, *Sexual Ethics*, 127.
72 Angelika Schaser, "Geschlecht strukturiert die Welt: Die Bedeutung des 19. Jahrhunderts für die Permanenz der Geschlechterhierarchie," in *Durchbruch der Moderne? Neue Perspektiven auf das 19. Jahrhundert*, ed. Birgit Aschmann (Frankfurt am Main: Campus, 2019), 186–191; Evans, *Sozialdemokratie und Frauenbewegung*, 99–100.
73 Due to my lack of language skills, this article can only be received through Timm Genett.
74 Robert Michels quoted after Genett, *Der Fremde im Krieg*, 59.
75 Michels, *Sexual Ethics*, 128.

discusses in detail in the last section of his book. For him, love is linked to sexuality: "Sexless love, whether in marriage or outside it, is stale and shallow."[76] The man would have a predisposition to polygamy, which can be a reason for infidelity. The woman, on the other hand, is not monogamous but "only" polyandrous. The greatest possible variance and passion in sexual intercourse reduces the probability of male infidelity.[77] Here it becomes clear what great importance Michels attaches to a sexually fulfilled married life, which he decouples from its purely reproductive purpose: "We must have the courage to confess that we love love and its ecstasy for its own sake."[78] According to Michels, in order to avoid any misunderstanding, the woman also had sexual needs, which were, however, denied to her by the Victorian sexual morals prevailing at the time.[79]

A major problem, which Michels had already emphasized in his criticism of bridal morals, is the lack of the gradual development of marriage. The bride is pushed almost seamlessly from the assumed virgin state into motherhood. A pregnancy in marriage usually occurs after the honeymoon. "Pregnancy, however, means an increasing reduction in the ability to enjoy life."[80] The married couple, who have hardly come closer to each other because of the bridal morals, cannot spend time together in exuberance during early pregnancy, and this would cloud the young marital happiness from the beginning. An important need of marriage is thus blocked from the very start: "In the first years of marriage, the husband initially unconsciously seeks his wife as a companion and comrade as well as his lover."[81] Instead, the young mother is torn in the "eternal three-part struggle between mother's duties and husband's duties and the woman's duties towards herself."[82]

This fate needed not be an inevitable one. Michels, on the other hand, sets out the guiding principle that "every man and woman has the right to prevent the procreation of children without renouncing physical love in any way."[83] Here Michels represents a radical democratic ideal of equality, which he applies to gender relations.[84] In order to realize this right, he advocates, among other things, Neo-Malthusianism (contraceptives), which also was a highly controver-

---

76 Ibid., 146.
77 Ibid., 155.
78 Ibid., 176.
79 Ibid., 188.
80 Ibid., 163.
81 Ibid., 164.
82 Ibid., 165.
83 Ibid., 167.
84 Genett, *Der Fremde im Kriege*, 63.

sial issue in the social democratic and women's movements at the time.[85] Although this is unnatural, an argument that was often used against contraceptives, all cultural achievements in the field of health education have this in themselves, according to Michels. "Neo-Malthusianism is a victory of human reason over animal irrationality."[86]

The "right not to have children" or conscious child planning would have several advantages. It could give the married couple time to live out their young happiness. Moreover, it would be a way for workers to escape the threat of poverty that a high number of children entails. Michels observes that a falling birth rate goes hand in hand with growing prosperity. This would also help to avoid "artificial abortions and infanticide, which are punishable everywhere."[87] Michels describes abortion as "excusable" due to the precarious situation of working-class families but does not advocate the right to abortion. The possibility of contraception would prevent this. However, the contraceptive methods would have to become even better for this purpose, as they did not completely rule out pregnancy.[88] Social Darwinist motives, which also increased in parts of the women's movement into racial hygiene variants of eugenics, play only a marginal role for Michels and should not be overrated.[89] For Michels, the reduction in the number of children or child planning has primarily private reasons, and beyond this also economic and moral reasons, but is in the end a purely "technical question."

Of fundamental importance to Michels was the general relationship between the married couple. A large majority of men would discourage the wife from developing her intellectual capacities and limit her professional development, a fact rooted in the "well-known general views on the duties of the wife as a housewife and mother, which are commonplace in the bourgeoisie of each country." If the woman is in gainful employment, she must at least not overshadow

---

[85] Contraceptives were rejected by leading social democrats such as August Bebel, Clara Zetkin, and Rosa Luxemburg (1871–1919) during the "birth strike debate" just before the First World War. Karl Kautsky, on the other hand, had taken an affirmative position on contraceptives since at least 1880, but he remained an exception in the party. However, the party position changed tentatively as a result of the "birth strike debate," as birth control was obviously a need of the working class. Evans, *Sozialdemokratie und Frauenbewegung*, 244–250.
[86] Michels, *Sexual Ethics*, 180.
[87] Ibid., 178.
[88] Ibid., 178–179.
[89] On racial hygiene discourses in the bourgeois women's movement, see Dietrich, *Weiße Weiblichkeiten*, 327–341. On forms of socialist eugenics, see Michael Schwartz, *Sozialistische Eugenik. Eugenische Sozialtechnologien in Debatten und Politik der deutschen Sozialdemokratie 1890–1933* (Bonn: Dietz, 1995).

the work and fame of the man. "The intellectualism of women is thus in many cases already limited by the egoism of men,"[90] which has led to the fact that there are relatively few intellectual women. At least it is not due to the supposed lack of female abilities or the corrupting effect of culture on the female sex, as some "male bluestockings" (*männliche Blaustrümpfe*) would claim.[91]

In reality, according to Michels, women are "far from being as different from men as the fanatical stagnators or backwarders of our social order imagine them to be."[92] In this way, Michels resolutely opposes the prevailing notion of bi-polar gender characters.[93] Gender inequality, on the other hand, would result, in addition to the egoism of men, from the double burden on women, which limits their scope for action. Thus, full employment makes it impossible to fulfill one's maternal duties, as Michels emphasizes in reference to a work by Marianne Weber. Nevertheless, both parties had parental duties to fulfill, which were by no means limited to the mother.

In counteracting this situation, Michels pleads—explicitly following Clara Zetkin—for a fairer division of labor in the household and in bringing up children in order to free women from their "inner struggle." Such a division of labor would not only facilitate the freer development of the woman, but would also broaden the husband's world of thought and give him an insight into the woman's "duties," of which he had previously only had vague ideas.[94] This "idea of a domestic division of labor, especially in bringing up children, is by no means unrealisable," says Michels.[95] This would enable the wife, but also the husband, to fulfill their duties toward their children, toward their spouse, and toward themselves.

In these statements, the individual development of the personality is at the center of Michels' argumentation, which is not only in the interest of the wife, who has been limited in her abilities up to now, but is also important for the relationship between the married couple as well as for the perfection of society. In doing so, Michels follows in the tradition of John Stuart Mill (1806–1873), who had already argued in a parliamentary speech on the right to vote for women in 1867 that women would be better able to bring up children and manage the

---

90 Michels, *Sexual Ethics*, 183.
91 Ibid., 184.
92 Ibid.
93 Karin Hausen, "Die Polarisierung der ‚Geschlechtscharaktere'. Eine Spiegelung der Dissoziation von Erwerbs- und Familienleben," in *Geschlechtergeschichte als Gesellschaftsgeschichte*, ed. Karin Hausen (Göttingen: Vandenhoeck & Ruprecht, 2012 [1976]), 19–49.
94 Michels, *Sexual Ethics*, 193.
95 Ibid., 195.

household if their intellectual development and socialization were not restricted to such an extent by society.[96] The educated woman would also be an added value for their husbands. As the couple spends a lot of time together due to the "domestic revolution," it would damage the man's character if the woman continued to be treated only as a "toy" or a "better servant" and not as a "conversation partner."[97] In the end, the whole of society would suffer.

Michels leaves no doubt that marriage, despite all its shortcomings, is the "best form of sexual conviviality" and the "necessary cell of every cultural life."[98] Michels' aim of "healing marriage" can only be achieved by "sharpening the sense of responsibility." Thus, on the horizon of Michels' diagnosis of the problem, his ideal conception of the new marriage, based on individuality as well as on equal "comradeship" and a fulfilled sex life, becomes apparent. The modern or "free woman" thus endows Michels with the attributes of a "proud, self-confident, co-creative companion."[99] Creating the legal and socio-economic framework for this was a political imperative.

Michels seems to have come quite close to the ideal of a "new marriage" with his own married life. His wife, Gisela Michels-Lindner (1878–1954), was also active in the SPD, organized a number of meetings in Marburg in 1905 at which she lectured, and in the following year also published in *Der Gleichheit* on the Italian women's movement.[100] In the foreword to *Sexual Ethics*, Michels describes his wife as a "loyal comrade" as well as a "faithful and independent companion," which is relatively congruent with the characteristics of the "new woman" he formulated and indicates that his position on the "woman question" was not limited to a theoretical discussion, but also represents an everyday practical guide. During his lifetime, Michels held fast to the ideal of marriage, even though it is not the only legitimate form of living together.[101]

---

96 John Stuart Mill, "Parlamentsrede über die Zulassung der Frauen zum Wahlrecht," in *Ausgewählte Werke*, vol. 1, eds. Ulrike Ackermann and Hans Jörg Schmidt (Hamburg: Murmann, 2012), 394–395.
97 Ibid.
98 Michels, *Sexual Ethics*, 128.
99 Ibid., 91.
100 Among others, see Gisela Michels-Linder, "Die sozialistische Frauenbewegung in Italien," *Die Gleichheit* 16, no. 22 (1906): 153.
101 "In sexual life, early marriage entered into out of love and keeping it pure is a social ideal that transcends all time." Michels, *Sittlichkeit in Ziffern?*, 219.

Robert Michels as a Border Crosser

The final task will be to situate Michels' positions on sexuality and marriage in the discourse of the time and not to leave it at the references made so far. "Sexuality was not a taboo subject," writes Ute Frevert, "but the subject of heated scientific and political controversies, not only in medical journals."[102] The subject of female sexuality as well as premarital and extramarital sexual intercourse was particularly controversial, on which, as described, Michels took a clear position. In contrast, the moral movement in the German Empire, which gained strength in the 1890s and consisted of very different political wings, devoted itself primarily to the problem of prostitution.[103] "They criticized the double morality of a society that criminalized prostitutes but left their male customers unscathed."[104] More far-reaching demands for a "new sexual morality," however, were demanded only by very few.

The avant-garde in the field of sexual reform was formed by the Association for Maternity Protection, founded in 1905 and headed by Helene Stöcker, which on the one hand wanted to improve the situation of illegitimate children and unmarried mothers and, on the other, advocated a "new sexual morality,"[105] which also led to conflicts within the association. On the first concern, both Max and Marianne Weber supported the association, in which Social Democrats such as August Bebel, Lily Braun, and Henriette Fürth (1861–1938) were also active.[106] However, the Weber family quickly distanced themselves from the association when it took a more offensive stance in favor of a reform of sexual morals. After Michels sent his article "Erotische Streifzüge" ("Erotic Forays"),[107] published in the association's magazine *Mutterschutz* in 1906, to Max Weber, the latter replied quite indignantly: "The specific Mutterschutz gang is an utterly confused bunch. After the babble of Stöcker, Borgius, etc. I withdrew my support. Crass hedonism and an ethics that would benefit only men as the goal of women ... that is simply nonsense."[108] The Bund Deutscher Frauenvereine (Federation of German Women's Associations), the national umbrella organiza-

---

102 Ute Frevert, *Frauen-Geschichte: Zwischen bürgerlicher Verbesserung und neuer Weiblichkeit* (Frankfurt am Main: Suhrkamp, 1986), 128.
103 Briatte, *Bevormundete Staatsbürgerinnen*, 103–116.
104 Frevert, *Frauen-Geschichte*, 132.
105 Briatte, *Bevormundete Staatsbürgerinnen*, 197.
106 Manfred Scharinger, *Proletarische Frauenbewegung: Kritische Bilanz und politische Lehren* (Vienna: RSO, 2009), 433.
107 Michels, "Erotische Streifzüge," 362–374.
108 Max Weber quoted after Bonnell, "Sexual Question," 99.

tion of the civil women's movement in Germany, also refused to accept the Association for Maternity Protection because of its "radical" positions.

Within *Sexual Ethics*, Michels advocates a "new sexual morality," but he clearly distances himself from the discourse of "free love." "Free love as an end in itself has long since become obsolete as a theorem."[109] Even the socialists who would have once paid homage to it renounced this practice and sailed back into the harbor of marriage. As a danger to the general public, "free love" would not be feasible but would fail in the face of reality. Apart from the fact that the idea of "free love" was never hegemonic in socialist thought, although it was advocated in early socialism by Charles Fourier (1772–1837), its socialist criticism is just as old.[110] What was also understood by this term in detail also diverged greatly. While "free love" was put forward by bourgeois and conservative critics as a fighting term and criticism of modernity against the radical bourgeois women's movement and social democracy, the few female social democrats who affirmatively referred to it associated it more with a criticism of the legal form of marriage, but not of monogamous marriage per se.[111] The sharp distinction made by Michels can therefore be seen more as a strategy of argumentation.

Sexuality was not discussed inordinately in the social democratic and proletarian women's movements. The US historian Robert Neuman emphasized that the SPD of the German Empire had advocated "sexual conservatism" despite its criticism of traditional moral concepts and bourgeois marriage.[112] This assessment is contradicted by Richard Evans, who praises Neuman's work as pioneering, but denies his judgment. The attributes "conservative" or "bourgeois" would not be suitable to describe the Social Democratic position, as this rating was too strongly influenced by later moral concepts.[113] Without presenting a final opinion, Michels himself remarked in an essay from 1927: "It would one day be an

---

109 Michels, *Sexual Ethics*, 127.

110 [A] contemporary critique was formulated at the time by the female Saint-Simonians, for example. Skadi Siiri Krause, "Die Saint-Simonistinnen zwischen Frauen- und Arbeiterbewegung," in *Geschlecht und Klassenkampf: Die "Frauenfrage" aus deutscher und internationaler Perspektive im 19. und 20. Jahrhundert*, ed. Vincent Streichhahn and Frank Jacob (Berlin: Metropol, 2020), 189–193.

111 Wally Zepler criticized that "free love" for most socialists "represents nothing more than a monogamous marriage freed from legal constraints." Wally Zepler, "Das psychische Problem in der Frauenfrage," *Sozialistische Monatshefte* 10, no. 4 (1906): 309.

112 Robert Neuman, "The Sexual Question and Social Democracy in Imperial Germany," *Journal of Social History* 7, no. 3 (1974): 272.

113 Evans, *Sozialdemokratie und Frauenbewegung*, 257–258.

interesting task to subject to a thorough examination the relationship between sexual morality and socialism or the modern labor movement."[114]

Leading social democrats such as August Bebel or Karl Kautsky (1854–1938), while emphasizing the naturalness of sexuality and explicitly granting it to women, restricted its legitimate exercise to marriage.[115] This position was shared by a majority of social democrats. There were only a few exceptions in the proletarian women's movement, such as Wally Zepler (1865–1940), Adelheid Popp (1869–1939), or Oda Olberg (1872–1955), who advocated a more open approach to sexuality in various gradations.[116] Overall, Robert Michels was therefore at the forefront of the sexual reform movement with his plea for a "new sexual morality." Apart from a few radical representatives of the bourgeois as well as the proletarian women's movement and a few bohemians, nobody went as far as he did in his views. The bond between sexuality and marriage was no longer absolute with Michels and a few comrades-in-arms. This was not simply a matter of fulfilling sexual needs but of reforming sexual morality in order to bring about a fundamental change in gender relations "so that women and men would be fundamentally equal and subject to the same morals."[117]

Even though the majority of social democrats did not represent such positions, they had been increasingly confronted with accusations from the bourgeoisie since the 1890s that they were responsible for the "dissolution of the family." Karl Kautsky countered this in his explanation of the 1891 Erfurt program of the SPD: "Nobody in the party thinks of 'abolishing' the family, of legally abolishing it and forcibly dissolving it. … What leads to dissolution is not the essence of cooperative production, but economic development."[118] Certainly, Karl Marx (1818–1883) and Friedrich Engels (1820–1895) advocated the thesis of the dissolution of the family in German ideology, but this was to be understood primarily as a description of destructive capitalist development and not as a political agenda.[119]

---

114 Michels, "Problem der Moralstatistik," 443.
115 Heinz Niggermann, *Emanzipation zwischen Sozialismus und Feminismus: Die sozialdemokratische Frauenbewegung im Kaiserreich* (Wuppertal: Peter Hammer, 1981), 237–282.
116 Oda Olberg, "Polemisches über Frauenfrage und Sozialismus," *Sozialistische Monatshefte* 9, no. 4 (1905): 309; Wally Zepler, "Die Frau der Zukunft und die freie Liebe," *Sozialistische Monatshefte* 3, no. 6 (1899): 290–300.
117 Briatte, *Bevormundete Staatsbürgerinnen*, 196.
118 Karl Kautsky, *Das Erfurter Programm in seinem grundsätzlichen Theil erläutert* (Stuttgart: Dietz, 1912 [1892]), 146.
119 "Historically, the bourgeois gives the family the character of the bourgeois family, in which boredom and money are the binding link, and which also includes the bourgeois dissolution of the family, which does not prevent the family itself from always continuing to exist. Its dirty existence has its counterpart in the holy concept of it in official phraseology and universal hypoc-

Within social democracy, monogamous marriage continued to serve as an ideal. However, this was to be put on a new foundation. According to Clara Zetkin, marriage was decomposed by economic and historical development.[120] This development was to be welcomed because "the family as an economic unit is disappearing and in its place the family as a moral unit." In this, "the woman, as a companion with equal rights, equal creation and equal aspirations, who strides forward with man, will be able to promote her individuality, but at the same time to fulfill her task as wife and mother to the highest degree."[121] For Niggermann, this is where Zetkin's humanistic-idealistic tradition is evident,[122] which can be seen as a common ground with Michels'.

A detailed picture of marriage under socialism was not sketched out by the social democratic actors at the time. Here they remained faithful to the unspoken ban on images (*Bilderverbot*), although some cursory remarks can be found among various social democrats. Oda Olberg, for example, took the view that monogamy would be "the predominant form of marriage in socialist society" but that "extramarital forms of sexual intercourse" would not be seen as immoral.[123] Engels, too, in his work *The Origin of the Family*, tends to advocate the model of a monogamous marriage in the socialist society of the future, although he abstains from a final judgment.[124] Marriage under socialism is defined by the actors primarily ex negativo. The legal and material inequality of the sexes cannot be the basis for the "new marriage." Its future foundation is based on autonomy and comradeship. In this respect, social democracy differed little from the ideas of the "radical" bourgeois women's movement.

---

risy." Karl Marx and Friedrich Engels, "Die deutsche Ideologie," in *MEW*, vol. 3 (Berlin: Dietz, 1969 [1845]), 164.

120 Clara Zetkin, "Nur mit der proletarischen Frau wird der Sozialismus siegen. Rede auf dem SPD-Parteitag in Gotha," in *Protokoll über die Verhandlungen des Parteitags der Sozialdemokratische Partei Deutschland, abgehalten zu Gotha vom 11. bis 16. Oktober 1896* (Berlin: Vorwärts, 1896), 160–168.

121 Ibid., 167.

122 Niggermann, *Emanzipation*, 241.

123 Olberg, "Polemisches," 309.

124 "What we can now conjecture about the way in which sexual relations will be ordered after the impending overthrow of capitalist production is mainly of a negative character, limited for the most part to what will disappear. But what will there be new? That will be answered when a new generation has grown up [...]. When these people are in the world, they will care precious little what anybody today thinks they ought to do; they will make their own practice and their corresponding public opinion about the practice of each individual – and that will be the end of it." Engels, *Ursprung der Familie*, 83.

Even those who relaxed the ties of sexuality to marriage, such as Michels and Stöcker, continued to regard monogamous marriage as ideal. Stöcker, for example, emphasized that the "new sexual morality" did not want to abolish either the family or the institution of marriage but that "living together between people who are personally attracted to each other, the trinity of father, mother, and child ... would always remain the highest ideal."[125] What they intended first and foremost was the "liberation" of love from its bourgeois compulsive character. A "free love" in the sense of unbridled sexuality, free of norms and values, as suggested by Helene Lange's critique of "feminist thought anarchy" and "hurrah eroticism" (*Hurra-Erotik*), was represented in reality by basically no one except in some circles of artistic and intellectual bohemians.[126] Overnight, as even Michels knew, his developed principles of the "new sexual morality" would not be realized. These would initially "only be able to have validity for a small elite of morally high standing people."[127]

The disputes about gender relations at the turn of the century were accompanied by a broad social crisis discourse in which "free love" functioned as a modern-critical cipher. The fear of disintegration and anomie caused by the threatening dissolution of social bonds was seen as the "doom of modern societies." The discourse about a "new sexual morality" appeared as an expression of this. According to Arni, the line of conflict ran between individualism and social obligation, which Michels and his comrades-in-arms had to take into account in their conceptions.[128] Michels solves this apparent contradiction, as has hopefully become clear, by understanding the "new sexual morality" as an ethical principle and moral goal, "whose aspiration, however, lies at the same time in the individual and collective interests of humanity."[129]

Conclusion

Sexual Ethics is definitely an opus that is immensely underestimated in its importance. Michels' starting point for his feminist-sexual reform writing was the criticism of bourgeois double morality, against the background of which a reform of the same is intended, which in its new form would serve as the moral basis of an

---

125 Helene Stöcker quoted after Briatte, *Bevormundete Staatsbürgerinnen*, 198.
126 Helene Lange, "Feministische Gedankenanarchie," in *Frauen und Sexualmoral*, ed. Marie-louise Janssen-Jureit (Frankfurt am Main: Fischer, 1996 [1909]), 147–155.
127 Michels, *Sexual Ethics*, 126.
128 Arni, "Liebesethik," 200.
129 Michels, *Sexual Ethics*, VIII.

egalitarian understanding of gender relations in modernity. As a sociological observer whose work "oscillates between the intention of political action and scientific description,"[130] Michels not only attempted to generate a gain in knowledge but also to intervene in political debates. In the present work, his critique of bourgeois marriage and sexual morality was also located in the contemporary discourse. The aim was to provide a contextualization that went beyond that of his previous reception.[131] Michels appeared at the beginning of the 20th century with a critical discussion of sexual morality at a time when the Association for Maternity Protection did not even exist. This does not mean, of course, that the discourse did not exist before either, but Michels set his own impulses in this debate. He was certainly inspired by activists of the women's movement and social democracy. However, the attempt to monolithically classify Michels must fail. It seems most appropriate to categorize him as a border crosser between the radical factions of the reform movement of the German Empire and whose *Sexual Ethics* deserves a more intensive academic debate in the future.

Works Cited

Archival Material

Correspondence from Robert Michels, Archivio Roberto Michels/Archivio Fondazione Luigi Einaudi (AFLE), Turin.

Secondary Sources

Anne-Laure, Briatte. *Bevormundete Staatsbürgerinnen: Die 'radikale' Frauenbewegung im Deutschen Kaiserreich*. Frankfurt am Main: Campus, 2020.

Arni, Caroline. "L'Amour en Europe: Ein Versuch über Robert Michels' vergleichende Liebeswissenschaft und den Liebesdiskurs in der Moderne." In *Der Eigensinn des Materials. Erkundungen sozialer Wirklichkeit: Festschrift für Claudia Honegger zum 60. Geburtstag*, edited by Caroline Arni, 71–89. Frankfurt am Main: Stroemfeld, 2007.

---

[130] Jasmin Siri, *Parteien: Zur Soziologie einer politischen Form* (Wiesbaden: Springer, 2012), 53.
[131] So it seems as banal as tautological for Kandal to simply judge without further specification: "Michels' discussions of sexuality, sexual morality, and the relations of the sexes had as its stimulus 'the new sexual ethic' advocated by feminists." Kandal, "Egalitarian Sexual Ethics," XXII.

Arni, Caroline. "Seelengesetze mit Gesellschaftswert. Weibliche Subjektwerdung und die Utopie menschlicher Perfektion in der feministisch-sexualreformerischen Liebesethik um 1900." *Feministische Studien* 27, no. 2 (2009): 196–209.

Bebel, August. "Die Frau und der Sozialismus." In *Ausgewählte Reden und Schriften*, vol. 10, edited by Internationales Institut für Sozialgeschichte Amsterdam. Munich: K. G. Sauer, 1996 [1879].

Bluhm, Harald and Skadi S. Krause. "Einleitung. Robert Michels' Soziologie des Parteiwesens. Oligarchien und Eliten – Die Kehrseiten moderner Demokratie." In *Robert Michels' Soziologie des Parteiwesens*, edited by Bluhm/Krause, 9–19. Wiesbaden: Springer, 2012.

Bonnell, Andrew. "Robert Michels, Max Weber, and the Sexual Question." *The European Legacy* 3, no. 6. (1998): 97–105.

Delap, Lucy. "The 'Woman Question' and the Origins of Feminism." In *The Cambridge History of Nineteenth-Century Political Thought,* edited by Gareth Stedman Jones, 319–348. Cambridge: Cambridge University Press, 2011.

Dietrich, Anette. *Weiße Weiblichkeiten: Konstruktionen von "Rasse" und Geschlecht im deutschen Kolonialismus*. Bielefeld: Transcript, 2007.

Engels, Friedrich. "Der Ursprung der Familie, des Privateigentums und des Staats." In *Marx-Engels-Werke*, vol. 21, 25–173. Berlin: Dietz, 1962 [1884].

Evans, Richard. *Sozialdemokratie und Frauenbewegung im deutschen Kaiserreich*. Bonn: Dietz, 1979.

Ferraris, Pino. "Questione femminile e morale sessuale nell'evoluzione politica di Roberto Michels." In *Roberto Michels. Economia – Sociologia – Politica*, edited by Riccardo Faucci, 97–122. Torino: Giappichelli 1989.

Frevert, Ute. *Frauen-Geschichte: Zwischen bürgerlicher Verbesserung und neuer Weiblichkeit*. Frankfurt am Main: Suhrkamp, 1986.

Genett, Timm. *Der Fremde im Kriege: Zur politischen Theorie und Biographie von Robert Michels 1876–1936*. Berlin: Akademie Verlag, 2008.

Genett, Timm. "Robert Michels. Pionier der sozialen Bewegungsforschung." In *Soziale Bewegungen zwischen Dynamik und Erstarrung*, edited by Timm Genett, 11–69. Berlin: Akademie Verlag, 2008.

Geske, Hans. "Oligarchie, Faschismus … Feminismus? Ein neuer Blick auf Robert Michels." In *Berliner Debatte Initial* 31, no. 3 (2020): 99–109.

Hausen, Karin. "Die Polarisierung der ‚Geschlechtscharaktere'. Eine Spiegelung der Dissoziation von Erwerbs- und Familienleben." In *Geschlechtergeschichte als Gesellschaftsgeschichte*, edited by Karin Hausen, 19–49. Göttingen: Vandenhoeck & Ruprecht, 2012 [1976].

Kandal, Terry R. "From Egalitarian Sexual Ethics to Gender Politics: An Evaluation of Michels' Contribution." In *Robert Michels: Sexual Ethics. A Study of Borderline Questions. With a new introduction by Terry R. Kandal*, xi–lxv. New York/London: Routledge, 2002.

Kandal, Terry R. "Profile. Rober Michels' Sexual Ethics." *Sociology* 38 (March/April 2001): 60–66.

Kandal, Terry R. *The Woman Question in Classical Sociology Theory*. Miami: Florida International University Press, 1988.

Kautsky, Karl. *Das Erfurter Programm in seinem grundsätzlichen Theil erläutert*. Stuttgart: Dietz, 1912 [1892].

Krause, Skadi Siiri. "Die Saint-Simonistinnen zwischen Frauen- und Arbeiterbewegung." In *Geschlecht und Klassenkampf. Die "Frauenfrage" aus deutscher und internationaler Perspektive im 19. und 20. Jahrhundert*, edited by Vincent Streichhahn and Frank Jacob, 185–201. Berlin: Metropol, 2020.

Lange, Helene. "Feministische Gedankenanarchie." In *Frauen und Sexualmoral*, edited by Marielouise Janssen-Jureit, 147–155. Frankfurt am Main: Fischer, 1996 [1909].

Marx, Karl and Friedrich Engels. "Die deutsche Ideologie." In *MEW*, vol. 3, 5–530. Berlin: Dietz, 1969 [1845].

Michels, Robert. "Altes und Neues zum Problem der Moralstatistik (Kritik der Geschlechtsmoralstatistik)." In *Archiv für Sozialwissenschaft und Sozialpolitik* 57, no. 2 (1927): 417–469, 701–745.

Michels, Robert. *Amour et Chasteté: Essais Sociologique*. Paris: Siard & Brière, 1914.

Michels, Robert. "Beitrag zum Problem der Moral." *Die neue Zeit* 1, no. 15 (1903): 470–475.

Michels, Robert. *Brautstandsmoral. Eine kritische Betrachtung*. Leipzig: Magazin Verlag, 1904.

Michels, Robert. "Das Weib und der Intellectualismus." *Dokumente der Frauen* 7, no. 4 (1902): 106–114.

Michels, Robert. "Der vierunddreißigste Bebel." *Die Gleichheit* 14, no. 15 (1904): 113–115.

Michels, Robert. "Die Arbeiterinnenbewegung in Italien." *Die Frau* 9, no. 6 (1902): 328–336.

Michels, Robert. "Die deutsche Frau im Beruf." *Die Gleichheit* 14, no. 11 (1904): 82–84.

Michels, Robert. *Die Grenzen der Geschlechtsmoral: Prolegomena. Gedanken und Untersuchungen*. Leipzig: Frauen-Verlag, 1911.

Michels, Robert. "Die Zwischenstufen der Ehrbarkeit." *Die neue Generation* 9 (September 1909): 351–359.

Michels, Robert. "Ein sexueller Kongreß in Italien." *Die neue Generation* 2 (1911): 63–70.

Michels, Robert. "Entstehung der Frauenfrage als soziale Frage." *Die Frauenbewegung* 9, no. 3 (1903): 17–18.

Michels, Robert. "Erotische Streifzüge: Deutsche und italienische Liebesformen. Aus dem Pariser Liebesleben." *Mutterschutz* 11, no. 9 (1906): 362–374.

Michels, Robert. "Frauenstimmrecht – schon heute eine Notwendigkeit." *Die Frauenbewegung* 8, no. 23 (1902): 177–178.

Michels, Robert. *I Limiti della Morale Sessuale: Prolegomena: Indagini e Pensieri*. Torino: Bocca, 1912.

Michels, Robert. "Neomalthusianismus." *Frauenzukunft* 1, no. 1 (1910): 42–55.

Michels, Robert. "Rückblick auf die Geschichte der proletarischen Frauenbewegung in Italien." *Die Gleichheit* 13, no. 1, 2–3; no. 2, 11–13; no. 5, 36–38; no. 8, 58–60; no. 11, 83–85; no. 17, 131–134 (all 1903).

Michels, Robert. *Sexual Ethics: A Study of Borderland Questions*. New York: Walter Scott, 1914.

Michels, Robert. *Sittlichkeit in Ziffern? Kritik der Moralstatistik*. Berlin: Duncker & Humblot, 1928.

Michels, Robert. *Zur Soziologie des Parteiwesens in der modernen Demokratie*. Leipzig: Klinkhardt, 1911.

Michels-Linder, Gisela. "Die sozialistische Frauenbewegung in Italien." *Die Gleichheit* 16, no. 22 (1906): 153.

Mill, John Stuart. "Parlamentsrede über die Zulassung der Frauen zum Wahlrecht." In *Ausgewählte Werke*, vol. 1, edited by Ulrike Ackermann and Hans Jörg Schmidt, 389–402. Hamburg: Murmann, 2012.
Mischung, Roland. "Religionsethnologie." In *Ethnologie. Einführung und Überblick*, edited by Bettina Beer and Hans Fischer, 213–236. Berlin: Reimer, 2012.
Mitzman, Arthur. *Sociology and Estrangement: Three Sociologists of Imperial Germany*. New York: Knopf, 1973.
Neuman, Robert. "The Sexual Question and Social Democracy in Imperial Germany." *Journal of Social History* 7, no. 3 (Spring 1974): 271–286.
Niggermann, Heinz. *Emanzipation zwischen Sozialismus und Feminismus: Die sozialdemokratische Frauenbewegung im Kaiserreich*. Wuppertal: Peter Hammer, 1981.
Nipperdey, Thomas. *Deutsche Gesellschaftsgeschichte, 1866–1918*, vol. 1: *Arbeitswelt und Bürgergeist*. München: Beck, 1991.
Olberg, Oda. "Polemisches über Frauenfrage und Sozialismus." *Sozialistische Monatshefte*, no. 4 (April 1905): 301–310.
Protokoll über die Verhandlungen des Parteitages der Sozialdemokratischen Partei Deutschlands. Abgehalten zu Bremen vom 18. bis 24. September 1904. Berlin: Vorwärts, 1904.
Schaser, Angelika. "Geschlecht strukturiert die Welt: Die Bedeutung des 19. Jahrhunderts für die Permanenz der Geschlechterhierarchie." In *Durchbruch der Moderne? Neue Perspektiven auf das 19. Jahrhundert*, edited by Birgit Aschmann, 171–198. Frankfurt am Main: Campus, 2019.
Scharinger, Manfred. *Proletarische Frauenbewegung: Kritische Bilanz und politische Lehren*. Wien: RSO, 2009.
Schwartz, Michael. *Sozialistische Eugenik: Eugenische Sozialtechnologien in Debatten und Politik der deutschen Sozialdemokratie 1890–1933*. Bonn: Dietz, 1995.
Siri, Jasmin. *Parteien: Zur Soziologie einer politischen Form*. Wiesbaden: Springer, 2012.
Van Gennep, Arnold. *Les rites de passage*. Paris: Deschamps, 1909.
Zepler, Wally. "Das psychische Problem in der Frauenfrage." *Sozialistische Monatshefte* 10, no. 4 (1906): 306–315.
Zepler, Wally. "Die Frau der Zukunft und die freie Liebe." *Sozialistische Monatshefte* 3, no. 6 (1899): 290–300.
Zetkin, Clara. "Nur mit der proletarischen Frau wird der Sozialismus siegen: Rede auf dem SPD-Parteitag in Gotha." In *Protokoll über die Verhandlungen des Parteitags der Sozialdemokratische Partei Deutschland, abgehalten zu Gotha vom 11. bis 16. Oktober 1896*, 160–168. Berlin: Vorwärts, 1896.

Frank Jacob
6 Marriage as Exploitation: Emma Goldman and the Anarchist Concept of Female Liberation

Asked in an interview in 1897 "What does anarchy hold out to me—a woman?" the famous American anarchist Emma Goldman (1869–1940)[1] replied: "More to [a] woman than to anyone else—everything which she has not—freedom and equality."[2] Goldman, whose feminist positions and role as a leading anarcha-feminist have been discussed in recent works,[3] was considered to be the "priest-

---

[1] Many biographical works and edited volumes about Goldman's life and impact have been published, including Paul Avrich and Karen Avrich, *Sasha and Emma: The Anarchist Odyssey of Alexander Berkman and Emma Goldman* (Cambridge, MA: Belknap Press, 2014); Richard Drinnon and Anna Maria Drinnon, eds., *Nowhere at Home: Letters from Exile of Emma Goldman and Alexander Berkman* (New York: Schocken Books, 1975); Richard Drinnon, *Rebel in Paradise: A Biography of Emma Goldman*, Phoenix edition (Chicago: University of Chicago Press, 1982 [1961]); Candace Falk, *Love, Anarchy and Emma Goldman* (New Brunswick, NJ: Rutgers University Press, 1990 [1984]); Bonnie Haaland, *Emma Goldman: Sexuality and the Impurity of the State* (Montréal et al.: Black Rose Books, 1993); Vivian Gornick, *Emma Goldman: Revolution as a Way of Life* (New Haven, CT: Yale University Press, 2011); Joseph Ishill, *Emma Goldman: A Challenging Rebel* (Berkeley Heights, NJ: Oriole Press, 1957); Frank Jacob, *Emma Goldman: Ein Leben für die Freiheit* (Berlin: Hentrich & Hentrich, 2021); Theresa Moritz and Albert Moritz, *The World's Most Dangerous Women: A New Biography of Emma Goldman* (Vancouver: Subway Books, 2002); David Porter, *Vision on Fire: Emma Goldman on the Spanish Revolution* (New Paltz, NY: Commonground Press, 1983); Alice Wexler, *Emma Goldman: An Intimate Life* (New York: Pantheon, 1984).
[2] Emma Goldman, "What Is There in Anarchy for Woman?" *St. Louis Post-Dispatch Sunday Magazine*, October 14, 1897, 9, in *Emma Goldman: A Documentary History of the American Years*, vol. 1: *Made for America, 1890–1901*, eds. Candace Falk et al. (Urbana/Chicago, IL: University of Illinois Press, 2008), 289.
[3] Kathy E. Ferguson, "Gender and Genre in Emma Goldman," *Signs* 36, no. 3 (2011): 733–757; Frank Jacob, "Anarchismus, Ehe und Sex: Emma Goldman (1869–1940) als Anarcha-Feministin," in *Geschlecht und Klassenkampf: Die "Frauenfrage" aus deutscher und internationaler Perspektive im 19. und 20. Jahrhundert*, eds. Vincent Streichhahn and Frank Jacob (Berlin: Metropol, 2020), 202–221; Donna M. Kowal, "Anarcha-Feminism," in *The Palgrave Handbook of Anarchism*, eds. Carl Levy and Matthew S. Adams (Cham: Palgrave Macmillan, 2019), 265–279; Donna M. Kowal, *Tongue of Fire: Emma Goldman, Public Womanhood, and the Sex Question* (Albany, NY: SUNY Press, 2016); Lori Jo Marso, "A Feminist Search for Love: Emma Goldman on the Politics of Marriage, Love, Sexuality and the Feminine," *Feminist Theory* 4, no. 3 (2003): 305–320; Penny A. Weiss and Loretta Kensinger, eds., *Feminist Interpretations of Emma Goldman* (University Park, PA: Pennsylvania State University Press, 2007).

OpenAccess. © 2021 Frank Jacob, published by De Gruyter. This work is licensed under the Creative Commons Attribution-NonCommercial-NoDerivatives 4.0 International License.
https://doi.org/10.1515/9783110751451-006

ess of anarchy"[4] by many of her contemporaries, and often her female appearance surprised the men who met her: "She is in every sense a womanly looking woman, with masculine mind and courage."[5] In fact, Goldman surprised many of her contemporaries, but not only with regard to her appearance but also with her ideas of unlimited freedom for everyone. She was praised as a "real champion of freedom"[6] by those who supported her political struggles against exploitation, the state, or the dominance of patriarchy in American society, but she was also considered the evil personification of anarchism,[7] which caused an "aura of menace around Emma Goldman."[8] Her criticism of the First World War and American imperialism,[9] as well as her support of the Russian Revolution, which she initially had high hopes for before realizing after her deportation to Soviet Russia that the revolutionary process had been corrupted by the Bolsheviks around Lenin,[10] made the well-known anarchist one of the main targets of the new laws the US government used during the war to suppress resistance against the state's official war policy. When Goldman and many of her anarchist friends were deported in 1919, it was the young J. Edgar Hoover (1895–1972) who personally oversaw that "two of the most dangerous anarchists in America"[11] were successfully expelled from the United States.

---

4 Goldman, "What Is There in Anarchy for Woman?" 289.
5 Ibid., 292.
6 Emma Goldman, An Anarchist Looks at Life, Text of a speech by Emma Goldman, held at Foyle's twenty-ninth literary luncheon (London, UK), March 1, 1933, Emma Goldman Papers, International Institute of Social History, Amsterdam (henceforth EGP-IISH), No. 191, 3.
7 Kowal, "Anarcha-Feminism," 274.
8 Kathy E. Ferguson, "Discourses of Danger: Locating Emma Goldman," *Political Theory* 36, no. 5 (2008): 743.
9 Frank Jacob, "Anarchistische Imperialismuskritik und staatliche Repression: Emma Goldman, Alexander Berkman und die Kritik an der politischen Ökonomie des Ersten Weltkrieges in den USA, 1917–1919," *Prokla* 50, no. 201 (2020): 681–695; Erika J. Pribanic-Smith and Jared Schroeder, *Emma Goldman's No-Conscription League and the First Amendment* (New York: Routledge, 2019).
10 Frank Jacob, "Anarchism and the Perversion of the Russian Revolution: The Accounts of Emma Goldman and Alexander Berkman," *Diacronie* 33, no. 1 (2018): https://doi.org/10.4000/diacronie.7405; Frank Jacob, "Der Anarchismus und die Russische Revolution – Emma Goldman und Alexander Berkman im Kampf gegen den Bolschewismus," *Ne znam: Zeitschrift für Anarchismusforschung* 7 (2018): 3–66; Frank Jacob, *Emma Goldman and the Russian Revolution: From Admiration to Frustration* (Berlin: De Gruyter, 2020); Frank Jacob, "From Aspiration to Frustration: Emma Goldman's Perception of the Russian Revolution," *American Communist History* 17, no. 2 (2018): 185–199.
11 J. Edgar Hoover, "Memorandum for Mr. Creighton," U.S. Department of Justice, August 23, 1919, 2, cited in Ferguson, "Discourses of Danger," 735.

Goldman would nevertheless continue her "rebellious life" and criticized not only Bolshevism but also Fascism and National Socialism in the years that followed the beginning of her exile.[12] Regardless of Goldman's many political struggles, the freedom of the modern woman was one essential aspect of her personal agenda, especially since women were far away from equality. For the anarchist Goldman, the woman "is the slave of her husband and her children. She should take her part in the business world the same as the man; she should be his equal before the world, as she is in the reality. She is capable as he, but when she labors, she gets less wages. Why? Because she wears skirts instead of trousers."[13] The patriarchy continued to abuse and exploit women for several reasons, which is why "[t]he woman, instead of being the household queen, told about in story books, is the servant, the mistress, and the slave of both husband and children. She loses her own individuality entirely, even her name she is not allowed to keep."[14] When, early on in her political life, Goldman began to criticize the exploitation of women by marriage as an institutionalized form of control in the name of the patriarchy, it was not surprising that she made enemies, who would later establish her public image as a "dangerous individual."[15] While this image stretched back to the assassination of US President William McKinley (1843–1901) and was intensified by a press campaign,[16] Goldman was probably one of the most influential anarchists in the United States and one of the anarcha-feminists whose ideas about equality made her quite appealing for feminists in later times as well.[17]

As American scholar Blaine McKinley emphasized, "[a]s men and women whose aspirations contrasted with those of most Americans, the anarchists saw the contradictions and inequalities of modern America,"[18] and Goldman expressed her criticism of these inequalities quite loudly and prominently. Like other anarchists, Goldman "offered a unique viewpoint on their times and experienced tensions that illuminated American society. Uncomfortable with the pre-

---

12 Frank Jacob, "Emma Goldmans Blick auf Bolschewismus, Faschismus und Nationalsozialismus: Eine anarchistische Perspektive auf den Totalitarismus der 1920er- und 1930er-Jahre," *Zeitschrift für Geschichtswissenschaft* 68, no. 10 (2019): 833–847.
13 Goldman, "What Is There in Anarchy for Woman?" 291.
14 Ibid.
15 Ferguson, "Discourses of Danger," 736.
16 Alex Kates Shulman, "Introduction," in *Red Emma Speaks: Selected Writings and Speeches by Emma Goldman*, ed. Alex Kates Shulman (New York: Vintage Books, 1972), 11–12.
17 Loretta Kensinger, "Radical Lessons: Thoughts on Emma Goldman, Chaos, Grief, and Political Violence Post-9/11/01," *Feminist Teacher* 20, no. 1 (2009): 52–53.
18 Blaine McKinley, "'The Quagmires of Necessity': American Anarchists and Dilemmas of Vocation," *American Quarterly* 34, no. 5 (1982): 503.

sent, they remained torn between the simpler past and the possible future."[19] However, and regardless of the political demands of her own political movement, Goldman could also observe a kind of anarcho-sexism, which was often expressed by male comrades who demanded equality and freedom, but only for men.[20] Or as Goldman herself worded it: "Even radials do not differ from the christians [sic]; they do not wish their wives to become radical; even they deem themselves necessary to her protection."[21] For the female anarchist, it was important that women gained emancipation from exploitative marriage structures and thereby sexual emancipation as well to become an essential part of the anarchist revolution of the future.[22] Donna M. Kowal, who studied Goldman's anarcha-feminist positions in great detail, highlights the feminist elements in her political agenda, as "Goldman's approach to anarchism emphasised the economic and psychosocial necessity of emancipating women, which she believed could only the accomplished through anarchism's ability to transcend artificial differences and class divisions between women and men."[23] Regardless of such views, Goldman also struggled with her political demands as they rarely tallied with her own life, in which the anarchist, e.g. in her relationship with Ben Reitman, remained what feminist Goldman biographer Alice Wexler called a "slave to sexual passion,"[24] seemingly unable to live up to her own ideals.[25]

The present chapter is nevertheless interested in Goldman's views on marriage and sexual liberation. While the former was considered to be an instrument of suppression, the latter, for the anarchist Goldman, meant a form of liberation of the female body and the female mind. After a short elaboration of Goldman's anarcha-feminist identity, this chapter will consequently take a closer look at her discourses about marriage and her ideas about the sexual liberation of women. It will thereby show that her thoughts about emancipation were quite ahead of her time and that freedom was one of the values Goldman would only consider and

---

19 Ibid., 503–504.
20 Lucy Nicholas, "Gender and Sexuality," in *The Palgrave Handbook of Anarchism*, eds. Carl Levy and Matthew S. Adams (Cham: Palgrave Macmillan, 2019), 605.
21 Emma Goldman, "The New Woman," *Free Society*, February 13, 1898, 2, in *Emma Goldman: A Documentary History of the American Years*, vol. 1: *Made for America, 1890–1901*, eds. Candace Falk et al. (Urbana/Chicago, IL: University of Illinois Press, 2008), 322.
22 On Goldman's concept of an anarchist revolution, see Frank Jacob, "An Anarchist Revolution? Emma Goldman as an Intellectual Revolutionary," *Journal for the Study of Radicalism* 15, no. 2 (2021), forthcoming.
23 Kowal, "Anarcha-Feminism," 274.
24 Wexler, *Emma Goldman*, 160.
25 Ferguson, "Gender and Genre," 735.

accept in its most total form and if applied or available for all, men and women alike.

Emma Goldman: An Early Anarcha-Feminist

Goldman was active in numerous ways: she was an anarchist revolutionary, but she also fought for the right of abortion, she was an anarchist, but also a proto-feminist. It is consequently appropriate consider one of her many different identities to be an anarcha-feminist one.[26] Kowal emphasized that "anarcha-feminists presented an alternative model of womanhood" and that

> Within the anarchist political and intellectual milieu of the late nineteenth and early twentieth centuries, anarcha-feminism emerged as a distinct, albeit loosely formed, 'school of thought' that was reflected in the transnational activism of anarchist women ... [who] tended to interpret the anarchist critique of authority through the lens of their experiences as women, especially constraints resulting from sexual double standards and the gendered division of labor.[27]

The label "anarcha-feminist" as such was, however, not used by these women themselves but later introduced by researchers who studied their cases.[28] It must nevertheless be seen as a consequence of the exclusion of women from political and public affairs, something that was not only criticized by female anarchists during the late 19th and early 20th centuries.[29] The stand against discrimination and for full emancipation nevertheless, as in other national contexts as well, led to a struggle within the predominantly male political movements, be they anarchist or socialist.[30]

---

[26] For a discussion of Goldman's different identities see Jacob, *Emma Goldman and the Russian Revolution*, 17–46 and the forthcoming Frank Jacob, *Emma Goldman: Die Identitäten einer Anarchistin* (Berlin: Hentrich & Hentrich, 2021).
[27] Kowal, "Anarcha-Feminism," 265.
[28] Ibid., 266.
[29] For a different example in the US context see Jowan A. Mohammed, "Mary Hunter Austin und die Forderungen nach einer Vernderung der Geschlechterrollen in den USA, 1914–1918," in *Geschlecht und Klassenkampf: Die "Frauenfrage" aus deutscher und internationaler Perspektive im 19. und 20. Jahrhundert*, eds. Vincent Streichhahn and Frank Jacob (Berlin: Metropol, 2020), 222–239.
[30] For a recent analysis of this question within German social democracy, see Vincent Streichhahn, "Zur 'Frauenfrage' und Sozialdemokratie im deutschen Kaiserreich Zwischen Antifeminismus und Emanzipation," in *Geschlecht und Klassenkampf: Die "Frauenfrage" aus deutscher und*

At the same time, "anarcha-feminist thought is not uniform"³¹ but as diverse as anarchism itself.³² Although the anarcha-feminists were also quite different with regard to their upbringing, social background, and the arguments they used, they were unified by "[r]ejecting compulsory marriage and motherhood, [and] they sought to enact their unconventional ideas of autonomous living and sexual agency."³³ Their aim was consequently to change the existent social order and gender norms alike, and it is no surprise that the "early anarchist feminist focus was on the rejection of state-sanctioned marriage but also on the imagination and prefiguration of alternative, non-dominative gender and sexual relations such as ideals of free love."³⁴ This does not, however, mean that there was no struggle among the anarcha-feminists, who would criticize each other. Voltairine de Cleyre (1866–1912),³⁵ for example, criticized Goldman for living off and not for the anarchist movement,³⁶ although the latter used hardly any money she made for her personal life, instead reinvesting most of her income from lectures into publications of friends and herself to support the anarchist movement further.³⁷

New York, where Goldman would start her activities as an anarchist speaker, was more than a metropolis of the United States in the late 19th century; it was a melting pot for anarchist immigrant communities from Germany, Italy, Czarist Russia, and other places,³⁸ whose ideas about "abolitionism, free thought, and the labor movement" were exchanged as they "were troubled by the economic inequalities, centralized power, and mass society they saw arising at the expense

---

internationaler Perspektive im 19. und 20. Jahrhundert, eds. Vincent Streichhahn and Frank Jacob (Berlin: Metropol, 2020), 48–77.
31 Kowal, "Anarcha-Feminism," 267.
32 Benjamin Franks, Nathan Jun and Leonard Williams, eds., *Anarchism: A Conceptual Approach* (New York/London: Routledge, 2018); Sean Sheehan, *Anarchism* (London: Reaktion, 2003).
33 Kowal, "Anarcha-Feminism," 275.
34 Nicholas, "Gender and Sexuality," 606–607.
35 Eugenia C. DeLamotte, *Gates of Freedom: Voltairine de Cleyre and the Revolution of the Mind* (Ann Arbor, MI: University of Michigan Press, 2004); Sharon Presley and Crispin Sartwell, *Exquisite Rebel: The Essays of Voltairine De Cleyre—Anarchist, Feminist, Genius* (Albany, NY: State University of New York Press, 2005).
36 Voltairine de Cleyre to Saul Yanovsky, October 18, 1910, Ishill Papers, Joseph Ishill Papers, Houghton Library, Harvard University; Voltairine de Cleyre to Joseph Cohen, October 26, 1910, Joseph Cohen Papers, Bund Archives of the Jewish Labor Movement, YIVO Archives, New York. Both letters are cited in McKinley, "The Quagmires," 519.
37 Ibid., 512 and 519–520.
38 Kenyon Zimmer, *Immigrants against the State: Yiddish and Italian Anarchism in America* (Urbana, IL: Illinois University Press, 2015).

of local self-sufficiency and personal initiative."³⁹ Especially for Jewish immigrants, America did not fulfill the expectations for a better life than the one they had left behind in Central and Eastern Europe, a region French historians Alain Brossat and Sylvia Klingberg referred to as "revolutionary Yiddishland"⁴⁰ and which Goldman had also intended to leave behind for a better life with her sister Helena in America.⁴¹ She described her own transformation in relation to the changing of her dreams, especially with regard to the harsh US experience later, as follows:

> Naturally, life presents itself in different forms to different ages. Between the age of eight and twelve I dreamed of becoming a Judith. I longed to avenge the sufferings of my people, the Jews, to cut off the head of their Holofernos. When I was fourteen I wanted to study medicine, so as to be able to help my fellow-beings. When I was fifteen I suffered from unrequited love, and I wanted to commit suicide in a romantic way by drinking a lot of vinegar. I thought that would make me look ethereal and interesting, very pale and poetic when in my grave, but at sixteen I decided on a more exalted death. I wanted to dance myself to death. ... Then came America, with its huge factories, the pedalling of a machine for ten hours a day at two dollars fifty a week.⁴²

For Jewish immigrants like Goldman, the United States represented the same misery they had tried to escape, and there was almost no difference with regard to poverty and sorrow.⁴³ When the female anarchist compared the lives of the Jewish immigrants in the "New World" with their former one in Europe, there was nothing much to cheer about: "There [in Russa] he must work like a galley slave whether he will or no. Here he is free—free to starve, free to be robbed and swindled on every hand. But the moment he seeks to organize labor, or assert his

---

39 McKinley, "The Quagmires," 504.
40 Alain Brossat and Sylvia Klingberg, *Revolutionary Yiddishland: A History of Jewish Radicalism*, trans. David Fernbach (London/New York: Verso, 2016). On the Jewish radical community in New York, also see Tony Michels, *A Fire in Their Hearts: Yiddish Socialists in New York* (Cambridge, MA/London: Harvard University Press, 2005); Frank Jacob, "Radical Trinity. Anarchist, Jew, or New Yorker?" in *Jewish Radicalisms: Historical Perspectives on a Phenomenon of Global Modernity*, eds. Frank Jacob and Sebastian Kunze (Berlin: De Gruyter Oldenbourg, 2019), 153–180.
41 Kowal remarks that Goldman "immigrated to the United States in 1886 to fell a restrictive Orthodox life." Kowal, "Anarcha-Feminism," 273.
42 Goldman, "An Anarchist Looks at Life," 4–5.
43 "A Woman Anarchist," *Pittsburgh Leader*, November 22, 1896, in *Emma Goldman: A Documentary History of the American Years*, vol. 1: *Made for America, 1890–1901*, eds. Candace Falk et al. (Urbana/Chicago, IL: University of Illinois Press, 2008), 243–244.

rights or strike for the defense of his dearest interests he is no longer free, but is apprehended and thrown in prison."⁴⁴

What must be understood here is that Goldman turned into an anarchist in the United States, meaning that her radical ideas and her identity as an anarchist were American in origin. When she was a young female in Russia, she dreamed of the land of opportunities: "There was still America, the gloriously free land where one is free to develop and to grow. The reception given immigrants even to-day is enough to outrage one's sensibilities, but forty years ago the treatment meted out of the people who pilgrimmed to America as to the promised land was so utterly appalling that it helped to deepen my hatred of man's inhumanity to man."⁴⁵ After a failed marriage⁴⁶ and her own "inauguration into the economic life in the States," due to which she had to work hard to make ends meet at the factory, she experienced "harsh treatment, [when the workers were] driven like slaves." And, almost natually, her "whole being rebelled"⁴⁷ against this form of unjust exploitation, as it was showing Goldman "how utterly corrupt and unscrupulous are those who grow rich on the toil of others. It also increased my contempts for the system which grinds human beings into gold dust."⁴⁸ In addition to this event, it was the Haymarket Tragedy⁴⁹—when anarchists were tried and executed based on suspicions but without any proof of being involved in a bomb attack on the police in Chicago in 1886— that "gave [her] feeling, form, and reality."⁵⁰ Goldman later claimed that "[t]he colossal crime of the State of Illinois, the bloodthirstiness of the press, the madness from [the] pulpit, and platform, the whole brutal business made a conscious Anarchist of me"⁵¹ and that "[t]he death of those Chicago martyrs was my spiritual birth: their ideal became the motive of my entire life."⁵² All in all, these events and experiences would turn the young immigrant into an anarchist, and after her deportation from the US in December 1919, she would continue to argue that "the exploitation of the masses is nowh[e]re quite so intensive as in

---

44 Ibid., 244.
45 Emma Goldman, "Why I am an Anarchist," n.d., EGP-IISH, No. 191, 2–3.
46 Deportation Hearings of Alexander Berkman and Emma Goldman, Stenographer's Minutes, December 8, 1919, Alexander Berkman Papers, Tamiment Library and Robert F. Wagner Labor Archives, New York University, New York City, NY, United States of America (henceforth ABP-TAM), TAM.067, Box 1, Folder 3, 28 and 30.
47 Ibid., 3.
48 Ibid.
49 Paul Avrich, *The Haymarket Tragedy* (Princeton, NJ: Princeton University Press, 1984).
50 Goldman, "Why I am an Anarchist," 3.
51 Ibid.
52 Goldman, "An Anarchist Looks at Life," 5.

the United States."⁵³ For the anarchist, it was obvious that the people there needed to embrace anarchist ideas to overcome the existent systemic problems because "[p]ower over others corrupts, brutalises and destroys the sense of proportion. It makes for conflict, strife and disintegration."⁵⁴

In contrast to many unknown anarchists⁵⁵ who were not as popular as Goldman or her lifelong companion Alexander Berkman (1870–1936), she could later afford to leave this hard experience of being exploited behind her to focus on her anarchist works as a publisher of the journal *Mother Earth*. At the same time, however, Goldman would be perceived as a dangerous woman, as the "dominant personality among American anarchists,"⁵⁶ and as a threat to the existent political and social order. When Berkman attempted to assassinate Henry Clay Frick (1849–1919), "the man responsible for the violence against striking workers at the Carnegie steel mills in Homestead, Pennsylvania"⁵⁷ in 1892, Goldman, who in general did not favor the use of violence, defended Berkman's decision, because "it was his belief that if the capitalists used Winchester rifles and bayonets on workingmen they should be answered with dynamite."⁵⁸ Berkman was nevertheless sentenced to spend 22 years in prison, but was released after 14 in 1906.⁵⁹ The moment he was able to leave prison, as Berkman described it,

> was a moment of supreme joy when I felt the heavy chains, that had bound me so long, give way with the final clang of the iron doors behind me and I suddenly found myself transported, as it were, from the dreary night of my prison-existence into the warm sunshine of the living day; and then, as I breathed the free air of the beautiful May morning—my first breath of freedom in fourteen years—it seemed to me as if a beautiful nature had waved her magic wand and marshalled her most alluring charms to welcome me into the world again.⁶⁰

---

53 Emma Goldman, "Good and Evil points in the Makeup of America," n.d. [1924], EGP-IISH, No. 189, 3.
54 Emma Goldman, "Anarchism and What It Really Stands For," n.d., EGP-IISH, No. 191, 5¹ᐟ².
55 On the different types of anarchists according to four categories related to their income and living conditions, see McKinley, "The Quagmires," 505.
56 Ibid., 516.
57 Ferguson, "Discourses of Danger," 744.
58 "Goldman's Cry Against Society," *Pittsburgh Post*, November 27, 1896, in *Emma Goldman: A Documentary History of the American Years*, vol. 1: *Made for America, 1890–1901*, eds. Candace Falk et al. (Urbana/Chicago, IL: University of Illinois Press, 2008), 249.
59 Alexander Berkman, *Prison Memoirs of an Anarchist* (New York: Mother Earth Publishing, 1912).
60 Alexander Berkman, "A Greeting," *Mother Earth* 1, no. 4 (1906), accessed October 17, 2019, http://dwardmac.pitzer.edu/Anarchist_Archives/goldman/ME/mev1n4.html.

Regardless of his time spent in prison, Berkman immediately joined the anarchist movement again and supported Goldman in her work for *Mother Earth*. The latter took the release of her friend as a reason to sum up the causes and events of 1892 for their readers:

> In looking over the events of 1892 and the causes that led up to the act of Alexander Berkman, one beholds Mammon seated upon a throne built of human bodies, without a trace of sympathy on its Gorgon brow for the creatures it controls. These victims bent and worn, with the reflex of the glow of the steel and iron furnaces in their haggard faces, carry their sacrificial offerings to the ever-insatiable monster, capitalism. In its greed, however, it reaches out for more; it neither sees the gleam of hate in the sunken eyes of its slaves, nor can it hear the murmurs of discontent and rebellion coming forth from their heaving breasts. Yet, discontent continues until one day it raises its mighty voice and demands to be heard: Human conditions! higher pay![61]

Goldman intended to use *Mother Earth* to awaken the political consciousness of the readers, who might get in contact with anarchist ideas for the first time. And it was her most important project, once she had decided to fully invest all her energy and financial capacity in this journal. In 1905, a year before *Mother Earth* was founded, Goldman had "borrowed money to open a facial and scalp massage parlor for middle-class, 'professional' women."[62] The parlor went well, and the anarchist Goldman made a profit for the first time. Maybe this was one reason for her to give up this opportunity when she was able to establish her own journal the next year. Finally, "[b]y earning her livelihood from the movement itself, she avoided the problems of a double life which had troubled her."[63] Although Goldman herself was never truly the "modern woman" she considered herself to be, *Mother Earth* was supposed to act as a platform of all kinds of anarchist ideas and to provide a possibility for the exchange of different views on society.[64] Goldman and Berkman themselves later formulated the raison d'être of *Mother Earth* as follows:

> As to the original *raison d'etre* of MOTHER EARTH, it was, first of all, to create a medium for the free expression of our ideas, a medium bold, defiant, and unafraid. That she has proved to the fullest, for neither friend nor foe has been able to gag her. Secondly, MOTHER EARTH was to serve as a gathering point, as it were, for those, who, struggling to free themselves from the absurdities of the Old, had not yet reached firm footing Suspended between heav-

---

61 E.[mma] G.[oldman], "Alexander Berkman," *Mother Earth* 1, no. 3 (1906), accessed October 17, 2019, http://www.gutenberg.org/files/27262/27262-h/27262-h.htm#Page_22.
62 McKinley, "The Quagmires," 517.
63 Ibid.
64 Ferguson, "Gender and Genre," 743–744.

en and hell, they have found in MOTHER EARTH the anchor of life. Thirdly, to infuse new blood into Anarchism, which—in America—had then been running at low ebb for quite some time. All these purposes, it may be said impartially, the magazine has served faithfully and well.[65]

Goldman used her journal to confront existent gender and social norms, as well as for political criticism of the US government. Referencing Michel Foucault, Kathy E. Ferguson called her "bold confrontations with authorities" acts of "anarchist parrhesia, fearless speech, a relentless truth-telling practice that risked her own security in pursuit of her 'beautiful ideal.'"[66]

One of the other aspects Goldman reflected upon in *Mother Earth* was the "Tragedy of Women's Emancipation."[67] She wanted to point out why women should have the same liberties as men and why equality was a precondition for true emancipation. Goldman emphasized that "[p]eace and harmony between the sexes, and individuals does not necessarily depend on a superficial equalization of human beings; nor does it call for the elimination of individual traits or peculiarities. The problem that confronts us, to-day, and which the nearest future is to solve, is how to be oneself, and yet in oneness with others, to feel deeply with all human beings and still retain one's own innate qualities."[68] The anarchist Goldman demanded that female emancipation should not be considered as a hostile project for society, because "man and woman can meet without antagonism and opposition. *The motto should, not be forgive one another; it should be, understand one another.*"[69]

It was emancipation that was supposed to "make it possible for [women] to be human in the truest sense," but to achieve it, "all artificial barriers should be broken and the road towards greater freedom cleared of every trace of centuries of submission and slavery."[70] The tragedy with regard to previous emancipation attempts, however, was clearly visible for Goldman, as

---

65 Emma Goldman and Alexander Berkman, "Our Sixth Birthday," *Mother Earth* 6, no. 1 (1911), accessed February 26, 2020, http://dwardmac.pitzer.edu/Anarchist_Archives/goldman/ME/mev6n1.html.
66 Ferguson, "Discourses of Danger," 738. For Foucault's text see Michel Foucault, *Fearless Speech*, ed. Joseph Pearson (Los Angeles: Semiotext(e), 2001), 19.
67 Emma Goldman, "Tragedy of Women's Emancipation," *Mother Earth* 1, no. 1 (1906): 9–17, http://dwardmac.pitzer.edu/Anarchist_Archives/goldman/ME/mev1n1.html#tra.
68 Ibid.
69 Ibid. My emphasis.
70 Ibid.

> the results so far achieved have isolated woman and have robbed her of the fountain springs of that happiness which is so essential to her. Merely external emancipation has made of the modern woman an artificial being …; anything except the forms which would be reached by the expression of their own inner qualities. Such artificially grown plants of the female sex are to be found in large numbers, especially in the so-called intellectual sphere of our life.[71]

Consequently, Goldman argued that "the emancipation of woman, as interpreted and practically applied to-day, has failed to reach that great end [i.e. true freedom and equality]. Now, woman is confronted with the necessity of emancipation from emancipation, if she really desires to be free. This may sound paradoxical, but is, nevertheless, only too true."[72] While "economic equality" could have been achieved in some professions, "[v]ery few [women] ever succeed, for it is a fact that women doctors, lawyers, architects and engineers are neither met with the same confidence, nor do they receive the same remuneration."[73]

The achievements of emancipation were consequently not good enough to have fully freed women from the suppression of the patriarchy, and Goldman would therefore criticize it by calling the previous emancipation a tragedy for women:

> The narrowness of the existing conception of woman's independence and emancipation; the dread of love for a man who is not her social equal; the fear that love will rob her of her freedom and independence, the horror that love or the joy of motherhood will only hinder her in the full exercise of her profession—all these together make of the emancipated modern woman a compulsory vestal, before whom life, with its great clarifying sorrows and its deep, entrancing joys, rolls on without touching or gripping her soul.[74]

In a letter to Berkman on 4 September 1925, i.e. almost 20 years later, Goldman would again emphasize the "tragedy of all of us modern women," which for her was based on the "fact that we are removed only by a very short period from our traditions, the traditions of being loved, cared for, protected, secured, and above all, the time when women could look forward to an old age of children, a home and someone to brighten their lives." For Goldman, it was clear that "[t]he modern woman cannot be the wife and mother in the old sense, and the new medium has not yet been devised, I mean the way of being wife, mother, friend and yet

---

71 Ibid.
72 Ibid.
73 Ibid.
74 Ibid.

retain one's complete freedom. Will it ever?"⁷⁵ Two aspects were essential for Goldman's view that emancipation had failed, namely the continuation of traditional means of patriarchic control, i.e. marriage, and the lack of sexual freedom for women. These two aspects shall now be taken into closer consideration.

Against Marriage

The continuation of the traditional views on marriage was, from Goldman's point of view, based on "the twin fantasies of protection and social mobility through [it]."⁷⁶ Women should rather be revolutionary and contest the contemporary perspective on marriage. Although such demands would also arouse criticism from her male anarchist comrades, Goldman did not back away from her demand that a true emancipation of women also needed to contest the existent idea of marriage. As Clare Hemmings, professor of feminist theory at the London School of Economics, worded it, "[f]or Goldman, marriage is the basis of private property and the particular oppression of women."⁷⁷ Marriage had turned out to be often nothing more than "an economic arrangement, an insurance pact"⁷⁸ for women, who were exploited in their marriage as they were as workers in the factories. Women would be dependent on men for the rest of their lives and doomed to live a life as parasite-like creatures, unable to achieve true freedom and equality as individuals.⁷⁹

In an article for *Firebrand* in 1897, Goldman expressed her views on marriage quite outspokenly: "From its very birth, up to our present day, men and women groan under the iron yoke of our marriage institution, and there seems to be no relief, no way out of it."⁸⁰ The relationship between women and men had been diminished to a capitalist form of exploitation because, as Goldman continued in her evaluation, "marriage relations, are the foundation of private property, ergo,

---

75 Letter to Alexander Berkman, September 4, 1925, in *Nowhere at Home: Letters from Exile of Emma Goldman and Alexander Berkman*, eds. Richard Drinnon and Anna Maria Drinnon (New York: Schocken Books, 1975), 130–133, cited in Ferguson, "Gender and Genre," 736.
76 Clare Hemmings, "In the Mood for Revolution: Emma Goldman's Passion," *New Literary History* 43, no. 3 (2012): 527.
77 Clare Hemmings, "Sexual Freedom and the Promise of Revolution: Emma Goldman's Passion," *Feminist Review* 106 (2014): 49.
78 Emma Goldman, *Marriage and Love* (New York: Mother Earth Publishing, 1911), 4.
79 Ibid.
80 Emma Goldman, "Marriage," *Firebrand*, July 18, 1897, 2, in *Emma Goldman: A Documentary History of the American Years*, vol. 1: *Made for America, 1890–1901*, eds. Candace Falk et al. (Urbana/Chicago, IL: University of Illinois Press, 2008), 269.

the foundation of our cruel and inhuman system."[81] Goldman considered marriage to be a tool of patriarchic control as "[i]t always gives the man the right and power over his wife, not only over her body, but also over her actions, her wishes; in fact, over her whole life."[82] The relationship between men and women was not equal but privileged for the former, who could exploit the latter as mother and housewife. With regard to the two sexes, it was "[p]ublic opinion [that] separate[d] their rights and duties, their honor and dishonor very strictly from each other."[83] At the same time, women were not granted their individual freedom, especially with regard to sex: "The subject of sex is a sealed book to the girl, because she has been given to understand that it is impure, immoral and indecent to even mention the sex question."[84] Women who were married were kept sexually uneducated on purpose to limit them in their liberation as females who could feel sexual pleasure as well. In addition to this form of exploitation of their bodies, women were also exploited in marriage because such relationships could hardly be called equal:

> Both, the man and the girl, marry for the same purpose, with the only exception that the man is not expected to give up his individuality, his name, his independence, whereas the girl has to sell herself, body and soul, for the pleasure of being someone's wife; hence they do not stand on equal terms, and where, there is no equality there can be no harmony. The consequence is that shortly after the first few months, or to make all allowance possible, after the first year, both come to the conclusion that marriage is a failure.[85]

It was therefore obvious for Goldman early on that marriage was an essential part of the systemic exploitation of women. She therefore could not believe that "many emancipated women prefer marriage with all its deficiencies to the narrowness of an unmarried life; narrow and unendurable because of the chains of moral and social prejudice that cramp and bind her nature."[86] The tragedy for Goldman was based on the fact that many women did not understand the full "meaning of emancipation. They thought that all that was needed was independence from external tyrannies; the internal tyrants, far more harmful to life and growth, such as ethical and social conventions, were left to take care of themselves; and they have taken care of themselves."[87] Full emancipation could con-

---

81 Ibid.
82 Ibid.
83 Ibid., 270.
84 Ibid.
85 Ibid., 271.
86 Goldman, "Tragedy of Women's Emancipation."
87 Ibid.

sequently not be achieved as long as women continued to live according to old-fashioned and outdated traditions like marriage that would force them to give up their individual freedom. Goldman therefore argued: "Indeed if the partial emancipation is to become a complete and true emancipation of woman it will have to do away with the ridiculous notion that to be loved, to be sweetheart and mother, is synonymous [sic] with being slave or subordinate. It will have to do away with the absurd notion of the dualism of the sexes, or that man and woman represent two antagonistic worlds."[88] Only together were women and men able to become equal, and only together and without any hierarchy could both be truly free. Kathy E. Ferguson summed up this vision of the US anarchist as follows:

> For Goldman, love between two people should create an intensified microcosm of the more general relation between individuals and the community in a liberated society. She envisioned anarchist love as creating bonds between free individuals that would enhance rather than confine each person. Similarly, she envisioned an anarchist society as a voluntary community of free, self-directing individuals, where individual growth and empowerment are nurtured through collective life.[89]

Regardless of her many later political endeavors, Goldman never gave up the hope for an honest and full emancipation of women, but in her later years she would continue to lecture about "The Tragedy of the Modern Woman."[90]

Goldman outlined that women had achieved political rights in the past, but the course of history had shown "that woman in politics is by no means better than man and her right of suffrage has helped her as little as it did most men to overcome outworn political, social, or moral values."[91] In particular, since women had been unable to leave the limiting forces of tradition behind, they had been unable to fully free themselves. It was women who still kept worshipping men to a level of self-denial: "When she [the modern woman] loves the man, she turns him into a god and surrounds him with a sacred hallow. In her blind idolization she falls to see that her deity is but human, all too human. The poor fool knows only too well that he is far from the hero imagined by his mother, wife, daughter, or mistress."[92] Yet instead of freeing the woman, the modern man would exploit her in multiple ways. Goldman also accused the modern women for their blind obedience, as they "were the most ardent support-

---

88 Ibid.
89 Ferguson, "Gender and Genre," 751.
90 Emma Goldman, "The Tragedy of the Modern Woman," n.d., EGP-IISH, No. 266.
91 Ibid., 1.
92 Ibid., 3.

ers of war to the extent of using their sex charms and persuasion to drive the youth of the land into the trenches and death."[93] And regardless of the political rights the suffragette movement had been able to secure in the past, "woman's political equality with man has contributed precious little to her inner emancipation."[94] At the same time, she continued to point out that the exploitation of women was not limited to their private life but also with regard to their working conditions: "As to the great mass of working girls and women, how much independence is gained if the narrowness and lack of freedom of the home is exchanged for the narrowness and lack of freedom of the factory, sweat-shop, department store, or office?"[95] The tragedy of the modern woman was consequently an exploitation that existed in a twofold way and could only be overcome by a political and social change.

The working conditions of poor women made it relatively unsurprising "that hundreds of girls are so willing to accept the first offer of marriage, sick and tired of their 'independence',"[96] although this decision would only lead to another form of exploitation. This "so-called independence which leads only to earning the merest subsistence is not so enticing, not so ideal, that one could expect woman to sacrifice everything for it. Our highly praised independence is, after all, but a slow process of dulling and stifling woman's nature, her low need, and her mother instinct."[97] The possibility to live free and independent was eventually given up due to the circumstances of being economically exploited in a capitalist system. The fact that representatives of the women's movement, especially the suffragettes, accepted the continuation of this system in exchange for a small share of political power was another of the reasons Goldman identified with regard to the tragedy of the modern woman: "Every movement that aims at the destruction of existing institutions and the replacement thereof with something more advanced, more perfect had followers who in theory stand for the most radical ideas, but who, nevertheless, in their every-day practice, are like the average philistine, feigning respectability and clamoring for the good opinion of their opponents. The suffragist and feminist movements made no exception."[98]

A true and full emancipation, however, needed more than just political rights. It needed freedom and equality, the two pillars of Goldman's interpreta-

---

93 Ibid., 7.
94 Ibid., $8^{1/2}$.
95 Ibid., $13^{1/2}$.
96 Ibid.
97 Ibid., 14.
98 Ibid., $18^{1/2}$.

tion of anarchism. The modern man, as she argued, "still wants woman as his housekeeper and caretaker of his home and his children. But he wants her in modern clothes."[99] The modern woman, on the other hand, "lacks courage to be inwardly free. Even with herself she is not frank."[100] Women in general did still accept the existent social norms and were therefore "still swayed by sentimental considerations. [The modern woman] still has too many gods. The result is lack of concentration and sticktoitiveness so essential to every goal one wishes to reach."[101] For Goldman, it was consequently foolish women who would pave the way for men while they denied their own freedom: "woman has not yet learned to march to victory regardless of the defeat of those in her way. Hence she has not reached greatness."[102] What kept women from fully emancipating was the fear of losing men's interest in them because, as Goldman continued in her argument, "the higher the mental development of [the modern] woman, the less possible it is for her to meet a congenial mate who will see in her, not only sex, but also the human being, the friend, the comrade and strong individuality, who cannot and ought not lose a single trait of her character."[103] If women were unable to be loved for their individuality but solely because they could be exploited, they would never be free, and "[i]f love does not know how to give and take without restrictions, it is not love, but a transaction that never fails to lay stress on a plus and a minus."[104] The modern woman, who "is in need of unhampered growth out of old traditions and habits"[105] therefore must resist traditional role models and disobey social expectations like marriage. For Goldman, it was instead "necessary that women learn to accept themselves and to value themselves as beings possessing a worth at least equal to that of the other sex, instead of unthinkingly accepting standards based on masculine psychology."[106] All in all, it was and still is important for a successful emancipation to "do away with the absurd notion of the conflict of the sexes, or that man and woman represent two antagonistic worlds."[107] These considerations are still important today and, as emphasized before, "[o]nly if the microcosms of romantic love and interpersonal relationships are freed from all forms of male

---

99 Ibid., 22.
100 Ibid., 29.
101 Ibid., 30.
102 Ibid., 31.
103 Ibid., 33.
104 Ibid., $36^{1/2}$.
105 Ibid., 39.
106 Ibid., 40.
107 Ibid., 41.

domination and dominance could a better and freer society be created."[108] To achieve this aim, Goldman, however, did not only want to increase awareness of the problems related to marriage as a traditional tool of patriarchic control over women; she also wanted women to gain their freedom with regard to their own sexuality and the possibilities to experience sexual pleasure.

For Sexual Liberation

Goldman was familiar with the works of German sexologist Magnus Hirschfeld (1868–1935),[109] and she "admired the brave struggle [Hirschfeld] ha[d] made for the rights of people who, by their very nature, can not find sex expression in what is commonly called 'the normal way'."[110] Goldman was interested in sexuality, as she considered it an important part of women's liberation. Like the American poet Walt Whitman (1819–1892), the anarchist highlighted "the beauty and wholesomeness of sex ... freed from the rags and tatters of hypocrisy."[111] Goldman's "insistence that women's experiences and sexual freedom must be incorporated into the heart of any sustainable revolution"[112] consequently does not surprise, as her appeal to the feminists of the 1960s and 1970s seemed to be quite natural, given this element of the anarchist's revolutionary considerations. Sexual liberation would allow women to break out of the social system that kept them hostages and exploited them physically and mentally. Only a free form of sexual self-expression would allow women equality with men, freeing their identities from the mother roles they were supposed to imitate in their lives after having been forced into marriage by social pressure. Goldman therefore, as Clare Hemmings has pointed out, "consistently situate[s] sexuality in a broad political context of the sexual division of labour, the institutions of marriage and the church, consumerism, patriotism and productive (as well as repro-

---

108 Jacob, "Anarchismus, Ehe und Sex," 216.
109 For Hirschfeld's life and work, see Manfred Herzer, *Magnus Hirschfeld und seine Zeit* (Berlin: De Gruyter, 2017).
110 Emma Goldman, "A Refutation Addressed to Dr. Magnus Hirschfeld," Berlin 1923, EGP-IISH, No. 208, 1. Some years later, Goldman would also meet Hirschfeld in Paris. Magnus Hirschfeld to Emma Goldman, Paris, November 24, 1933, EGP-IISH, No. 98.
111 Emma Goldman, "Walt Whitman" (1916), in *The Emma Goldman Papers: A Microfilm Edition*, ed. Candace Falk with Ronald J. Zborayetal, reel 54 (Alexandria, VA: Chadwyck-Healey, 1990), 2, cited in Ferguson, "Gender and Genre," 747.
112 Hemmings, "Sexual Freedom," 44.

ductive) labour, [and] she frames sexual freedom as both the basis of new relationships between men and women and as a model for a new political future."[113]

To achieve freedom and equality, the basis and aim for Goldman's anarchist vision was important for sexual identity as well, because sexuality had to be separated from any form of capitalist exploitation to allow for a better, i.e. freer, life. While left intellectuals had been "suspicious of attention to desire and pleasure,"[114] Goldman embraced these aspects and made them an essential part of her political agenda. Beyond their daughter- or mother-identity, women should consider their sexuality and sexual pleasure as a way to express themselves as females, who should naturally not be restricted by traditional roles with regard to their desire. If sexuality continued to be considered as something unrelated to the suppression of women, it would not allow women to break the co-constitution of sexuality and labor and its impact on different ways of exploitation.[115] Sexual freedom was a precondition for every passionate revolutionary, and a famous episode from Goldman's life emphasizes that she would not accept being part of an unpassionate liberation movement:

> At the dances I was one of the most untiring and gayest. One evening a cousin of Sasha [Alexander Berkman], a young boy, took me aside. With a grave face, as if he were about to announce the death of a dear comrade, he whispered to me that it did not behoove an agitator to dance. Certainly not with such reckless abandon, anyway. It was undignified for one who was on the way to become a force in the anarchist movement. My frivolity would only hurt the Cause. I grew furious at the impudent interference of the boy. I told him to mind his own business, I was tired of having the Cause constantly thrown into my face. I did not believe that a Cause which stood for a beautiful ideal, for anarchism, for release and freedom from conventions and prejudice, should demand the denial of life and joy. I insisted that our Cause could not expect me to become a nun and that the movement should not be turned into a cloister. If it meant that, I did not want it. "I want freedom, the right to self-expression, everybody's right to beautiful, radiant things." Anarchism meant that to me, and I would live it in spite of the whole world—prisons, persecution, everything. Yes, even in spite of the condemnation of my own closest comrades I would live my beautiful ideal.[116]

---

113 Ibid.
114 Lisa Rofel, "Queer Positions, Queerying Asian Studies," *Positions* 20, no. 1 (2012): 185, cited in ibid., 46.
115 For a detailed discussion of this interrelationship, see Emma Goldman, *The White Slave Traffic* (New York: Mother Earth Publishing, 1909).
116 Emma Goldman, *Living My Life* (New York: Knopf, 1931), accessed December 17, 2018, https://www.theanarchistlibrary.org/library/emma-goldman-living-my-life, ch. 5.

This call for freedom included sexual freedom, as the life of women was one determined by "sorrow, misery [and] humiliation"[117] in relation to their sex. Hemmings emphasized how Goldman interpreted the co-dependency between sexuality and capitalist exploitation as follows:

> Goldman locates the economy of women's sexuality firmly within the means of production and the exploitation of surplus labour. Women are not only commodities themselves, but also producers of the next generation of exploitable labour, within the twin evils of capitalism and militarism. Not only is women's experience of sex and love one of ignorant misery, her reproductive labour is bound as to what President Roosevelt saw as a national duty to provide offspring for the nation.[118]

The capitalist exploitation of women made Goldman also realize that birth control was a form of empowerment for women, who could decide on their own when and how to have children, without dooming the next generation to become a cog in the machine of the overall capitalist exploitation mechanism.[119] The revolutionary transformation of society consequently needed a transformation of the idea of marriage, and related to this a reconsideration of female sexuality, especially by women themselves. She was not the only left intellectual who consequently considered the orgasm to be an experience of liberation.[120] The sexual revolution Goldman envisioned would have ended the inequality between men and women and instead would pave the way to a unification of the sexes in the struggle against capitalism and for a better future for all.

For Goldman, sex was "woven into every fabric of human life and lays its finger on every custom. To the debit side of the sex account we must charge many silly stupidities and some of the foulest injustices which go to make the thing we call human culture the amazing and variegated mosaic that it is."[121] She nevertheless demanded "the free sane acceptance of the human body, in all its faculties" because this acceptance presented "the master-key to the art of the future."[122] In contrast to men, women still suffered from all kinds of lim-

---

117 Goldman, "Marriage."
118 Hemmings, "Sexual Freedom," 50.
119 Emma Goldman, "The Social Aspects of Birth Control," *Mother Earth* 11, no. 2 (1916): 468–475.
120 Wilhem Reich, *Die Funktion des Orgasmus: Zur Psychopathologie und zur Soziologie des Geschlechtslebens* (Vienna: Internationaler Psychoanalytischer Verlag, 1927); Wilhelm Reich, *Die sexuelle Revolution: Zur charakterlichen Selbststeuerung des Menschen* (Frankfurt am Main: Fischer, 1966).
121 Emma Goldman, "The Element of Sex in Life," n.d., EGP-IISH, No. 213, 7–8.
122 Ibid., 12.

itations: "The man rarely starves sexually. The flourishing business of prostitution is proof for that."[123] It was traditions, like marriage, that demanded this kind of self-restriction for women because "[s]ociety demands that the young adult man and woman (especially woman) shall repress the sex-impulse for a number of years—often for the whole of their life."[124] The common opinion therefore emphasized that "[s]ex is disgraceful for nice girls,"[125] and young women were supposed to preserve their virginity for marriage instead of freeing their body and mind by experiencing sexual pleasure. While women consequently suffered from marriage and other role-model-related restrictions, "[m]ost men are brought up to believe that woman must be taken and not give herself gladly and joyously in love and passion. That also prevents the more sensitive of the male species to give themselves freely—they are afraid to outrage and shock the sensibilities and innocence of their wives."[126]

As long as sex was supposed to be a taboo for women and not a pleasure to enjoy, there was neither a chance for emancipation nor one for a revolution that could change society as a whole. Or, as Goldman worded it with regard to the negative impact of sexual restrictions:

> Take frigidity in some women largely due to the deadening effect of the sex taboo. Such women cannot even if they try desperately respond to the sex urge in the man. In fact, the very thought of the sexual embrace to such women is torture. Even if the man lacks refinement and imposes his needs on his wife he will find no satisfaction. In the end he seeks gratification elsewhere. There is quite a percentage of married men among the clientele of prostitution. Sex is more powerful than all decisions. The man will grow indifferent and in the end insist on divorce.[127]

Goldman consequently asked for an unlimited and unconditional sexual liberation for women: "Let us get rid of the mock modesty so prevalent on the surface of polite society, let us liberate sex from falsehood and degradation."[128] It is unfortunate that this liberation has not yet been achieved and that countless women around the world still suffer from the same exploitation of their sexuality with regard to labor-related and marriage-related exploitation by capitalism and men alike.

---

123 Ibid., 14.
124 Ibid., 15.
125 Ibid., 21.
126 Ibid., 24.
127 Ibid., 26–27.
128 Ibid., 50.

Conclusion

Emma Goldman, as a strong anarchist woman, "wanted a world without jealousy, insecurity, or possessiveness, and she fought those feelings in herself, with limited success."[129] Having experienced the exploitation of women in the US garment industry as well as a rather unsuccessful marriage, she knew how hard it was for female workers and wives to gain equality and freedom. Goldman therefore dedicated her political struggle as an anarchist toward a revolution that would free women and men alike, because only as equal partners would they be able to change the world. When Goldman fought against the traditional idea of marriage, as it had been representing the yoke that prevented women from liberation, she without any doubt fought against the exploitation of the idea of love as a precondition for human relationships, but not love as such. Goldman loved her life, and she wanted women to love themselves as well. A free sexual experience of love and pleasure was important for the passionate revolutionary, as it was essential for the female anarchist that the individual freedom of women was not limited by antiquated and outdated models of companionship, i.e. marriage.

However, many of her demands came too early, and Goldman would not live long enough to witness the consequences of some of her demands in later years. Yet, when she wrote to Rose Pesotta, an anarcha-feminist union organizer and vice-president of the International Ladies Garment Workers Union, in 1935, Goldman had not given up her hope that the anarchist movement would eventually be able to trigger change: "Yes, our movement is in a bad state. The old ones have either died out or have become hoary with age. And the young ones are in the Communist ranks. There is unfortunately no one who could gather them up even if they were interested in our ideas. My only consolation is the certainty that the present trend to dictatorship is not for all times. Our ideas will have their day in the world court, though I may not live to see it. You are so much younger, you probably will."[130] The fact that Goldman's writings were revived in the second half of the 20th century and continue to appeal to feminists all over the world even today highlights how important her ideas were with regard to true emancipation based on freedom and equality. One can therefore only hope that Goldman's demands will eventually be addressed in the 21st century, liberating women and men alike to face the causes for the existence of sorrow and misery in the world: exploitation and inequality, which is unfortunately still, around a century after Goldman expressed her thoughts, a gender inequality.

---

129 Ferguson, "Gender and Genre," 751.
130 Emma Goldman to Rose Pesotta, Montreal, March 7, 1935, EGP-IISH, No. 129, 2.

Works Cited

Unpublished Sources

International Insitute for Social History, Amsterdam, The Netherlands

Emma Goldman Papers

Tamiment Library and Robert F. Wagner Labor Archives, New York University, New York City, NY, United States of America

Alexander Berkman Papers, TAM.067

Published Primary and Secondary Works

"A Woman Anarchist." In *Emma Goldman. A Documentary History of the American Years*, vol. 1: *Made for America, 1890–1901*, edited by Candace Falk et al., 243–246. Urbana/Chicago, IL: Illinois University Press, 2008.

"Goldman's Cry Against Society." In *Emma Goldman: A Documentary History of the American Years*, vol. 1: *Made for America, 1890–1901*, edited by Candace Falk et al., 249. Urbana/Chicago, IL: University of Illinois Press, 2008.

Avrich, Paul. *The Haymarket Tragedy*. Princeton, NJ: Princeton University Press, 1984.

Avrich, Paul and Karen Avrich. *Sasha and Emma: The Anarchist Odyssey of Alexander Berkman and Emma Goldman*. Cambridge, MA: Harvard University Press, 2012.

Berkman, Alexander. "A Greeting." *Mother Earth* 1, no. 4 (1906). Accessed October 17, 2019. http://dwardmac.pitzer.edu/Anarchist_Archives/goldman/ME/mev1n4.html.

Berkman, Alexander. *Prison Memoirs of an Anarchist*. New York: Mother Earth, 1912.

Brossat, Alain and Sylvia Klingberg. *Revolutionary Yiddishland: A History of Jewish Radicalism*. Translated by David Fernbach. London/New York: Verso, 2016.

DeLamotte, Eugenia C. *Gates of Freedom: Voltairine de Cleyre and the Revolution of the Mind*. Ann Arbor, MI: University of Michigan Press, 2004.

Drinnon, Richard. *Rebel in Paradise: A Biography of Emma Goldman*. Phoenix edition. Chicago: University of Chicago Press, 1982 [1961].

Drinnon, Richard and Anna Maria Drinnon, eds. *Nowhere at Home: Letters from Exile of Emma Goldman and Alexander Berkman*. New York: Schocken Books, 1975.

Falk, Candace. *Love, Anarchy, and Emma Goldman*. Rev. ed. New Brunswick, NJ: Rutgers University Press, 1990 [1984].

Falk, Candace et al., eds. *Emma Goldman: A Documentary History of the American Years*, vol. 1: *Made for America, 1890–1901*. Urbana/Chicago, IL: University of Illinois Press, 2008.

Ferguson, Kathy E. "Discourses of Danger: Locating Emma Goldman." *Political Theory* 36, no. 5 (2008): 735–761.

Ferguson, Kathy E. "Gender and Genre in Emma Goldman." *Signs* 36, no. 3 (2011): 733–757.

Foucault, Michel. *Fearless Speech*. Edited by Joseph Pearson. Los Angeles: Semiotext(e), 2001.
Franks, Benjamin, Nathan Jun and Leonard Williams, eds. *Anarchism: A Conceptual Approach*. New York/London: Routledge, 2018.
G.[oldman], E.[mma]. "Alexander Berkman." *Mother Earth* 1, no. 3 (1906): 22 – 24. Accessed October 17, 2019. http://www.gutenberg.org/files/27262/27262-h/27262-h.htm#Page_22.
Goldman, Emma. *Living My Life*. New York: Knopf, 1931. Accessed December 17, 2018. https://theanarchistlibrary.org/library/emma-goldman-living-my-life.
Goldman, Emma. "Marriage." In *Emma Goldman: A Documentary History of the American Years*, vol. 1: *Made for America, 1890 – 1901*, edited by Candace Falk et al., 269 – 273. Urbana/Chicago, IL: Illinois University Press, 2008.
Goldman, Emma. *Marriage and Love*. New York: Mother Earth, 1911.
Goldman, Emma. "The New Woman." In *Emma Goldman: A Documentary History of the American Years*, vol. 1: *Made for America, 1890 – 1901*, edited by Candace Falk et al., 322 – 323. Urbana/Chicago, IL: Illinois University Press, 2008.
Goldman, Emma. "The Social Aspects of Birth Control." *Mother Earth* 11, no. 2 (1916): 468 – 475
Goldman, Emma. "The Tragedy of Women's Emancipation." *Mother Earth* 1, no. 1 (1906): 9 – 18, http://dwardmac.pitzer.edu/Anarchist_Archives/goldman/ME/mev1n1.html#tra.
Goldman, Emma. *The White Slave Traffic*. New York: Mother Earth, 1909.
Goldman, Emma. "Walt Whitman. 1916. " In *The Emma Goldman Papers: A Microfilm Edition*, edited by Candace Falk with Ronald J. Zborayetal, reel 54. Alexandria, VA: Chadwyck-Healey, 1990.
Goldman, Emma. "What Is There in Anarchy for Woman?" In *Emma Goldman: A Documentary History of the American Years*, vol. 1: *Made for America, 1890 – 1901*, edited by Candace Falk et al., 289 – 292. Urbana/Chicago, IL: Illinois University Press, 2008.
Goldman, Emma and Alexander Berkman. "Our Sixth Birthday." *Mother Earth* 6, no. 1 (1911). Accessed February 26, 2020. http://dwardmac.pitzer.edu/Anarchist_Archives/goldman/ME/mev6n1.html.
Gornick, Vivian. *Emma Goldman: Revolution as a Way of Life*. New Haven, CT: Yale University Press, 2011.
Haaland, Bonnie. *Emma Goldman: Sexuality and the Impurity of the State*. Montréal et al.: Black Rose Books, 1993.
Hemmings, Clare. "In the Mood for Revolution: Emma Goldman's Passion." *New Literary History* 43, no. 3 (2012): 527 – 545.
Hemmings, Clare. "Sexual Freedom and the Promise of Revolution: Emma Goldman's Passion." *Feminist Review* 106 (2014): 43 – 59.
Herzer, Manfred. *Magnus Hirschfeld und seine Zeit*. Berlin: De Gruyter, 2017.
Ishill, Joseph. *Emma Goldman: A Challenging Rebel*. Berkeley Heights, NJ: Oriole Press, 1957.
Jacob, Frank. "An Anarchist Revolution? Emma Goldman as an Intellectual Revolutionary." *Journal for the Study of Radicalism* 15, no. 2 (2021). Forthcoming.
Jacob, Frank. "Anarchism and the Perversion of the Russian Revolution: The Accounts of Emma Goldman and Alexander Berkman." *Diacronie* 33, no. 1 (2018): https://doi.org/10.4000/diacronie.7405.
Jacob, Frank. "Anarchismus, Ehe und Sex: Emma Goldman (1869 – 1940) als Anarcha-Feministin." In *Geschlecht und Klassenkampf: Die "Frauenfrage" aus deutscher*

und internationaler Perspektive im 19. und 20. Jahrhundert, edited by Vincent Streichhahn and Frank Jacob., 202–221. Berlin: Metropol, 2020.

Jacob, Frank. "Anarchistische Imperialismuskritik und staatliche Repression: Emma Goldman, Alexander Berkman und die Kritik an der politischen Ökonomie des Ersten Weltkrieges in den USA, 1917–1919." *Prokla* 50, no. 201 (2020): 681–695.

Jacob, Frank. "Der Anarchismus und die Russische Revolution – Emma Goldman und Alexander Berkman im Kampf gegen den Bolschewismus." *Ne znam: Zeitschrift für Anarchismusforschung* 7 (2018): 3–66.

Jacob, Frank. *Emma Goldman and the Russian Revolution: From Admiration to Frustration* Berlin: De Gruyter, 2020.

Jacob, Frank. *Emma Goldman: Die Identitäten einer Anarchistin*. Berlin: Hentrich & Hentrich, 2021.

Jacob, Frank. *Emma Goldman: Ein Leben für die Freiheit*. Berlin: Hentrich & Hentrich, 2021.

Jacob, Frank. "Emma Goldmans Blick auf Bolschewismus, Faschismus und Nationalsozialismus: Eine anarchistische Perspektive auf den Totalitarismus der 1920er- und 1930er-Jahre." *Zeitschrift für Geschichtswissenschaft* 68, no. 10 (2019): 833–847.

Jacob, Frank. "From Aspiration to Frustration: Emma Goldman's Perception of the Russian Revolution." *American Communist History* 17, no. 2 (2018): 185–199.

Jacob, Frank. "Radical Trinity: Anarchist, Jew, or New Yorker?" In *Jewish Radicalisms: Historical Perspectives on a Phenomenon of Global Modernity*, edited by Frank Jacob and Sebastian Kunze, 153–180. Berlin: De Gruyter, 2019.

Kensinger, Loretta. "Radical Lessons: Thoughts on Emma Goldman, Chaos, Grief, and Political Violence Post–9/11/01." *Feminist Teacher* 20, no. 1 (2009): 50–70.

Kowal, Donna M. "Anarcha-Feminism." In *The Palgrave Handbook of Anarchism*, edited by Carl Levy and Matthew S. Adams, 265–279. Cham: Palgrave Macmillan, 2019.

Kowal, Donna M. *Tongue of Fire: Emma Goldman, Public Womanhood, and the Sex Question*. Albany, NY: SUNY Press, 2016.

Marso, Lori Jo. "A Feminist Search for Love: Emma Goldman on the Politics of Marriage, Love, Sexuality and the Feminine." *Feminist Theory* 4, no. 3 (2003): 305–320.

McKinley, Blaine. "'The Quagmires of Necessity': American Anarchists and Dilemmas of Vocation." *American Quarterly* 34, no. 5 (1982): 503–523.

Michels, Tony. *A Fire in Their Hearts: Yiddish Socialists in New York*. Cambridge, MA/London: Harvard University Press, 2005.

Mohammed, Jowan A. "Mary Hunter Austin und die Forderungen nach einer Veränderung der Geschlechterrollen in den USA, 1914–1918." In *Geschlecht und Klassenkampf: Die "Frauenfrage" aus deutscher und internationaler Perspektive im 19. und 20. Jahrhundert*, edited by Vincent Streichhahn and Frank Jacob, 222–239. Berlin: Metropol, 2020.

Moritz, Theresa and Albert Moritz. *The World's Most Dangerous Woman*. Vancouver: Subway Books, 2001.

Nicholas, Lucy. "Gender and Sexuality." In *The Palgrave Handbook of Anarchism*, edited by Carl Levy and Matthew S. Adams, 603–621. Cham: Palgrave Macmillan, 2019.

Porter, David, ed. *Vision on Fire: Emma Goldman on the Spanish Revolution*. 3rd ed. New Paltz, NY: Commonground Press, 1985 [1983].

Presley, Sharon and Crispin Sartwell. *Exquisite Rebel: The Essays of Voltairine De Cleyre— Anarchist, Feminist, Genius*. Albany, NY: State University of New York Press, 2005.

Pribanic-Smith, Erika J. and Jared Schroeder. *Emma Goldman's No-Conscription League and the First Amendment*. New York: Routledge, 2019.
Reich, Wilhem. *Die Funktion des Orgasmus: Zur Psychopathologie und zur Soziologie des Geschlechtslebens*. Vienna: Internationaler Psychoanalytischer Verlag, 1927.
Reich, Wilhelm. *Die sexuelle Revolution: Zur charakterlichen Selbststeuerung des Menschen*. Frankfurt am Main: Fischer, 1966.
Rofel, Lisa. "Queer Positions, Queerying Asian Studies." *Positions* 20, no. 1 (2012): 183–193.
Sheehan, Sean. *Anarchism*. London: Reaktion, 2003.
Shulman, Alex Kates. "Introduction." In *Red Emma Speaks: Selected Writings and Speeches by Emma Goldman*, edited by Alex Kates Shulman. New York: Vintage Books, 1972.
Streichhahn, Vincent. "Zur 'Frauenfrage' und Sozialdemokratie im deutschen Kaiserreich: Zwischen Antifeminismus und Emanzipation." In *Geschlecht und Klassenkampf: Die "Frauenfrage" aus deutscher und internationaler Perspektive im 19. und 20. Jahrhundert*, edited by Vincent Streichhahn and Frank Jacob, 48–77. Berlin: Metropol, 2020.
Weiss, Penny A. and Loretta Kensinger, eds. *Feminist Interpretations of Emma Goldman*. University Park, PA: Pennsylvania State University Press, 2007.
Wexler, Alice. Emma Goldman: An Intimate Life. New York: Pantheon Books, 1984.
Zimmer, Kenyon. *Immigrants against the State: Yiddish and Italian Anarchism in America*. Urbana, IL: Illinois University Press, 2015

Jowan A. Mohammed

7 To End the Yoke of Marriage: Mary Hunter Austin and the Struggle Against Patriarchal Norms

Introduction

For the author Mary Hunter Austin (1868–1934), the most important thing that a woman should achieve was being able to take care of herself by her own labor. Austin considered this claim not to be a recommendation but an encouragement for women. She herself was a strong advocate for every woman being able to take care of themselves and of their economic independence, no matter if a woman was working for her husband in the house or for someone else in the factory or office. This independence was important and should be achieved by "the married women just as much as [by] the unmarried ones."[1] The home was not a place to be on display like an ornament for women, Austin believed, but a place to gather oneself to excel in the outside world, and the way to such an achievement was based on the trinity of equal marriage, labor, and the ownership of one's own citizenship. The road to this idea's fulfillment was a long one, impacted by one's family, social norms like marriage or divorce, and a life led according to eclecticism and a hunger for change. The many ways Austin contributed to the female struggles in relation to gender norms, sexuality, marital issues, and other social problems were notable both in her own time as well as today. The politically left author was in general a strong advocate for love and kinship, but she also pointed to ways these things could be improved.

Mary Hunter Austin was born 9 September 1868 in Carlinville, Illinois as the fourth of six children of George Hunter (1830–1878) and Susanna Graham Hunter (1842–1896). Although especially her mother was everything but encouraging with regard to Austin's education, she graduated from college with a teaching degree, and she further evolved while lecturing and writing in the years to come. Austin was first and foremost a landscape writer who advocated for Native American rights, and she was later deemed proto-feminist in New York City and rediscovered by modern scholars.[2]

---

[1] "Mrs. Well Known Says," *The Hattiesburg News*, January 18, 1911: 5.
[2] For further reading, see Jowan A. Mohammed, "Mary Hunter Austin und die Forderungen nach einer Veränderung der Geschlechterrollen in den USA, 1914–1918," in *Geschlecht und Klas-*

ð OpenAccess. © 2021 Jowan A. Mohammed, published by De Gruyter. This work is licensed under the Creative Commons Attribution-NonCommercial-NoDerivatives 4.0 International License.
https://doi.org/10.1515/9783110751451-007

Her personal life went through many ups and downs, and Austin wrote on these experiences in several of her works. Her relationships with men, e.g. her father, her brother, and later on her husband, would determine her later criticism of existent gender roles and marriage as a tool of patriarchic exploitation in particular.

While her father had been supportive and loving prior to his death, Austin's older brother was in many ways selfish, although the competition with him urged her to improve and adapt in life. Austin and her brother Jim went to school together, creating even more tension and competition as she was younger but similarly ambitious. After the death of her father, the young girl believed that her brother, the new man of the house, was the favorite of her mother. He got all the attention and accommodations, while Austin was expected to not make a fuss and to know her place as a woman both in the family and in the society of the late 19th century. The present chapter intends to take a closer look at Austin's struggle against existent gender roles and marriage-related norms in the United States in the last decades of the 19th century and the early ones of the 20th century. It will therefore examine Austin's life before her works and respective reflections about the said roles and norms are taken into closer consideration.

Austin's Life and Her Experiences with Patriarchy

In her autobiography *Earth Horizon* (1932), Austin recalls her engagement with the women's suffragette movement as a result of the imbalanced relationship between women and men. What fueled her fire to become hard-headed was based on a personal story regarding the unfair demands that were put on her by her mother to submit to whatever her brother had decided upon as a rule for the household, e.g. "a four-minute egg."[3] The author later recalled the family's reactions to her divergence by not conforming to the idea that she had to eat the same soft-boiled egg as everyone else. The experience of soft-boiled eggs unsettled her in the morning, and upon asking if her egg could be boiled a minute or two longer, the question was not received positively but led to a conflict between her individual wishes and the patriarchic norms of her home. It became a constant annoyance and led to comments from Jim, such as "somehow you never

---

senkampf: Die "Frauenfrage" aus deutscher und internationaler Perspektive im 19. und 20. Jahrhundert, eds. Vincent Streichhahn and Frank Jacob (Berlin: Metropol, 2020), 222–239.
3 Mary Hunter Austin, *Earth Horizon: An Autobiography* (Boston/New York: Houghton Mifflin, 1932), 129.

seem to have any feeling for what a home should be,"⁴ or her mother, who argued, "Oh, Mary, why do you always have to have something different from the rest of the family."⁵ The rest of the family obviously had no problem with following the patriarchic decision of Austin's older brother, but the young girl felt cheated out of a possible choice.

In 1890, after graduating with a teaching degree, it was made clear that she had been excluded from her family's farm ventures and financial interests. The young woman deemed this decision to be absolutely unfair, as she considered it only right that she and her older brother would get an equal amount of help to start their lives. The hurt made the young Austin realize that her "only" option to build a life of her own was to get married—as a husband would provide safety in life that she herself could not provide alone.⁶ These issues had been criticized by other early feminists, e.g. the anarchist Emma Goldman (1869–1940), who argued that marriage would not provide a safe environment for mistreated girls but would establish just another form of patriarchic exploitation.⁷ Marriage was consequently also a destructive change for Austin in many ways because, prior to her decision, it was not an option or important for her, especially not since she had put so much effort into finishing her studies, despite sickness and delays.⁸ Austin would later reflect upon this step as follows:

> [I]t wouldn't just naturally present itself to the modern young woman that this meant Mary wasn't to nullify the effort of her schooling by getting married immediately on leaving school. Mary often knew her mother's contemporaries to shake their head over girls whose mothers had been known to train their resources to put them through college. "What a waste,' they said; 'they'll only get married as soon as they're out.' But the implications of emphasis on the word *man* went deeper and revealed what not one of the women who used it would admit, that the secret concern of women of that time was family limitation.⁹

Austin here describes how she had been wasting her education on a man, promising her mother she would not "throw it all away" if the latter just helped her through it. Her narration of this time is harsh and critical: "as I recall those later nineteenth-century decades, all the disabilities of excessive child-bearing were

---

4 Ibid.
5 Ibid.
6 Augusta Fink, *I-Mary: A Biography of Mary Austin* (Tuscon, AZ: University of Arizona Press, 1983), 54.
7 For a detailed discussion of Goldman's view about marriage, see Frank Jacob's chapter in the present volume.
8 Austin, *Earth Horizon*, 162.
9 Ibid.

charged to the horrid appetites of husband."[10] Austin's criticism of a lack of intelligence when discussing family limitations was rather ahead of her time. In 1932, she wrote that educated women had not yet "come into use" and that she had "cheerfully" promised her mother not to waste the resources spent on her education on marriage but would rather "make something of her education," while she was secretly also wishing for five children to match the social demands for women at that time.[11] It becomes clear that there was a shift in ideas about the ideal of family and marriage in Austin's time, i.e. between the late 1880s and 1930s, and the transformation of old toward new types of family dynamics took place during these decades and could be witnessed by Austin. The majority of women did not work besides their husbands until the 1920s.[12] All family systems had structures and obligations, while political rights and labor division suited the social dominance of men with regard to the existent "structures" of each family. The socio-economic relationship within the family would naturally, for Austin too, represent the first instance to generate the social role of a woman.[13]

Prior to marrying Stafford Wallace (1862–1931), Mary's wish for a family structure of her own was not something she was particularly looking for, and her dating life was not an exciting one, as she later recalls:

> Toward the end of sophomore year, one of them [the young men in Austin's neighborhood] had let her know handsomely that she met all the requirements of what a preachers' wife should be, and he thought they might as well be engaged. Confronted with the enormity of telling a serious young man that she'd rather be dead than married to him [...].[14]

This shows that she never married out of desperation or settled just for anybody, but rather came to the decision of marriage at a point where she saw it as the most pragmatic decision, one she would take according to her own terms. In the summer of 1890, she became engaged, which her mother deemed as her daughter "going out of the family."[15] Around this time, perhaps somewhat self-assured, Austin describes herself at 22 years old and recently engaged as "more than ordinarily intelligent about everything but other people."[16] When it came to her new courtship, she was excited, but she also went into her mar-

---

10 Ibid., 163.
11 Ibid.
12 Stephanie Coontz, "Introduction," in *American Families: A Multicultural Reader*, eds. Stephanie Coontz, Maya Parson and Gabrielle Raley (New York: Routledge, 1999), xii.
13 Ibid., xv.
14 Austin, *Earth Horizon*, 172–173.
15 Ibid., 218.
16 Ibid., 220.

riage with the self-awareness of a young educated woman. Her knowledge about the social institution of marriage made her approach toward it rather diplomatic:

> She hadn't taken the first man that asked her, nor at the first time of asking. She had engaged herself to a young man of similar social background of her own, and with a university education. She had been entirely frank as to her intention toward a writing career. She had not concealed the fact of her lack of physical robustness, which she hoped to compensate for by teaching, if necessary, until writing began to pay.

In short, Austin expected her husband to understand that he had not married an unequal wife, but a woman who demanded equality and her own professional outlook for the future.

She gained newfound confidence when she met Stafford Wallace Austin. He was seven years older than her, and Austin described him as "very absent minded but [an] extremely intellectual man."[17] This absent-mindedness set the tone for the rest of their relationship; despite some intellectual stimulus and the practical properties to build a life, there was little romance, which we see in later years affecting the author's opinions in media portrayals about mate-love and successful relationships. Her relationship with Wallace was consequently nothing more than a "modest love."[18]

This "modest love" never went through any proper flourishment and was more than unsatisfactory as time passed,[19] thus allowing Austin's selfishness of only caring for her own needs, which she had adjusted repeatedly due to boundaries or negotiations during the engagement, preventing the marriage from lasting. After all, marriage seemed not to comfort Austin, who demanded more for her life than being someone's wife. Despite her relatively "free reign," she was not intellectually stimulated by the marriage, but was eventually left rather bored. At the same time, she contributed close to nothing in terms of domestic tasks, leaving her house in a subpar standard. Despite the lack of much joy, success, or structure in their marriage, the couple's first and only child, named Ruth, was born in the spring of 1892.[20] The ideal marriage with five children and a loving husband, which Austin had secretly hoped for as a girl, was consequently nowhere in sight.

Austin, who perhaps never would have married if not out of necessity, was ultimately thrown into a marriage and her submission to a husband, as it was

---

17 Ibid., 54–55.
18 Ibid., 56.
19 Abraham Hoffman, "Mary Austin, Stafford Austin, and the Owens Valley," *Journal of the Southwest* 53, no. 3/4 (2011): 307.
20 Fink, *I-Mary*, 59–63.

dictated by social norms which the female writer would later contest in her works. Evidentially, this marriage was one of the things that made Austin "special" in a way, because it eventually led to a finalized divorce and turned her into an unconventional woman of her time.[21]

The milestones that were the most celebrated, in contrast to those of her domestic life (such as the birth of her child, etc.), were the ones related to her writing career; the accomplishment of selling her first two short stories gave Austin a great sense of triumph and confidence, and she described it (i.e. the quality of her creative effort) as "this opening movement of an activity that was to mean more to me than anything that was ever to happen to me; quietly as I suppose all growing things begin... there was that stream of knowingness which ever since adolescence I had felt going on in me."[22] In terms of how this affected her marriage, it was positive to some extent as well as problematic in others. The confidence in her achievements as a writer gave her the comfort to follow her husband anywhere in his venture to secure a living, knowing that she could always write.[23] In her third year of marriage, it was Austin who secured a good life financially, a possibility "brought up in a university town where people of intelligence and taste contrive, on incomes little better than those of highly skilled labor to achieve for themselves security and certain of appurtenances of good living,"[24] which was something her husband did not possess. The expectations of a man who was educated and "on her level" was rather disappointing when he was not someone who could hold his end of the union, leaving his wife in a stressful situation where she felt she had to step up more than a wife ought to do at those times. This was positive in the sense that Austin broke barriers by working and making a living, however it also drove a wedge between her and her husband as the relationship became dull and disappointing. Her marriage was eventually determined by a lack of balance and distrust because the partners did not work as a team; while they existed within the same space, they were totally distant from each other.

Moreover, the author was also consumed by her writing and spent the subsequent years following the decisions of her husband when he decided to move to wherever he saw fit to work, e.g. to the Owens Valley.[25] Although the marriage was already dull in numerous ways, Wallace supported Austin's goals of becom-

---

[21] Karen Langlois, "Mary Austin and Andrew Forbes: Poetry, Photography, and the Eastern Sierra," *California History* 85, no. 1 (2007): 42.
[22] Fink, *I-Mary*, 62.
[23] Ibid., 64.
[24] Austin, *Earth Horizon*, 239.
[25] Ibid.

ing a writer, and it was in that regard that she found the most joy, especially since her husband seemed to provide the support she had never gotten from her family.[26]

An important friend she made at this point in her life, during which she was overwhelmed by her need to write, teaching, taking care of her daughter Ruth, and disagreeing with her husband, who did not wish her to take too many teaching commitments so she could be at his disposal at home, was Miss Williams.[27] Miss Williams taught at an Indian School located in a reservation, and it was through her that Mary got the opportunity to connect with the Native American population close by and got the benefit of visiting them on their land. The friendship gave her both the companionship she was not getting from Wallace and was also fruitful for her thoughts and writings. During this time, Austin was made aware of the abuse and mistreatment the Native Americans in the area (Paiute) were suffering from.[28] Specifically, the attacks on and sexual abuse of native women in a practice called *mahala* chasings,[29] in which Native American girls working in town as housekeepers were attacked and raped on their way home from work, made Austin furious. Often, the young women and girls were not only raped but also harshly beaten.[30] To observe such injustices matured Austin considerably, in addition to her own divorce at a time in which this was not "normal."

Marriage and Gender Norms in Austin's Works

The occurrences of a divorce matured something in Austin, and her pen(wo)manship began to move beyond its early focus on Native American tales, mining, and sheepherding traditions in the regions she had lived in. This shift came when her marriage began to break around 1905. Her literary skills ripened into a new stage, focusing more on the hardship of women's lives in the West, a prime example being one of the stories in *Lost Borders* (1909), "The Bitterness

---

26 Ibid.
27 Fink, *I-Mary*, 83.
28 Ibid., 84–87.
29 Janis P. Stout, *Picturing a Different West: Vision, Illustration, and the Tradition of Cather and Austin* (Lubbock, TX: Texas Tech University Press, 2007), 84. Also see Melody Graulich, ed. *Western Trails: A Collection of Short Stories by Mary Austin* (Reno, NV: University of Nevada Press, 1987), 9; Glenda Riley, *A Place to Grow: Women in the American West* (Arlington Heights: Harlan Davidson, 1992), 189.
30 Fink, *I-Mary*, 84.

of Women," which explores domestic relations gone wrong.[31] It paints a picture and explores how in "the treacherous desert country men are lost, children die, [and] women who wish to become wives and mothers live wasted lives."[32] This is the point from which the writer further evolves and deliberates more broadly on the theme of women not making a life for themselves without a man, into which she is not only projecting her own life but also putting other women's experiences into words, among whom are the Native American women she encountered in the desert as well as her mentors such as the novelist Charlotte Perkins Gilman (1860–1935).[33] Gilman served as a prime example of *what* Mary wanted to be: someone who had suffered an unhappy marriage, who had been accused of being an unsuitable mother, and who had had to give her children over into someone else's care, yet who was still fighting for the social and economic liberation of women and for a transformation of existent gender roles.[34]

Austin would then also spend almost two years traveling in Europe, especially in Italy, and she also visited London. During her European years she met and became friends with individuals such as George Bernard Shaw (1856–1950), W. B. Yeats (1865–1939), and H. G. Wells (1866–1946), who were people she absorbed strength from.[35] Her "feminist" intellectuality and properties developed greatly due to her attending a British socialist meeting of the Fabian Society in London.[36] This society was appealing not only because of the influential literary individuals that were involved but also because of their support for Austin's fundamental aims, i.e. politics for women and their concerns; the Fabian Society was in support of the suffragette movement in Great Britain.[37]

---

[31] Karen S. Langlois, "A Fresh Voice from the West: Mary Austin, California, and American Literary Magazines, 1892–1910," *California History* 69, no. 1 (1990): 32–33.
[32] Ibid., 33.
[33] On Gilman's life and work see, among others, Catherin J. Golden and Joanna Schneider Zangrando, eds., *The Mixed Legacy of Charlotte Perkins Gilman* (Newark, DE: The University of Delaware Press, 2000).
[34] Fink, *I-Mary*, 84–100.
[35] Blanche H. Gelfant, "'Lives' of Women Writers: Cather, Austin, Porter/and Willa, Mary, Katherine Anne," *NOVEL: A Forum on Fiction* 18, no. 1 (1984): 66.
[36] Benay Blend, "Mary Austin and the Western Conservation Movement: 1900–1927," *Journal of the Southwest* 30, no. 1 (1988): 13.
[37] Derril Keith Curry Lance, "The Suffragette Movement in Great Britain: A Study of the Factors Influencing the Strategy Choices of the Women's Social and Political Union, 1903–1918" (MA Thesis, University of North Texas, 1977), 61.

In *Mary Austin's Regionalism: Reflections on Gender, Genre, and Geography*,[38] German scholar Heike Schaefer sheds light on Austin's take on the dilemma and "bitterness" of women in various stages of life, e.g. marriage and the domesticity of that institution.

Austin often examined different dilemmas women had to face in society, particularly when they (much like herself) were self-determined, professionally ambitious, and family-oriented women, who were, however, limited by the existent gender roles and the social expectations for women.[39] In her personal life, Austin had to choose between family life and her career, which is exactly the same narrative many of her protagonists have to follow as society does not allow them to "have it all." Independent and norm-defying characters are a staple in Austin's literature and reflect both who she was herself and whom she wished to become.

Mary Hunter Austin's personal story consequently deserves to be studied closely because it is not only the base for her own career as a successful writer but also the base for her stories. The people with whom she interacted influenced her intellectually but also challenged her identity as a woman, both positively and negatively, and it is in these interactions we find many answers to why she fought for gender equality and contributed to changes to gender roles.

Austin's mother would, instead of encouraging her daughter, blame possession for being the reason for the girl's odd behavior, a fact that created even more distance between them.[40] As a woman with the responsibility for her household, she did not understand or appreciate Mary's vivid imagination and her lack of self-control in speaking whatever was on her mind, dismissing social cues of politeness—much to her mother's frustration and dismay.[41] The lack of female connection resulted in some level of mental isolation, and from an early age Austin developed an alter-ego, a braver and bolder version of herself referred to as "I-Mary," which to her was more than just Mary-by-herself. She (I-Mary) had no need to be understood and did not mind being different: "To be I-Mary was more solid and satisfying than to be Mary-by-herself."[42] She protect-

---

38 Heike Schaefer, *Mary Austin's Regionalism: Reflections on Gender, Genre, and Geography* (Charlottesville, VA: University of Virginia Press, 2004), 244.
39 Ibid. For a detailed analysis of Mary Hunter Austin's impact on gender roles in the US, see Mohammed, "Mary Hunter Austin."
40 Fink, *I-Mary*, 9.
41 For further reading on the relationship between Austin and her mother, see Elizabeth Wright, "Mary Hunter Austin (1868–1934)," in *American Women Writer 1900–1945: A Bio-Bibliographical Critical Sourcebook*, ed. Laurie Champion (Connecticut: Greenwood Publishing Group, 2000): 13–19.
42 Austin, *Earth Horizon*, 47.

ed herself with this kind of armor and felt brave whenever she needed to be stern and confident during the upcoming years of her life into adulthood

The American academic Esther Stineman writes that "Austin had many reasons to write her story, not the least among them was to vindicate herself from the onus of deserting her husband and placing her child in an institution, personal agonies that colored her writing and career."[43] The sorrow of a failed marriage was probably something Austin could recover from, as her years in New York were greatly determined by the contact with like-minded women (i.e. free women), but a child in an institution that she could not give a proper life to by herself was another sorrow only a mother could feel. Perhaps it is not too presumptuous to claim that everything Austin did and wrote, whether it was about love, marriage, war, or a particular landscape, was a way of taking control of her identity as a woman and improving her own self at a crossroads. She claimed that she felt misunderstood and that writing was a way for her to express herself in a wholesome manner and pay her respects to all the things she saw in a way that others did not.[44]

Austin had been peculiar in many ways from an early age, and this statement remains valid when it came to the opposite sex, because despite having an interest in boys, they seemed less keen on her—later this became a proud moment for her, as she used this to focus on her career and intellect. In adulthood, "Austin's views seemed impractical to economists, legislators, and businessmen who focused on the economic possibilities of the Southwest,"[45] but she was still passionate to the point where the impracticality did not matter, and the cause made sense; indeed, it was this drive that she took with her further into her living years. Throughout her life, Austin became tremendously dedicated to finding solutions and putting an end to the conflict between nature and culture; she saw people as a reflection of the land and the wilderness of individuals linked to the wilderness of the flora and fauna. Austin's ideas and the idea of the socially constructed gender as we define it in our time are similar in many regards as they attempt to let go of limitations. Gender (and nature in Austin's case) should not be construed as an unchanging identity but be remotely constituted in time, defined by the space through a performative—vague and wild.[46] Much like how we as humans exist and insist on our presence, Austin defined nature

---

43 Esther Lanigan Stineman, "Mary Austin Rediscovered," *Journal of the Southwest* 30, no. 4 (1988): 550.
44 Austin, *Earth Horizon*, 47.
45 Blend, "Mary Austin and the Western Conservation Movement," 21.
46 Judith Butler, *Gender Trouble: Feminism and the Subversion of Identity* (New York/London: Routledge, 2006), 140.

as something that "insists on itself."[47] Despite the hardship the Hunters experienced in the land, the young woman was content because the unconventional society felt more suited to her.[48] The term *normal* to specify averageness was not something that had yet been categorized, however the idea that there was a human norm, and that this norm was "the average man," was set; thus, a display of difference from women was categorized as a weakness of the female sex and of their intelligence both mentally and physically.[49] She defined and criticized stereotypes of women at the time by being outspoken on matters where women did not have a big role, such as the environmental issues present in her activism and literature, and is described as creating a "feminist alternative to the masculinist myths of the far West as a place where men achieved heroism either by conquering the wilderness or by communing with it in solitary ecstasy."[50] Austin desired to find the fundamental value of nature, and thereby herself as a woman, and therefore she wished to overcome hierarchical traditions in Western culture that imply that the desert is a wasteland or that men control nature, and in the process, she became an advocate for Native American rights as well as gender equality.[51] These values of hers started in the early stages of her youth and were cultivated all through her life as she matured. One can argue that because of the lack of emotional support from her family, and later in life, her husband as well, she looked to the flora and fauna of the desert for clues to survive under difficult conditions. Nature became her safe zone and focus point alike, especially since she must have felt alone quite often. Independent and self-defined, even borderline selfish and self-centered, her attitude often made her an outcast in the various Western towns where she lived during her lifetime. Consequently, Austin shared with other desert appreciators the strong sense of herself as a nonconformist who sought comfort in the spirituality provided by the land.[52]

Despite having a husband/marriage, it was in other women that Austin found companionship for most of her adult life. These women all fought for something, often correlating with the author's own battles and later activism.

---

47 Blend, "Mary Austin and the Western Conservation Movement," 16–17.
48 Ibid.
49 Melody Graulich, "Mary, Mary, Quite Contrary," *The Women's Review of Books* 1, no. 4 (1984): 16–17.
50 Lois Rudnick, "Review: Feminist on the Frontier," *The Women's Review of Books* 7, no. 7 (1990): 22.
51 Vera L. Norwood, "Heroines of Nature: Four Women Respond to the American Landscape," *Environmental Review* 8, no. 1 (1984): 41.
52 Blend, "Mary Austin and the Western Conservation Movement," 16–17.

Some of the women the author encountered in her lifetime were inspirations and some were comforts in their similarity to her. Austin also "never attempted to separate her art from her politics,"[53] and going against what was considered "normal" determined Austin's life as an activist. This is clearly the case as it influenced the writer in her journey of self-discovery within the areas of politics and her socio-cultural understandings. Her political views on society were impacted by the injustice she saw in the male-dominated (i.e. patriarchic) culture she was surrounded by. "Austin was always a political activist – so much so that her career as a writer may have suffered because of her commitment to a variety of social causes which seem now presciently in advance of her time."[54] Almost above all else, Austin was a firm believer that men's experience could not speak for women, as she thought that women's vision for "selfhood" was considerably different from men's.[55] These ideas also inspired her grand, almost scandalous ideas, such as the freedom of choice in mating and the role of marriage bureaus.[56] Marriage bureaus were organizations that men and women joined in order to find a husband or a wife. Essentially, the idea was to sign up to arrange the meeting of a potential husband or wife who wished for the same thing. Based on Austin's plea to make these state-run (a municipal matter) shows that they were seen as helping to give people more options; it showcases that the bureaus would increase the number of more successful marriages that would not end in divorce. The production of marriage certificates had become an efficient business by the 1900s, and clerics had books containing blank marriage certificates that were ready to go in minutes, making them efficient machineries.[57] In 1912, *The New York Times* published the notion to "make marriage a trade"[58] as it was printed that in both "Jersey City and Newark," i.e. City Halls, "marriages had become a traffic. In both of the municipal buildings there are clerks employed in department offices who are also Justices of the Peace. The marrying clerks have had the License Bureau 'shadowed' for the love-lorn…"[59] Austin was a firm believer that "the real romance is the right marriage," and the idea of "mu-

---

53 Graulich, "Mary, Mary, Quite Contrary," 16–17.
54 Gelfant, "'Lives' of Women Writers," 69.
55 Graulich, "Mary, Mary, Quite Contrary," 17.
56 Doris E. Fleischman, "Mary Austin Thinks Freedom of Choice in Mating Is Merely Nominal Here, Therefore the Novelist Urges Municipal Marriage Bureaus," *New York Tribune*, December 18, 1914, 7.
57 "Marriage Bureau Complete," *The New York Times*, December 5, 1900, 5.
58 "Make Marriage a Trade," *The New York Times*, January 6, 1912, 10.
59 Ibid.

nicipal 'soul mating'"⁶⁰ would contribute to solving many socio-economic problems. "To love, to be loved, to marry and to keep on loving – that is the only perfect and possible ideal for men and women."⁶¹ The author encouraged the idea that town/city halls should not only be for the business of the marrying but also for the meeting: "there is no reason why each town should not have large halls or public meeting rooms where, under municipal chaperonage, the social life of the young may be married on."⁶² The idea was that it would help young people "start right" in their pursuit of perfect partnerships which would ensure success in all aspects of life. Marriage, both before, during, and after, should be a matter that society concerned itself with, according to the author, who in 1913 firmly stated that "society should stand by [a] woman raising [a] family."⁶³ The bearing and raising of children, which women did, was something she saw as the highest form of service, to which a woman gives 20 years of her life. During that time, "she has a right to expect society to stand by and see that the security of her married life is not a disturbed by any trivial or unworthy occasion."⁶⁴ The author's opinions on marriage and motherhood can be divided into two parts. Firstly, a woman's worth is not only that of her belonging to the first man who asks for her hand in marriage and of her ability to reproduce. Secondly, and most importantly, a woman is to marry—but after careful consideration and on the basis of love. Motherhood, although not the only thing to determine the value of a woman, should be regarded as the highest of sacrifices and treated with respect and ensured security.

In her writings, there was always a narrative in which the protagonist had to make the hard choice between love and career, family and the self, and so on, and thus it is not so strange that she would encourage something like "municipal marriage bureaus." Austin argues that there is nothing wrong or disreputable about openly seeking a mate and wishing for such marriage bureaus to arrange relationships legitimized by the state. The author actually believed that the state did not do enough for married people, besides giving its name to sanction marriages, but no one could go to the state for advice or aid in what she labeled "the most important business of this world."⁶⁵ Although there were plenty

---

60 "Municipal 'Soul Mating.'" *Bryan Daily Eagle*, March 4, 1914, 4; the same article was also published on the same day in *The Daily Star Mirror*.
61 Ibid.
62 Ibid.
63 Mary Austin, "Mary Austin Says White Slave Trials Mark Dawn of New Era for Women," *The San Francisco Call*, September 5, 1913, 3.
64 Ibid.
65 Fleischman, "Mary Austin Thinks Freedom," *New York Tribune*, December 18, 1914, 7.

of private marriage bureaus, that alone was not good enough for Austin, who considered them to be merely matrimonial agencies, which were all creditable in accomplishment. This demand, however, could obviously lead to misunderstandings: "In the modern era of freedom of choice it seems a step back to continentalism, the idea of having one's mate picked out for him. But it is just that freedom of selection which Mrs. Austin desires to augment in her scheme. The further we get away from barbarism and ignore it the more we realize the necessity of freedom of selection in our marital relation."[66]

Austin argued on the basis of the "average person having no chance in marriage," having asked "many," who all confirmed that there was not a great selection, while most only had one option or suitable acquaintance: "how can they be expected to make happy marriages if they are forced to marry the one person man or woman they know?"[67] It is somewhat difficult to fully understand what Austin truly wished to achieve by such a "sacred business"; the best possible love? Or the best possible business/practical outcome of a union between a man and a woman? "People wouldn't be unhappy if they were sure they loved each other when they married. It is only those who marry for other reasons than love that swell the numbers of the divorce list. And there is a very great number of them."[68]

The idea that men and women marry for "a home," or at least their idea of one, should not be the only incentive when choosing a mate. Additionally, she labeled many young men and women as "tragic" because it was a group of hard-working people whom time had passed by and who lacked the option of finding anyone available. Overall, the idea of making marriage the responsibility of the state was a pragmatic idea of Austin, but it also shows clear evidence of perhaps saving others from the fate of her own life. Maybe she had hoped that such bureaus could prevent unhappy and unequal relationships, like the one she had experienced herself. Austin encouraged the investigation of people's characters in these bureaus and not just taking any and everybody at face value. In a way, such arguments emphasize that Austin had a rather scientific approach to marriage, which should be considered a pragmatic choice according to the partner's profile rather than a purely love-related decision. Only such a form of state-orchestrated marriage could have prevented exploitation of any form as well. The idea of municipal meeting halls for young people, "under municipal chaperonage,"[69] was also a rather clever plan toward labor: "a married woman is out of

---

66 Ibid.
67 Ibid.
68 Ibid.
69 "Municipal 'Soul Mating,'" *Bryan Daily Eagle*, March 4, 1914, 4.

her job when her children are sixteen or eighteen years old, or surely when they become married. State chaperon would be a most delightful occupation. She had experienced in being a personal mother, and she will enjoy being kind of a public mother." This was a rather clever ploy toward both helping people find "practical and suitable" partners as they become presented with more options and securing women an occupation upon their expiration as mothers—since that was a woman's shelf-life; girl, wife, mother, and then out of purpose. The state as the overseeing institution would consequently guarantee that women would be granted a safe and secure marriage with a suitable partner. Maybe Austin had hoped that equality could be secured that way, as the traditional and exploitational patriarchic marriage would eventually end through this practice.

The Modern Woman and (Demolishing) the Institution of Marriage

In 1895, American journalist and author Elizabeth Bisland (1861–1929) wrote that "criticism of the marriage relation is in the air"[70] and how fiction was the arena in which these discussions were being held. Many women like Austin would begin to discuss these matters in the upcoming years, as well as the traditional roots and gender roles that had determined family matters for so long.[71] Bisland makes the argument that mutual affection for a child is what essentially held a family together. The argument is that a father's love was cultivated, while the love of a mother was instinctive.[72] In Austin's own childhood, however, her mother was emotionally distanced, although this is a rather subjective narrative bestowed upon us in the author's autobiography and can probably be argued in many cases as dramatic/exaggerated. Overall, her father was her emotional support, and her loss after his early death was a loss no one else could fill.

With Bisland's argument of cultivation and instinctive love and Austin's own experience with missing a parent (i.e. a key role), one would assume that she fell into the norm after the birth of her own child. However, her daughter was born (in 1892) with a mental disability, which created distance, stress, and what was perceived as a personal maternal and marital failure—she was shamed by her own mother, who believed this was some sort of punishment/judgment upon

---

[70] Elizabeth Bisland, "The Modern Woman and Marriage," *The North American Review* 160, no. 463 (1895): 753.
[71] Ibid.
[72] Ibid.

the author.⁷³ Her own life and marriage not working out exceptionally well in its earlier years, Austin went on to advocate for successful love and marriage, and, as someone who had experienced it "all,"⁷⁴ built the basis of her ideal partnership on more practical things, such as work and income. Her circle in New York and the people she corresponded with encouraged these ideas and a change of gender norms.

While living in New York, Austin befriended the rich supporter of the arts, Mabel Dodge Luhan (1879–1962), who arranged "evenings," as she called them.⁷⁵ A remarkable group of people attended these events, such as suffragist, actress, and poet Ida Rauh (1877–1970), labor leader and feminist Elisabeth Gurley Flynn (1890–1964), writer and activist Max Eastman (1883–1969), writer and social reformer John Collier (1884–1968), and political commentator and reporter Walter Lipmann (1889–1974), just to mention a few among the socialists, journalists of all kinds, trade unionists, anarchists, artists, clubwomen, suffragists, poets, psychoanalysts, "and even an occasional murderer."⁷⁶ It was here that Austin met people who made her feel "normal," because she was surrounded by other outsiders, which surely encouraged her deeds toward modernity.

One of the events was particularly arranged for "dangerous characters," which included the Russian-Jewish anarchists Emma Goldman and Alexander Berkman (1870–1936).⁷⁷ Also present was Elizabeth Gurley Flynn, who was the person responsible for introducing Austin to Goldman.⁷⁸ Evenings such as this, in the company of most radical individuals, created bonds across class and ideologies⁷⁹ and were without any doubt fruitful for Austin's growing determination and acted as inspirations.

Goldman was one of the most recognizable radical faces of the anarchist movement prior to the First World War, having been arrested multiple times and known as "the high priestess of anarchy,"⁸⁰ becoming the ultimate symbol of anarchist protest in the early 20th century in addition to her writing/editing

---

73 Fink, *I-Mary*, 70–78.
74 Mary Hunter Austin, *Love and The Soul Maker* (New York: D. Appleton and Company, 1914).
75 Fink, *I-Mary*, 167–168.
76 Ibid., 168.
77 Emily Hahn, *Mable* (New York: Houghton Mifflin Company, 1977), 67–71. For further reading on notable individuals in New York at that time, see Emily Hahn, *Romanic Rebels: An Informal History of Bohemianism in America* (New York: Houghton Mifflin Company, 1967).
78 Austin, *Earth Horizon*, 326.
79 Allen Churchill, *The Improper Bohemians* (New York: E.P Dutton and Company 1959), 56–58.
80 Jeffrey A. Johnson, "Aliens, Enemy Aliens, and Minors: Anti-Radicalism and the Jewish Left," in *Historicizing Fear: Ignorance, Vilification, and Othering*, eds. Travis D. Boyce and Winsome M. Chunnu (Boulder, CO: University Press of Colorado, 2020), 200.

in the anarchist journal *Mother Earth* (established in 1906).[81] It is therefore interesting in many ways how Goldman and Austin came to cultivate a friendship in which being an outspoken and profound individual was respected and celebrated.

Although both women were politically left, the mainstream media treated them differently in relation to the US entry into the First World War. Goldman was stereotypically depicted as "a money-hungry Jew" wishing to profit off her publication (i.e. *Mother* Earth), described as a money-grabbing opportunist and "shrewd [individual] ... who for many years has made anarchy a well paying [sic] profession."[82] Although Austin wrote for a living as well, she was not accused of the same.

Around the same time as Goldman was being ostracized and villainized due to the nationalist tensions that had been created due to the war,[83] Austin was celebrated for her works, e.g. "Sex Emancipation Through War,"[84] a political essay published in 1918 which can best be described as a feminist work. In it, the author reflects on how women are in need of emancipation through work, which would secure safety for them because the social structures were all far too accommodating for the man. Austin especially thought of economic exploitation in relation to female gender identity and conveyed the idea of how it is but a superstition that the work a human being does or may do is determined by sex. She argues against the social value of a woman being established by what some man thinks of her and how it is utterly ridiculous that the man must be the sole provider for the family. This is a clear criticism against existent family structures, i.e. marriage, in which there is a homemaker (woman) and a bread-winner (man); women's emancipation would solve it "all."[85]

Mobilization for war as a form of independence for women was among the things that female crusaders had in common; the notion that every American woman, rich or poor, married or single should be able to earn her own living was a collective thought among the likes of Austin.[86] The idea was that labor would ensure a freedom that would protect against "old maid's fate," which

---

81 Ibid.
82 Ibid.
83 For further reading on Goldman's alienation in America, see Frank Jacob, *Emma Goldman and The Russian Revolution: From Admiration to Frustration* (Berlin: De Gruyter, 2020), 85–118.
84 Mary Austin, "Sex Emancipation Through War" in *Beyond Borders: The Selected Essays of Mary Austin*, ed. Reuben J. Ellis (Carbondale, IL: Southern Illinois University Press, 1997), 44–55.
85 "The May Forum," *Chicago Eagle*, May 11, 1918, 5.
86 Marguerite Moors Marshall, "Mobilizing the American Girl into an Industrial Reserve Force is Insurance Against Old Maid's Fate," *The Evening World*, March 6, 1917, 3.

was to be avoided, as marriage was inevitable for survival but also something that was going through social change, as social reforms were shaping society and women's roles in new ways.

Well-educated, middle-class women such as Austin played a key role in pushing progressive reforms and fighting this idea of "old maid's fate." The club movements helped women develop public opinion and carve out a space for themselves, and increasingly gained a political voice even without the right to vote (yet).[87] Among the places in which activism played out and sustained itself was in networks of female friends who wished to make social reform, not marriage, the focus of their lives (e.g. wealthy women joining immigrant women workers in an effort for the right to vote, unionization, and the improvement of factory conditions).[88] Women's social reform solidarity maintained a great level of purposefulness because the interests of women and children became a federal matter through these social welfare networks,[89] e.g. the idea that arranging good marriages through bureaus on a municipal level such as those Austin advocated to benefit women in getting a balanced and equal marriage was part of the collective effort toward all aspects of social change for the objective prosperity of all partners equally.

Austin did not dismiss the need for sexes (i.e. man being man and woman being woman), as she contends that there are undoubtedly important and unchangeable differences between the abilities of the two, but argued that the war had been a good thing because it had demonstrated that the differences are not that fundamental in the grand scheme of things[90] (e.g. working as a woman and earning wages): "in other words, it is not so much brains as nervous stability that is required."[91]

Despite Austin being a leftist who should have been more critical of war, she considered it to be a good opportunity for change. Maybe this made her chaotic and someone who played on all fields, or maybe she was just eclectic and pas-

---

87 Ellen Skinner, *Women and the National Experience: Primary Sources in American History* (Boston/New York: Addison-Wesley Educational Publishers Inc., 1996), 115.
88 Ibid., 149.
89 Ibid., 172.
90 Birgitta Bader-Zaar, "Controversy: War-related Changes in Gender Relations: The Issue of Women's Citizenship," in *1914–1918-online: International Encyclopedia of the First World War*, eds. Ute Daniel, Peter Gatrell, Oliver Janz, Heather Jones, Jennifer Keene, Alan Kramer, and Bill Nasson, issued by Freie Universität Berlin, October 8, 2014, accessed March 3, 2021, https://encyclopedia.1914-1918-online.net/article/controversy_war-related_changes_in_gender_relations_the_issue_of_womens_citizenship.
91 Austin, "Sex Emancipation," 49. For further reading on women and their employment conditions, see Skinner, *Women and the National Experience*, 172–176.

sionate, but overall, she demanded change with regard to the social core structures. The narrative of "Sex Emancipation" is not critical of the war, nor does it have a negative narration toward men (and a positive one toward women); however, it determines the idea that women (married or not) are more than capable of doing jobs that have traditionally been non-female friendly—this also applies to the female role in existent family structures, determined by pre-set roles for husbands and wives.

The criticism she presents is related to the assumption that a woman has no value to society except the one a man assigns her—making her the object of his desire and the mother of his household:

> There is no history of the development of the idea that a woman has no value to society except that which man gives her, as the object of his desire and the mother of his children.... Men sacrifice themselves to womanhood, its racial function; they sacrifice themselves and the world to their love for a particular woman. But whoever heard of a man putting himself aside because the world needed some woman's gift for architecture, or biology, or sociology, more than it needed *his* contribution.[92]

Much like her criticism from girlhood about women throwing away their education to marry, wasting the resources spent on their education, she also blames men for this: "men have never hesitated to take a woman out of society and insist that every gift, every possible contribution of hers to general human welfare shall be excised, aborted, done with."[93] This is a clear disapproval of the social structures that rule that a woman belongs to a man—whether it be a husband, father, or brother to decide as he pleases. Austin stood for the idea that the world was a very feminine place, meaning a mother's place, making it conceptive, brooding, nourishing, and a place of infinite patience and elusiveness.[94] However, although it might come across as her dismissing marriage, she was critical of its norms rather than its existence as such. She fought so that the social structure of marriage did not define the entirety of women's value or discredit their positions as equal citizens.

In her fiction, she spoke freely, although she was somewhat afraid people assumed her social criticism came from a person who did not know love or the hunger to speak about it (for change): "few men understand what that hun-

---

92 Ibid., 50.
93 Ibid.
94 Teena Gabrielson, "Woman-Thought, Social Capital, and the Generative State: Mary Austin and the Integrative Civic Ideal in Progressive Thought," *American Journal of Political Science* 50, no. 3 (2006): 656.

ger is in women … like the opium-eater's for his drug."[95] In her youth she did not just settle for any man, and she was greatly impacted by her mother. In later years, this particular issue comes up in *Earth Horizon* when Austin reflects upon meeting Henrietta Rodman (1877–1923), a feminist school teacher who drew the author to the struggle of making a place for married school teachers.[96]

Her personal life and fiction greatly affected each other, and in a newspaper interview, Austin states that the motivation behind her books about the topic of love (e.g. *Love and The Soul-Maker*) was the need for books that would help people avoid "such a muddle of our loving. Women want such a book, and men need it."[97] In an interview about *Love and The Soul-Maker*, the author addresses the notion that parental love is not something that just comes for free with romantic love:

> All the things that marriage ought not to do for us may be gathered under the one head of not discrediting our social values. This is the sole criterion of particular marriages with which society had any concern – are parties to it worth more or less to us? … Nature has experimented with matings a thousand way across the field of life; welded the essential elements in one, divided them, united them in ephemeral tragedy, swept the respective instruments apart though wider and wider ranges of unmatched experience, brought them together for longer and more complicated contacts.[98]

Passion between men and women, Austin claimed, was not just nature's preface to mother- and fatherhood. Romantic love in itself is "the oldest need and strongest instinct of the human race."[99] Austin presents the prerogative that mate-love (i.e. romantic love between the two sexes) had been so dim in the past that parenthood was looked at as a miracle and the driving force, which in turn made it utterly detached from the romantic love of the husband and wife. The author's wish to shed light on the importance of romantic love is perhaps strongly driven by her own misfortunate marriage; "marriage is an agreement between any pair to practice mate love towards one another with intention."[100] In many ways, the author is chaotic in what her point is; is love and romance the intention? Or is she pressing the importance of going into a romance with clear intentions?

---

95 Austin, *Love and The Soul Maker*, 2.
96 Ibid.
97 Ibid., 8.
98 Ibid., 174–175.
99 Nixola Greeley-Smith, "Mary Austin Discovers Love-Grafters 'Birds of Speckled Feathers'," *The Day Book*, June 10, 1914, 10.
100 Ibid.

In her literature, whether political or autobiographical, Austin fought tooth and nail for a bigger change. Perhaps it was to achieve redemption for her own failed marriage, or perhaps it was to save others from the same fate she had gone through. Another notable work that takes a similar critical approach to the institution of marriage is *A Woman Of Genius* (1912).[101] The narrative of the work reveals her sense about large female talents and ambitions on the one hand and the demands of love and domesticity on the other; in many ways, it is a tug of war between the self and the demands of the patriarchal society. Ultimately, the idea is that the price of conventional marriage is the destruction of one of the partners.[102]

In *The Ford* (1917), one can read passages such as "women have a much keener sense of real values,"[103] which is something Austin always emphasized: "take marriage, for instance; – a woman will marry a man because he is clean and honest and will make a good father for her children, but a man won't marry a woman unless she makes him feel a certain way."[104] This dates back to her 1914 interviews about marriage bureaus and "girls marrying for a home."[105] What the author is presenting are the different intentions based on gender; women think practically about their future, planning for the long-run of family and safety, while men could be self-serving when choosing a mate as they were the providers based on the social constructions of gender and marital structures: "Love in man may change his relation to society, but in woman it changes the woman."[106]

The ideas in her fiction, in addition to being inspired by her own life prior to 1914, became influenced by the outbreak of the First World War. In addition to her advocacy on marriage for the benefit (social value) of both genders equally, she also implemented this into ideas of how to improve democracy. The war, for example, excluded women, which she strongly advised against, because the idea that democracy could only thrive on the basis of husbands who went to war was not something that society could truly benefit from, according to Austin. She argued that

---

101 Mary Austin, *A Woman of Genius* (New York: Doubleday, Page & Company, 1912).
102 Lee R. Edwards and Arlyn Diamond, *American Voices: American Women* (New York: Bard Books, 1973), 15–16.
103 Mary Austin, *The Ford* (Boston/New York: Houghton Mifflin, 1917), 233.
104 Ibid.
105 Fleischman, "Mary Austin Thinks Freedom of Choice," 7.
106 "By and About Women," *The Day Book* (Chicago, IL), June 5, 1914.

> [c]ivilization as we have it now is one-eyed and one-handed. It is kept going by man's way of seeing things, and man's way of dealing with the things that he sees ... man's method in approaching a new issue is to throw out a hypothesis, a general supposition of what seems likely or desirable to prove true.... This is what women have to stand squarely; not their ability to see the world in the same way men see it, but the importance and validity of their seeing it some other way.[107]

Despite the loudest messages presented by Austin in different instances of her works, it all boiled down to the idea that women should march to the beat of their own drum. This idea challenged the conformity of the time that marriage was a necessity, and Austin rather demanded it be re-defined and restructured to fit the modern woman. A woman should not have to choose between a career and a family, a home or a dull love life, and in later years the author wished for a change to be applied not only to women in marriage and love relationships but also to women's place in society as a whole: "What we women must also hold is the place America has set in the first line of democratic thinking,"[108] because man's intelligence and dominance ought not to be the only valid one in the family, in society, and in labor relations.[109]

Conclusion

Mary Hunter Austin was a strong independent woman at a time when spousal approval was important to be "whole." At times, she needed validation, which she was able to seek and find in her writing more than in a man after her marriage ended. She wanted a society that valued women inside and outside of marriage just as much, as a man was not the only fulfillment a woman ought to achieve in her lifetime. Austin, at the age of 22, "knew more about the marriage as a social institution than most young women of her years" and did not "take the first man that asked her, nor at the first time of asking."[110]

Perhaps her ideas were too advanced for her time, although she expressed them exactly at a crossroads in social history where society needed women like Austin to criticize social institutions, e.g. that of marriage, which were demanded to be transformed for the benefit of women and society's better future. The female writer fought for social change in all aspects of her life; citizenship, gender roles, and all other institutions that ought to limit women or tell them

---

107 Mary Austin, *The Young Woman Citizen* (New York: The Woman's Press, 1918), 17–19.
108 Ibid., 9.
109 Ibid., 16.
110 Austin, *Earth Horizon*, 220.

they were "less valuable." Marriage was not something she believed should limit women or something that they should just settle for out of necessity, and she encouraged ideals of independent paid work for women that was supposed to lead toward emancipation. This would benefit the modern woman in her independence, as well choosing a mate with caution, rather than taking "the first man that asked" or at "the first time of asking."[111] Women should be free and economically independent enough to make a wise decision that matched their own demands, not the necessities dictated by an exploitative society, whose patriarchic character dictated the roles women were supposed and allowed to play by. Due to her demands, it is relatively unsurprising that Austin was rediscovered as an important voice by Second Wave feminists in later years, who expressed similar demands with regard to equality and the end of patriarchically determined marriages.

Works Cited

Newspapers and Periodicals

Bryan Daily Eagle
Chicago Eagle
New York Tribune
The Daily Star Mirror
The Day Book
The Evening World
The Hattiesburg News
The New York Times
The San Francisco Call

Published Sources and Secondary Works

Austin, Mary Hunter. *A Woman of Genius*. New York: Doubleday, Page & Company, 1912.
Austin, Mary Hunter. *Love and The Soul Maker*. New York: D. Appleton and Company, 1914.
Austin, Mary Hunter. *The Ford*. Boston/New York: Houghton Mifflin, 1917.
Austin, Mary Hunter. *The Young Woman Citizen*. New York: The Woman's Press, 1918.
Austin, Mary Hunter. *Earth Horizon: An Autobiography*. Boston/New York: Houghton Mifflin, 1932.

---

111 Ibid.

Austin, Mary. "Sex Emancipation Through War." In *Beyond Borders: The Selected Essays of Mary Austin*, edited by Reuben J. Ellis, 44–55. Carbondale, IL: Southern Illinois University Press, 1997.

Bader-Zaar, Birgitta. "Controversy: War-related Changes in Gender Relations: The Issue of Women's Citizenship." In *1914–1918-online: International Encyclopedia of the First World War*, edited by Ute Daniel, Peter Gatrell, Oliver Janz, Heather Jones, Jennifer Keene, Alan Kramer, and Bill Nasson. Accessed March 3, 2021. https://encyclopedia.1914-1918-online.net/article/controversy_war-related_changes_in_gender_relations_the_issue_of_womens_citizenship.

Blend, Benay. "Mary Austin and the Western Conservation Movement: 1900–1927." *Journal of the Southwest* 30, no. 1 (1988): 12–34.

Bisland, Elizabeth. "The Modern Woman and Marriage." *The North American Review* 160, no. 463 (1895): 753–755.

Butler, Judith. *Gender Trouble: Feminism and the Subversion of Identity*. New York/London: Routledge, 2006.

Churchill, Allen. *The Improper Bohemians*. New York: E.P Dutton and Company, 1959.

Coontz, Stephanie, Maya Parson and Gabrielle Raley, eds. *American Families: A Multicultural Reader*. New York: Routledge, 1999.

Edwards, Lee R. and Arlyn Diamond, *American Voices: American Women*. New York: Bard Books, 1973.

Fink, Augusta. *I-Mary: A Biography of Mary Austin*. Tuscon, AZ: University of Arizona Press, 1983.

Gabrielson, Teena. "Woman-Thought, Social Capital, and the Generative State: Mary Austin and the Integrative Civic Ideal in Progressive Thought." *American Journal of Political Science* 50, no. 3 (2006): 650–663.

Gelfant, Blanche H. "'Lives' of Women Writers: Cather, Austin, Porter / and Willa, Mary, Katherine Anne." *NOVEL: A Forum on Fiction* 18, no. 1 (1984): 64–80.

Golde, Catherin J. and Joanna Schneider Zangrando, eds. *The Mixed Legacy of Charlotte Perkins Gilman*. Newark, DE: University of Delaware Press, 2000.

Graulich, Melody, ed. *Western Trails: A Collection of Short Stories by Mary Austin*. Reno, NV: University of Nevada Press, 1987.

Graulich, Melody. "Mary, Mary, Quite Contrary." *The Women's Review of Books* 1, no. 4 (1984): 16–17.

Hahn, Emily. *Mabel*. New York: Houghton Mifflin Company, 1977.

Hahn, Emily. *Romanic Rebels: An Informal History of Bohemianism in America*. New York: Houghton Mifflin Company, 1967.

Hoffman, Abraham. "Mary Austin, Stafford Austin, and the Owens Valley." *Journal of the Southwest* 53, no. 2/3 (2011): 305–322.

Jacob, Frank. *Emma Goldman and The Russian Revolution: From Admiration to Frustration*. Berlin: De Gruyter, 2020.

Jacob, Frank. "Klassendiskurs und Geschlechterrollen im Japan der Taishō-Zeit (1912 1926)." In *Geschlecht und Klassenkampf: Die "Frauenfrage" aus deutscher und internationaler Perspektive im 19. und 20. Jahrhundert*, edited by Vincent Streichhahn and Frank Jacob, 305–335. Berlin: Metropol, 2020.

Johnson, Jeffrey A. "Aliens, Enemy Aliens, and Minors: Anti-Radicalism and the Jewish Left." In *Historicizing Fear: Ignorance, Vilification, and Othering*, edited by Travis D. Boyce and Winsome M. Chunnu, 193–206. Boulder, CO: University Press of Colorado, 2020.

Lance, Derril Keith Curry. "The Suffragette Movement in Great Britain: A Study of the Factors Influencing the Strategy Choices of the Women's Social and Political Union, 1913–1918." MA thesis, University of North Texas, 1977.

Langlois, Karen S. "A Fresh Voice from the West: Mary Austin, California, and American Literary Magazines, 1892–1910." *California History* 69, no. 1 (1990): 22–35.

Langlois, Karen S. "Mary Austin and Andrew Forbes: Poetry, Photography, and the Eastern Sierra." *California History* 85, no. 1 (2007): 24–43.

Mohammed, Jowan A. "Mary Hunter Austin und die Forderungen nach einer Veränderung der Geschlechterrollen in den USA, 1914–1918." In *Geschlecht und Klassenkampf: Die "Frauenfrage" aus deutscher und internationaler Perspektive im 19. und 20. Jahrhundert*, edited by Vincent Streichhahn and Frank Jacob, 222–239. Berlin: Metropol, 2020.

Norwood, Vera L. "Heroines of Nature: Four Women Respond to the American Landscape." *Environmental Review* 8, no. 1 (1984): 34–56.

Riley, Glenda. *A Place to Grow: Women in the American West*. Arlington Heights: Harlan Davidson, 1992.

Rudnick, Lois. "Feminist on the Frontier." Review of *Mary Austin: Songs of a Maverick*, by Esther Lanigan Stineman. *The Women's Review of Books* 7, no. 7 (1990): 22.

Schaefer, Heike. *Mary Austin's Regionalism: Reflections on Gender, Genre, and Geography*. Charlottesville, VA: University of Virginia Press, 2004.

Skinner, Ellen. *Women and the National Experience: Primary Sources in American History*. Boston/New York: Addison-Wesley Educational Publishers Inc., 1996.

Stineman, Esther Lanigan. "Mary Austin Rediscovered." *Journal of the Southwest* 30, no. 4 (1988): 545–551.

Stout, Janis P. *Picturing a Different West: Vision, Illustration, and the Tradition of Cather and Austin*. Lubbock, TX: Texas Tech University Press, 2007.

Wright, Elizabeth. "Mary Hunter Austin (1868–1934)." In *American Women Writers 1900–1945: A Bio-Bibliographical Critical Sourcebook*, edited by Laurie Champion, 13–19. Westport, CT: Greenwood Publishing Group, 2000.

Section III: **Marriage Discourses in Literature**

Jamie Callison
8 Redefining Marriage in Interwar Britain: Internal Transformation and Personal Sacrifice in the Poetry of H.D.

[My therapist] threw his weight about, said I was going away because Mrs. Simpson left for the continent, which is pretty silly; as R.A. is doing the Mrs. Simpson dash for liberty as far as I can gather.[1]

Going through divorce proceedings in England in 1938, the American ex-patriot and modernist poet Hilda Doolittle (H.D., 1886–1961) saw her experience reflected in the case of Edward VIII (1894–1972) and her compatriot, the socialite and two-time divorcee Wallis Simpson (1896–1986). Given the Anglican opposition to divorce, Edward was unable to square his decision to marry Simpson with his role as head of the Church of England. He thus decided to abdicate the throne. The scandal gripped the nation. The "dash" to which H.D. refers was Simpson's retreat to France, following the public revelation of Edward's intention, in a bid to avoid media scrutiny. H.D.'s own divorce was granted and generated far less public attention. She would never marry again. Indeed, the letter suggests that Edward's obsession with marriage was ripe for ridicule. H.D.'s letter groans with embarrassment at the parallels suggested by Simpson's actions and her fears about the notoriety that her own divorce might attract. The poet saw parallels, too, between the romantic yearnings of Edward and those of her own soon-to-be ex-husband, the serial eloper and fellow modernist writer, Richard Aldington, who, she observed, was soon to be enjoying his "fourth honeymoon in the heal and toe of Italy and its environs."[2]

Seen through the lens of this letter, all four figures seem absurd for wasting so much time on marriage. In the 20th-century avant-garde circles in which H.D. moved, there was an attempt to do without the institution altogether. When it was practiced by members of this group, marriage might well function as a way of providing legal standing for unconventional familial structures and erotic connections. In the 1920s, for instance, H.D.'s long-term companion Bryher (i.e., Annie Winifred Ellerman [1894–1983]) married H.D.'s lover Kenneth Macpherson

---

1 H.D. "To Bryher," February 6, 1937, H.D. Papers, Yale Collection of American Literature, Beinecke Rare Book and Manuscript Library, Yale University, YCAL MSS 24, III, 48, 1201 YCAL MSS 24 (henceforth H.D. Papers), Series III: Personal Papers, Box 48, Folder 1201.
2 H.D., "To Bryher."

OpenAccess. © 2021 Jamie Callison, published by De Gruyter. This work is licensed under the Creative Commons Attribution-NonCommercial-NoDerivatives 4.0 International License.
https://doi.org/10.1515/9783110751451-008

(1902–1971)—H.D. and Aldington themselves having been long separated—and together Bryher and Macpherson adopted H.D.'s daughter, Perdita.[3] This quartet lived together, often expanding the household further to include Macpherson's male lovers. Aldington's desire for a serial, if at times overlapping, monogamy recognized by law looks, from this perspective, quaint. Building on this and similar legacies in the second half of the 20th century, second-wave feminism, from Simone de Beauvoir to Betty Friedan, chronicled the exhausting limitations of heterosexual marriage and sought to imagine alternative ways of living.[4] A similar impulse was reflected in various gay subcultures and the critical thought these generated with a particular focus on the exclusionary logic upon which marriage relied.[5] Not all lives looked like H.D.'s, but she was among the vanguard of broader social change.

These narrative elements slot into a wider story. Marriage was an institution underwritten by religious institutions. After the First World War, the Church of England was able to mobilize its supporters to stave off, at least for a time, a liberalization of divorce laws.[6] By the late 1930s, however, it no longer mustered sufficient support to retain the existing arrangement. Church teaching on marriage and divorce and the legal framework that reinforced it decoupled. Lacking control of what by then were becoming secular institutions, the Church watched as the lives of its congregants and former congregants came to reflect patterns increasingly at odds with its own teaching. In turn, far fewer people chose to voluntarily bind themselves to this teaching. This is the basic structure of secularization as outlined by Peter Berger in *The Sacred Canopy* (1984). Religion is seriously eroded once the secular state takes control of the institutions formerly run by churches and becomes a matter of individual choice.[7]

With her wry comment about the royals, H.D. appears invested in this narrative, and yet marriage makes a surprise reappearance in one of her major works, *Helen in Egypt* (1961). This work is a modern epic poem, reflecting on the Trojan War in quite different ways to those found in Homer and written a dec-

---

3 See Barbara Guest, *Herself Defined: The Poet H.D. and Her World* (Garden City, NY: Doubleday, 1984), 202–206.
4 See Jane F. Gerhard, *Desiring Revolution: Second-Wave Feminism and the Rewriting of Twentieth-Century American Sexual Thought* (New York: Columbia University Press, 2001), 13–50.
5 Michael Warner, *The Trouble with Normal: Sex, Politics, and the Ethics of Queer Life* (Cambridge, MA: Harvard University Press, 2000), 81–148.
6 Caitriona Beaumont, "Moral Dilemmas and Women's Rights: The Attitude of the Mothers' Union and Catholic Women's League to Divorce, Birth Control and Abortion in England, 1928–1939," *Women's History Review* 16, no. 4 (2007): 467.
7 Peter L. Berger, *The Sacred Canopy: Elements of a Sociological Theory of Religion* (Garden City, NY: Doubleday, 1984), 127–154.

ade or so after her belated divorce. Helen chooses to bind herself in a form of marriage with Achilles at the close of the poem. H.D.'s thinking in this was informed by the French comparative literature scholar and cultural critic Denis de Rougemont, particularly his work *L'Amour et l'Occident* (1939) or as it appeared in the English translation H.D. used alongside the French, *Passion and Society*. De Rougemont's work was one of a number of texts that thought through the implications of the 20th century's liberalization of divorce laws for marriage in general and particularly for what Cosmo Lang (1864–1945), the Archbishop of Canterbury who did much to force Edward's abdication, called the "Christian principles of marriage."[8] The influence of this branch of thinking on H.D., who was neither a practicing Christian nor inclined to pro-marriage arguments, reveals a limitation in 20th-century social thought and opens up one particular line of post-secular critique of the contemporary emphasis on autonomy and self-development.[9] In what follows I survey, first, the legal and social contexts for H.D.'s own divorce before moving on to the Christian response to these dynamics as represented in *Passion and Society*. Finally, I show how these ideas affected H.D.'s work and reflect key fault lines evident in the idea of the secular.

Christian Marriage and its Discontents

H.D. thought about her own marriage to Aldington as a war casualty. The couple had married in 1913 as young poets and leading figures in the Imagist poetic group that their fellow writer, publicist, and ultimately political propagandist for Mussolini, Ezra Pound, helped shape. This literary couple, in the early months of their marriage, spent idyllic holidays in Greece, and in London they wrote poetry together, contributed to journals, and worked on translations at the British Museum Reading Room. This all changed when the First World War came. H.D. suffered a traumatic stillbirth and almost died in 1915, and Aldington was conscripted in 1917 and went off to the front. Describing what followed in her *roman-à-clef Bid Me To Live*, H.D. noted how Aldington returned with what she called, in the lightly fictionalized account of events from that period, an "over-physical sensuality" or, as she put more directly in her petitioner's

---

8 Cosmo Lang, "Past and Present: Lang's Abdication Broadcast," in Robert Beaken, *Cosmo Lang: Archbishop in War and Crisis* (London: I.B. Tauris, 2012), 265.
9 See Charles Taylor, "What does Secularism Mean?" in *Dilemmas and Contradictions: Selected Essays* (Cambridge, MA: Harvard University Press, 2011), 303–325.

statement for her later divorce proceedings, "[he] became very oversexed."[10] On leave from the army, Aldington began a sexual relationship with Arabella York, *Bid Me to Live's* Bella, another member of their artistic circle and fellow resident at their London boarding house. Unable to live in such proximity to York, H.D. left London with her own lover, Cecil Gray, and ultimately became pregnant with Gray's child, Perdita.[11] Against this backdrop, Aldington and H.D. separated permanently and ultimately contentiously after a failed attempt at reconciliation in 1919.

A central trauma for H.D. involved Aldington first agreeing to be named as Perdita's father on the child's birth certificate and then later threatening to expose the fraud, laying H.D., or so she feared, open to legal consequences. Her anxieties about Aldington's intentions toward the child were a factor in Bryher and Macpherson's later decision to adopt Perdita.[12] H.D. wrote about this incident in her petitioner's statement: "I was in an extremely weak state of health after pneumonia [brought on by Spanish flu] and a dangerous confinement. On the second night after my return [to Aldington in 1919] suddenly out of nowhere his attitude completely changed and he threatened me with divorce proceedings and also with the legal consequences of registering the baby in his name."[13] The emotional conflict is evident in the correction. Is the erasure of "threatened me physically" evidence of a momentary and soon-regretted hyperbole or a second thought with one eye on managing Aldington's feelings? In any case, the conjunction of the physical threat and Aldington's sudden reneging underscores the degree to which H.D. was hurt and taken aback by the shift in position.

The shock imprinted itself on H.D.'s imagination. *Helen in Egypt* opens with a meeting between Helen and Achilles, the latter having "*lately arrived from Troy and the carnage of battle*" [H.D.'s italics].[14] Achilles is confused, staring into the fire and grappling around for answers: "who are we? who are you? /where is this desolate coast?/ who am I? am I a ghost?" (*HE*, 16). Suddenly, he grasps her throat "with his fingers' remorseless steel" (*HE*, 17). Achilles's listlessness and

---

10 H.D., *Bid Me to Live*, ed. Caroline Zilboorg (Gainesville: University of Florida Press, 2011), 33; Hilda Doolittle, "Petitioner's Statement," H.D. Papers, Yale Collection of American Literature, Beinecke Rare Book and Manuscript Library, Yale University, YCAL MSS 24, Series III: Personal Papers, Box 48, Folder 1201, 1.
11 Doolittle, "Petitioner's Statement," 5.
12 Guest, *Herself Defined*, 203.
13 Doolittle, "Petitioner's Statement," 6.
14 H.D., *Helen in Egypt* (New York: New Directions, 1961). 13. Hereafter referred to as *HE* with reference given in the body of the text.

instability owe something to the trauma of the battlefield, which H.D., through Aldington, knew of from personal experience. The biographical constriction of her own airways at the hands of the Spanish flu and Aldington's act of violence come together in the poem's portrait of Achilles's attempted strangulation. Helen spends the rest of the book trying to understand both what brought her and Achilles together and why he acted in this way at their first meeting. For an H.D. critic like Rachel Blau DuPlessis, this is merely an example of "romantic thralldom" in evidence across H.D.'s work, but therapeutically, perhaps, the scene offers H.D. the opportunity to connect with a returning soldier in a way that proved elusive with her husband.[15] This essay argues that this reconsideration was made possible, at least in part, by the way in which marriage came to be discussed in the run-up to the Second World War.

In 1919, after the failed reconciliation, H.D. had little access to divorce. Under English law, husbands were permitted to divorce wives on the grounds of adultery, but this was not reciprocal. This very visible legal inequality served as a rallying call for both the National Union of Societies for Equal Citizenship (NUSEC) and the Woman's Creative Guild, whose protests were instrumental in the passing of a 1923 bill that extended adultery provision to both parties.[16] When H.D. and Aldington divorced in 1938, the grounds were those made possible by the 1923 bill, namely Aldington's adultery.

The 1923 legal changes nevertheless had unintended consequences. They gave rise to what became known as "the hotel bill" divorce. This practice was famously sent up in Evelyn Waugh's novel, *A Handful of Dust* (1934), where the protagonist Tony pays Milly, a prostitute, to travel with him to Brighton so as to be discovered in a room alone with him by the hotel staff. This event was thereafter to be cited in his wife's petition for divorce as evidence of his adultery. In the novel, the paper-thin nature of the ruse is exposed when Milly decides to bring her young daughter along to the supposedly romantic tryst.[17] Outrage at this manipulation of the system was one of the chief factors behind

---

[15] Rachel Blau DuPlessis, "Romantic Thralldom in H. D.," *Contemporary Literature* 20, no. 2 (Spring 1979): 179.

[16] Lawmakers were also swayed by contemporary fears about the spread of venereal disease; the double standard enshrined in the existing law tacitly condoned male adultery, and lawmakers felt that without fear of becoming subject to divorce proceedings, husbands naturally inclined toward promiscuity in a way that was liable to damage public health. See Ann Sumner Holmes, "The Double Standard in the English Divorce Laws, 1857–1923," *Law & Social Inquiry* 20, no. 2 (1995): 601–620.

[17] See Henry Kha, "The Spectacle of Divorce Law in Evelyn Waugh's *A Handful of Dust* and A. P. Herbert's *Holy Deadlock*," *Law & Literature* 30, no. 2 (2018): 267–285.

a further extension to divorce provisions introduced by the Matrimonial Causes Act (1937) and ensured that the Church of England did not oppose the legislation as it had earlier bills. Archbishop Lang grudgingly explained that "as a statesman he believed that the 1937 bill provided a 'timely and valuable remedy' for many abuses, yet as a clergyman he could not support any bill in favor of divorce" and abstained from the vote in the House of Lords.[18] This extended the number of grounds upon which a petition for divorce could be granted and ultimately reflected the recommendations of a Royal Commission set up to investigate the issue and convened just prior to the First World War.[19]

While not opposing the bill, the Church of England did not offer it enthusiastic support. Lang played an important role in securing Edward VIII's abdication on the grounds that the head of the Church of England could not conduct his personal life in a manner that challenged institutional views on the indissolubility of marriage.[20] Following the radio broadcast of Edward's abdication speech, Lang himself took to the airwaves to comment on the episode:

> Even more strange and sad it is that he should have sought his happiness in a manner inconsistent with the Christian principles of marriage, and within a social circle whose standards and ways of life are alien to all the best instincts and traditions of his people. Let those who belong to this circle know that today they stand rebuked by the judgement of the Nation which had loved King Edward. I have shrunk from saying these words, but I have felt compelled for the sake of sincerity and truth to say them.[21]

The BBC received some 250 complaints following the broadcast, typically accusing Lang of "kicking a man while he's down" and defending Edward's right to personal happiness.[22] For Christians, the recognition of the degree to which the Church's attitudes to marriage were out of step with public opinion led to a variety of attempts to think through the "Christian principles of marriage," which for Lang are simply assumed and not explicated in any way. The context of the speech equates these "principles" almost entirely with opposition to divorce. As early as 1920, the novelist, literary critic, and Christian thinker Charles Williams observed that the Church had traditionally offered little in the way of positive guidance on marriage, and instead confined "herself to exhorting the

---

[18] Beaumont, "Moral Dilemmas and Women's Rights," 469.
[19] See Lawrence Stone, *Road to Divorce: English 1530–1987* (Oxford: Oxford University Press, 1990), 397–398.
[20] Beaken, *Cosmo Lang*, 118.
[21] Lang, "Past and Present," 265.
[22] Beaken, *Cosmo Lang*, 140.

newly married pair to observe their moral duties and their ecclesiastical [sic], and to repudiating divorce more or less strenuously."[23]

The decoupling of law and theology offered an opportunity for a rethink. Williams's own suggestion was a thoroughgoing sacramentalizing of sexual intercourse, which "is, or at least is capable of being in a remote but real sense, a symbol of the Crucifixion," although his ideas received little support and he proved unable to find a publisher for them.[24] Two other Oxford-based writers, Martin D'Arcy and C.S. Lewis, also contributed to this Christian re-evaluation of love. Both D'Arcy's *The Mind and Heart of Love: Lion and Unicorn* (1945) and Lewis's *The Four Loves* (1960) responded to a contemporary work by a Swedish theologian, Anders Nygren, *Agape and Eros* (1930), which had attempted to disentangle Christian love of God (agape) from the Greek celebration of desire (eros). In different ways, both D'Arcy and Lewis made the case for the significance to marriage of various forms of love, agape and eros among them.

These accounts of hitherto unexpounded principles responded not only to changes in the law but also to various non-Christian discourses of marriage. The title of Marie Stopes's *Married Love* (1918) is both euphemistic—the married love in question is heterosexual penetrative sexual intercourse—and indicative of a growing call for marriages to become far more reciprocal in tenor. The book united these ideas insofar as it traced many marital difficulties to a misunderstanding of female sexuality. It put forward an understanding of female arousal as cyclical and thus distinct from the constant background hum of the male equivalent. Stopes urged both parties in a given relationship to accommodate themselves to these rhythms in service of a more fulfilling marriage. True to Stopes's own scientific training, this understanding of arousal was couched in the terminology of modern experimental science, but *Married Love* also included passages rhapsodizing in a spiritual register on, among other things, simultaneous orgasm and conception:

> When two who are mated in every respect burn with the fire of the innumerable forces within them, which set their bodies longing towards each other with the desire to inter-penetrate and to encompass one another, the fusion of joy and rapture is not purely physical. The half swooning sense of flux which overtakes the spirit in that eternal moment at the apex of rapture sweeps into its flaming tides the whole essence of the man and woman, and as it were, the heat of the contact vapourises their consciousness so that it fills the whole of cosmic space. For the moment they are identified with the divine thoughts, the waves of eternal force, which to the Mystic often appear in terms of golden light. From

---

23 Charles Williams, *Outlines of Romantic Theology* (Grand Rapids, MI: Eerdmans, 1990), 9.
24 Ibid., 24.

their mutual penetration into the realms of supreme joy the two lovers bring back with them a spark of that light which we call life.
And unto them a child is born.[25]

Paul Peppis has shown how *Married Love* endeavored to appeal to two different constituencies: proponents of free love and defenders of social purity.[26] From this perspective, the insistence that this "joy and rapture is not purely physical" but rather "eternal" and "cosmic" and the fact that intercourse is connected to conception is weighted to find favor among the latter—although the link between the intensity of the described sexual experience and the biblical echo of "unto them a child is born" (Isaiah 9:6–7) is notably underdeveloped. Is Stopes, for instance, suggesting a link between simultaneous orgasm and conception, or between a focus on conception and the intensity of sexual experience? More than that, though, the allusion to Isaiah and the fact that these climaxing lovers are "identified with the divine thoughts, the waves of eternal force, which to the Mystic often appear in terms of golden light" goes beyond mouthing reassuring pieties. Sex, here, is not merely necessary to a happy marriage, but rather a channel for spiritual growth. Stopes's account of an orgasm-induced altered state of consciousness is pulled up by the hedging of "as it were," and yet it is unclear how "the heat of contact vapourises their consciousness so it fills the whole of cosmic space" is any more figurative than the "half swooning sense of flux which overtakes the spirit in that eternal moment at the apex of rapture sweeps into its flaming tides the whole essence of the man and woman" that precedes it. Both parts of the sentence make claims as to the transformative effects of sex. In recognition of not only Stopes's attempt to appeal to the social purity constituency but also the pragmatic accommodations necessary given her cyclical account of female desire, marriage is the forum in which these sexual encounters become possible, and they facilitate a form of spiritual self-development.

Stopes's American contemporary, the feminist writer and activist Florence Tuttle, outlined an idea of "spiritual marriage" that also drew on ideas of self-development, although her account reflects a greater interest in the psychological exercise of the will and combines this with an interest that Stopes also indulged elsewhere in a particular form of eugenics. Tuttle's *The Awakening of Woman: Suggestions from the Psychic Side of Feminism* (1915) presents a brief account of human evolution, arguing that it did not end with the emergence of rea-

---

25 Marie Stopes, *Married Love: A New Contribution to the Solution of Sex Difficulties* (London: Fifield, 1918), 77–78.
26 See Paul Peppis, *Sciences of Modernism: Ethnography, Sexology, and Psychology* (Oxford: Oxford University Press, 2013), 166.

son and mankind's problem-solving capacities. There was, Tuttle contends, a corresponding spiritual development, which she conceives of largely as a capacity for altruism.[27] Marriage, for her, needs to recognize this spiritual stage of human development, and this involves an appreciation that

> ... marriage is a psychical as well as a physical contract. It implies complete and united character selection. Character denotes those dominating qualities that the individual has trouped to constitute personality. Character becomes, thus, spiritual capital, an investment in qualities we choose to possess. (*AW*, 157)

Tuttle centers her understanding of marriage on the idea of choice. Both parties choose a partner on the basis of a shared vision of truth, rather than physical characteristics or through financial or parental compulsion (*AW*, 158–159). Her vision of a spiritual marriage is one in which two people with complementary worldviews come together to work on a shared project. "For two people to see the same truth, to pool their vision and jointly work for it," she argues, "is to enrobe life with a new color and enthusiasm" (*AW*, 162). Working toward this common goal, perfectly in step, such spiritual marriages will enable the human race to ascend higher into an increasingly complex and developed state. This understanding arises from the significance she accords the exercise of the will. Her evolutionary account ends with the declaration that "evolution sweeps aside all discussions and declares that man [...] stands at the pinnacle of creation, his future bounded only by the circumference of his own will" (*AW*, 155).

While it is not entirely clear that such an understanding of human development is best squared with the institution of marriage—is this unbounded human capacity not better served alone?—Tuttle reconciles the two perspectives via her understanding of evolutionary development. The exercise of the will becomes an increasingly complex, and thus developmentally higher, activity through this coming together of two distinct yet harmonized wills. By contrast, a woman constrained in marriage by parental or financial considerations is barred from exercising her own will and consequently fails to ascend, harming not only the woman's own self-development, but also the conditions of society at large. Spiritual marriages had a eugenic impact insofar as the developmental ascent of the well-matched couple issues in better adapted children, while poorly chosen marriage would not help raise the level of the overall human stock.

---

27 Florence Guertin Tuttle, *The Awakening of Woman: Suggestions from the Psychic Side of Feminism* (New York: Abingdon, 1915), 154. Hereafter referred to as *AW* with reference given in the body of the text.

Thus, marriage for both Stopes and Tuttle feeds into what the historian Lucy Delap calls the avant-garde feminism of "internal transformation."[28] Organizations like the NUSEC challenged the Church of England's stranglehold on marriage law, and further legal campaigns for broader grounds for divorce were largely successful in disentangling theological or scriptural opposition to divorce from the legal code. Yet Stopes and Tuttle represent another dimension for thinking about marriage focused not so much on legal constraints as the idea of marriage as an interpersonal phenomenon taking place between two people at a particular time. To describe this, the language of equality central to legal debates was put aside in favor of the language of self-development. This helped address the problematic ideas of personal sacrifice, of wife and mother, for the good of the family or, as Virginia Woolf put it, thinking of the famous Victorian symbol, "killing the Angel in the House."[29] In this new marriage discourse, marriage is a means for self-actualization rather than the end of it. Yet, this particular perspective issued in challenges from both de Rougemont's *Passion and Society* and H.D.'s *Helen in Egypt*. Both authors were skeptical about the emphasis on personal autonomy in these secular understandings of marriage.

Many Loves: Denis de Rougemont on Eros and Agape

De Rougemont's *Passion and Society* was by turns theological survey, historical narrative, literary analysis, and cultural critique. De Rougemont sought to isolate the theological and ritual underpinnings of an understanding of love stemming from the Cathars, a dualist sect in 12th-century France condemned as heretical by the Roman Catholic Church and closely associated with the lives and work of the troubadour poets.[30] From there, he argued that the Catharist view of love exerted continued influence on contemporary attitudes toward romance, distorting, in doing so, modern views of marriage. The Cathars were, he suggested, an unnamed third party in many of the divorces of his day. The influence stemmed from a society-wide overvaluation of romantic passion: "Men and

---

28 Lucy Delap, *The Feminist Avant-Garde: Transatlantic Encounters of the Early Twentieth Century* (Cambridge: Cambridge University Press, 2007), 6–7.
29 Virginia Woolf, "Professions for Women," in *Collected Essays*, 2 vols. (London: Hogarth Press, 1966), 2:286.
30 For a comparable narrative drawing on similar sources, see Ezra Pound, "Psychology and Troubadours," *Quest* 4, no. 1 (October 1912): 37–53.

women today, in being creatures of passion, expect an overwhelming love to produce some revelation either regarding themselves or about life at large."³¹ A relationship acts as a conduit for some revelation inaccessible in single life and has remarkably little to do with the romantic partner. De Rougemont saw this fascination with passion at work in numerous modern endeavors to uncover primal instincts and drives, to peel back layers of cultivation in order to uncover what was deepest, basest, most fundamental in the psyche.

This contemporary fascination with passion was, de Rougemont goes on, the "last vestige of the primitive mysticism" associated with the Cathars (*PS*, 293). This mysticism was derived from the classical idea of eros, which he understood as "complete Desire, luminous Aspiration, the primitive religious soaring carried to its loftiest pitch, to the extreme exigency of purity which is also the extreme exigency of Unity" (*PS*, 74). The emphasis on the otherworldly, non-mediated here differentiates this version of eros from its more common equation with sexual love, which—in Diotima's famous speech in Plato's *Symposium*—acts as a stage in the ascent from the physical to the metaphysical. Such an outlook did, of course, have Christian descendant. Dante's feelings for Beatrice represent one prominent example. The "effort" of Dante and his contemporaries, the poet and critic T.S. Eliot argued, "was to enlarge the boundary of human love so as to make it a stage in the progress toward the divine."³² In the world of eros as de Rougemont understands it, sex was only ever a distraction. Eros is characterized as a desire to leave the created world, which seems tarnished, evil, limited, and to achieve a mystical reunion with the world of spirit from which humankind properly came. The steps of eros, then, do not so much bring a pilgrim closer to what is divine as allow him to peek out over the top and ultimately, in doing so, to visualize his own annihilation.

The Christian counterpart to eros is agape. If passion attempts to soar beyond the earthly realm, then agape takes place in time, fully mediated by earthly experience: "the symbol of Love is no longer the infinite *passion* of a soul in quest of light, but the *marriage* of Christ and the Church" (*PS*, 83). He goes on to stress the duties that attend the lover in the here and now:

---

31 Denis de Rougemont, *Passion and Society*, trans. Montgomery Belgion (London: Faber & Faber, 1940), 293. H.D.'s copy is held at the Beinecke Library, Yale University, http://hdl.han dle.net/10079/bibid/602571. Hereafter referred to as *PS* with reference given in the body of the text.
32 T.S. Eliot, "The Clark Lectures. Lectures on the Metaphysical Poetry of the Seventeenth Century with Special Reference to Donne, Crashaw and Cowley," in *The Complete Prose of T. S. Eliot: The Critical Edition*, ed. Ronald Schuchard, 8 vols., 2:707, Project Muse, accessed November 20, 2020, https://about.muse.jhu.edu/muse/eliot-prose/.

> The mistake lies in supposing that "the real thing", the longing for which has now become an obsession, is there to be found. It is not lying in wait for us on the far side of a surrender to enervated instinct and resentful flesh. It is not hidden, but lost. The only way to recover it is by building it up afresh, thanks to an effort that shall go against passion—that is to say, by some action, a putting in order, a purification, that will bring us back to the sober mean. (*PS*, 241)

Passion, the desire to connect with "the real thing" hidden behind appearances, prevents the lover from ever seeing the beloved. Love becomes an essay at self-fulfillment. Agape, by contrast, takes the worldly present as its starting point and develops a relationship; it consists of "some action, a putting in order, a purification." Marriage is the key undertaking here, although de Rougemont's recommendation of the "sober mean" stands in stark contrast with the idea of wedded bliss. Indeed, he goes on to define marriage as a "wager" (*PS*, 311), a term that emphasizes the risk it involves. Despite the best intentions of all involved, the project one works toward, the relationship one attempts to build, could fail. Opening up creates vulnerability and agape resides in this ever-present exposure to potential loss.

Eros and agape can be understood as consecutive stages: the former associated with the classical world, the latter ushered in with the advent of Christendom. De Rougemont broadly subscribes to this periodization, but the Cathars complicated this timeline by cultivating classical eros in the midst of the Holy Roman Empire, sowing their beliefs and practices across Europe. Eros was not only an idea. The Cathars had instead an entire *worldview and set of practices* tied to it, and it was this broader cultural influence that shaped much of the literature of romance. *Passion and Society* opens with an analysis of the myth of the "parting lovers," Tristan and Iseult, whose adulterous love breaks apart a kingdom. Attending to not only the social upheaval the pair countenance in pursuit of love but also the limited time they spend with each other in various versions of the story, de Rougemont contends "Tristan and Iseult do not love one another ... *What they love is love and being in love*" (*PS*, 51). These lovers are party to a love that, far from celebrating an embodied other, uses that other as a conduit for the aforementioned "primitive soaring"; their relationship is marked by "a desire that never relapses, that nothing can satisfy"—the lovers have no real interest in each other, thinking only of a reunion with spirit (*PS*, 74). These assumptions inform the doctrine of the "*fruitfulness of suffering*" central to the Catharist worldview and practice (*PS*, 247).

While the contemporary lionization of passion harked back to the heretical revival of eros, its modern instantiation was inevitably dissociated from the religious group that had shaped it. Modern romance was, in other words, what the Victorian anthropologist Edward Tyler called a "survival"—a ritual practice or saying separated from its original context in such a way as to have lost its meaning.³³ Relationships can never deliver on their salvific, revelatory promises precisely because these claims are religious in origin, shaped by a theological, ritual, and cultural context inaccessible to us. Modern relationships are cut off from this religious nexus of meaning, and the desire and the resulting failure can only ever be disorientating.

Against "Tender Kisses, the Soft Caresses": Love and War in H.D.

> What did Rico matter with his blood-stream,
> his sex fixations, his man-is-man, woman-is-woman?
> This was not true.³⁴

De Rougemont's ideas found counterparts in the character of Rico in *Bid Me to Live*, H.D.'s portrait of D.H. Lawrence. Rico searches for what de Rougemont calls the "real thing" of passion. This pursuit recalls Eliot's own account of Lawrence, whom he saw as attempting to descend to the lowest levels of consciousness, stripping off accumulated and ultimately decadent layers of civilized appearance in order to achieve a worldview undistorted by contemporary fashions.³⁵ De Rougemont later mouths what he takes to be Lawrence's deeply unsympathetic outlook:

> You made woman into a kind of divinity—coquettish, cruel, and vampiric. Your fatal women, your adulterous women, and your women made arid by virtue, have emptied life of all delight for us. We shall get our own back on them. Woman is first and foremost a female. We are going to make her drag herself to the domineering male on her belly. Instead of describing courtesy, we shall praise the cunning of animal desire, the complete obsession of the mind by sex. And our vast bestial innocence will rid us of your liking for sin, which is but a disease of the procreative instinct. ... Your taboos are sacrileges on the real divinity, which is Life. And life is instinct released from mind, a great solar power that crushes and magnifies the prolific man, the magnificent unleashed bully. (*PS*, 240)

---

33 See Edward Burnett Tylor, *Primitive Culture: Researches into the Development of Mythology, Philosophy, Religion, Language, Art, and Custom*, 2 vols. (London: John Murray, 1871), 1:70–139; see also Timothy Larsen, *The Slain God: Anthropologists and the Christian Faith* (Oxford: Oxford University Press, 2014), 22–27.
34 H.D., *Bid Me to Live*, 35
35 "He wished to go as low as possible in the scale of human consciousness, in order to find something that he could assure himself was real." T.S. Eliot, *After Strange Gods: A Primer of Modern Heresy*, in *Complete Prose*, 5:487.

The critic unites H.D.'s concern with Lawrence's talk of "women-consciousness" ("women is first and foremost a female") and his "sex obsession" ("the cunning of animal desire, the complete obsession of the mind by sex") and Eliot's sense of the significance of Lawrence's search for the real outside of civilizational norms ("Your taboos are sacrileges on the real divinity, which is Life"). What is new here is the violence or the deliberate perversity of these glorifiers of instinct in their plan to "drag [woman] to the domineering male on her belly." *Bid Me to Live* also serves as a challenge to this exemplar of what the philosopher Charles Taylor calls a subtraction narrative.[36]

H.D. read *Passion and Society* after she had written *Bid Me to Live*, so she was doubtless pleased to find her own intuitions confirmed in her critical counterpart; the Lawrence chapter, for instance, is extensively highlighted in H.D.'s own edition of the book. H.D.'s post-1940s works betray de Rougemont's influence. H.D.'s renewed interest in the Moravian Christianity of her childhood, evidenced in novels like *The Gift* and *The Mystery*, for instance, can be traced to de Rougemont's discussion of the sect. *Helen in Egypt*, too, is shaped by the competing understandings of relationships outlined in *Passion in Society*. One central component of the poem's narrative involves the eponymous hero turning her back on what Susan Stanford Friedman calls a "joyous act of springtime love," apparently taking de Rougemont's commitment to a romantic sobriety to heart.[37] The poem stages the respective pulls of Paris and Achilles on Helen's attentions—with the Trojan calling out for his former lover in a way that remains unmatched by Achilles:

> why, why would you deny
> the peace, the sanctity
> of this small room,
>
> the lantern there by the door?
> why must you recall
> the white fire of unnumbered stars,
>
> rather than that single taper
> burning in an onyx jar,
> where you swore
>
> never, never to return,
> ("return the wanton to Greece"),
> where we swore together

---

36 Charles Taylor, *A Secular Age* (Cambridge, MA: Harvard University Press, 2007), 572–575.
37 Susan Stanford Friedman, *Psyche Reborn: The Emergence of H.D.* (Bloomington, IN: Indiana University Press, 1981), 255.

> defiance of Achilles
> and the thousand spears,
> we alone would compel the Fates,
>
> we chosen of Cytheraea;
> can you forget the pact?
> why would you recall another?
> (*HE*, 141–142)

Paris opposes the candlelit intimacy of their love affair in the "sanctity/ of this small room" with the cosmic intensity of Helen's yearning for Achilles, comparable, perhaps, to Iseult's desire for Tristan. He works hard to formalize this most famous of adulterous unions through repeated reference to the vows they "swore," their unique and special status ("we alone would compel the Fates,/ we chosen of Cytheraea"), and the shift over the course of the passage from the second person—why have "you" betrayed me?—to the first-person plural—"we" made a commitment to live in opposition to the martial death cult of Greece represented by "Achilles/ and the thousand spears." The references to the warmly lit haunts of the Paris-Helen romance (the "lantern," "the onyx jar") underscore the earthly nature of the relationship in contrast with what Paris takes to be the insubstantial nature of Helen's connection with Achilles, lit by "the white fire of unnumbered stars." A fact most evident in the rhetoric of the passage itself; Paris pleads and suffers for Helen's love, while Achilles remains withdrawn, removed, distant.

Paris's description of Helen's bedazzlement remembers Helen and Achilles's first meeting. On the beach where Helen first catches sight of him, Achilles is described as the "*Star in the night*" (*HE*, 17) to whom, we later learn, "god willed" Helen be joined (*HE*, 102); later, too, Achilles's mother, the nymph Thetis, advises Helen to "*Seek not another Star*" (*HE*, 178). Achilles finds himself in the firmament, far removed from the proximity and intimacy that characterized the Helen-Paris romance. Throughout the poem, Helen struggles with this idea of a luminous Achilles, but in the third poem of the book—where the character becomes a "realist"—the language shifts. The verse becomes clear-sighted about what is demanded of its eponymous hero:

> the sun and the seasons changed,
> and as the flower-leaves that drift
> from a tree were the numberless
>
> tender kisses, the soft caresses,
> given and received; none of these
> came into the story. (*HE*, 289)

The unwinding of a simile that compares the volume and delicacy of falling leaves to a lover's caress contemplates the sensuality of a romantic partnership. Nevertheless, this represents only the briefest of moments. The poem quickly jerks free from the reverie in the syntactic recapitulation of "none of these/ came into the story." All that one would hope from a marriage can be put out of mind. The conventions of romance are briefly entertained, "tender kisses, the soft caresses," before their dismissal in favor of the "epic, heroic" (*HE*, 289). De Rougemont's assessment of marriage as a necessarily "sober" undertaking is felt in the studied grimness of these lines.

As a character in H.D.'s work, Helen's peers are Veronica, the eponymous hero of *Pilate's Wife*, and Mary of *Trilogy*, both of whom offer feminist and revisionist versions of mythic stories. In both of these, a female on the character of the myth or story is brought to the center and given an inner life otherwise absent from the record. The Helen of the final book of *Helen in Egypt* is different. She renounces at the close a version of Delap's avant-garde feminism centered on "the self-liberation of elites, through the cultivation of the will and personality [...] a desire to seek liberation [...] through internal transformation of one's psyche and sexual being."[38] These concerns are channeled by *Pilate's Wife*, for example, with Veronica closing the novel with the observation that "It [Jesus's putative execution and actual escape] was so few days ago that it had happened (three?) but already Jesus had created a new heaven, a new earth; merely, she said to herself, by being beautiful."[39] The demythologizing impulse here, the re-description of the story of Jesus in terms of aesthetics, "by being beautiful," enables the novel to focus on the transformation of Veronica's inner life rather than the change wrought on society or new understandings of the relationship between God and his creation. By the close of the novel, she is no longer the urbane, bored, decadent figure she was at the outset. In *Helen in Egypt,* Helen spends the first two books reflecting upon the gradience of her inner life, envisioning the kinds of change through which Veronica goes, but the marriage ends all that. She gives over the possibility of further "internal transformation[s]" or what Terry Eagleton calls "the consoling illusion that fulfilment can be achieved without fundamental rupture and rebirth," and she chooses instead to act, to join herself to Achilles.[40]

Helen's decision to commit to Achilles is made against the backdrop of war, the threat of which is always bubbling up in the poem. In a choral section, the

---

[38] Delap, *Feminist Avant-Garde*, 6–7.
[39] H.D., *Pilate's Wife* (New York: New Directions, 2000), 134.
[40] Terry Eagleton, *Radical Sacrifice* (New Haven, CT: Yale University Press, 2018), 8.

complexity of the relationship between love and war is played out in the sound patterns of the verse so that "the rhythms must speak for themselves" (*HE*, 178):

> War, Ares, Achilles, Amor;
> ...
> could Achilles be the father of Amor,
> Begotten of Love and of War? (*HE*, 179)

In the thread of nouns, proper and otherwise—"War, Ares, Achilles, Amor"—love and war are linked through both the assonance that facilitates the entry of a new god of love ("Amor") into a list constructed from terms associated with battle ("War, Ares, Achilles") and the cross-language rhyme of the English "War" and the Latin "Amor." In this auditory similarity, one might hear a hint of the unity to which Friedman attends, and yet rhymes work through both similarity and difference; identical words do not rhyme, and the difference here is further underlined by the fact that the rhyme moves across linguistic boundaries.[41] The auditory connection suggests that a change in one area affects the other. "Was Troy lost for a kiss,/ or a run of notes on a lyre?" (*HE*, 230), Helen asks elsewhere, a question that can be read as merely rhetorical. As with W.B. Yeats's lyric "The Sorrow of Love," it is the tragedy of Helen's "red mournful lips." The inevitable connection between love and war serves as the inspiration for art, inspiration that, for Yeats, frees man from mere slavish mimesis of nature.[42] There is a timelessness to the situation: love, war, and art are part of a cycle that cannot be broken, and *Helen in Egypt* is merely the latest iteration. H.D.'s work is nevertheless as much dramatic poem as it is lyric and narrative. While relaying the poet's reflections on love and war and re-telling the story of the fall of Troy, the poem also expresses the perspectives of its characters. Read in Helen's voice, these lines do not merely articulate a universal resignation in the face of the inevitability of the process; "'Was Troy lost for a kiss/ or a run of notes on a lyre?' I won't let that happen again," Helen seems to say. Helen and Achilles's union is not a perpetuation of the aforementioned cycle, but a challenge to it. Unlike de Rougemont's Tristan and Iseult, whose passion tears apart a kingdom, Achilles and Helen's marriage represents an attempt to halt the cycle to which the poem draws attention.

---

41 Rhyme "is the phonological correlation of differing semantic units at distinctive points in verse." "Rhyme," *The Princeton Handbook of Poetic Terms*, 3rd ed., eds. Roland Greene and Stephen Cushman (Princeton, NJ: Princeton University Press, 2016), 294.
42 W.B. Yeats, "The Sorrow of Love," in *The Collected Poems of W.B. Yeats*, New Ed., ed. Richard J. Finneran (London: Macmillan, 1989), 40.

The climax of *Helen in Egypt* depicts not the internal transformation of the character, but the loss of self for a greater good. Informed by de Rougemont and the broader attempt to think about marriage in terms other than indissolubility, H.D. has Helen give up ideals that she herself—and, indeed, many of her readers—held dear, representing a turn away from the fascination with what Delap's calls the feminism of "inward transformation" that runs through Stopes, Tuttle, and indeed much of H.D.'s own *oeuvre* and the earlier books of *Helen in Egypt* itself.

Conclusion

In her personal life, H.D. exemplified many of the broader sociological trends in and around marriage. She contributed to the burgeoning divorce statistics and later rejected marriage altogether, scoffing at those who remained attracted to the institution. At various points, she was part of a broader avant-garde resistance to the forms of life represented by marriage. Yet, for all that, she was critical of the increasingly individualistic, self-developmental, and in de Rougemont's view, nihilistic attitudes to marriage in contemporary thinking about the institution. This ambivalence represents complicated attitudes toward the secular. Tuttle, Stopes, and others outlined forms of marriage in which the couple helped each other grow and develop. H.D. and Aldington had subscribed to such views themselves. And yet, the 20th century's wars intervened, and this arrangement proved painfully insufficient. Secularism emphasized individual autonomy and helped remake relationships after this pattern through a 20th-century critique of traditional understandings of marriage. De Rougemont's critique responded to this remade romantic world, pointed out its limitations, and sought to offer an alternative understanding that, for H.D., chimed with the way in which love and war had collided in her own life. The very oddness of the poem's ending can be best understood not so much as a failed attempt at feminine liberation after the pattern of Blau DuPlessis's "romantic thralldom" as a bracing alternative to a number of the assumptions running through early 20th-century feminist accounts of marriage.

Works Cited

Archival Sources

Doolittle, Hilda (H.D.). *Papers*. Yale Collection of American Literature, Beinecke Rare Book and Manuscript Library.

Secondary Sources

Beaken, Robert. *Cosmo Lang: Archbishop in War and Crisis*. London: I.B. Tauris, 2012.
Beaumont, Caitriona. "Moral Dilemmas and Women's Rights: the attitude of the Mothers' Union and Catholic Women's League to divorce, birth control and abortion in England, 1928–1939." *Women's History Review* 16, no. 4 (2007): 463–485.
Berger, Peter L. *The Sacred Canopy: Elements of a Sociological Theory of Religion*. Garden City, NY: Doubleday, 1984.
Blau DuPlessis, Rachel. "Romantic Thralldom in H.D." *Contemporary Literature* 20, no. 2 (Spring 1979): 178–203.
Doolittle, Hilda (H.D.). *Bid Me to Live*. Edited by Caroline Zilboorg. Gainesville: University of Florida Press, 2011.
Doolittle, Hilda (H.D.). *Helen in Egypt*. New York: New Directions, 1961.
Doolittle, Hilda (H.D.). *Pilate's Wife*. New York: New Directions, 2000.
Eagleton, Terry. *Radical Sacrifice*. New Haven, CT: Yale University Press, 2018.
Eliot, T.S. *After Strange Gods: A Primer of Modern Heresy*. In *The Complete Prose of T. S. Eliot: The Critical Edition*, vol. 4, edited by Ronald Schuchard. Project Muse. https://about.muse.jhu.edu/muse/eliot-prose/.
Eliot, T.S. "The Clark Lectures. Lectures on the Metaphysical Poetry of the Seventeenth Century with Special Reference to Donne, Crashaw and Cowley." In *The Complete Prose of T. S. Eliot: The Critical Edition*, vol. 2, edited by Ronald Schuchard. Project Muse. https://about.muse.jhu.edu/muse/eliot-prose/.
Gerhard, Jane F. *Desiring Revolution: Second-Wave Feminism and the Rewriting of Twentieth-Century American Sexual Thought*. New York: Columbia University Press, 2001.
Greene, Roland and Stephen Cushman, eds. *The Princeton Handbook of Poetic Terms*. 3rd ed. Princeton, NJ: Princeton University Press, 2016.
Guest, Barbara. *Herself Defined: The Poet H.D. and Her World*. Garden City, NY: Doubleday, 1984.
Kha, Henry. "The Spectacle of Divorce Law in Evelyn Waugh's *A Handful of Dust* and A. P. Herbert's *Holy Deadlock*." *Law & Literature* 30, no. 2 (2018): 267–285.
Lang, Cosmo. "Past and Present: Lang's Abdication Broadcast." In Robert Beaken, *Cosmo Lang: Archbishop in War and Crisis*, 263–267. London: I.B. Tauris, 2012.
Larsen, Timothy. *The Slain God: Anthropologists and the Christian Faith*. Oxford: Oxford University Press, 2014.
Peppis, Paul. *Sciences of Modernism: Ethnography, Sexology, and Psychology*. Oxford: Oxford University Press, 2013.
Pound, Ezra. "Psychology and Troubadours." *Quest* 4, no. 1 (October 1912): 37–53.

Rougemont, Denis de. *Passion and Society*. Translated by Montgomery Belgion. London: Faber & Faber, 1940.

Stanford Friedman, Susan. *Psyche Reborn: The Emergence of H.D.* Bloomington, IN: Indiana University Press, 1981.

Stone, Lawrence. *Road to Divorce: English 1530–1987*. Oxford: Oxford University Press, 1990.

Stopes, Marie. *Married Love: A New Contribution to the Solution of Sex Difficulties*. London: Fifield, 1918.

Sumner Holmes, Ann. "The Double Standard in the English Divorce Laws, 1857–1923." *Law & Social Inquiry* 20, no. 2 (Spring 1995): 601–620.

Taylor, Charles. *A Secular Age*. Cambridge MA: Harvard University Press, 2007.

Taylor, Charles. "What does Secularism Mean?" In *Dilemmas and Contradictions*, 303–325. Cambridge, MA: Harvard University Press, 2011.

Tuttle, Florence Guertin. *The Awakening of Woman: Suggestions from the Psychic Side of Feminism*. New York: Abingdon, 1915.

Tylor, Edward Burnett. *Primitive Culture: Researches into the Development of Mythology, Philosophy, Religion, Language, Art, and Custom*. 2 vols. London: John Murray, 1871.

Warner, Michael. *The Trouble with Normal: Sex, Politics, and the Ethics of Queer Life*. Cambridge, MA: Harvard University Press, 2000.

Williams, Charles. *Outlines of Romantic Theology*. Grand Rapids, MI: Eerdmans, 1990.

Woolf, Virginia. "Professions for Women." In *Collected Essays*. 2 vols. London: Hogarth Press, 1966.

Yeats, W.B. *The Collected Poems of W.B. Yeats*. Edited by Richard J. Finneran. New Ed. London: Macmillan, 1989.

Jessica Allen Hanssen
9 Scenes from a Marriage: *The Age of Innocence* as Discourse on the Transactional Value of Marriage

Introduction

Edith Wharton's 1920 novel *The Age of Innocence*[1] is an innovative masterwork of tension and suspense; even the most domestic of its descriptions only heighten the reader's anticipation to find out what happens next. Frankly, it does not have the most unusual plot: a privileged young man marries one woman out of duty while believing he is in love with an exotic yet inaccessible other, and is forced to deal with the emotional and social consequences of the choices he makes for the rest of his life. Indeed, the themes of vanity and fallibility against the passage of time have been covered in long form by such heavy-hitters as Johann Wolfgang von Goethe, Marcel Proust, and Henry James. Yet *The Age of Innocence* is remarkable in its expression of the at-the-time insignificant moments which ultimately define a person's, marriage's, or culture's destiny. Wharton's contribution to the novelistic genre comes from the singular and thoughtful way she builds psychological tension through narrative focalization, thus allowing characterization and discourse to emerge through connecting with her reader's knowledge as well as her own lived experience.

Through establishing how Wharton explores a complex marital situation through a selective inclusion of significant cultural forces such as visual arts and earlier American literature into the narrative and builds mood through expanding interpretative spaces at key junctures in the novel, we can establish how *The Age of Innocence* stands as a powerful and still-influential document on the nature of transaction in marriage discourse in 20th-century American literature. This chapter will therefore present both biographical and literary historical data that establishes the context for Wharton's work. It will also briefly introduce and explore some cultural developments of the early 20th century, such as the rise of psychoanalysis and secularization, which itself might be understood as transactional in nature, that might have impacted a contemporary audience's awareness of marriage discourse. These will then inform an interpreta-

---

[1] All primary quotations from *The Age of Innocence* are taken from Edith Wharton, *The Age of Innocence* (New York: Penguin Classics, 1996 [1920]).

OpenAccess. © 2021 Jessica Allen Hanssen, published by De Gruyter. This work is licensed under the Creative Commons Attribution-NonCommercial-NoDerivatives 4.0 International License.
https://doi.org/10.1515/9783110751451-009

tive analysis built on a close reading of key elements of the marriage of protagonist Newland Archer and his wife, May Welland Archer, in *The Age of Innocence*, leading to a thus-informed discussion of the novel's significance to marriage discourse in later 20th-century American fiction.

Wharton's *Tableau Vivant*

Edith Wharton's place in American society, born in Old New York and raised among a moneyed and privileged elite yet denied a formal education, as would have been proper for women of her class and time, led her to struggle as a younger woman with a feeling of living the *tableau vivant*—living in imitation of the real thing, as numerous biographers such as R. W. B. Lewis and more recently Hermione Lee have observed.[2] She uses the novel form as a means for narrativizing her internal conflict and as a protest against it. Wharton's descriptive yet exacting writing style is remembered not least for her representation, through words, of the *tableau vivant*, the living picture. The *tableau vivant* was a popular form of entertainment in the 19th century, in which people would don elaborate costumes and pose as living waxworks in front of carefully constructed sets intended to represent paintings. For example, one of her most enduring characters, Lily Bart of *The House of Mirth* (1902),[3] famously participates in a *tableau vivant* and enjoys being on display for her friends to admire, but when the admiration stops, so does her sense of wellbeing, with disastrous results.

Wharton herself was the subject of numerous portraits as an infant and child, as though her principal value was to sit still and look pretty, without too much thought given to what she might have to say. Emily J. Orlando, having studied Wharton's attitude and ideas on visual art, notes that Wharton's heroines progress "from victim to agents in the visual marketplace"[4] and that she often alludes to art and art collecting as part of a "scathing critique" of a male-centered society.[5] The very title *The Age of Innocence* is taken from a 1788 painting by Sir Joshua Reynolds (Fig. 1), who was much admired by Wharton's fellow New Yorker Washington Irving and his London social set, notably

---

[2] Richard Warrington Baldwin Lewis, *Edith Wharton: A Biography* (New York: Harper & Row, 1975); Hermione Lee, *Edith Wharton* (New York: Vintage Books, 2008).
[3] Edith Wharton, *The House of Mirth* (New York: Charles Scribner's Sons, 1905).
[4] Emily J. Orlando, *Edith Wharton and the Visual Arts* (Tuscaloosa: University of Alabama Press, 2007), 24.
[5] Orlando, *Visual Arts*, 4.

Charles Leslie and Sir Walter Scott (an author young Edith was expressly forbidden from reading until she was married[6]). The painting is of a young girl with reddish hair, perhaps five or six years old and not unlike Wharton herself at about that age (Fig. 2), looking off into the distance as though lost in thought. By using this painting as the starting point for her novel, Wharton ironically suggests that one is innocent, or devoid of the necessity of social code, only in childhood; that there can be no "age of innocence" beyond that point, and especially within the context and boundaries of marriage. Yet even the child, whom we love to believe is devoid of code and can be read like a book, has her own secret thoughts. Wharton herself reflected wistfully over her own childhood: "I have often sighed, in looking back at my childhood, to think how pitiful a provision was made for the life of the imagination behind those uniform brownstone facades,"[7] that irony being that this sentiment was brought on by a memory of seeing her first courtesan glamorously debarking a brougham at seventeen, the forms and colors of the woman and her carriage moving young Edith in their "elegance and mystery," but being sharply told to turn her head away by her mother,[8] as though profession and agency are contagious and visually transmitted. No matter how hard Newland Archer, May Welland Archer, or Wharton herself try to remember a time of innocence, once we leave childhood it is gone from us forever, if it ever existed in the first place. For women—and, not without connection but also not within the scope of this discussion, the enslaved—, this change was traditionally further signaled and cemented by the adoption of her husband's family name. The static image of the young girl, the very opposite of the *tableau vivant* motif she later became famous for, sends all of these messages at the same time.

Fortunately for American literature, Wharton received an early opportunity to travel abroad, thus inspiring her life-long interest in art and architecture and her future aesthetic sensibilities. Biographer Hermione Lee refers to Wharton's move to Europe when Edith was four years old as "the crucial first moment," when "nothing was the same afterwards."[9] She gained, even at such a young age, a sense of story and grandeur that she carried with her throughout her life, as reflected in her writing. Upon her return to America, and when beginning her career, Wharton sought to conquer what she saw as the complacency of

---

6 Lee, *Edith Wharton*, 38.
7 Edith Wharton, "A Little Girl's New York," *Harper's Magazine* 176 (March 1938): 356–364, repr. *The Age of Innocence: A Norton Critical Edition*, ed. Candace Waid (New York: W. W. Norton, 2002), 232–247. Subsequent citations refer to the Norton edition.
8 Wharton, "Little Girl's New York," 235.
9 Lee, *Edith Wharton*, 16.

Fig. 1: *The Age of Innocence* by Joshua Reynolds (1788).

her own class toward matters of genuine importance, such as art, literature, philosophy, and science. Her writings on design and architecture, both American and European, were particularly well informed and influential,[10] as was her war reportage from France, as Peter Buitenhuis documents.[11] Her unique vantage, as well as her undeniable curiosity about the world around her, led her to become one of the most astute observers of society's manners and mores, both in fiction and in non-fiction.

---

10 Edith Wharton and Ogden Codman Jr., *The Decoration of Houses* (New York: Charles Scribner's Sons, 1897).
11 Peter Buitenhuis, "Edith Wharton and the First World War," *American Quarterly* 18, no. 3 (Autumn 1966): 493–505.

Fig. 2: *Edith Jones at Age Five* by Edward Harrison May (1870).

The Age of Innocence (1920)

The Age of Innocence is Wharton's eighth full-length novel and certainly her best known. It elegantly portrays desire and betrayal in 1870s New York, a setting rife with social and economic anxiety, even among the upper classes. The novel begins as Newland Archer, a young lawyer and avid man-about-town, prepares to marry May Welland, a young debutante from a respectable and wealthy old family. Their marriage would have been completely conventional and expected, and the prospect of it was welcomed by all as a means of continuance of the established social order. Before their engagement is announced, however, he meets May's cousin, the mysterious Countess Ellen Olenska, who has returned to

New York after a long and somewhat scandalous absence, and Ellen's nonconventional style and suggestion of sexual liberation instantly appeal to Newland. The conflict of the novel arises as Newland attempts to balance his desire for Ellen with his responsibility to his (now) wife May and the emotional challenges he encounters as he naively attempts to manipulate the world to his liking.

The contemporary reception for *The Age of Innocence* was overwhelmingly positive, as Helen Killoran observes.[12] Critics noted the novel's accurate attention to literary craft, precise attention to details of setting, and its historically accurate encapsulation of a changing American way of life.[13] It seems, however, that many contemporary readers, doubtlessly seduced by the fantastic descriptions of Gilded Age fashion or the encoded entendres of 1870s upper-class society, might have missed the novel's sharp critique of its characters and their culture: when *The Age of Innocence* won the 1921 Pulitzer Prize, it was commended for being "the American novel published during the year which shall best present the wholesome atmosphere of American life, and the highest standard of American manners and manhood."[14] Clearly, Wharton did not mean for Newland and May Archer's decadent lifestyle or loveless, transactional marriage to present any kind of ideal, and wrote (in a letter to Sinclair Lewis): "When I discovered that I was being rewarded—by one of our leading Universities—for uplifting American morals, I confess I did despair."[15]

Wharton's Feminism

Wharton certainly observed the societal shift between the late 19th and early 20th centuries when it came to women's roles in marriage. Françoise Basch provides a comprehensive historical review of the various movements and ideologies that are the background for the primary setting of *Age*,[16] including the various forms of institutional oppression (economic, hegemonic, and marital) that many early American feminists fought against, but there is scant evidence that

---

[12] Helen Killoran, *The Critical Reception of Edith Wharton* (Rochester, NY: Camden House, 2001).
[13] Killoran, *Critical Reception*, 90.
[14] Mike Pride, "Edith Wharton's 'The Age of Innocence' Celebrates its 100th Anniversary," *The Pulitzer Prizes*, https://www.pulitzer.org/article/edith-whartons-age-innocence-celebrates-its-100th-anniversary.
[15] Pride, "100th Anniversary."
[16] Françoise Basch, "Women's Rights and the Wrongs of Marriage in Mid-Nineteenth-Century America," *History Workshop Journal* 22, no. 1 (Autumn 1986): 18–40.

Wharton was much engaged with these or with their impact on the emergent idea of the "New Woman." She had little use for outward manifestations of feminist ideology and was known to have refuted these in her personal[17] and professional[18] correspondence. Wharton's relationship to the feminism of her time was indeed complex, and not always as strident as a contemporary reader might prefer it to have been. One might even call it ambivalent. There is, however, also a subtle feminist discourse at work which permeates and influences Wharton's approach to narrative. Her feminism, if we can even call it that, is a quiet one, which reflects the complexities of the lived experience of women rather than treating them as either victims or proto-New Woman resistance fighters. Other critics have called attention to Wharton's engagement with the "New Woman" archetype, including, among others, Ellen Dupree,[19] and of particular relevance to this discussion, Sevinç Elaman-Garner, who claims that the juxtaposition of "the multiplicity of contending voices and perspectives on women, marriage and divorce,"[20] particularly regarding Ellen Olenska, adds nuance and depth to the archetype exactly because it does not present a clear or stereotypical vision of her intrinsic motivation. Wharton's fiction, and *The Age of Innocence* in particular, portrays women as complex characters who undertake various types of rebellion and must endure the consequences of their choices, just as the men of their set must; Wharton saw authentic characterization of sensitive and courageous people as her literary project,[21] and the success of this project stands as a testament to her lived experience, if not necessarily her stated values.

Again, it is not the intention of this chapter, or within its scope, to present a general overview of all the gender studies that have influenced a feminist reading of Wharton,[22] but a brief consideration of the impact of recent gender studies of Wharton is nonetheless essential. In particular, the 1991 study by Carol J. Sin-

---

17 Lewis, *Biography*, 476.
18 Edith Wharton, *The Writing of Fiction* (New York: Charles Scribner's Sons, 1925).
19 Ellen Dupree, "The New Woman, Progressivism, and the Woman Writer in Edith Wharton's 'The Fruit of the Tree,'" *American Literary Realism, 1870–1910* 31, no. 2 (Winter 1999): 44–62.
20 Sevinç Elaman-Garner, "Contradictory Depictions of the New Woman: Reading Edith Wharton's *The Age of Innocence* as a Dialogic Novel," *European Journal of American Studies* 11, no. 2 (Summer 2016): 17.
21 Wharton, *Writing of Fiction*, 20–21.
22 See Sandra M. Gilbert and Susan Gubar, *The Madwoman in the Attic: The Woman Writer and the Nineteenth-Century Literary Imagination* (New Haven, CT: Yale University Press, 1979); Elaine Showalter, *Sexual Anarchy: Gender and Culture at the Fin de Siècle* (New York: Penguin Books, 1991); Cynthia Griffin Wolff, *A Feast of Words: The Triumph of Edith Wharton* (New York: Oxford University Press, 1977).

gley and Susan E. Sweeney of "anxious power"²³ in Wharton's short story "Pomegranate Seed" (1931) becomes relevant here. For Singley and Sweeney, this "anxious power" derives in part from Wharton's personal "ambivalence toward the forbidden power of language" as stemming from a lingering childhood trauma,²⁴ and that the various actions women take in this story—be they reading, writing, or even dying—"also signa[l] Wharton's ambivalence toward female art and authorship"²⁵ and that, notably, any act of a woman's creative fulfillment comes at a cost. In *Age*, which comes a full ten years before "Pomegranate Seed," Wharton does not yet broach the theme so directly, but *Age* nevertheless engages the "forbidden power of language"; much of this engagement, and thus its "anxious power," takes place in the focalization, and not in the plot itself.

Early Literary Precedents

While Wharton's themes, style, and attention to focalization have frequently been compared to her relative contemporaries, notably Henry James, to whom this chapter will return, a relatively overlooked but potentially fruitful vein of comparison perhaps reaches back still further, to Nathaniel Hawthorne in particular. Although they do not share the same gender, social, or economic backgrounds, or the same historical context for their fiction, they both share an emphasis on the lived experience, one which returns frequently to the intricacies of marriage and the problems of choice. They both also use their historically centered fiction to tell stories about present-day America, such as Hawthorne did in *The Scarlet Letter* (1850), in which he used the background of colonial America and especially the historical context of the Salem witch trials to explore the limitations of religion and sexual liberation in his contemporary reality,²⁶ and also in short stories such as "The Minister's Black Veil" (1832)²⁷ and "Young Goodman Brown" (1835).²⁸

---

23 A phrase itself adapted from Gilbert and Gubar, *Madwoman*.
24 Carol J. Singley and Susan Elizabeth Sweeney, eds., *Anxious Power: Reading, Writing, and Ambivalence in Narrative by Women* (New York: State University of New York Press, 1993), 197.
25 Singley and Sweeney, *Anxious Power*, 214.
26 Nathaniel Hawthorne, *The Scarlet Letter*, 1850, vol. 1 of *The Centenary Edition of the Works of Nathaniel Hawthorne*, ed. William Charvat et al., 23 vols. (Columbus: Ohio State University Press, 1962–1997).
27 Nathaniel Hawthorne, "The Minister's Black Veil," 1836, in *Twice-Told Tales*, vol. 9 of *The Centenary Edition of the Works of Nathaniel Hawthorne*, ed. William Charvat et al., 23 vols. (Columbus: Ohio State University Press, 1962–1997), 37–53.

Additionally, both Wharton and Hawthorne share a keen awareness of the connection of visual art to the written narrative; Rita K. Gollin, in her essay studying Hawthorne's relationship to the visual arts, notes that "Nathaniel Hawthorne was born into a confident and rapidly expanding America where … there were no major collections of art, no government patronage or the arts nor generous private patrons."[29] His movement toward the exploration of American landscapes and themes was as reactionary as it was essential; for Hawthorne, "America" itself came to represent freedom from a stifling artistic tradition and also a safe distance from which to reflect upon the rest of the artistic universe. This awareness of Hawthorne's artistic concerns speaks to Wharton's approach to her own fiction, in which she frequently incorporates elements of the rest of the artistic world, for example painting, sculpture, music, and architecture, as a metaphor for the opposition of the static and the dynamic, in literature as well as in culture. Having navigated a by-then more explicitly developed system of patronage and the business side of the American arts world than Hawthorne, however, Wharton also includes reference to these realities as essential context for her outlook on the connection of art and society.

Finally, it is worth noting, by way of comparison, that Hawthorne's approach to the representation of marriage, feminism, and women's rights, which can be seen in his short stories, novels, and essays as indirect but palpable social critique, predates and clearly informs Wharton's. Hawthorne certainly draws upon an "anxious power" in his characterization of Hester Prynne and Goodwife Faith Brown, and many other women characters. In this sense, Wharton's approach to feminism builds on Hawthorne's early awareness and also informs it from her lived experience, as Margaret B. McDowell observes: "because of her sympathy with her women characters and her insight into their lives, she reveals an implicit feminism as they relate, ordinarily at some disadvantage, to individual men or to a society which men control and dominate."[30]

For these reasons, it is notable that Wharton staged her contemporary war novel in Antebellum America, as this bears structural and narrative similarity to Hawthorne's *The Marble Faun* (1860), a novel which also transposes decidedly American concerns about art, justice, and morality to, in this case, Italy, and,

---

28 Nathaniel Hawthorne, "Young Goodman Brown," 1835, in *Mosses from an Old Manse*, vol. 10 of *The Centenary Edition of the Works of Nathaniel Hawthorne*, ed. William Charvat et al., 23 vols. (Columbus: Ohio State University Press, 1962–1997), 74–90.
29 Rita K. Gollin, "Hawthorne and the Visual Arts," in *A Historical Guide to Nathaniel Hawthorne*, ed. Larry J. Reynolds (Oxford: Oxford University Press, 2001), 109.
30 Margaret B. McDowell, "Viewing the Custom of Her Country: Edith Wharton's Feminism," *Contemporary Literature* 15, no. 4 (Autumn 1974): 521–538.

revealingly, a novel that everyone at the Archer house has read.[31] *The Age of Innocence*, in fact, bears out more than a little similarity to Hawthorne's last romance, both of which chronicle the nature of a closely quartered, never-consummated, bizarre love triangle as it plays out (or not) as war becomes imminent. The connection of the Italian setting of *The Marble Faun* to *The Age of Innocence* therefore provides revelatory context for Newland Archer's actions and behavior.

Throughout the novel, Newland Archer connects his romantic impulses with Italy, imagining that one day he and May will "read *Faust* together ... by the Italian lakes."[32] He does not, of course, pull this association out of thin air; he learns it at the opera house, that palace of illusion and shimmer which Wharton's narrator witheringly describes as a world in which the "German text of French operas sung by Swedish sopranos should be translated into Italian for the clearer understanding of English-speaking audiences."[33] He never does make it to Italy with May, however, as reality kicks in and their honeymoon tour of Europe consists largely of duty calls to distant family and visits to dressmakers and tailors. The real reason that they do not go to Italy, however, is that Newland is unable to imagine his naïve May in "that particular setting"[34]; it is as though for him Italy has connotations with which he does not wish to burden her—or himself. Italy becomes for Newland the sought-for, an exercise in self-denial.

This self-denial also carries, to Wharton's contemporary reader, deep psychoanalytic connections to, for example, Freud's fear of train travel as he describes it in *The Interpretation of Dreams* (1901), which he eventually, he claims, conquers by tracing it to an early incident in which he became aroused observing his (pregnant) mother washing herself on a train. Before he conquered his fear, however, it prevented Freud from traveling to Rome to look upon the monuments, which was one of his most ardent desires. Although Newland does manage to make the European passage, he does not make it to Italy, representative of an unconscious repression of his desires and also, potentially, of the stranglehold his mother and her domineering ways have on his marriage and other life choices.

By the time Newland and May are well established in marriage, and Archer is deep into his infatuation with Ellen Olenska, he still holds the belief that somewhere outside of the confines of America, there is some kind of magical country where he could be free to love Ellen without restraint. In chapter 29,

---

31 Wharton, *Age*, 27.
32 Wharton, *Age*, 6.
33 Wharton, *Age*, 4.
34 Wharton, *Age*, 159.

tucked inside May's wedding-gift carriage with Ellen, he attempts to express his yearning to physically abandon his reality. While he is unable to properly articulate his desire, Ellen asks directly: "Is it your idea that I should live with you as your mistress—since I can't be your wife?"[35] Her ability, whether deriving from more or less sophistication than Archer possesses, to succinctly state the facts, and particularly the word "mistress," without any sort of ambiguity shocks Newland into a revelation, as he then declares to Ellen: "I want—I want somehow to get away with you into a world where words like that—categories like that—don't exist. Where we shall be simply two human beings who love each other, who are the whole of life to each other, and nothing else on earth will matter."[36] Ellen immediately calls his bluff, however, and seems to anticipate his association of romance and lack of social code with the Mediterranean: "Oh, my dear— where is that country? Have you ever been there ... I know so many who have tried to find it; and believe me, they all got out at wayside stations: at places like Boulogne, or Pisa, or Monte Carlo."[37] Ellen, with this brief catalog, deflates Newland's sincere-sounding desire as the kind of Eurotrash fantasy that only a naïve American could muster. While Hawthorne's young artists go to Rome seeking artistic—and social—freedom but find instead a world of darkness, lethargy, and seclusion, Wharton takes this idea one step further and does not allow Newland Archer the latitude to make his own discoveries. He is trapped in a world of his own creation but which is devoid of even fantasy. And while Newland's entire sense of well-being stems from having a comfortable place within a clearly defined social tradition, Ellen Olenska, as Cynthia Griffin Wolff notes, has "learned the terrible and inexorable toll that tradition takes,"[38] also bearing similarities to other of Hawthorne's doomed pairings: Goodman Brown and Faith, Mr. Hooper and Elizabeth, or Arthur Dimmesdale and Hester Prynne.

Hawthorne, however, is not the only canonical American reference for *The Age of Innocence*, and in a world where the ancestors of the old Dutch "Patroons," synthesized into the cold yet essential social arbiters the van der Luydens, reign supreme, it is perhaps not surprising that Wharton would also reach to Washington Irving for inspiration, as he, too, was an astute participant in and chronicler of the social mores of the New York of his time. Notice, for example, the playful way Wharton incorporates "Rip Van Winkle," that fabled old man of Old New York, into the story. While Irving is mentioned only in passing as

---

35 Wharton, *Age*, 238.
36 Wharton, *Age*, 238.
37 Wharton, *Age*, 238–239.
38 Wolff, *Feast of Words*, 426.

a writer that even (or only!) your mother can love, that Newland Archer's story drops off in chapter 33 when he learns of May's pregnancy and resumes in chapter 34—nearly thirty years after his marriage to May—structurally evokes the paralepsis of Rip's famous mountain siesta, and the refrain of "Why, this used to be one of the old Cesnola rooms!"[39] he hears at the Metropolitan Museum closely resembles Rip's discombobulated response, upon waking, to the metamorphosis of the King George The Third Inn to the Union Hotel, now replete with stars and stripes: "all of this was strange and incomprehensible."[40] For those who know and appreciate Irving's work and the American mythology he created, or even his life situation (in which, having experienced first a fall and then a stratospheric rise in social standing, he remained a lifelong bachelor after the tragic death of his fiancée), a whole story is told in the interstice between chapters 33 and 34.

As Rip does, Newland indeed "wakes up" in a new world, a New Land, even, and like Rip Van Winkle's framing narrator Geoffrey Crayon goes abroad to escape it, in his case to Paris, that old haunt of beauty and romance and decadence, but he cannot seem to shake the old social standards. At the moment when it is at last safe for Newland to express his true feelings for Ellen Olenska—May is dead, New York is on the far side of the Atlantic, and even his grown son Dallas approves of the reunion—Newland remains planted on a bench outside of Ellen's apartment building, content to let a closing curtain be his only sign of her existence. "It's more real to me here than if I went up," he says sitting there, articulating his life-long impulse to value the image of a thing more than the thing itself.[41] This moment was foreshadowed in chapter 30, when Newland Archer, two years after his marriage and desperately trying to conceal his growing distaste for May in what he saw as a "perpetual tepid honeymoon,"[42] insisted on opening the curtains to his library and looking out over the city of New York, on Washington Square, no less, on an icy night, breathing in the cold air while "getting the sense of other lives not his own, and a whole world beyond his world."[43] He takes a particular delight in not looking at May while doing so, just as Rip takes delight in abandoning his wife, whose opinions he valued as much as Newland seems to value May's, for the cold and remote Catskills. It is, of course, notable that Irving presents Rip van Winkle's wife,

---

[39] Wharton, *Age*, 284.
[40] Washington Irving, "Rip Van Winkle," in *The Sketch Book of Geoffrey Crayon*, 1819–20, repr. *The Legend of Sleepy Hollow and Other Stories: Or, The Sketch Book of Geoffrey Crayon, Gent.*, intro. Alice Hoffman (New York: Random House, 2001), 35.
[41] Wharton, *Age*, 298.
[42] Wharton, *Age*, 35.
[43] Wharton, *Age*, 242.

Dame van Winkle, as focalized through Rip's unfair and naïve perception of her as mean and shrewish, but also, quietly and from outside the narrative, allows the reader to appreciate her intellectual superiority, independence, and willingness to let Rip stew in his own juices; this duality informs Wharton's outlook on Newland and May's focalization as well. While Wharton's influences were broad, and also European, the deep structural connections to early American literature set the tone for and add rich context to her settings, social observations, and indirect characterizations.

Metatextual Cultural Forces

One of the many observations Wharton not only made but narrativized was the glacial pace at which large-scale societal shifts slowly but inevitably affect the insulated lives of her characters. *The Age of Innocence* comes at an interesting juncture when it comes to American attitudes on marriage. While it is mostly set in the 1870s (with a proleptic jump to the early 1900s at the very end) and documents the customs and conventions of its setting with precision, *Age* is nevertheless very much of its time in terms of its metatextual influences. The impact of psychoanalysis on the American cultural landscape, for example, began to become more pronounced in the early 1920s, while religious influence began to weaken somewhat.[44] These forces, although neither of them are explicitly

---

[44] The rise of psychoanalysis as a cultural force can be neatly tied to Freud's 1909 visit to the United States. By 1920, psychoanalysis was well established among the New York elite, as documented by Sanford Gifford, "The Psychoanalytic Movement in the United States, 1906–1991," in *History of Psychiatry and Medical Psychology*, eds. Edwin R. Wallace and John Gach (New York: Springer, 2008), 629–656. This timeline intersects with the rise of secularization as understood by Peter L. Berger as "the process by which sectors of society and culture are removed from the domination of religious institutions and symbols." Berger, *The Sacred Canopy: Elements of a Sociological Theory of Religion* (Garden City, NY: Doubleday, 1967), 107. While church remained a significant social class indicator in elite New York, it is notable that the Archers had a family pew at the most grand and prestigious of New York's Episcopal churches, Grace Church. It was completed in 1846, as was, just down Broadway, A. T. Stewart Dry Goods Store, a.k.a. the five-story "Marble Palace," the country's first department store, giving the ladies who lunch an equally grand place to shop while still dressed in their Sunday finest: see Harry E. Resseguie, "Alexander Turney Stewart and the Development of the Department Store, 1823–1876," *Business History Review* 39, no. 3 (Autumn 1965): 301–322. This apparent turn away from religion, or at least toward an equally appealing consumerism, only slightly anticipates Weber's later and influential theories about the Protestant ethic, a notion to which Wharton perhaps alludes: "in a world where all else had reeled on its foundations the 'Grace Church wedding' remained an unchanged institution." Wharton, *Age*, 284.

mentioned much at all in *Age*, nevertheless reach a nexus within. Something is lost, and something is also gained, as one philosophy begins to overtake another, and *The Age of Innocence* dwells right at their intersection and places the transactional marriage of Newland Archer and May Welland right in this crucial cultural moment. In this sense, Newland and May, representing at times alternating outlooks on both tradition and possibility, and with the economic freedom to explore issues from more than one perspective, personalize a culture war that might not otherwise be immediately accessible.

Whereas religious tradition had generally been the significant organizational structure for one's life and a prime motivator for marriage, the turn of the 20th century presents the rise of new ways to understand one's sense of self and which have implications on *The Age of Innocence* and its creation and examination of a marriage discourse. Although the novel's 1870s setting does not allow for direct engagement with behaviorism in the plot, the 1920 publication does invite metacontextual consideration of how psychological behaviorism, an offshoot of the rise of psychoanalysis in general, begins to displace religion and to infiltrate the function of marriage in the Archers' lives. Behaviorism in general seeks to externalize the inner life of the mind as a series of behaviors, which can then be classified and, potentially, understood as an evidence-based reasoning for learning through conditioning one's responses to one's environment.[45] Pavlov's animal experiments, perhaps under his objection, nevertheless formed a strong contemporary basis for how human behavior can be conditioned, and James Watson's refinements were a hot subject for debate throughout the 1910s.[46] Whereas psychology as a science was and is difficult for laypeople to grasp, behaviorism provided access to many of its tenets in a readily understood form. There is scant research to indicate that Wharton was much interested in the debate, but it is clear that she knew about it and applied this knowledge to Newland Archer's characterization, who drew on, in the classification of his social set, "the new ideas in his scientific books, and the much-cited instance of the Kentucky cave-fish, which had ceased to develop eyes because they had no use for them."[47] People, like a given species, can be understood, and they can also, upon necessity, adapt to their situation.

---

[45] George Graham, "Behaviorism," in *Stanford Encyclopedia of Philosophy*, ed. Edward N. Zalta, Stanford University, 1997–, article published May 26, 2000, last modified March 19, 2019, https://plato.stanford.edu/archives/spr2019/entries/behaviorism/.

[46] Richard F. Rakos, "John B. Watson's 1913 'Behaviorist manifesto': Setting the Stage for Behaviorism's Social Action Legacy," *Revista Mexicana de Análisis de la Conducta* 39, no. 2 (2013): 99–118.

[47] Wharton, *Age*, 56.

For someone like Newland, behaviorism functioned much like a religion, in that it provided a means of exploring the essence of personhood and routes to resolution, but with the added tangibility of reinforcement. Additionally, whereas the idea of sinfulness and (self-)deception had also traditionally been the realm of the church, and thus cloaked in mystery and ambiguity and relying upon an intercessory framework for redemption, the idea that one can identify and correct one's own unseemly behavior through self-introspection and direct action, without the potential discomfort of engagement with an intercessor, was undoubtedly a liberating concept for its practitioners. Similar to religion, behaviorism focuses on the ways in which a person can experience transformation, self-improvement, or change, but without the implied judgment of the church or its followers. For the upper-class characters Wharton writes about, in which the static immutability of wealth and status is key, true transformation, perhaps, is ultimately undesirable or even impossible, and at best it is conflated into economic transaction—one might "transform" oneself with a trip to Paris, a new jewel, a new carriage, a well-appointed study, or a new lover. Even as religion itself does not provide much social prestige to the novel's characters, it remains central to the function of high society as an outward symbol of conservatism, as a small price to pay for carrying on in one's private excesses. It is notable that the only time Newland attends church in the novel is on the occasion of his own wedding, and his discomfort is palpable.

Yearnings toward self-improvement are certainly implied in *Age,* and this is part of the reason that Newland and May drift apart. Newland's entire worldview, though deeply steeped in the traditional, is also informed by a scientist's desire to categorize and classify, and for Newland to be able to successfully achieve classification of others is a way for him to advance his sense of self and well-being, without necessarily having to reflect on his own behavior. The ways he treats May, other people, and especially Ellen Olenska are affected by Newland's tendencies toward the superficially categorical. Once he has categorized a person, his words, deeds, gifts, and so on all fall into order, or so he thinks, and he gets a certain patriarchal satisfaction from this. Part of Newland's problem is the way in which he assigns meaning to the things and people around him, as though he is classifying them for a collection before putting them away. Scholarly examination or meditation is not his style. While he is indeed a fast reader of people, perhaps coming from his perceived "intellectual and artistic superiority,"[48] he can be too hasty. Once he has placed a label on someone, the label becomes indelible, and in fact supplants the person in his mind. This is why, for

---

48 Wharton, *Age,* 7.

example, he is unable to see Ellen's deep social insecurity and relative inexperience, he made up his mind from the first time he saw her black satin dress and her Josephine hairstyle that she was glamorous and exotic, as opposed to "innocent" May with her white dresses and pinned-up curls. Since the narrator is more sophisticated than Newland himself, we are able to sense the ambiguity of these symbols and images so much more readily than Newland, creating a sense of knowing and dramatic irony. And yet, the principles of behaviorism go two ways, and Newland rarely, and only at the novel's conclusion, turns to self-examination. His behaviorist tendencies, for the most part, focus only outward, toward what he can immediately grasp or control.

In this sense, May and Ellen both appear to be more comfortable with the introspective. What they individually want from Newland cannot be readily classified or hastily bought. May's outlook on her marriage is simultaneously more conservative and more liberal than Newland's. She knows the informal but fixed rules of marriage in her class and does not expect or need to challenge them. When she finds herself a victim of Newland's easy characterization of her as "innocent" of his indiscretion with Ellen, she takes comfort in her own intuitive sophistication and self-actualization and allows Newland the discomfort of coming to an independent realization that she does not actually depend on him for much of anything. Her wealth is independent, her social standing is her own: Newland has more at stake than she does and must change his behavior accordingly. Likewise, while Newland might have categorized Ellen as a fallen temptress that he could lift back into societal grace (and quietly receive gratitude for), this categorization does not take into account Ellen's deeply introspective nature and her trusting ability to relate her emotional state to others, including May, which also forces change on Newland's part. He could not conceive of them as united because he had separated them so strongly. Wharton's great irony here is that while impulses derived from behaviorism might have been appealing to men seeking a way to uphold a patriarchal order without the strictures of religious piety, it is the women in *The Age of Innocence* who demonstrate by far the deeper psychological awareness.

Discussion: Transactional and Tangible Distance

All of these factors—Wharton's upbringing, her artistic and literary influences, her rejection of politics, and her knowledge of how emergent cultural forces such as psychoanalysis can shape but not define a discourse—cumulatively enable *The Age of Innocence* to serve as a strong presentation of how the idea of distance, in setting, focalization, and symbolism, creates a sense of marriage as transactional. The social standard which Wharton so ably expresses in *The Age of Innocence* is based primarily on the idea of distance and the simultaneous but differently motivated drive each of the novel's main characters feel to maintain, above all, a sense of control through manipulating it. Pamela Knights[49] has written extensively about the various social codes at play in the novel and how they serve to disembody the character from his or her life, but not with specific referent to the idea of distance. In order to describe the social code which defines Newland Archer and is simultaneously his undoing, Wharton relies on certain images to express this distance. In this brief discussion, I will seek to tie Wharton's various influences together in order to explore and illuminate specific examples of how the sensory elements of sport, flowers, and food function to enforce the ideas of transactional distance within the Archers' marriage.

Obviously, the image of archery is of primary importance, given the charactonym "Archer." A great deal of critical ink has been spilled describing the allegorical significance of Archer as it relates to May Archer's resemblance to Artemis, especially given Wharton's study of Frazer's *The Golden Bough* (1890, with a third and final version in 1906–1915), and frequent mythological allusions are made throughout the book to suggest that May is like Artemis, virgin goddess of the hunt. A similar comparison can be made with Newland Archer and Artemis's twin Apollo, also an archer, who was charged with, among many tasks, being the patron defender of herds and flocks; Archer's obsession with people, places, and things being "right" speaks to his role as society's shepherd. Here, however, the connection which Wharton wishes us to make is, of course, with Isabel Archer, heroine of Henry James's *The Portrait of a Lady* (1881). It is well established, notably by American feminist literary scholar Cynthia Griffin Wolff[50] and later by 19th-century literary scholar Cushing Strout,[51] that James was a profound influence on Wharton's subject matter and writing style, and Isabel Archer, James's fullest representation of the "true American girl," was widely admired by the international reading public as "the pride of America" and had become a well-known character in the newly developed American literature by the time Wharton began writing novels. There are obvious similarities in the setting and social milieu of *The Portrait of a Lady* and *The Age of Innocence*, yet

---

49 Pamela Knights, "Forms of Disembodiment: The Social Subject in *The Age of Innocence*," in *The Cambridge Companion to Edith Wharton*, ed. Millicent Bell (Cambridge: Cambridge University Press, 1995), 20–46.
50 Wolff, *Feast of Words*.
51 Cushing Strout, "Complementary Portraits: James's *Lady* and Wharton's *Age*," in *Edith Wharton's The Age of Innocence*, ed. Harold Bloom (Philadelphia, PA: Chelsea House Publishers, 2005), 3–11.

while *Age* is informed by *Portrait*, it does not seem derivative; Strout maintains that to see it this way is "patronizing" of Wharton and her achievements, or "merely being a clever disciple of James."[52] Wharton takes her Archer one step further than does James, and while conjuring up all the virtues of James's Isabel, adds to May a sense of artificiality which is no less "American" than her cheerfulness, self-confidence, or wholesomeness. Lacking none of Isabel Archer's outer qualities, but devoid of James's false and somewhat patriarchal perceptions about the "freedom" of the American girl, May Archer represents an updated image of manufactured femininity, offered up for consumption for a husband and a society who have no real understanding of the depth of her emotions. Everything from her appearance in the archery contest at the exclusive Newport Country Club (notably, a club to which Ellen Olenska did not belong), to her Parisian white summer dress and diamond arrow brooch, to Newland's internalized anger at his friend's admiration of her appearance, as though she exists and dresses only for Newland for to admire, symbolizes this duality. Yet just as archery looks easy until you try it, May's façade is flawless and hides great amounts of skill, patience, and determination. Even in her ribbon-accented corset, and while displaying perfect archer's form, she radiates the glow that comes from knowing that, even if Newland was no longer in the picture, her access to the club and its social set would remain, as well as that Newland is not as free to pursue Ellen as he thinks he might be because she also carries, unbeknownst to all except her, his child. Newland is free to categorize and interpret May however he likes, but his time is limited, and so she keeps her distance for now, knowing the exact speed at which her arrow will land.

Also expressing the discourse of marital distance through coded imagery is the frequent reference to various flowers and exotic foods. We use the phrase "hothouse flower" today to mean a cultivated, delicate personality that would not survive outside of its unnatural habitat, and, though not to the extent as in Wharton's day or the time of the novel, we still send flowers at times of social importance: courtship, weddings, childbirth, celebration, illness, and death. What do we value about a bouquet of flowers? They are fragrant, beautiful, and expensive. Grown in greenhouses or special fields as the objects of intense care, they are cut in their prime, and generally delivered by messenger, just to bring us temporary sensorial pleasure. We essentially enjoy their delicate corpses for a day or two and then toss them aside as soon as their mortality becomes too obvious. They are purely a metaphor for social transaction. In the 1882 reference work *Our Deportment*, which offers a guide to the "manners, conduct, and

---

52 Strout, "Complementary Portraits," 4.

dress of the most refined society," John Young suggests that flowers can be as expressive of meaning as a poem, and he claims that there are specific meanings attached to certain flowers by "universal consent."[53] While some of the so-called meanings of flowers on his list go back to Roman times, others seem more arbitrary, yet the idea that a flower sends a certain encoded message is one that would certainly have resonated with Newland Archer's set.

The frequent and specific references to various flowers in *The Age of Innocence* sensorily capture the idea of the commodification of personality and Newland Archer's distance from the life around him. He chooses lily-of-the-valley to represent May Welland, sending her a delicately ribboned bunch every day, and bright yellow roses to represent Ellen Olenska, spontaneously sending her large bouquets with no card. He seems to believe that the lily-of-the-valley symbolizes May's innocence and purity, which he wants on schedule, while the yellow roses represent Ellen's exotic allure, which he wants at whim. Yet, as Edith Wharton, and anyone with her social background, likely knew from books such as *Our Deportment*, the lily-of-the-valley was widely understood to symbolize the return of happiness,[54] while the yellow rose stood for the decrease of love.[55] So Newland Archer manages to send one message while believing he is sending entirely another; the "innocence" of the novel's title is his.

In *The Age of Innocence*, the symbolic value of flowers frequently becomes lost, and in no place more so than at the end of Part I, in which Newland Archer stands at the altar waiting to be married. Whereas one would expect him to await his beloved bride May with excitement and eagerness, he instead finds himself noticing everything else around him, such as the music, the ghostly faces in the crowd, and the noises and murmurs in the air, and May herself is reduced to "a vision of a cloud of tulle and orange-blossoms floating nearer and nearer." I find this image to be rather horrific in its disambiguation of May, and while orange-blossoms are traditionally the flower of brides, representing chastity,[56] there is something decidedly sinister in the defamiliarization of traditional American bridal imagery here, as though Newland wishes to disassociate himself with his marriage even before it occurs. Knights argues that at this point, the "signs come adrift from their meanings,"[57] but it is not certain that they were ever connected for Archer. The irony of all this disassociation comes to him at the end of

---

[53] John H. Young, *Our Deportment; or, The Manners, Conduct and Dress of the Most Refined Society* (New York: F. B. Dickerson & Co, 1885), 126.
[54] Young, *Our Deportment*, 417.
[55] Young, *Our Deportment*, 420.
[56] Young, *Our Deportment*, 416.
[57] Knights, "Forms of Disembodiment," 35.

the novel when he realizes "something he knew he had missed: the flower of life."[58] Which flower would that be? It is never stated.

One could make a similar case for the exotic foods served at the frequent parties Archer and his set ceaselessly attend and host. Content to dine on the humblest and most poorly prepared of meals while at home, Archer treats his dinner guests to asparagus "from Florida," terrapin soup, and the Roman punch which Mrs. Archer believes makes "all the difference."[59] Looking at what "Roman punch" would have been made of, it is an appallingly sweet, tasteless concoction of sweet wines, fruits, lemonade, merengue, and sugar;[60] it does not sound appetizing in the slightest to a palate more sophisticated than a child's. Its appeal, apparently, comes from its fanciful service, in a bowl shaped to resemble "the heart of a red rose, or … the bosom of a swan, or the cup of a lily, or the 'right little, tight little' life saving boat," the bowl itself being the finest china, glazed pottery, or even ice,[61] and reserved for only this purpose. The exoticism of the foods, and his ability to afford to serve them, simultaneously emphasizes Archer's comfort with his posh surroundings and yet his need to fill his life with imported things and imported people: Ellen Olenska is the guest of honor at this particular "farewell" dinner. In Archer's world, people are also judged according to the kinds of food they serve and to which company they serve them: dining becomes a transaction of food for the pleasure of classification. For example, the van der Luydens, the absolute upper crust of New York society, are famous for rarely dining out, preferring their own dinner company to that of others. The matriarch Mrs. Manson Mingott, who is May and Ellen's grandmother (and a stand-in for Edith Wharton's own), is equally famous for the penury of her kitchen despite her vast bulk and fortune. The vulgar-yet-accepted Beauforts serve "hot canvas-back ducks and vintage wines"[62] at their dinners, presumably to make up for Julius Beaufort's unknown social origins. May's mother Mrs. Welland serves meals utterly lacking in appeal but made up for in the amount of gossip that one might hear over her table. And social climbers like Mrs. Lemuel Struthers do not seem even to bother with meals at all but serve champagne to one and all! The people around Newland Archer oc-

---

58 Wharton, *Age*, 286.
59 Wharton, *Age*, 270.
60 "Real Roman Punch: How a Drink Made Exclusively for the Pope Became General," *Morning Union* 44, no. 5956, February 7, 1890, https://cdnc.ucr.edu/?a=d&d=MU18900207.2.3&e=---en-20--1--txt-txIN---1.
61 Mary Elizabeth Wilson Sherwood, *Manners and Social Usages* (New York: Harper & Brothers, 1887), 268.
62 Wharton, *Age*, 17–18.

cupy themselves with assessing the meaning of the foods people serve with zeal, yet do not discuss these meanings publicly, for that would be an unspeakable violation of the unspoken social code of the List of 400 which defined their social status. The very phrase "keeping up with the Joneses," after all, was introduced into American slang as a reference to Edith Wharton's extended family,[63] who would have known a thing or two about expensive parties and the transactional value of things that express distance.

By the end of the novel, Newland Archer recognizes that the various forms of distance in his life are in step with the changing society. Consider the marriage of his son Dallas to Fanny Beaufort, daughter of a scandalous, fallen man and his former mistress:

> Nothing could more clearly give the measure of the distance that the world had travelled. People nowadays were too busy—busy with reforms and 'movements', with fads and fetishes and frivolities—to bother much about their neighbors. And of what account was anybody's past, in this kaleidoscope where all the social atoms spun around in the same place?[64]

With this observation, the idea of distance ironically brings us closer to the narrative than ever, as we recognize something of what we think of as our own cultural peculiarities. "Dash it, Dad, don't be prehistoric!" begs Dallas,[65] failing to understand the engrained codes that keep Newland from making the move toward Ellen. Despite his obvious approval of the marriage of Dallas to Fanny, Newland cannot bring himself to apply the same standards to himself, choosing instead a stance of isolation that defies his own self-characterization as, above all, one who belongs.

Conclusion

This chapter has addressed the innovative ways in which *The Age of Innocence* by Edith Wharton develops a holistic and original discourse on American marriage through her simultaneous engagement with and disengagement from significant cultural forces such as visual arts, earlier American literature, and emerging 20th-century attitudes toward psychoanalysis and secularization, and exemplified this engagement with examples from the text in order to illumi-

---

63 Carol J. Singley, ed., *A Historical Guide to Edith Wharton* (Oxford: Oxford University Press, 2003), 5.
64 Wharton, *Age*, 291.
65 Wharton, *Age*, 293.

nate the subtleties of her narrative focalization as they shape a transactional view on marriage. Thinking about *The Age of Innocence* from a historical standpoint, and by way of conclusion, one takes from Archer's final reflection on his distance from his own world—and his own marriage—a connection to Wharton's own post-war sense of distance, loss, and alienation. Written after she personally experienced the aftermath of World War I as a volunteer in the war relief effort, and also after the dissolution of her own marriage following her husband's extended mental illness and her own romantic affair,[66] she struggled to reconcile the physical and emotional consequences of the war with the culture and lifestyle she had known before its start. An unfinished poem of hers simultaneously expresses her patriotism and her skepticism: "France! To give thee, o my more than country / Give thee of my blood's abundance all."[67] In this sense, her conservative yet liberal concerns here anticipate those of the younger Lost Generation writers, who also found themselves culturally and spiritually uprooted as a result of World War I and also exploring the meaning of marriage. In this sense, her outlook as she expresses it in *The Age of Innocence* does not seem radically different than, or even anticipates, that of Hemingway or Fitzgerald, who are in a certain sense her literary heirs. The subtle yet conscious focalization Wharton employs throughout *The Age of Innocence*, and the depth of characterization this enables, is neatly divided between these writers, Hemingway inheriting her wartime dramatic ambiguity and willingness to expand gender roles, as he did in *The Sun Also Rises* (1926),[68] and Fitzgerald, practically a Whartonian character himself, taking her idea of the transactional values within a marriage to its artistic height in *Tender is the Night* (1934).[69]

Works Cited

Basch, Françoise. "Women's Rights and the Wrongs of Marriage in Mid-Nineteenth-Century America." *History Workshop Journal* 22, no. 1 (Autumn 1986): 18–40. https://doi.org/10.1093/hwj/22.1.18.

Berger, Peter L. *The Sacred Canopy: Elements of a Sociological Theory of Religion*. Garden City, NY: Doubleday, 1967.

---

66 Mary Virginia Davis, "Edith Wharton," in *Magill's Survey of American Literature*, vol. 6, *Steinbeck–Zindel, Appendixes, Indexes*, edited by Steven G. Kellman, rev. ed. (Pasadena, CA: Salem Press, 2007), 2663–2667.
67 Lee, *Edith Wharton*, 450.
68 Ernest Hemingway, *The Sun Also Rises* (New York: Modern Library, 1926).
69 F. Scott Fitzgerald, *Tender is the Night* (New York: Scribner, 1934).

Buitenhuis, Peter. "Edith Wharton and the First World War." *American Quarterly* 18, no. 3 (Autumn 1966): 493–505. https://doi.org/10.2307/2710850.

Davis, Mary Virginia. "Edith Wharton." In *Magill's Survey of American Literature*, vol. 6, *Steinbeck–Zindel, Appendixes, Indexes*, edited by Steven G. Kellman, 2663–2667. Revised edition. Pasadena, CA: Salem Press, 2007.

Dupree, Ellen. "The New Woman, Progressivism, and the Woman Writer in Edith Wharton's 'The Fruit of the Tree.'" *American Literary Realism, 1870–1910* 31, no. 2 (Winter 1999): 44–62.

Elaman-Garner, Sevinç. "Contradictory Depictions of the New Woman: Reading Edith Wharton's *The Age of Innocence* as a Dialogic Novel." *European Journal of American Studies* 11, no. 2 (Summer 2016). https://doi.org/10.4000/ejas.11552.

Fitzgerald, F. Scott. *Tender is the Night*. New York: Scribner, 1934.

Gifford, Sanford. "The Psychoanalytic Movement in the United States, 1906–1991." In *History of Psychiatry and Medical Psychology*, edited by Edwin R. Wallace and John Gach, 629–656. New York: Springer, 2008. https://doi.org/10.1007/978-0-387-34708-0_21.

Gilbert, Sandra M., and Susan Gubar. *The Madwoman in the Attic: The Woman Writer and the Nineteenth-Century Literary Imagination*. New Haven, CT: Yale University Press, 1979.

Gollin, Rita K. "Hawthorne and the Visual Arts." In *A Historical Guide to Nathaniel Hawthorne*, edited by Larry J. Reynolds, 109–133. Oxford: Oxford University Press, 2001.

Graham, George. "Behaviorism." In *Stanford Encyclopedia of Philosophy*, edited by Edward N. Zalta. Stanford University, 1997–. Published May 26, 2000. Last modified March 19, 2019. https://plato.stanford.edu/archives/spr2019/entries/behaviorism/.

Hawthorne, Nathaniel. "The Minister's Black Veil." 1836. In *Twice-Told Tales*, 37–53. Vol. 9 of *The Centenary Edition of the Works of Nathaniel Hawthorne*, edited by William Charvat, Roy Harvey Pearce, and Claude M. Simpson. 23 vols. Columbus: Ohio State University Press, 1962–97.

Hawthorne, Nathaniel. *The Marble Faun*. 1860. Vol. 9 of *The Centenary Edition of the Works of Nathaniel Hawthorne*, edited by William Charvat, Roy Harvey Pearce, and Claude M. Simpson. 23 vols. Columbus: Ohio State University Press, 1962–1997.

Hawthorne, Nathaniel, *The Scarlet Letter*. 1850. Vol. 1 of *The Centenary Edition of the Works of Nathaniel Hawthorne*, edited by William Charvat, Roy Harvey Pearce, and Claude M. Simpson. 23 vols. Columbus: Ohio State University Press, 1962–1997.

Hawthorne, Nathaniel, "Young Goodman Brown." 1835. In *Mosses from an Old Manse*, 74–90. Vol. 10 of *The Centenary Edition of the Works of Nathaniel Hawthorne*, edited by William Charvat, Roy Harvey Pearce, and Claude M. Simpson. 23 vols. Columbus: Ohio State University Press, 1962–1997.

Hemingway, Ernest. *The Sun Also Rises*. New York: Modern Library, 1926.

Irving, Washington. "Rip Van Winkle." In *The Sketch Book of Geoffrey Crayon*. 1819–20. Reprinted in *The Legend of Sleepy Hollow and Other Stories: Or, The Sketch Book of Geoffrey Crayon, Gent*. Introduction by Alice Hoffman. New York: Random House, 2001.

Killoran, Helen. *The Critical Reception of Edith Wharton*. Rochester, NY: Camden House, 2001.

Knights, Pamela. "Forms of Disembodiment: The Social Subject in *The Age of Innocence*." In *The Cambridge Companion to Edith Wharton*, edited by Millicent Bell, 20–46. Cambridge: Cambridge University Press, 1995.

Lee, Hermione. *Edith Wharton*. New York: Vintage Books, 2008.

Lewis, Richard Warrington Baldwin. *Edith Wharton: A Biography.* New York: Harper & Row, 1975.

McDowell, Margaret B. "Viewing the Custom of Her Country: Edith Wharton's Feminism." *Contemporary Literature* 15, no. 4 (Autumn 1974): 521–538. https://doi.org/10.2307/1207776.

Orlando, Emily J. *Edith Wharton and the Visual Arts.* Tuscaloosa: University of Alabama Press, 2007.

Pride, Mike. "Edith Wharton's 'The Age of Innocence' Celebrates its 100th Anniversary." *The Pulitzer Prizes.* Accessed February 22, 2021. https://www.pulitzer.org/article/edith-whartons-age-innocence-celebrates-its-100th-anniversary.

Rakos, Richard F. "John B. Watson's 1913 'Behaviorist manifesto': Setting the Stage for Behaviorism's Social Action Legacy." *Revista Mexicana de Análisis de la Conducta* 39, no. 2 (2013): 99–118.

"Real Roman Punch: How a Drink Made Exclusively for the Pope Became General." *Morning Union* 44, no. 5956. February 7, 1890. https://cdnc.ucr.edu/?a=d&d=MU18900207.2.3&e=—--en-20--1--txt-txIN——1.

Resseguie, Harry E. "Alexander Turney Stewart and the Development of the Department Store, 1823–1876," *Business History Review* 39, no. 3 (Autumn 1965): 301–322. https://doi.org/10.2307/3112143.

Sherwood, Mary Elizabeth Wilson. *Manners and Social Usages.* New York: Harper & Brothers, 1887.

Showalter, Elaine. *Sexual Anarchy: Gender and Culture at the Fin de Siècle.* New York: Penguin Books, 1991.

Singley, Carol J., ed. *A Historical Guide to Edith Wharton.* Oxford: Oxford University Press, 2003.

Singley, Carol J., and Susan Elizabeth Sweeney, eds. *Anxious Power: Reading, Writing, and Ambivalence in Narrative by Women.* New York: State University of New York Press, 1993.

Strout, Cushing. "Complementary Portraits: James's *Lady* and Wharton's *Age.*" In *Edith Wharton's The Age of Innocence*, edited by Harold Bloom, 3–11. Philadelphia, PA: Chelsea House Publishers, 2005.

Wharton, Edith, *The Age of Innocence.* New York: Penguin Classics, 1996 [1920].

Wharton, Edith. *The House of Mirth.* New York: Charles Scribner's Sons, 1905.

Wharton, Edith. "A Little Girl's New York." *Harper's Magazine* 176 (March 1938): 356–364. Reprinted in *The Age of Innocence: A Norton Critical Edition*, edited by Candace Waid, 232–247. New York: W. W. Norton, 2002.

Wharton, Edith. *The Writing of Fiction.* New York: Charles Scribner's Sons, 1925.

Wharton, Edith, and Ogden Codman Jr. *The Decoration of Houses.* New York: Charles Scribner's Sons, 1897.

Wolff, Cynthia Griffin. *A Feast of Words: The Triumph of Edith Wharton.* New York: Oxford University Press, 1977.

Young, John H. *Our Deportment; or, The Manners, Conduct and Dress of the Most Refined Society.* New York: F. B. Dickerson & Co, 1885.

Margaret Stetz

10 "Marriages are just performances": Staging Fashion, Comedy, and Feminism in *Love, Loss and What I Wore*

> "All mothers want their daughters to get married.
> To most mothers, a daughter in a marriage that's just okay
> is better than a daughter who's single and happy."
> – Ilene Beckerman
> *Mother of the Bride: The Dream, the Reality, the Search for a Perfect Dress* (2000)[1]

The trajectories of white middle-class American women's lives underwent a radical revision in the late 20th and early 21st centuries. No longer were they necessarily pointed toward heterosexual marriage; no longer were they expected to end in the domestic sphere. As a reflection of these changing conditions, literary works issued by the mainstream publishing world offered numerous expressions of dissident social and sexual attitudes, including exposés of marriage as an oppressive, patriarchal institution. Pro-marriage texts, however, especially those making arguments for marriage on grounds related to reasons other than romance, by no means vanished from the scene; instead, they assumed new forms. As this study will suggest by focusing on one such text in two different versions—the first an illustrated memoir by Ilene Beckerman; the second a playscript by Nora and Delia Ephron, created over a decade later—they took aim at a middlebrow, mass-market, and largely female audience, employing comic irony for its ability to entertain, sentimental representations of familial bonds for their emotional effect, and an emphasis on fashion for its power to draw in and draw together women readers and spectators. In doing so, they reshaped the rationale for marriage, presenting it as an institution redeemed by its potential to connect women with one another.

---

[1] Ilene Beckerman, *Mother of the Bride: The Dream, the Reality, the Search for a Perfect Dress* (Chapel Hill, NC: Algonquin, 2000), 1.

OpenAccess. © 2021 Margaret Stetz, published by De Gruyter. This work is licensed under the Creative Commons Attribution-NonCommercial-NoDerivatives 4.0 International License.
https://doi.org/10.1515/9783110751451-010

Love, Loss, and What I Wore: A Commercial Phenomenon

With no history of authorship and no training as an artist, Ilene Beckerman (b. 1935, née Ilene Edelstein) surprised the American publishing industry in 1995 with the success of her bestselling illustrated memoir, *Love, Loss, and What I Wore*. Almost everything about it was unusual. Compact in size (13 x 17 cm) and relatively brief in length (140 pp.), it employed a distinctive format, with each left-hand page containing a short text (in some cases, comprising as few as 10 to 30 words) and each facing page offering a simple, almost crude line drawing of a clothed figure that was, in most cases, a representation of Beckerman herself at different ages. The narrative charted her progress through the stages of her life, each one of which was tied to a specific item of dress that Beckerman both described and drew from memory, as she traced her history as a middle-class Jewish woman growing up in New York City and its suburbs.

Most of the final third of the book, however, was dedicated to the subject of the clothes associated with her two failed marriages. Surprisingly, neither union had begun with the bride in the sort of white gown that usually featured in weddings of the 1950s and 1960s—at least in the case of first marriages—and equally surprisingly, both had ended in divorces that Beckerman herself appeared to have initiated. The memoir concluded, nonetheless, with the author describing her contentment in domestic terms, as having had the satisfaction of attending the weddings of two daughters and, at age sixty, of enjoying sessions of dressing up with her four-year-old granddaughter, using a drawer filled with cosmetics and boxes of clothes preserved from her own younger years. Although the dust-jacket copy identified Beckerman as the vice-president of an advertising agency, there was no mention of this career within the text itself; everything focused instead upon personal relations, and especially on familial ones, as her source of identity and pride.

Throughout Beckerman's memoir, the tone of the prose was witty and understated, with frequent comic touches that were often dry to the point of being acerbic. This was particularly true when the subject at hand was one of the writer's two unhappy marriages. (*Love, Loss, and What I Wore* did not cover the period of her third, later-in-life marriage.) The narrative's ending, however, underlined a sentimental strain, emphasizing the satisfactions of continuity in family life and the rewards of an intergenerational sharing—but only through the maternal line—of pleasure in dress, as expressed in the author's delight as her granddaughter adorned herself in traditionally feminine garments. In this way, Beckerman's was a nostalgic, if not retrograde text. Indeed, it was almost a throwback, in terms of its heteronormative assumptions and embrace of conventional ideas of gender and gendered roles, to the earlier historical eras, from the 1940s onward, that it recorded through a personal lens. Beckerman's was a fondly remembered world of Girl Scout troops, ballet classes, proms and other school dances, and occasional outings to the "ladies'" sections of New York department stores.

Arriving in the mid-1990s, a time when American women had made enormous gains in legal status, dramatic changes in their expressions of gender, and explorations of diverse sexualities, *Love, Loss, and What I Wore*, despite or perhaps because of its somewhat dated perspective, proved an unexpected hit. It was curiously popular from the first, accruing huge amounts of publicity for its author and large profits for Algonquin Books, its publisher. It spawned, moreover, a raft of follow-up texts by Beckerman, all in a similar pocket-sized format and with the same combination of sparse text and her own deliberately amateurish line drawings. These included *What We Do for Love* (1997), a reflection on the men at the center of her disappointing romances and marriages; *Mother of the Bride* (2000), an account of the elaborate planning undertaken for her eldest daughter's wedding; *Makeovers at the Beauty Counter of Happiness* (2005), a meditation on her youth occasioned by anxiety over an upcoming reunion of her single-sex high-school class; and *The Smartest Woman I Know* (2011), a tribute to the grandmother who had raised both her and her sister, following the death of their mother and abandonment by their father. Each volume affirmed the importance of family life to women, in particular, and of the married state both as a necessary prelude to reproduction and a guarantor of continuity, regardless of whether some marriages turned out badly.

If the 1990s was the decade of "zines"—i.e., of deliberately non-professional-seeming and individualistic publishing ventures with a handcrafted aesthetic—*Love, Loss, and What I Wore* had the look of a related phenomenon; yet, in terms of its implicit ideology, it was an anti-zine and perhaps even a sign of backlash. Whereas American zine productions were often connected to the radical feminist movements of the so-called "riot grrrls" [sic] and committed to disruption of the gendered social order,[2] Ilene Beckerman's 1997 memoir represented the antithesis of such revolutionary aims. It celebrated white middle-class social ambitions, the pleasure of capitalistic acquisitions of material goods (literally) in the form of dresses and other objects associated with the fashion industry, and the satisfactions available to women within the frameworks of moth-

---

2 Caroline K. Kaltefleiter, "Start Your Own Revolution: Agency and Action of the Riot Grrrl Network," *International Journal of Sociology and Social Policy* 36, no. 11/12 (2016): 808–823.

erhood and grandmotherhood—all made possible by heterosexual marriages, even after such marriages ended.

So popular with the mainstream American reading public did *Love, Loss, and What I Wore* become that, soon after its release in 1995, it was optioned by the Hollywood screenwriter/director Nora Ephron (1941–2012) and her sister Delia Ephron (b. 1944), both of whom were specialists in comedies about the lives of women. Their goal was not to turn it into a film, however, but a play, yet a funny thing happened, so to speak, on the way to the theater. A long delay occurred in the adaptation of the original text, allowing for and even necessitating other kinds of transformation by the time of its first production in 2008.

If Beckerman's memoir embodied a belated response to and in some respects a reaction against Second Wave feminism, the Ephrons' dramatization showed signs of the positive influence of Third Wave feminism. Even as they incorporated elements of that movement, however, the Ephron sisters mainstreamed it by stripping some of its more challenging elements and rendering it more palatable for a middlebrow playgoing public. In the process, they also recuperated the notion of marriage for their 21st-century audience, going further than Beckerman had to remove it from the sphere of heterosexual romance and to recast it as an institution that cemented and celebrated relations between and among women instead. When late in the play a wedding dress appeared as one of the featured items of clothing, it was in a section titled "Brides," in plural form, because the marriage was that of two lesbians.

Marriage and American Second Wave Feminism

In the title work from *Snapshots of a Daughter-in-Law: Poems from 1954–1962*, the groundbreaking volume that in 1963 helped to introduce Second Wave feminism to American literature, Adrienne Rich (1929–2012) depicted dresses in general and the mementos associated with bridal wear at heterosexual weddings in particular as oppressive trappings—literally, as emblems of the *entrapment* of middle-class white women. The older female figure in Rich's poem, lost in nostalgia, her "mind ... moldering like wedding-cake," has her new clothes made on the pattern of those worn in the days before her marriage, when she still had social value. Meanwhile, the younger female speaker thinks bitterly of "mildewed orange flowers,"³ meaning the traditional orange blossoms featured at weddings ever since Queen Victoria's marriage to Prince Albert in the mid-19th century.⁴ These rotting floral decorations are part of the "commodious/steamer-trunk of tempora and mores" that have been conflated with ideas of what is natural and necessary for all women—a code of unwritten but seemingly inescapable social laws.⁵ As the critic Maggie Doherty has put the matter, "The poem is decidedly feminine, replete with images uniquely horrifying to women readers," fusing reminders of domesticity and marital life with "burdens" and "enclosures," even as it drives toward the possibility of "escape."⁶

Almost simultaneously in 1963, the social critic Betty Friedan (1921–2006) published *The Feminine Mystique* and famously opened her polemic with a chapter titled "The Problem That Has No Name." By this, she meant a deep "dissatisfaction" with their restriction to the domestic sphere that an entire post-Second World War generation of white, middle-class, heterosexual women in the U.S. had felt but had been forced to suppress.⁷ Even as this sense of unfulfillment, frustration, and despair spread silently, the number of women who succumbed to the pressure to become "housewives" grew: "By the end of the nineteen-fifties, the average marriage age of women in America dropped to 20, and was still dropping, into the teens. Fourteen million girls were engaged by 17."⁸

Interestingly, Friedan linked this closing of horizons and elimination of any alternatives to heterosexual marriage for women to the subject of the clothed body and to deliberate efforts to reduce the space that it occupied. As she noted, women in the early 1960s were consuming a diet drink "called Metrecal, instead of food, to shrink to the size of the thin young models. Department-store buyers reported that American women, since 1939, had become three and four sizes smaller. 'Women are out to fit the clothes, instead of vice-versa,' one buyer said."⁹ At the same time, what Adrienne Rich would later term "compulsory heterosexuality" and with it the drive toward marriage was being imposed on

---

3 Adrienne Rich, "Snapshots of a Daughter-in-Law," accessed November 28, 2020, https://genius.com/Adrienne-rich-snapshots-of-a-daughter-in-law-annotated.
4 Katie Frost, "The One Royal Wedding Tradition You Probably Never Knew About," *Good Housekeeping*, November 5, 2018, https://www.goodhousekeeping.com/uk/news/a577089/orange-blossom-royal-wedding-brides/.
5 Rich, "Snapshots of a Daughter-in-Law."
6 Maggie Doherty, "Look at Me Now: The Evolution of Adrienne Rich," *New Yorker*, November 30, 2020, 84.
7 Betty Friedan, *The Feminine Mystique* (New York: W. W. Norton, 1963), 15.
8 Ibid., 16.
9 Ibid., 17.

girls at ever younger ages and often associated with items of clothing.[10] Friedan cited, in *The Feminine Mystique*, a 1960 "advertisement for a child's dress, sizes 3–6x" from the *New York Times* that featured these words, meant to appeal to the parents of primary school-aged daughters: "She Too Can Join the Man-Trap Set."[11]

By the mid-1960s, the discontent articulated by Friedan's book had fueled a resolve among many of its readers to move from individual recognition of "The Problem" to organized protests on a large scale. These were directed against both the social attitudes that relegated women's energies to so-called "full-time homemaking" and the legal limitations on their rights that underpinned the insistence upon marriage-and-motherhood as women's sole approved social function. A new spirit of activism, identified as Second Wave feminism, soon appeared in the U.S., and it spread across the lines of race, class, and sexual orientation. In 1966, it resulted in the founding of the National Organization for Women, a.k.a "NOW." It would also generate actions ranging from the reintroduction in Congress of the Equal Rights Amendment in 1971 to the creation in 1972 of *Ms.*, a mass-market periodical edited by the journalist and activist Gloria Steinem (b. 1934) that combined feminist politics with works drawn from across the arts. The magazine's title, moreover, enshrined an effort to eliminate from official governmental forms and from informal discourse alike the use of honorifics such as "Mrs." and "Miss" that automatically labeled all women—and only women—according to marital status. At the same time, Second Wave feminists of the late 1960s and 1970s recognized the linkage between liberation and clothing, advocating for their right to wear trousers, rather than skirts, in venues ranging from research libraries, to courts of law, to the floor of the U.S. Congress.[12]

Many thousands, and eventually millions, of American women either participated actively in political initiatives or gave support through their membership in feminist organizations and subscriptions to feminist periodicals. Countless others benefited both directly and indirectly, as they took advantage of the oppor-

---

[10] See Adrienne Rich, "Compulsory Heterosexuality and Lesbian Existence," *Signs: Journal of Women in Culture and Society* 5, no. 4 (1980): 631–660.
[11] Friedan, *The Feminine Mystique*, 16.
[12] For more about this important period of social change, see Sally Ann Drucker, "Betty Friedan: The Three Waves of Feminism," *Ohio Humanities*, April 27, 2018, http://www.ohiohumanities.org/betty-friedan-the-three-waves-of-feminism/; also Ruth Rosen, *The World Split Open: How the Modern Women's Movement Changed America* (New York: Viking, 2000). Rosen refers, for instance, to an incident in the 1970s when a male judge in New York City "ordered a female attorney, dressed in a tailored, designer pants suit and silk blouse, to leave his courtroom and not to return until she wore a skirted suit." See Rosen, *The World Split Open*, 163.

tunities opened by this Second Wave movement. Middle-class white women, in particular, felt freer to pursue higher education and forge careers while seeking divorces or not marrying at all, and women of all sexual orientations could explore erotic relationships outside of marriage without automatically being subject to the same degree of extreme stigmatization and demonization that had prevailed when, for instance, a woman's sexual history could be introduced into divorce proceedings as evidence of her unfitness to retain custody of her children.

Ilene Beckerman: Left Ashore During the Second Wave

Such feminist awakenings (known at the time as "consciousness-raising") were not, however, universally shared experiences, as Ilene Beckerman suggested implicitly throughout *Love, Loss, and What I Wore* and then made clear explicitly in one of her follow-up volumes, *Mother of the Bride* (2000). In the latter, Beckerman described with comic irony her own situation in the late 1960s and early 1970s: "I had gone from being a powerless daughter to a powerless wife to a powerless mother – all too quickly. I had been so busy changing diapers, I didn't have time to read *The Feminine Mystique*. I had been so busy trying to look like Gloria Steinem, I didn't have time to read Gloria Steinem."[13] It was one of the few moments in her published works where Beckerman made any overt political references to the feminist stirrings that were going on around her, while she was occupied with marriage, a household, and a family of five children born in quick succession (in her second union). These statements were also unusual for hinting, through repetition of the adjective "powerless" in connection with each of these gendered roles, at her own awareness of the existence of any possible injustice at the heart of family life or anger in reaction to it.

Certainly, there was little evidence anywhere in *Love, Loss, and What I Wore* that Beckerman had been, during the period of Second Wave feminism, in sympathy with what Susan Kingsley Kent has described as its adherents' pursuit of "changes in the law, the social and economic system, and the culture that would 'liberate' them from current conceptions of femininity that … locked them into stifling, unfulfilling, slavish positions, and often made them vulnerable to sexual

---

13 Beckerman, *Mother of the Bride*, 115.

predations from men."¹⁴ Although Beckerman's 1995 memoir may have hinted at a degree of agency and self-direction consistent with these attitudes, especially in its implication that the choice to end both of her first two marriages had been hers, she later revised this picture in her 1997 sequel, *What We Do for Love*. There, Beckerman revealed that her decision to seek a divorce from her first husband happened only after he already had left her, and that her initial response, rather than a welcome sense of release or empowerment, had been a mental breakdown that culminated in a suicide attempt and brief hospitalization in a psychiatric institution.¹⁵ Having come of age during what Lauren S. Cardon classifies as a "postwar period marked [by] a 'return to normalcy' during which businesses, colleges, advertisements, television programs, and the fashion industry conspired to put women back in the home," Beckerman had absorbed its "passive mode of femininity."¹⁶ To lose the security of her role as a wife was to become, at the age of 23, so socially and psychically unmoored as to be incapable of surviving without medical intervention. Even in this instance, however, as Beckerman reported in *What We Do for Love*, while disillusioned with her first marriage, she was not disillusioned about marriage as an institution and was buoyed by the advice of a woman friend and peer: "Dora kept telling me to get a divorce. She said I was still young and I could do better"¹⁷—meaning that she could find a worthier man to be her next husband.

Neither Ilene Beckerman nor "Dora," it seems, had freed herself at the time from the injunction offered by Anne Fogarty in her influential 1959 manual, *Wife Dressing: The Fine Art of Being a Well Dressed Wife*, to "remember that you are an appendage of your husband, Adam's rib that was separated from him ... and now spiritually returned to his side,"¹⁸ and there is reason to question the degree to which Beckerman ever renounced this internalized subordination or the feeling of incompleteness when not married. Especially for those of Beckerman's generation, who were born in the 1930s, a willingness to live outside of Second Wave political consciousness, or even in opposition to it, was more common than feminists of any generation might wish to acknowledge. As we see from the retrogressive generalization that opened her illustrated volume, *Mother of the Bride* (which also serves as the epigraph to my chapter)—i.e., "All mothers want their

---

14 Susan Kingsley Kent, *Gender: A World History* (Oxford: Oxford University Press, 2021), 132.
15 Ilene Beckerman, *What We Do for Love* (Chapel Hill, NC: Algonquin, 1997), 54–65.
16 Lauren S. Cardon, *Fashion and Fiction: Self-Transformation in Twentieth-Century American Literature* (Charlottesville, VA: University of Virginia Press, 2016), 182.
17 Beckerman, *What We Do for Love*, 65.
18 Anne Fogarty, *Wife Dressing: The Fine Art of Being a Well-Dressed Wife* (New York: Glitterati, 2008 [1959]), 25.

daughters to get married. To most mothers, a daughter in a marriage that's just okay is better than a daughter who's single and happy"[19]—Beckerman could eventually reach the point of recognizing that it was possible to be both single and happy, while still believing this truth should be outweighed by the imperative for every woman to marry. It was an observation simultaneously humorous in tone and serious in content, as demonstrated by the rest of the memoir, which detailed the planning of her own oldest daughter's wedding. As Beckerman would go on to state in that same work from 2000, "When I was in my twenties, you were supposed to get married. I never had to say, 'I'm just a housewife.' I never regretted not having a career. You only get a few years to be the mother of young children."[20] This sentiment became her ultimate defense of marriage: not as an institution associated with heterosexual desire or with lasting romance, but as the one that enabled full-time motherhood.

While embodying what, from Lauren S. Cardon's later critical perspective, might be called a passive femininity, the persona that Beckerman presented in her 1995 book *Love, Loss, and What I Wore* was nonetheless active in purely consumerist terms, as expressed through clothes shopping. A celebration of the exercise of individual taste through the selection and purchase of clothing, as well as a positive statement about the importance of preserving the memories associated with specific garments worn in the past, *Love, Loss, and What I Wore* proved both resonant and rewarding to large segments of American women readers. In January 1996, a few short months after the volume's initial publication, Alex Witchel noted in the *New York Times* that it had a first printing of 40,000 and was already going into a second.[21] Beckerman's depoliticized approach to her subject—i.e., a summary of her life, as seen through a procession of (illustrated) articles of dress—offered a comforting and largely unchallenging literary and visual experience to mainstream audiences. When it came to the topic of high heels, for instance, there was none of the angst captured by Richard Thompson Ford in his assertion that "[i]f any single item of clothing can contain the controversies, contradictions, pleasures, pain, and prejudice of gendered clothing, it is the high-heeled shoe" or in his analysis of it as the epitome "of conventional femininity, required in many contexts by custom and express prescription."[22] Becker-

---

19 Beckerman, *Mother of the Bride*, 1.
20 Ibid., 116.
21 Alex Witchel, "Shopping with Ilene Beckerman; Wearing Her Life on Her Sleeve," *New York Times*, January 24, 1996, http://www.nytimes.com/1996/01/24/garden/shopping-with-ilene-beckerman-wearing-her-life-on-her-sleeve.html.
22 Richard Thompson Ford, *Dress Codes: How the Laws of Fashion Made History* (New York: Simon & Schuster, 2021), 233.

man merely supplied instead a stick-figure drawing of herself in black and a matter-of-fact statement about the role that such an item of fashion had played in her first marriage: "Black dress with cut-out necklace and matching bolero jacket. Harry always liked me to wear my hair off my face. I could wear very high heels with Harry because he was so tall."[23] What came through in her narrative was the simple pleasure of having owned these shoes, to be shared with women readers who also wished to enjoy the memory of wearing high heels while being free, at least temporarily, of the need to consider the fraught gendered social issues attached to them (in this case, why a woman was never supposed to be taller than her male partner).

As Shahidha Bari observes in *Dressed: The Secret Life of Clothes*, "to walk in the world as a woman is to be made available for assessment."[24] Beckerman's text, in contrast, provided a brief, amusing respite from such painful external scrutiny and from any attendant self-consciousness. It encouraged audiences of middle-class white women, in particular, to feel free to recall, as Beckerman herself did, the beauty of the "gorgeous green taffeta strapless gown" with a skirt "extravagantly full" that her sister had worn "to our cousin's wedding"[25] while avoiding the question of how such Christian Dior-inspired "New Look" dresses of the late 1940s had been deployed both to romanticize heterosexual marriage ceremonies and to construct a disabling vision of postwar Western femininity as purely decorative.

Beckerman's 1995 memoir deliberately steered clear of politics in another area, as well. As the promotional copy inside the dust jacket of the first edition announced, the persona Beckerman *fashioned* was that of an "Everywoman": "Like all of us, she likes to look nice while she's pursuing happiness"; she "invites us to reflect on our own lives and remember what we wore."[26] This universalizing project, however, required Beckerman to downplay her Jewish identity. Although *Love, Loss, and What I Wore* was divided into sections according to decades, nowhere in the one labeled "The 1940s" was there any mention of what it meant to be growing up in a Jewish family during the period of the Holocaust and the founding of the State of Israel. Such references would have particularized her history and risked making the volume less of a glass in which readers of a different heritage could believe their own past was being reflected. Only decades later, in her 2011 tribute to her maternal grandmother, *The Smartest*

---

23 Ilene Beckerman, *Love, Loss, and What I Wore* (Chapel Hill, NC: Algonquin, 1995), 100.
24 Shahidha Bari, *Dressed: The Secret Life of Clothes* (London: Jonathan Cape, 2019), 55.
25 Beckerman, *Love, Loss, and What I Wore*, 34.
26 Beckerman, *Love, Loss, and What I Wore*, front flap.

Woman I Know, were there oblique references to a larger political framework when Beckerman discussed the unease that her grandparents exhibited, even while seemingly safe in New York City: "But every bone in their body was Jewish, and despite living in this wonderful land of opportunity, they were always on guard. The next Hitler or Stalin could be waiting around the corner on 64th Street."[27] The humorous turn at the end of this serious statement mirrored the even more determinedly comic treatment of religion and ethnicity in the earlier *Love, Loss, and What I Wore*, where these elements were deployed for laughs and connected throughout with each of Beckerman's two failed marriages. To the first of her weddings, we are told, "My grandfather wouldn't come because he thought Harry was too old for me and because he was Catholic"[28]; to her second wedding, this time to a man who was also a Jew, "My grandfather wouldn't come. He was still mad at me for marrying Harry."[29]

Turning religious affiliation in the context of marriage into a punchline enabled Beckerman both to raise the subject of difference and to keep it from interfering with the construction of herself as an "Everywoman," in whom each white, middle-class women reader might potentially see herself. This was important to the selling of *Love, Loss, and What I Wore* as a text aimed at the middlebrow market, with the middlebrow text constituting, according to David Cardiff, a form of "entertainment" both "universal and particular in its appeal," offering every audience member the illusion of being an "exclusive initiate."[30] As Timothy Aubry has explained, "to elicit identification from the reader" is often the "central strategy [...] associated with middlebrow literature,"[31] and Beckerman succeeded well at inspiring such identification. The reviewer for the *New York Times Book Review* noted at the time of its first publication that "[p]aging through the book is like rummaging through your own attic. Some of the items [of clothing described] will make you smile nostalgically, others will make you cringe in shame."[32] Acknowledging the book's power to serve as a bond with and also among its women readers, she confessed her own "re-

---

27 Ilene Beckerman, *The Smartest Woman I Know* (Chapel Hill, NC: Algonquin, 2011), 8.
28 Beckerman, *Love, Loss, and What I Wore*, 96.
29 Ibid., 106.
30 David Cardiff, "Mass Middlebrow Laughter: The Origins of BBC Comedy," *Media, Culture and Society* 10 (1988): 41.
31 Timothy Aubry, "Erica Jong's Textual Bulimia: *Fear of Flying* and the Politics of Middlebrow Consumption," *Journal of Popular Culture* 42, no. 3 (2009): 420.
32 Ellen Feldman, "Pumps and Circumstance: A Sartorial Memoir Conjures Up a Life in Terms of How It Was Clothed," *New York Times Book Review*, January 7, 1996, 28.

solve to send a copy" of Beckerman's illustrated memoir "to several childhood chums, and my sisters, and a lot of other friends."[33]

Staging *Love, Loss and What I Wore* and Mainstreaming Third Wave Feminism

When it appeared in 1995, Beckerman's volume may indeed have functioned as a gift book, exchanged frequently among white middle-class American women friends and relations in general, but it also drew the immediate attention of a particular pair of sisters, Nora and Delia Ephron. Both were prominent and commercially successful as novelists, journalists, essayists, and writers for mainstream theater and Hollywood films, as well as film producers (and one of the two sisters, Nora, was also a director of films). It was Nora Ephron, however, who enjoyed wider renown. At the point when they optioned *Love, Loss, and What I Wore* soon after its publication, Nora Ephron's career as a screenwriter was associated in the public mind with heteronormative romantic comedies, thanks to the enormously popular film *When Harry Met Sally* (1989)—part of a genre sometimes dismissively labeled as "chick flicks." Her fame was even greater for a 1983 novel and then for her own 1986 screenplay based on it: *Heartburn*, a bitterly funny, lightly fictionalized autobiographical account of a marriage between two high-profile figures gone bad, due to adultery by the husband. Though Nora Ephron may have been the better known of the two sisters, Delia Ephron was also widely recognized as a commercially viable, middlebrow author whose subjects, too, often centered on the problems that arose in and from marriage. Her *Funny Sauce: Essays about Family Life* (1986), for instance, dealt humorously with issues such as divorce, the challenges of step-parenting, and joint custody of children. By 1995, therefore, each Ephron sister had excelled at work that foregrounded heterosexual pairings, either building toward marriage or locked in marriages that were messily dissolving; each writer was especially interested, moreover, in representing the perspectives and emotions of the women characters, as these romances were forming or coming apart. By focusing on the situations of middle-class white women, while emphasizing what was personal and downplaying larger political implications, Nora and Delia Ephron—who, like Ilene Beckerman, were Jewish writers with a strong sense of comedy—had been able to appeal to the same sort of fan base that, in 1995, Beckerman was now attracting. It was hardly surprising that they would have seen at

---

33 Ibid.

once the commercial possibilities in adapting *Love, Loss, and What I Wore* to another medium and would have tried to ensure that they would be the ones to undertake this.

In her 2013 volume of autobiographical essays titled *Sister Mother Husband Dog*, Delia Ephron outlined briefly the background to this long gestation, which finally resulted in the publication of their script for a theatrical version of Beckerman's memoir in 2008 and its professional debut onstage a year later:

> Nora found the book [*Love, Loss, and What I Wore*] and fell in love with it. And she knew it was a play, a *Vagina Monologues* sort of thing. And I am eternally grateful, because it was pure joy. Eventually.
> We always called it *The Vagina Monologues* without the vaginas [...].
> We optioned the book in 1996, and the play opened Off-Broadway in 2009. Fourteen years later. The world's longest birth.[34]

The finished product, which bore only a small resemblance to Beckerman's original text, reflected a shift in attitudes that had occurred over that period of time in American culture—i.e., the mainstreaming of a new feminist movement known as the Third Wave. In its dramatic form, moreover, as Delia Ephron herself acknowledged, this version of *Love, Loss, and What I Wore* modeled itself closely on what was perhaps the most successful theatrical outgrowth of Third Wave feminism, Eve Ensler's *The Vagina Monologues*. During the process of making this transition to the stage, Ilene Beckerman's text ceased to be the story of one "unliberated" middle-class, mid-century woman whose life had been dominated by social pressure to marry and whose personal satisfaction had come instead from a combination of motherhood and the pleasures of clothes shopping and dressing, for the Ephron sisters opened it up to accommodate other experiences, desires, and sources of fulfillment. In doing so, they were both responding to and reaffirming changes in American women's lives and also in attitudes regarding marriage.

Third Wave feminism, like its Second Wave predecessor, began at the margins, but rapidly moved toward the center of public awareness, beginning that progress in the early 1990s. Unlike the Second Wave, this Third Wave was led by women of color and queer women, who emphasized that the category of "women" was by no means a unified or homogeneous one, nor were all women oppressed equally. Neither were women oppressed only by something called patriarchy; racism and homophobia, for instance, were just as destructive (and could be found even in communities of privileged white, heterosexual

---

34 Delia Ephron, "Collaboration," in *Sister Mother Husband Dog* (New York: Penguin, 2013), 215.

women who identified with the Second Wave). As R. Claire Snyder has suggested, however, in a 2008 essay on the movement for the feminist journal *Signs*, one thing that the Third Wave did share with the Second was a belief in the importance of individual perceptions and histories—of the role of "the personal story" in political activism.[35] The difference lay in the highlighting and the valuing of difference itself. Snyder went on to explain that, as a reaction "to the collapse of the category of 'women,'" the Third Wave had brought to the fore "personal narratives that illustrate an intersectional and multiperspectival version of feminism" and, "as a consequence of the rise of postmodernism," it had "embrace[d] multivocality over synthesis."[36]

With the rise of the Third Wave, there were also shifts in the targets and goals of feminist activism. No longer was marriage itself viewed, as it has been by Betty Friedan and her contemporaries, as the primary social force placing constraints upon middle-class women's lives by limiting their access to economic independence and confining their labor to the household. There was instead increasing concern, from the 1990s on, with another threat: what later came to be known as GBV (gender-based violence), including sexual assault and, within the framework of marriage, domestic violence. Attention to the latter was heightened, in the mid-1990s, by the widely publicized revelations, during O. J. Simpson's murder trial and acquittal, of complaints regarding physical abuse that his dead ex-wife had made to the police while they were married.[37]

The Vagina Monologues (1996), a play constructed by Eve Ensler as a series of first-person monologues by a diverse group of women characters and drawn from the playwright's own interviews with a number of women from different communities, was integrally linked to this new focus on the subject of sexual violence, which had accompanied the emergence of the Third Wave. More than merely a work of theater, it became, in the words of Christine M. Cooper, "a worldwide phenomenon" and a "mass culture event, performed hundreds of times each year" over the following decade.[38] Its popularity was fueled by its direct connection to activism. With benefit performances often timed to coincide with Valentine's Day, it served as "the motor behind V-Day, an antiviolence organization with the declared mission of ending violence against women and

---

[35] R. Claire Snyder, "What Is Third-Wave Feminism? A New Directions Essay," *Signs: Journal of Women in Culture and Society* 34, no. 1 (2008): 184.
[36] Ibid., 175.
[37] Maryclaire Dale, "O. J. Simpson Case Helped to Bring Spousal Abuse Out of Shadows," *AP News*, June 12, 2019, https://apnews.com/article/c85957bb9c764313a88659b5837f5245.
[38] Christine M. Cooper, "Worrying about Vaginas: Feminism and Eve Ensler's *The Vagina Monologues*," *Signs: Journal of Women in Culture and Society* 32, no. 3 (2007): 727.

girls, once and for all, everywhere."³⁹ What *The Vagina Monologues* also shared with Third Wave feminism was an insistence upon the importance of, to use R. Claire Snyder's term, "multivocality," a principle made literal in the play through its use of a series of personal narratives spoken by "a wide range of voices, distinguished by age, race or ethnicity, region, economic status, and sexual orientation."⁴⁰ The mood and tone of these speeches ranged from serious to comic.

It was this dramatic work that Nora and Ephron decided to emulate when adapting Ilene Beckerman's illustrated memoir for the stage. The humorous name they employed for their own version of *Love, Loss and What I Wore*— "*The Vagina Monologues* without the vaginas"⁴¹—was no mere joke. While a few recognizable episodes from the narrative of Beckerman—referred to throughout the play by her nickname of "Gingy" (for her red hair)—were still present as a framing device, they were no longer the sole or even the chief focus. Substituting for them and drawing the audience's attention instead was a series of monologues by characters of differing social identities and backgrounds, all of whom recounted their love affairs (some with happy endings, some with tragic ones) with specific items of clothing and frequently deployed comic techniques when doing so. The storytellers ranged from a Latinx woman recalling the gang insignia-decorated sweater that she had worn with pride at age fifteen; to a survivor of stranger-rape during her freshman year at U. C. Berkeley, who found strength in remembering the pairs of boots she had loved both before and after her assault; to the former owner of a 1960s paper dress designed by Betsy Johnson that had been ruined by an unexpected rush of menstrual blood at a dinner party; to a former cancer patient who spoke of how concentrating on the prospect of eventually wearing, after surgical breast reconstruction, a woman friend's gift of a white lace bra helped her to get through the nightmare of a mastectomy.

As in Ensler's play, the memories recounted by the characters in the Ephrons' *Love, Loss and What I Wore* (which inexplicably dropped from its title the so-called "Oxford comma" punctuation after the word "Loss") were mostly of a kind associated with bodies marked as female. But also, as in Ensler's *The Vagina Monologues*, there were limits as to the diversity of the representations of womanhood. Although the Ephron sisters' clothing-related monologues were clearly influenced by Third Wave feminism, that influence only went so far. Third Wave theorists had asserted the crucial role in feminist discourse of race in general and of

---

39 Ibid.
40 Ibid., 728.
41 Ephron, "Collaboration," 215.

Blackness in particular, along with the pressing need to examine and expose white racism. But race, while present as a subject, had not been the central issue in Ensler's play, and it was most definitely underrepresented in the Ephrons' later stagework, too. This was obvious from the cast list for its first production, which occurred at the Westside Theater in New York City on 1 October 2009. Indeed, all of the multiple roles were taken by white celebrity performers: Tyne Daly, Rosie O'Donnell, Samantha Bee, Katie Finneran, and Natasha Lyonne.[42] The sole role written for a woman of color—the part of Nancy, the Latinx ex-gang member (which reinforced a problematic racial stereotype)—was played by Lyonne, an actor of French and Hungarian Jewish heritage. Just as Ilene Beckerman's original text had made it easy for white, middle-class women to identify with her narrative and had encouraged such identification, so the Ephrons' adaptation seemed especially inviting to audiences of the same demographic, who got only a diluted version of Third Wave multivocality and a distinct emphasis instead on whiteness.

One topic, however, did move the play beyond a narrow and conservative perspective: the intersection of marriage with sexual orientation. In the segment of their *Love, Loss and What I Wore* titled "Brides," which came late in the action, the Ephron sisters tackled overtly a major political controversy that was still very much unsettled and undecided in 2008/2009—i.e., the issue of same-sex unions. The construction of this episode introduced the topic only gradually, though, perhaps as a sop to the sensibilities of middlebrow, mainstream theatergoers, who were led gently toward it, rather than confronted with it.

"Brides" began with two women onstage, each one looking at and speaking alternately to the audience in succession:

> LISA. I never thought I would get married.
>
> AMANDA. I'm not somebody who dreamed of my wedding from a young age. I did not have visions. I just wanted a dress I could twirl around in.
>
> LISA. But two months before my wedding I saw an ad that said, "Wedding Dress Sample Sale." So Saturday at 11 A.M. I was standing with 40 other brides-to-be in front of a store called "Brides 2 Be." They opened the doors and, stampede [...].
>
> AMANDA. I went to all the San Francisco department stores and tried on white bridal dresses with satin tops and big fancy bottoms. It was like going back centuries [...].[43]

---

42 Nora Ephron and Delia Ephron, *Love, Loss and What I Wore* (New York: Dramatists Play Service, 2008), 5.
43 Ibid., 42.

Only after further description of the difficulties in finding suitable attire for the ceremony did Lisa, the first of the two characters, reveal the greater complication associated with preparations for her wedding:

> LISA. I've been dealing with my parents' homophobia since I was a young teenager. I thought they were going to get there, but when I told them I was getting married, they hit the roof. But my fiancée's mother was great. Right after we told her the news, she came right over with an old plastic sandwich bag full of family rings. She said to me, "I want you to pick the ring you want to get married in."[44]

This revelation came almost at the end of the "Brides" section, when the audience members would have been fully involved already in the fate of these two characters and, presumably, sympathetic to their very ordinary and universal concerns with finding the right clothes and accessories for a wedding. It arrived with a stage direction that referred to the actions of Lisa: "(*She turns to Amanda.*)"[45] The character's change in position was followed immediately by Lisa's spoken words—"I, Lisa, take thee Amanda, to be my partner for life, to love, honor, be faithful to through good times and bad, as long as we both shall live"—and by Amanda's recitation of the identical vow.[46] "Brides" then concluded with a more openly political sentiment than anything found elsewhere in Nora and Delia Ephron's play or in Ilene Beckerman's 1995 memoir. This took the form of a statement by her mother that Amanda quoted—a retort to Lisa's mother, who had asked everyone repeatedly why it was necessary for this couple to marry: "'Why'd they have to do this?' And my mom said, 'To honor their relationship.'"[47]

The timing of this segment of the play was significant, as was the location of the two characters in it, indicated through Amanda's reference to going "to all the San Francisco department stores."[48] In February 2004, Gavin Newsom, then Mayor of San Francisco, had announced that same-sex marriages would be recognized as legal in that city. Within a month, more than 3,600 same-sex weddings had been performed.[49] This triggered a homophobic backlash in the State of California, resulting in California voters passing a ban ("Prop 8") on

---

44 Ibid., 42–43.
45 Ibid., 43.
46 Ibid., 43–44.
47 Ibid., 44.
48 Ibid., 42.
49 Rachel Gordon, "State Lawmaker Joins S. F.'s Gay Wedding Waltz," *San Francisco Chronicle*, March 9, 2004, https://www.sfgate.com/news/article/State-lawmaker-joins-S-F-s-gay-wedding-waltz-2783567.php.

these marriages in 2008, the same year in which Nora and Delia Ephron completed and published their script for *Love, Loss and What I Wore*.[50] With its negative presentation of maternal homophobia, its countering of that with an expression of maternal support for marriage as a necessary way to "honor" a same-sex "relationship," and its centering of a romantic story of lesbian love and commitment—all tied to a shopping experience likely to be familiar to an audience of middle-class women theatergoers, involving the hunt for the perfect wedding dress—this section of the Ephrons' play constituted a direct, if discreet, political intervention.

Such overt activism on behalf of what was called the "marriage equality" movement showed the impress of Third Wave feminism, with its strong commitment to advancing queer women's rights. Yet even here, the Ephrons' *Love, Loss and What I Wore* was far less daring and more safely mainstream than its theatrical inspiration, *The Vagina Monologues*. Ensler had risked ire and condemnation with her infamous "The Little Coochie Snorcher That Could" monologue—a sexually explicit defense by an adult speaker of her erotic encounter, when a young teenager, with an older woman as a liberating experience. What the Ephrons offered was far blander: a Third Wave-inflected production with much of the tang of salt removed from the Wave. The stage directions for the final part of "Brides," which had the characters of Amanda and Lisa turn to one another before repeating their marriage vows, did not, after all, instruct the performers to re-enact the kiss that usually followed those words during a wedding ceremony; neither was there any expression in the dialogue of the role of sexual desire in their union. Nothing onstage, in fact, potentially challenged too directly the sensibilities of a middlebrow audience; everything remained "respectable" according to traditional class-based standards. Yet this short scene was still a far cry from, and an advance upon, the determinedly apolitical narrative of Ilene Beckerman's memoir, with its avoidance of any mention of the Second Wave feminist ideologies that were roiling American society at the historical moment when she became a wife (twice) and then a mother.

Where Beckerman's illustrated memoir and the Ephron sisters' loose adaptation of it did overlap was in their critical, somewhat jaded representations of relations between husbands and wives within heterosexual marriage and their juxtapositions of these with vibrant, vital (non-sexual) connections between women bound by ties of blood and/or friendship. This latter emphasis, shared by the two texts, came together in the final "Gingy" section, "Scene 28," of

---

50 Not until 2015 would a ruling by the US Supreme Court legalize same-sex marriage in all fifty states.

the Ephrons' *Love, Loss and What I Wore*, which drew directly upon Beckerman's work and assigned an explanation of authorial intent to their stand-in for the writer:

> GINGY. After I finished making all these drawings and writing all the bits and pieces that went with them [...] I made some copies [...] and gave them to my children and to my two best friends. I was so happy, you have no idea. It was the story of my life. My mother was in it, and my grandmother, and my Aunt Babbie. It was as if they were still alive. They were acknowledged. Because when my sister dies, no one but me will know who they were.[51]

In contrast, the Ephrons' adaptation presented the same character's history of heterosexual love affairs and marriages in a flat, one-sentence-long recitation of names, followed by a more enthusiastic declaration of emotion for an item of clothing by a woman designer: "So there it was. First Walter, then Harry, then Al, then Stanley. *(A Diane von Furstenberg dress.)* I loved this print jersey Diane von Furstenberg wrap dress. It was easy to put on and very comfortable and if you gained a few pounds it still fit."[52]

The subject of weight and the damaging psychological pressure that women who were closely bound could exert upon one another formed the bridge into the Ephron sisters' most damning portrait of marriage. "Scene 20," titled "Fat/Thin," was, like "Brides," composed as a set of alternating speeches. But unlike the lesbian couple in "Brides," here the two figures directly addressing the audience, "Mary" and "Eve," had no relation to one another and seemed not to be aware of one another's monologues. Unusually, too, each was joined onstage by an additional speaking character—"Mary's Mother" and a woman psychiatrist, identified only as "Eve's Shrink."

From Mary, who described herself as "big as a house," the audience learned that her mother had expressed alarm about the size of her daughter's body, encouraged her to enter into a marriage that was loveless, and passed on to Mary her own "ivory satin" wedding dress from a high-end New York department store.[53] That same dress, which would be lent to all the women in this family for their weddings, proved a token of ill fortune. In Mary's words, "[w]e all got divorced, my whole family, everyone except my mother who stayed married to my father for fifty-six miserable years."[54]

In counterpoint to this narrative, Eve's was the story of someone underweight and depressed, who had been urged by her psychiatrist to remain in

---

51 Ephron and Ephron, *Love, Loss and What I Wore*, 49.
52 Ibid., 34.
53 Ibid., 36.
54 Ibid., 37.

an unsatisfactory union on the grounds that being married was necessary for a woman's psychological health. Her own experience, however, had taught her the opposite lesson:

> EVE. I have a picture of me and my first husband together [...] I was wearing my lime green winter coat, so short, with a plaid scarf, and I look really happy. But I was never happy with David. Whenever I see that picture, I always think how photos lie and how many marriages are just performances.[55]

Despite the insistence by her "shrink" that Eve really was in love with her husband but was "just too neurotic to realize it," Eve did achieve contentment in this monologue by becoming a writer and by freeing herself from each of the unbearable weights in her life: "David and I got divorced. And I left my shrink. (*To shrink.*) I mean, fuck you."[56] The line was designed to elicit a laugh from the audience and also to encourage the spectators to applaud, cheering on the character who had liberated herself from two kinds of destructive relationships. As they learned, too, Eve's writing would connect her explicitly to women's culture and potentially to audience members who identified themselves as crafters, for her first book was about the art of crocheting.

Mary's and Eve's situations, as conceived by the Ephron sisters, seemed in some ways an echo of an earlier time in American social history, when heterosexual marriage (as many Freudian analysts affirmed) was assumed to be every woman's proper destiny. In rejecting this imperative, "Fat/Thin" appeared to be paying homage not to Third Wave feminism, but to the Second Wave with which Ilene Beckerman's original source text had refused to engage; yet its resolution was by no means wholly anti-marriage, for it also tempered the critique. Almost as an afterthought, this segment concluded with the characters of Mary and Eve reporting that they later made second marriages—not in white bridal gowns, but in, respectively, "my mother's navy blue suit" and "a shocking pink Mexican cotton skirt and a white Mexican blouse, off the shoulder"—and had found in these unions the fabled "happily ever after."[57] Throughout *Love, Loss and What I Wore*, as middlebrow playwrights determined to promote maximum identification between the spectators and the performers onstage and, wherever possible, to avoid offending any faction of their audience, Nora Ephron and Delia Ephron tried, so to speak, to have their wedding cake and eat it, too.

---

55 Ibid., 36.
56 Ibid., 37.
57 Ibid., 37.

Conclusion

Cynthia Kuhn and Cindy Carlson have suggested in *Styling Texts: Dress and Fashion in Literature* (2007) that fashion "reflects and responds to society simultaneously; indeed, it conveys tensions particularly well."[58] Throughout the latter part of the 20th century and the beginning of the 21st, few American institutions have been so fraught with tensions as marriage. Literary texts that focus on fashion, therefore, would seem logical vehicles for examining the problems inherent in this legal and social bulwark, as well as for exploring its positive potential. Nevertheless, Clair Hughes reminds us that "a concern for dress in art or literature ... is still regularly dismissed as female and frivolous."[59] In 1995, when writing and illustrating *Love, Loss, and What I Wore*, however, Ilene Beckerman did not merely risk such a categorization of her work but embraced it; so, too, did Nora Ephron and Delia Ephron in their later stage adaptation of her narrative. Ultimately, while neither version of *Love, Loss, and What I Wore* celebrated marriage as it has frequently presented itself, in conventional and oppressive forms, each found differing ways to recuperate its possibilities, particularly as a source of bonding between and among women. Even from the perspective of the present moment when, as Rhonda Garelick has pointed out, a surprising degree of "ingrained misogyny" endures that "denigrates women's culture as irrelevant, wasteful, and destructive," such a project stands out for its courage.[60]

Works Cited

Aubry, Timothy. "Erica Jong's Textual Bulimia: *Fear of Flying* and the Politics of Middlebrow Consumption." *Journal of Popular Culture* 42, no. 3 (2009): 419–441.
Bari, Shahidha. *Dressed: The Secret Life of Clothes*. London: Jonathan Cape, 2019.
Beckerman, Ilene. *Love, Loss, and What I Wore*. Chapel Hill, NC: Algonquin, 1995.
Beckerman, Ilene. *Makeovers at the Beauty Counter of Happiness*. Chapel Hill, NC: Algonquin, 2005.
Beckerman, Ilene. *Mother of the Bride: The Dream, the Reality, the Search for a Perfect Dress*. Chapel Hill, NC: Algonquin, 2000.
Beckerman, Ilene. *The Smartest Woman I Know*. Chapel Hill, NC: Algonquin, 2011.

---

58 Cynthia Kuhn and Cindy Carlson, "Introduction," in *Styling Texts: Dress and Fashion in Literature*, eds. Cynthia Kuhn and Cindy Carlson (Youngstown, NY: Cambria Press, 2007), 9.
59 Clair Hughes, *Dressed in Fiction* (Oxford: Berg, 2005), 184.
60 Rhonda Garelick, "Fashion Will Not Disappear. It Will Transform," *New York Times*, December 22, 2020, https://www.nytimes.com/2020/12/22/opinion/covid-fashion-athleisure.html?action=click&module=Opinion&pgtype=Homepage.

Beckerman, Ilene. *What We Do for Love*. Chapel Hill, NC: Algonquin, 1997.
Cardiff, David. "Mass Middlebrow Laughter: The Origins of BBC Comedy." *Media, Culture and Society* 10 (1988): 41–60.
Cardon, Lauren S. *Fashion and Fiction: Self-Transformation in Twentieth-Century American Literature*. Charlottesville, VA: University of Virginia Press, 2016.
Cooper, Christine M. "Worrying about Vaginas: Feminism and Eve Ensler's *The Vagina Monologues*." *Signs: Journal of Women in Culture and Society* 32, no. 3 (2007): 727–758.
Dale, Maryclaire. "O. J. Simpson Case Helped to Bring Spousal Abuse Out of Shadows." *AP News*. June 12, 2019. https://apnews.com/article/c85957bb9c764313a88659b5837f5245.
Doherty, Maggie. "Look at Me Now: The Evolution of Adrienne Rich." *New Yorker*. November 30, 2020, 81–86.
Drucker, Sally Ann. "Betty Friedan: The Three Waves of Feminism." *Ohio Humanities*, April 27, 2018. http://www.ohiohumanities.org/betty-friedan-the-three-waves-of-feminism/.
Ephron, Delia. "Collaboration." In *Sister Mother Husband Dog*, 189–221. New York: Penguin, 2013.
Ephron, Nora and Delia Ephron. *Love, Loss and What I Wore*. New York: Dramatists Play Service, 2008.
Fogarty, Anne. *Wife Dressing: The Fine Art of Being a Well-Dressed Wife*. New York: Glitterati, 2008 [1959].
Ford, Richard Thompson. *Dress Codes: How the Laws of Fashion Made History*. New York: Simon & Schuster, 2021.
Friedan, Betty. *The Feminine Mystique*. New York: W. W. Norton, 1963.
Frost, Katie. "The One Royal Wedding Tradition You Probably Never Knew About." *Good Housekeeping*. November 5, 2018. https://www.goodhousekeeping.com/uk/news/a577089/orange-blossom-royal-wedding-brides/.
Garelick, Rhonda. "Fashion Will Not Disappear. It Will Transform." *New York Times*. December 22, 2020. https://www.nytimes.com/2020/12/22/opinion/covid-fashion-athleisure.html?action=click&module=Opinion&pgtype=Homepage.
Gordon, Rachel. "State Lawmaker Joins S. F.'s Gay Wedding Waltz." *San Francisco Chronicle*. March 9, 2004. https://www.sfgate.com/news/article/State-lawmaker-joins-S-F-s-gay-wedding-waltz-2783567.php.
Hughes, Clair. *Dressed in Fiction*. Oxford: Berg, 2005.
Kaltefleiter, Caroline K. "Start Your Own Revolution: Agency and Action of the Riot Grrrl Network." *International Journal of Sociology and Social Policy* 36, no. 11/12 (2016): 808–823.
Kent, Susan Kingsley. *Gender: A World History*. Oxford: Oxford University Press, 2021.
Kuhn, Cynthia and Cindy Carlson. "Introduction." In *Styling Texts: Dress and Fashion in Literature*, edited by Cynthia Kuhn and Cindy Carlson, 1–11. Youngstown, NY: Cambria Press, 2007.
Rich, Adrienne. "Compulsory Heterosexuality and Lesbian Existence." *Signs: Journal of Women in Culture and Society* 5, no. 4 (Summer 1980): 631–660.
Rich, Adrienne. "Snapshots of a Daughter-in-Law." Accessed November 28, 2020. https://genius.com/Adrienne-rich-snapshots-of-a-daughter-in-law-annotated.
Rosen, Ruth. *The World Split Open: How the Modern Women's Movement Changed America*. New York: Viking, 2000.

Snyder, R. Claire. "What Is Third-Wave Feminism? A New Directions Essay." *Signs: Journal of Women in Culture and Society* 34, no. 1 (2008): 175–196.

Witchel, Alex. "Shopping with Ilene Beckerman; Wearing Her Life on Her Sleeve." *New York Times*. January 24, 1996. http://www.nytimes.com/1996/01/24/garden/shopping-with-ilene-beckerman-wearing-her-life-on-her-sleeve.html.

Contributors

Jamie Callison is an Associate Professor of British and American Literature at Nord University, Norway. His work has appeared in journals such as *Literature and Theology*, *Modernist Cultures* and *ELH*. His co-edited (with Thomas Goldpaugh) edition of *The Grail Mass* – a previously unpublished, book-length poem by the modernist writer David Jones – was published by Bloomsbury Academic in 2018. His monograph *Modernism and Religion: Mysticism and Orthodoxy in the Long Poem* is forthcoming with Edinburgh University Press.

Mariela Fargas Peñarrocha is a professor at the University of Barcelona, Department of History and Archaeology. She holds a doctorate in Early Modern History and graduated in Law from the same University. Her research has focused on the history of the family, the history of marriage and also about the situation and the experiences of women in Catalonia-Barcelona in the 16th and 17th centuries. Her works especially analyzed family and marriage conflicts, institutionalized litigation, and violence in everyday life. She is also a researcher at the ADHUC Research Center for Theory, Gender, Sexuality (University of Barcelona).

Jessica Allen Hanssen (Dr. philos., University of Oslo, 2010) is an Associate Professor and the Faculty Coordinator for the Bachelor of English degree at Nord University, Bodø, Norway. Hanssen teaches the 19th century in British and American Studies for Bachelor of English and teacher education students. She also teaches two specialty courses, American Fiction after 1945 and Crime Fiction, for advanced bachelor students. Her primary areas of research interest are American literature, especially 19th and early 20th-century fiction, short-story theory, narratology, young adult fiction, and middle grades English education. Recent publications on literary themes include work on Washington Irving (2016), Nathaniel Hawthorne (2016), Mary Shelley (2018), and David Foster Wallace (2021). Additionally, her education research focuses on the intersection of critical theory and middle grades English education and the early introduction of critical reading, and especially reader-response and narratology-based teaching strategies, into the Norwegian national curriculum.

Frank Jacob is Professor of Global History at Nord Universitet, Norway. He studied History and Japanese Studies at the universities of Würzburg, Germany and Ōsaka, Japan. His main fields of research include transnational anarchism, revolution theory, and modern Japanese History. Jacob is the author or editor of more than 80 books and his recent works include *Emma Goldman and the Russian Revolution* (De Gruyter, 2020), *Rosa Luxemburg: Living and Thinking the Revolution* (Büchner, 2021), and *East Asia and the First World War* (De Gruyter, 2022).

Jowan A. Mohammed, an avid researcher interested in women's history and World War One, lives in Norway and is a PhD student at Nord University, where she works on her dissertation project "Women as War Critics in the Urban Space: A study of Social Change in Times of War." Her monograph *Mary Hunter Austin: A Female Writer's Protest Against the First World War in the United States* (Vernon Press, 2021) was her debut on the life and works of Mary Hunter Austin (1868–1934), which also served as the inspiration for her contribution to this edited collection.

Sabine Müller is Professor of Ancient History at Marburg University. She studied Medieval and Modern History, Art History, and Ancient History. Her research focuses on the Persian Empire, Argead Macedonia, the Hellenistic Empires, Macedonian royal women, Lukian of Samosata, and reception studies. Her publications include the monographs *Die Argeaden* (2016), *Perdikkas II. – Retter Makedoniens* (2017), and *Alexander der Große – Eroberung – Politik – Rezeption* (2019). She is co-editor of the *Lexicon of Argead Makedonia* (2020) and *The Routledge Companion to Women and Monarchy in the Ancient Mediterranean World* (2021).

Marion Röwekamp is a historian (Dr. phil. Hist., University of Munich, 2008) and a full-time lawyer. She is holding the Wilhelm and Alexander von Humboldt Chair of the DAAD at the Colegio de México in Mexico City. Previously, she worked several times in the USA (2000/2001 Columbia University, New York City, 2007 Five Women College Studies and Research Center, South Hadley, MA, 2009/2010 John F. Kennedy Fellow at the Center for European Studies, Harvard University), in Mexico (Colegio de México, Instituto de Investigaciones Históricas of UNAM in Mexico City) and the Latin American Institute of the Free University of Berlin. She hasd published various books and articles in the areas of women's legal history, exile and memory studies several nation contexts, namely Germany, Spain, Mexico and the US. Her latest book *New Perspectives on European Women's Legal History* was published 2017 (co-ed. with Sara L. Kimble, Routledge).

Margaret D. Stetz is the Mae and Robert Carter Professor of Women's Studies and Professor of Humanities at the University of Delaware, USA. Along with several exhibition catalogues, edited collections, and monographs, she has published more than 130 essays on topics such as Victorian feminism, nineteenth-century publishing history, the politics of animated films, British modernist literature, the "comfort women" of WWII, neo-Victorianism, and women's comedies. Her articles on dress and gender have appeared in journals such as *Working with English* (2009), *RaVoN [Romanticism and Victorianism on the Net]* (2009), and *Humanities Bulletin* (2019), and in volumes such as *Crossings in Text and Textile* (UPNE, 2015), the *Blackwell Encyclopedia of Victorian Literature* (2015), *Long Shadows* (Northwestern University Press, 2016), *Neo-Victorian Humour* (Brill 2017), and *Fashion and Authorship* (Palgrave Macmillan, 2020).

Vincent Streichhahn is a PhD student at the University of Halle and is working on the theory and practice of the "women's question" within German Social Democracy during the imperial period. As a political scientist, he is dedicated to the gender order of modernity as well as to the the social movements of the 19th and early 20th centuries.

Index

Achaimenid 31, 38, 39
Achilles 189–91, 200–3
adultery 9, 80, 191, 242
Aegean 43
agape 193, 196–8
Aldington, R. 187–91, 204
America 115, 134, 135, 139, 140, 143, 180, 209, 214–16, 223, 235
Amor 68, 203
Amyntas 35, 36
anarchist 134–43, 145, 147, 150, 151, 154, 161, 174, 175
– movement 138, 142, 151, 154, 174
Antoninus, M. A. 41, 42
Archer, M. W. 208, 209, 211, 218, 220–6
Archer, N. 208, 209, 211, 216, 217, 220, 223, 225–7
Arsinoë 44, 45
Astete, G. de 56, 60, 62
Athens 28n8, 29–31, 35
Austin, M. H. 18, 159–81
autonomy 6, 107, 108, 126, 189, 196, 204

BDF 82, 83, 88–90
Bebel, A. 8, 111, 120n85, 123, 125
Beckerman, I. 231–4, 237–42, 245, 251
behaviorism 220–2
Berkman, A. 141, 142, 144, 151, 173
BGB 78–83, 85, 90
borderland problems 110, 111, 113
bourgeois 2, 8, 107, 108, 109n23, 110, 111, 113–17, 124–8
bride 1, 29, 30, 40, 115, 116, 119, 225, 232, 233, 237, 238
Bund Deutscher Frauenvereine see BDF
Bürgerliches Gesetzbuch see BGB

Camós, M. A. de 57, 58, 60, 61
capitalism 142, 152, 153
Cathars 196–8
Catholisism 52, 53, 93
Cervantes, M. de 67, 68
childhood 173, 200, 209, 214, 242

Church 4, 5, 10, 62, 63, 78, 82, 92, 116, 150, 188, 196, 197, 219n44, 221
– of England 187, 188, 192, 196
citizens 4, 10, 74, 76–8, 80, 83, 84, 86–8, 90, 95, 177
Civil Code 82, 83, 118
– Austrian 80
– French 78
– German 78, 81
– Prussian 80
companion 119, 122, 126, 141, 187
conflict 13, 27, 51, 53, 59, 62, 64, 70, 87, 93, 127, 141, 149, 159, 168, 190, 208, 212
court 36n47, 43, 51, 52, 57, 154
courtship 66, 67, 162, 224
Crayon, G. 218
creation 6, 45, 126, 195, 201, 217, 220, 236
crisis 11, 12, 85, 109, 127
culture 70, 80, 90, 121, 152, 168–70, 212, 215, 220, 228, 237, 243, 244, 250, 251
– patriarchal 54, 58, 170
Cytheraea 201

Dareios I 31–3
Dareios III 38, 39, 44
daughter 30, 32, 33, 35, 37–40, 43, 44, 65, 67, 114, 147, 151, 162, 165, 167, 173, 188, 191, 227, 231, 237, 239
death 16, 26, 29, 31, 39, 44, 45, 57, 65, 79, 92, 139, 140, 148, 151, 160, 173, 201, 218, 224, 233
democracy 76, 77, 93, 94, 105, 106, 179
– social 18, 105, 106, 108n18, 113, 118, 124, 126, 128
desire 116, 151, 177, 188, 193, 194, 197–202, 211, 212, 217, 221, 239, 248
Diodoros 40
diplomacy 4, 27, 29, 45
Dittmar, L. 73, 74
divorce 5, 10–12, 34, 35, 42, 57, 67, 80, 81, 85, 89–93, 95, 109n23, 153, 159,

---

OpenAccess. © 2021, published by De Gruyter. [CC BY-NC-ND] This work is licensed under the Creative Commons Attribution-NonCommercial-NoDerivatives 4.0 International License.
https://doi.org/10.1515/9783110751451-012

164, 165, 170, 172, 187–93, 196, 204, 213, 237, 238, 242
domestic 9, 51, 52, 54, 58, 61, 64, 66, 78, 84, 95, 118, 121, 122, 163, 164, 166, 207, 231, 232, 235, 244
dynasty 29, 31, 32, 35, 43

economic 3, 8, 16, 17, 27, 65, 70, 77, 78, 90, 91, 95, 109, 117n69, 118, 120, 125, 126, 136, 138, 140, 144–6, 166, 16, 175, 211–12, 214, 220, 221, 237
– equality 94, 144
– independence 84, 159, 244
– power 65
– status 25, 245
education 7, 52, 54, 55, 57, 58, 60, 92, 110–13, 120, 159, 161–63, 177, 208, 237
Edward VIII 187, 192
Elagabalus 41, 42
emancipation 91, 136, 137, 143–49, 153, 154, 175, 177, 181
– of women 78, 145, 147
Engels, F. 8, 9, 117n67, 125, 126
Ephron, Delia & Nora 231, 234, 242, 243, 245, 246, 248–51
eros 193, 196–8
erotic 2, 111, 123, 187, 237, 248
eugenics 85, 120, 194
Europe 4n23, 52, 78, 139, 166, 198, 209, 216
evolution 54, 117, 194, 195
exile 31, 44, 135
exotic 207, 222, 224–6
exogamy 29

faith 54, 61, 62
fashion 19, 84, 85, 212, 231, 233, 238, 240, 251
feminism 1, 16, 19, 75, 137, 188, 194, 196, 202, 204, 212, 213, 215, 216, 231, 244
– Second Wave 188, 234, 236, 237
– Third Wave 234, 242, 243, 245, 248, 250
Ferguson, K. E. 143, 147
fiction 11, 173, 177–9, 208, 210, 213–15
fight 58, 75–7, 89

First World War 12, 120n85, 134, 174, 175, 179, 188, 189, 192
France 110, 115, 187, 196, 210, 228
GBV (gender-based violence) 244
gender 17, 57, 59, 68, 73, 76, 85, 87, 90, 93, 107, 121, 168, 175, 179, 213, 214, 233
– equality 16, 18, 86, 167, 169
– inequality 53, 118, 121, 154
– norms 12, 14, 17, 138, 143, 159, 165, 174
– relations 12, 18, 83, 87, 106, 107, 109, 112–14, 119, 125, 127, 128
– roles 12, 17, 54, 66, 84, 160, 166, 167, 173, 179, 228
Genett, T. 106, 107, 111, 113, 114
German National People's Party see DNVP
German People's Party see DVP
German Social Democratic Party see SPD
Germany 74–6, 78, 83, 85, 91, 94, 106, 107, 110, 115, 124, 138
– Imperial 18, 73, 74, 77
– Weimar Republic 18, 73, 76, 83, 90
God 41, 42, 44, 56, 58, 61–4, 73, 95, 147, 193, 201, 203
Goldman, E. 18, 133–54, 161, 174–5
Guevara, F. A. de 56, 58–60

harmony 42, 51–3, 56, 60, 143, 146
Hawthorne, N. 214, 215, 217
heterosexual 108, 188, 193, 231, 234–5, 239, 240, 242, 243, 248–50
Hirschfeld, M. 150
homophobia 243, 247, 248
honeymoon 119, 187, 216, 218

identity 1, 8, 13, 82, 136, 140, 151, 167, 168, 175, 232, 240
illegitimate 79, 85, 92, 93, 113, 123
immoral 2, 116, 126, 146
independent 6, 13, 68, 118, 122, 148, 167, 169, 180, 181, 222
inequality see gender inequality
inheritance 33n32, 65, 81, 92, 117n69
institution 3, 5, 14, 15, 17, 62, 110, 145, 167, 168, 173, 187, 188 204, 231, 234, 238, 239

– of marriage 2, 127, 163, 173, 179, 195
– social 9, 90, 91, 93, 163, 180
Irving, W. 208, 217, 218
Italy 68, 110, 114, 115, 138, 166, 187, 215, 216

justice 64, 74, 90, 95, 215
judgment 64, 124, 126, 173, 221

Kandal, R. 106, 114, 128n131
Kassandros 39, 40
Kautsky, K. 120n85, 125
Kowal, D. M. 136, 137
Krause, S. S. 107
Kyros II 32, 33

labor 107, 125, 138, 139, 151, 153, 159, 164, 172, 174, 175, 180, 244
– division of 93, 118, 121, 137, 162
LGBTQ+ 4, 13
liberation 127, 133, 136, 146, 150–4, 166, 202, 204, 236
– sexual 18, 136, 150, 153, 212, 214
London 145, 166, 189, 190, 208
lovers 1, 17, 66, 188, 194, 198
Lykourgos 29, 30
Lynkestian 36

Macedonia 25, 26, 28, 35–7, 39, 44
Mardonios 33
marriage 31, 33–5, 37, 39–46, 51–70, 73, 74, 77, 79–82, 84–6, 90–5, 109–11, 114, 116, 117n69, 118, 119, 122–7, 135, 136, 138, 140, 145–50, 152–4, 159–81, 187–9, 191–8, 202–4, 207–9, 211–20, 222, 223, 225, 227, 228, 231, 232, 234–44, 246–51,
– alliance, alliances 27–9, 31, 33, 36, 38, 39
– bureaus 170, 171, 179
– bourgeois 107, 113, 124, 128
– clandestine 52, 62
– law 80–2, 92, 118, 196
– monogamous 9, 124, 126, 127
– new 122, 126, 196
– peace in 56, 60–2

– policy 28, 31–3, 35, 38, 39, 41, 42, 45, 36, 69
McKinley, B. 136
McKinley. W. 136
monarchy 115
monogamy 117n69, 126, 188
motherhood 119, 138, 144, 171, 236, 239, 243
Munk, M. 89

nature 7–9, 14, 16, 26, 94, 95, 110, 141, 146, 150, 168, 169, 178, 191, 201, 203, 207, 216 , 222,
– women's 61, 76, 148
New York 138, 159, 168, 174, 208, 211, 212, 217–219n44, 226, 232, 233, 241, 246, 249
nobility 52, 53, 67
norms *see* gender norms

obedience 53, 57, 63, 66, 69, 147
obsession 70, 187, 198–200, 223
Olenska, E. 211, 213, 216–18
Olympias 36–9
orgasm 152, 193, 194
Oxyartes 38

pantheon 41
parents 43, 57, 58, 60, 62, 63, 66–8, 81, 115, 236, 247
Paris 200, 201, 218, 221
patriarchy 13, 15, 17, 77, 79, 134, 135, 144, 160, 243
Peisistratos 29–31, 38
Persian 17, 29, 31–3, 38, 39, 43, 44
Pfülf, A. 89
Philip II 35–40
poem 188, 189, 200–4, 225, 228, 234, 235
polygamy 28, 40, 45, 119
Ptolemy II 38, 44, 45

queer 243, 248

rape 10, 116, 245
rebellion 38n59, 142, 213
Reichstag 81, 88–93

religion 188, 214, 219n44, 220, 221, 241
Renaissance 51, 52, 59, 62
revolution 74, 83, 108, 122, 134, 136, 150, 152–4
Rhodes 43
Riehl, W. H. 73
romantic 5, 11, 13–17, 19, 139, 187, 196, 197, 200, 202, 204, 216, 228, 242, 248
– love 149, 178
– thralldom 191, 204
Rome 26, 41, 42, 216, 217
Russia 91, 134, 138, 140

sacrament 52, 56–8, 62, 68, 82, 92
sacrifice 6, 19, 31, 148, 177, 187, 196
Second World War 13, 191, 235
separation 57, 78, 90, 92, 115
sex 9, 11, 15, 17, 66, 74, 87, 111, 112, 121, 122, 144, 146, 148–50, 152, 153, 168, 169, 175, 177, 194, 197, 199, 200, 233, 247, 248
Simpson, W. 187
slave 135, 136, 139, 147
Snyder, R. C. 244
socialism 8, 93, 124–6, 135
soul 25, 65, 66, 144, 146, 171, 197
SPD 88, 91, 108n18, 122, 124, 125
spiritual 2, 35, 40, 140, 193–5
suffrage 74–6, 83, 84, 88, 94, 110, 147
suffragette movement 148, 161, 166

Teispid 32, 33
Thessalonike 39–41
throne 29, 32, 33, 35, 42, 45 142, 187
tradition 42, 65, 111, 121, 126, 147, 215, 217, 220
tragedy 143, 144, 146–8, 178, 203
Tuttle, F. 194–6, 204
tyranny 29–31

unconventional 138, 164, 169, 187

union 1, 2, 5, 17, 42, 52, 53, 56–8, 61, 62, 70, 78, 95, 154, 164, 172, 203, 232, 237, 248, 250
United States 14, 134, 135, 138–41, 160, 219n44
unmarried 15, 85, 113, 123, 146, 159

values 3, 17, 66, 78, 127, 136, 147, 169, 178, 179, 213, 228
vampiric 199
Victorian 119, 196, 198
victory 9, 83, 120, 149
violence 57, 58, 68, 116, 141, 191, 200, 244
– sexual 16, 244
virginity 116, 153
vote 75, 94, 121, 176, 192

Wallace, S. 162–5
war 45, 56, 60, 84, 86, 91, 134, 148, 168, 175–7, 179, 188, 189, 199, 202–4, 210, 215, 216, 220, 228 *see also* First World War, Second World War
Weber, Max 106, 113, 123
Weber, Marianne 121, 123
wedding 46, 66, 67, 115–17, 217, 221, 233, 234, 239–41, 246–50
Weimar Republic *see* Germany
Wharton, E. 19, 207–9, 212–15, 217–21, 223–5, 227, 228
Whitman, W. 150

Xenophon 52
Xerxes 33

Yeats, W. B. 166, 203
Yiddishland 139

Zayas, M. de 69
Zepler, W. 124n111, 125
Zetkin, C. 112, 120n85, 121, 126